The Student's Guide to
Shakespeare

William McKenzie

EDINBURGH
University Press

Edinburgh University Press is one of the leading university presses in the UK. We publish academic books and journals in our selected subject areas across the humanities and social sciences, combining cutting-edge scholarship with high editorial and production values to produce academic works of lasting importance. For more information visit our website: edinburghuniversitypress.com

Edinburgh University Press Ltd
The Tun – Holyrood Road, 12(2f) Jackson's Entry, Edinburgh EH8 8PJ

Typeset in Gill Sans Nova
by R. J. Footring Ltd, Derby, and
Printed and bound in the United States of America

A CIP record for this book is available from the British Library

ISBN 978 1 4744 1351 0 (hardback)
ISBN 978 1 4744 1352 7 (webready PDF)
ISBN 978 1 4744 1353 4 (paperback)
ISBN 978 1 4744 1354 1 (epub)

Contents

Acknowledgements

It is a real pleasure to acknowledge here the help I have received during the writing of this book. I only regret that space prevents me from including all the (many) friends and colleagues with whom I have exchanged ideas over a long process. I suspect that such a list might double the length of the book. A special mention, however, for the undergraduate and MA students I worked with at Royal Holloway University of London, 2007–2009, under the expert mentorship of Ewan Fernie and Kiernan Ryan and with the valuable peer-support of John Miles and Theodora Papadopoulou. Many of the ideas set out here started to emerge during this time. I would also like to thank Sean McEvoy, who first proposed this project to me, demonstrated saintly patience as it slowly took shape, and made invaluable comments on the typescript. St Hilda's College, Wadham College, and Brasenose College at the University of Oxford all offered warm, happy, and stimulating intellectual environments. And the staff at EUP, namely James Dale, Carla Hepburn, Michelle Houston, Zuzana Ihnatova, Jackie Jones, Rebecca Mackenzie, and Adela Rauchova, gently and cheerfully guided me through the various stages of publication. The anonymous readers' suggestions were astute and extremely useful, and I incorporated them gratefully. Eliza Wright copy-edited the typescript with great accuracy, thoroughness, and efficiency. My family all offered real support throughout. Any errors or inaccuracies that have survived into the finished book I of course acknowledge mine. If you spot any, please do get in touch with me via the publishers so that we might address them.

Historical chronology

Key date	Shakespeare's life events	Shakespeare's plays/poems*	Selective theatrical/ cultural context	Historical events
1564	William Shakespeare born (c. 23 April)			
1567			Golding's English translation of Ovid's *Metamorphoses* (Shakespeare's favourite book?)	
1588			Montaigne, *Essais* (2nd edn) Marlowe, *Dr Faustus*	Spanish Armada fails to invade England
1589	Shakespeare arrives in London	Two Gentlemen of Verona	Marlowe, *Jew of Malta* staged	Henri III of France murdered
1590		Taming of the Shrew Henry VI Part 2	Marlowe, *Tamburlaine* staged	Anne of Denmark crowned Queen of Scotland
1591	James Burbage moves Admiral's Men to the Rose Theatre	Henry VI Part 3 Henry VI Part 1 Titus Andronicus	Sidney, *Astrophil and Stella* Marlowe, *The Massacre at Paris*	
1592		Richard III staged Edward III	Greene's *Groatsworth of Wit* Marlowe, *Edward II*	Outbreak of bubonic plague closes the theatres
1593		Venus and Adonis	Arrest warrant issued for Christopher Marlowe	
1594	With the theatres reopened Lord Hunsdon reconstitutes his theatre company as the Lord Chamberlain's Men	Lucrece Love's Labour's Lost The Comedy of Errors		Lopez affair Theatres reopened Henri IV converts to Catholicism, recognised as king by all of France
1595		Richard II Romeo and Juliet A Midsummer Night's Dream		Francis Drake departs on his final voyage
1596		King John The Merchant of Venice Henry IV Part 1	Sketch of the Swan Theatre by Johannes de Witt	

1597	Moves out of Bishopsgate Buys New Place in Stratford	The Merry Wives of Windsor Henry IV Part 2	Edward Alleyn, Marlowe's 'star' actor, retires from acting
1598	Acts in Ben Jonson's Every Man in His Humour (Curtain Theatre)	Much Ado About Nothing	Jonson, Every Man in His Humour
1599	Globe Theatre built in Southwark	Henry V Julius Caesar Hamlet	Death of Edmund Spenser Jonson, Every Man out of His Humour
1600		As You Like It	
1601		Twelfth Night The Phoenix and the Turtle	
1602		Troilus and Cressida	
1603	The newly crowned King James gives Shakespeare's company a royal patent, making them the King's Men	Measure for Measure Othello Sir Thomas More	Thomas Heywood, A Woman Killed with Kindness Death of Elizabeth I/Accession of James I
1605		King Lear Timon of Athens	Gunpowder plot
1606		Macbeth Anthony and Cleopatra All's Well that Ends Well	Jonson, Volpone
1607		Pericles, Prince of Tyre	Monteverdi, Orfeo
1608	The King's Men acquire the Blackfriars Theatre	Coriolanus	Another outbreak of plague closes the theatres
1609		Shakespeare's Sonnets and A Lover's Complaint published The Winter's Tale	
1610		Cymbeline The Tempest	Chapman, Bussy d'Ambois Jonson, The Alchemist
1611			King James Bible published
1613	Globe Theatre burns down	Henry VIII or All is True	Beaumont and Fletcher, The Maid's Tragedy Middleton, A Chaste Maid in Cheapside
1616	Death of William Shakespeare (c. 23 April)		
1623		First Folio published	

*Approximate date of first composition unless otherwise stated.

Glossary

Canonical   A 'canonical' text is one that has been confidently and consensually attributed to its named author.

Catchword   In early printed texts, the first word of the following page, set aside from the main text, to enable printers to check the book has been assembled correctly.

Compositor   A print-worker who set type, that is to say, arranged the lettered blocks, from which multiple copies of books were printed. Compositors often worked collaboratively to produce texts more quickly, and could sometimes introduce mistakes.

Control text   The version of a text from which a modern edition is prepared.

Discovery space   A space set into the *frons scenae*, concealed from view by a curtain. When revealed, the space could contain, for example, Polonius's dead body (*Hamlet*), Hermione's statue (*The Winter's Tale*) or Miranda and Ferdinand playing chess (*The Tempest*).

Fair copy   As suggested by Hamlet when he tells Horatio he 'Devised a new commission, wrote it *fair*' (V, ii, 32), a 'fair copy' is a text that has been carefully written out by the playwright or professional scribe, or 'scrivener' (see *Richard III*, III, vi).

Folio   A type of book where each sheet of paper is folded over once to make two leaves, or four recto–verso pages.

Foul papers   Working copies of a play that were amended during the rehearsal and performance process.

Frons scenae   The wall at the back of the stage, often with a curtain concealing the 'discovery space', and doors leading back to the 'tiring house'.

Locus   A term from Robert Weimann's *Author's Pen and Actor's Voice* (2000: 184). Broadly speaking, the *locus* is a space associated with higher-born characters: 'a site for the dominant discourse of honour, chastity, magnanimity and warlike resolution', often depicted by actions taking place on the upper stage.

Octavo   A type of book where each sheet of paper is folded over three times to make sixteen recto–verso pages.

Platea   Another term from Weimann. The *platea* is the literally and figuratively lower space, where Hamlet and Hal descend to address persons of poorer social standing.

Promptbook   A document in either fair or foul copy that incorporated stage directions, notes on props and special effects, and revisions, including those requested by state authorities. Characters' names were often replaced with actors' names.

Scribal copy   A copy of the text prepared by a 'scrivener' or scribe.

Stationers' Register   The account-books of the Company of Stationers, to which all printers were legally obliged to belong. The Register recorded fees paid for rights for printing new works, as well as fines levied for those who printed without permission.

Substantive text   Said of an edition based on a writer's own manuscript. Contrast 'derivative text', which is based on an earlier printed version.

Tiring house   The room where actors changed costume or 'attired', behind the *frons scenae*, and from which offstage sound effects could be heard (often signalled by the stage direction 'sound within').

Bibliography

Weimann, R. (2000), *Author's Pen and Actor's Voice: Playing and Writing Shakespeare's Theatre*, Cambridge: Cambridge University Press.

How this book will work

This book focuses on the plays most often taught on undergraduate courses, according to data collated by the Higher Education Academy English Subject Centre. For breadth of coverage eight of Shakespeare's history plays are discussed in two chapters, each covering one 'tetralogy': four plays relaying a single, continuous narrative. Each chapter should take about thirty to forty-five minutes to read. You should then have a good enough working knowledge of the play to write an exam answer, contribute to a seminar, or to start planning a piece of coursework. The plays are divided into their conventional genres, and then covered in the order in which they were written, with the exception of the histories, set in order of the events they depict. Each chapter title bears the title of the play or plays covered. It also gives a date, or frequently a range of dates: the most likely date for when the manuscript was completed, then that of the first recorded performance and, finally, when the text was printed, if printed before the 1623 First Folio. For the chapters on the histories, the date range refers to the date of composition for the first play to the first performances of the last.

The chapters on the individual tragedies, comedies and late plays each contain nine sections and a bibliography. The chapters on the histories are organised slightly differently because they deal with continuous tetralogies, not individual plays: these contain eight sections and a bibliography. The first section of each chapter gives a 'Plot summary' to enable you to get a good overall sense of the play(s) right away, by detailing clearly and succinctly what happens when. This will give you things to say in essays and class discussions, and is crucial for exams. The act, scene and line references are to a particular scholarly edition, specified at the beginning of each chapter.

The second section of each chapter is called 'Characters' and focuses one by one on a play's *dramatis personae*, as the Folio editors called them, listing the scenes in which each appears. This section seeks to help students dealing with 'characterological' questions ('analyse the role of Iago in *Othello*') or actors thinking about their character's individual 'journey' through the play. Characters may develop, like Hal, or regress, like Anthony. Sometimes I have reversed the expected order of priority, discussing, say, Cleopatra before Anthony, or Juliet before Romeo. These decisions are intended to help students question the criteria through which the relative 'importance' of characters is established. Straightforwardly quantitative measures like numbers of appearances, lines spoken or soliloquies are convincing when, say, affirming the undoubted centrality of Prince Hamlet in *Hamlet*. But sometimes the *quality* of onstage time counts, not the quantity. The witches in *Macbeth*, Tybalt in

Romeo and Juliet, or Shylock in *The Merchant of Venice*, all appear only infrequently but play important thematic and structural roles.

Another issue arises when looking at Shakespeare's *dramatis personae* in isolation from each other: some seem to be more 'character'-like than others. Shakespeare depicts in a masterly way what the late Joel Fineman called the 'subjectivity effect', representing verbally a recognisably human psychology working in real time, a 'rounded character'. But in Shakespeare's time human personalities were not characterised in precisely this way: the word 'character' in Shakespeare's work chiefly had the meaning, still familiar to us, of a numerical or alphabetical symbol. Correspondingly, it is far from sure if all Shakespearean 'characters' are endowed with a 'character' in our modern sense. Lear's Fool, for example, reveals none of the background information from which such a psychological profile might be con-structed. We know nothing of his family or his previous life; his riddling speech comments on external events rather than his interiority. He is therefore a function rather than a character (as Stanley Wells rightly observes), contributing to how the play subtly shades an individual family drama with folkloric, even archetypal signifi-cance (see Chapter 5). Many of Shakespeare's *dramatis personae* blend these various modes of identity, especially the clowns. Pompey in *Measure for Measure* personifies a whole social class. Falstaff in the *Henry IV* tetralogy arguably personifies a whole mode of being. Shakespeare's representations of human beings range from acute psychological accuracy to broad social allegory.

It is also worth remembering that while the *dramatis personae* are studied here in isolation, they are, obviously, most often interacting with each other. Their 'charac-ters' might shift according to this or that social situation. In *Measure for Measure*, for example, Claudio behaves very differently to the Duke and to Isabella. The events portrayed in Shakespeare's plays also scrutinise the idea that a character retains a consistent, logical and coherent pattern (or 'personality') regardless of what happens to him or her. In *Macbeth*, *Hamlet* and *Henry V*, for example, people leap out of their own lives, behaving with radical unpredictability. The 'character' section should therefore be seen as introductory. It helps to get to know the play, but a play's meaning is by no means exhausted by the sum of its isolated characters.

The third section is called 'Play structure' and takes a step back to see how the play as a whole is constructed. How and why, for example, is information released to or withdrawn from an audience? This section explores the interrelation of the individual units into which editors divide the play, like acts or scenes, and a play's dramatic or thematic symmetries. This might relate to the location – *Hamlet* is tightly restrained to Elsinore, *Anthony and Cleopatra* ranges across continents – use of stage space and narrative pacing. The chapters on the histories do not contain this section because they deal with sets of plays rather than individually structured units. I there-fore discuss in those chapters the creative and theatrical ways Shakespeare shapes his historical sources, such as the Chronicles of Raphael Holinshed, Edward Hall and Thomas More.

The fourth section focuses on language. Samuel Johnson grumpily noted Shake-speare 'quibbled' with words for the sake of it (see Mahood [1957] (2003): 9), but

John Dover Wilson more charitably observed, 'When Shakespeare used a word, all of its possibilities were alive in his mind' (quoted in Wilson 2007: 51–2). This section thus traces such verbal adventures as words play through the play. This may involve following a single word like 'nothing' in *King Lear* or 'honest' in *Othello*, or a recurrent strand of figurative language like animal imagery. The section also explores how prose and verse work independently and in relation to each other, entailing attention to Shakespearean versification. Shakespeare's rhythms do not always follow orthodox iambic pentameter, where five unstressed and five stressed syllables alternate in each line. He varies and innovates on this rhythm in various ways, often to convey a sense of emotional expressiveness or urgent, dramatic purpose. Enjambed or 'run-on' lines, for example, where the sentence 'runs on' over the end of the iambic pentameter line, may, according to context and circumstance, express deep thought (as in Macbeth's first soliloquy) or distress (as in Hamlet's). At such moments poetic form is part of the psychological content. Perhaps form and content never can nor should be wholly separated. Shakespeare's language is always motivated. In his plays everyone, always, seeks somehow to persuade someone else. Shakespeare's characters thus regularly use the rhetorical figures trained into Elizabethan grammar-school and university students to make them persuasive orators. Taking some examples from sonnet 43 (unless otherwise stated), these figures might include: *anadiplosis* or repeating words in a new clause ('thy noble son is *mad. Mad* I call it' *Hamlet*, II, ii, 92–3) ; *anthimeria* or transforming nouns to verbs ('*uncle* me no *uncle*', *Richard II*, II, ii, 86); *antistasis* or repeating words in different senses ('darkly *bright* [adj.], are *bright* [adv.] in dark directed'); *catachresis* or strained metaphor ('in thy piteous *heart* plant thou thine *ear*', *Richard II*, V, iii, 125); *chiasmus* or a reversal in the order of words in two otherwise parallel phrases ('*Fair* is **foul** and **foul** is *fair*', *Macbeth*, I, i, 9); *epanalepsis* or repeating a word at the beginning and end of a line ('*Old* Gaunt indeed, and gaunt in being *old*', *Richard II*, II, i, 74); *epizeuxis* or repeating words without separation ('those whose *shadow shadows* **form form**'); *gradatio* or repeating at the start of a new clause a word from the last ('My conscience hath a thousand several *tongues*, / And every *tongue* brings in a several *tale*, / And every *tale* condemns me for a villain', *Richard III*, V, v, 172–4); *polyptoton* or repetition of words from the same root but with different endings ('*darkly* [...] *dark*'); *polysyndeton* or excessive use of conjunctions for rhythmical effect ('tomorrow, *and* tomorrow, *and* tomorrow', *Macbeth*, V, v, 18); and *symploce* or repeating words at the beginnings and ends of a series of clauses ('He heareth *not*, he stirreth *not*, he moveth *not*', *Romeo and Juliet*, II, i, 16). Elizabethan handbooks like George Puttenham's *Arte of English Poesie* (published in 1589) gave exhaustive lists of such figures. Song and music, used especially frequently in, say, *Twelfth Night*, is also discussed in this section.

The fifth section of each chapter is called 'Themes'. Admittedly there is some overlap in Shakespeare between themes and language. 'Nothing' is frequently repeated in *King Lear* to draw attention to the nothingness at the heart of this bleakest and most desolate of plays. Shakespeare may even make a theme of language itself, as when Juliet famously asks 'what's in a name?' (II, i, 86). But this fifth section explores more widely the large-scale and urgent conceptual issues the plays invoke. Each play represents variations on what might be termed 'metath-emes': concepts which, despite the differences introduced by later editors between histories, comedies and tragedies, run powerfully throughout the whole of Shake-speare's work. At their broadest, all the plays (and the poems) deal in some way with love, power, subversion, gender, race, sexuality, religion, conflict and social class. I would also say that Shakespeare thinks deeply about how skills associated with theatrical performance seep into the so-called 'real' world. The melancholic in *As You Like It*, Jaques, states in one of Shakespeare's most famous speeches that 'All the world's a stage' (II, vii, 138). Roleplay and disguise help people get what they want, from the most sympathetic lover like Helena in *All's Well that Ends Well*, to the most Machiavellian of murderous politicians like Richard III. But Shakespeare's ob-session with performance extends to performing an action as well as playing a role. His plays often stage irreversible events and observe how people respond. Duncan cannot be un-murdered. King Lear cannot become un-mad. Lovers cannot un-fall in love. The plays thus stage tensions between predestined fortune and people's power to change it.

The sixth section of each chapter is called 'Texts and contexts'. It sets out first the textual history of each play, focusing on variations between different versions exploring what might significantly affect our understanding. It secondly outlines social, intellectual and historical contexts that are useful for an understanding of the play. Shakespeare, despite his genius, did not write in a vacuum. Indeed, much Shakespeare criticism, at its broadest, is effectively a variation on the 'nature vs nurture' debate (the phrase itself comes from *The Tempest*, IV, i, 188–9). To what degree is artistic achievement the 'pure genius' of a 'great man'? To what degree is it just a clever, or fortuitous, alignment of already existing material? The information set out here is intended to help students arrive at their own positions.

The seventh section offers a history of the play in performance. Due to limited space it prioritises recent English-speaking productions, most often from the UK, where I am based. Particular focus will be given to how contemporary practitioners have made Shakespeare 'talk' to their own time, stressing that Shakespearean performances on stage and film are events where aesthetic and stylised artistry is in-separable from sociological critique. Shakespeare performance absorbs, displays, and actively contributes to modern cultural trends and movements. Portrayals of Shake-speare's women, especially Ophelia and Desdemona, have reflected and engaged with questions arising from successive waves of feminism, while productions of *The Tempest*, *Othello* and *The Merchant of Venice* unavoidably take, however implicitly, a position in relation to contemporary debates about racism and racial identity. These, however, are only the most visible examples. Productions of all Shakespeare's plays can provoke and actively influence urgent questions about the present.

The eighth section surveys the most important texts in the reception history of a given play. For reasons of space, I have often limited these surveys to very recent publications, peer-reviewed articles that students can access online via an institu-tional login. Most often these texts are works of literary criticism, but sometimes they will be literary adaptations, which may be no less illuminating.

The discussion questions in the ninth section are intended to help guide students' thinking, to serve as revision aids, to test exam skills as mock questions or to stimulate seminar discussion. This can be especially useful if it gets a bit quiet in the seminar room. Questions that can be applicable to any play include: who does the play side with? How are sympathies or antipathies created? (Via soliloquy, for example?) Are the speaking persons representations of actual human beings, or allegories of the kinds of forces, passions and desires that move us all? Or even both? In other words, do the plays depict not, or not only, an actual geographical space, but a kind of interiorised window into how our minds work?

Bibliography

Mahood, M. [1957] (2003), *Shakespeare's Wordplay*, London: Routledge.

Wilson, R. (2007), *Shakespeare in French Theory: King of Shadows*, London/New York: Routledge.

Introduction

This book tries to help busy students of Shakespeare by giving, quickly and access-ibly, the information necessary when preparing a seminar discussion or presentation, or revising for exams. It also raises the kinds of intellectually adventurous ques-tions that examiners ask candidates to grapple with in their written work. This introduction starts with a brief biography ('Who was Shakespeare?'), which focuses selectively on the most relevant details for the tasks students are commonly asked to perform. The following section ('How is Shakespeare?') introduces issues fun-damental to any thoughtful engagement with Shakespeare by seeing Shakespeare as the initiator of a collaborative, creative process that I call 'the construction of Shakespearean meaning'. This process, which involves, amongst many others, actors, directors, editors, readers, audience members (and students, of course), is today more energetic and stimulating than ever.

'Who was Shakespeare?' William Shakespeare 1564–1616

William Shakespeare born in Stratford-upon-Avon in 1564. His baptism at the town's Holy Trinity Church was dated 26 April, and the birth is usually dated back to 23 April because the record of his death on 23 April 1616 says he had reached his fifty-third year. There is no documentary evidence that William attended the town's grammar school, re-established by King Edward VI in 1553, but it is likely that William's father, John Shakespeare, a leather-worker who later rose to the status of bailiff, or mayor, would have had the means and the wish to give his son a good education. There is, moreover, clear reference in Shakespeare's plays to the kinds of classical texts taught on the school curriculum. *The Comedy of Errors*, for example, is based on the confused-identity comedy *Menaechmi* by the Latin playwright Plautus. And Ovid, author of a compendium of mythological stories of transforma-tion entitled *The Metamorphoses*, exerts a strong influence on Shakespeare's work throughout his career from his first tragedy *Titus Andronicus* (first performed around 1591) to his last single-authored play *The Tempest* (c. 1610). Boys left grammar school at fifteen. Details of Shakespeare's late adolescence are hazy, but at eighteen he married the twenty-six-year-old Anne Hathaway. Their first child Susannah was baptised six months later in 1583. She had been conceived outside wedlock. William and Anne's next two children, the twins Hamnet and Judith, were baptised in 1585.

There is another period of hazy information between 1585 and 1592, from the ages of twenty-one to twenty-eight, often termed the 'Lost Years'.

By 1592, however, Robert Greene had punningly mentioned 'an upstart crow' who is 'by his own conceit the only Shake-scene in a country' (Greene [1592] 1996: 19). Shakespeare had by this time established himself in London, a *fin-de-siècle* boomtown whose population had nearly trebled in the last fifty years. There are records of him living in Bishopsgate until 1597. Recent statistical and stylistic analysis has mooted that Shakespeare corroborated during this period with other playwrights on *Edward III* (added to the Oxford Shakespeare in 2005) and *Arden of Faversham*, George Peele on *Titus Andronicus*, and Thomas Nashe on *Henry the Sixth Part One*. From 1592 to 1594, when the London theatres closed to stop the spread of plague, Shakespeare composed two successful tragic narrative poems, both based on episodes from Ovidian texts, *Venus and Adonis* and *The Rape of Lucrece*. On the reopening of the theatres in 1594 the Queen's Lord Chamberlain Henry Carey, Lord Hunsdon, set up a theatre company (the Lord Chamberlain's Men) with whom Shakespeare was involved from a very early stage, if not the beginning. Members had stakes in theatre companies, and Shakespeare's 10 per cent share made him between £200 and £700 a year, not a fortune but more than any other playwright. At times of financial need the company sold their playbooks for printing and some of Shakespeare's plays circulated in 'Quarto' form. In 1597 he bought New Place, the second-biggest house in Stratford-upon-Avon. This period was not without its sadnesses. In 1596 his son Hamnet died. Biographically minded critics think this a powerful influence on the writing of *Hamlet*. As a Lord Chamberlain's Man Shakespeare produced on average two plays a year and carried out acting duties. His reputation grew yet further. The Lord's Chamberlain's Men performed before the Queen at court.

In 1598 the landlord at The Theatre, the first successful professional playhouse, increased the rent and then decided to tear down the building. Shakespeare's company thus under cover of night dismantled The Theatre and transported the timbers from Shoreditch to Southwark to build the Globe Theatre, opened in 1599. The Globe attracted healthy audiences. In 1603 Elizabeth I died and the new King James I gave Shakespeare's company royal patronage. They became the King's Men that year. The King's Men performed for the court 187 times in the thirteen years between James's accession and Shakespeare's death: more than once a month. With James's support Shakespeare could afford to slow his output, producing an average of one play a year. These plays tend to be more serious: 'problem plays', like *Measure for Measure* and *All's Well that Ends Well*, and the tragedies *Othello*, *Macbeth* and *King Lear*. In 1605 Shakespeare bought an expensive share in the tithes of Stratford-upon-Avon, procuring him a comfortable income of £40 a year. From about 1606, after a long period of exclusive sole authorship, it seems that Shakespeare made a partial return to collaboration. *Pericles* (1607) was co-written with George Wilkins, the tragedy *Timon of Athens* with Thomas Middleton, and *The Two Noble Kinsmen*, *Henry VIII, or All is True* and a lost play *Cardenio* with John Fletcher.

In 1608 the King's Men bought the Blackfriars Theatre, an indoor, more exclusive and technologically advanced playing space. This may have led Shakespeare to experiment with more ambitiously spectacular plays like *The Tempest*. On 29 June 1613 an accident with a cannon during a performance of Shakespeare's *Henry VIII* led to a fire that put the Globe out of action. From that point on Shakespeare's output dried up. Whether the two events are more than coincidental is a matter for conjecture. William Shakespeare died between 23 and 25 April 1616. He left a will, bequeathing the bulk of his property to his eldest daughter Susannah, but also arranging an independent income for Susannah's younger sister Judith, following various indiscretions committed by her husband. As was common at the time he left money to buy mourning rings to three theatrical collaborators: Richard Burbage, Henry Condell and John Hemmings. Shakespeare left his wife Anne simply his 'second best bed'. Precisely what this means about Shakespeare's relationship with his wife of over twenty years is a mystery. In any event, Anne Shakespeare continued to live in New Place, probably cared for by her daughter.

'How is Shakespeare?' Constructing Shakespearean meaning from his time to ours

As almost goes without saying, and as shown by the recent commemorations of the 400th anniversary of his death (23 April 2016), Shakespeare is a cultural phenomenon. His popularity shows no sign of abating. Shakespeare was successful in his own lifetime but his work now has a global reach that extends well beyond his original London playhouses. To set up the kinds of questions a Shakespeare student may ask when considering the reasons for his works' continued influence and power, I want to think of the construction of Shakespearean meaning as a collaborative process: initiated of course by the man William Shakespeare, but by no means limited to or exhausted by him. Shakespearean meaning is constructed from a vast number of variously perceptible or imperceptible decisions, taken by many people. These decisions can be located in three overlapping domains: the Shakespearean text, theatrical or cinematic production, and the wider cultural space in which Shakespeare's plays are read and seen, which includes literary criticism.

From stage to page and back again: the Shakespearean 'text'

As noted above, Shakespeare collaborated with other playwrights in the early and late periods of his career. But even though he also wrote many plays alone, this is not to say that there is a single, 'pure' Shakespearean play. The different versions of, say, the plays in the *Henry VI* tetralogy, *Romeo and Juliet*, *Hamlet* or *King Lear* (to name but a few), would suggest that Shakespeare himself revised his artworks depending on what worked in performance. Shakespeare is thus his own first distorter. But distortions or interference in the Shakespearean text may have also occurred at any other step in the complicated process of transferring Shakespeare's words from stage to page. At its simplest, this process may have occurred as follows. Shakespeare would compose his play, alone and while working with his fellow actors. A 'holotext', often a prompt book, would emerge as the single version on which performances were based, and to which actors could refer if they forgot their lines. Such working copies, messily tweaked or amended as performances and rehearsals went on, are known as 'foul' papers, a term first used by the King's Men in 1625. A professional scribe or 'scrivener', such as Ralph Crane, would then write up the text neatly as 'fair papers', to help the printers set the text as quickly and accurately as possible.

In practice, however, the process did not always work as smoothly. Corrections could be made at any stage and then only imperfectly reflected, or missed out entirely, as the book was printed. Even more drastically, sometimes Shakespearean texts were based on pirated or illegally distributed manuscripts, as is suspected to have happened with the first known printed version of *Hamlet*, which contains some almost comical discrepancies from the play's most celebrated lines: 'To be or not to be, ay, that's the point'. The purity or authority of Shakespeare's earliest printed texts is therefore difficult to verify. Only eighteen of his plays were published in his lifetime, often in multiple and differing versions. A further eighteen were only published after his death in the 1623 collected edition of his plays (two years in the making) now known as the 'First Folio'. *Pericles*, the thirty-seventh and final play confidently ascribed to Shakespeare, was only added to a later edition. We have a few signatures and a short extract from *Sir Thomas More* agreed to be in Shakespeare's hand, but no Shakespearean manuscripts against which these printed texts can be checked.

Shakespeare's works are therefore, in Jacques Derrida's phrase, 'still-living palimpsest[s]' (Derrida 1992: 433). They are unavoidably mediated by other people's decisions. Sometimes, however, the signs of such mediation are obvious enough for readers to detect. Ralph Crane the scrivener, for example, characteristically added punctuation to the text as he wrote it out. The First Folio's editors, Shakespeare's long-time colleagues John Hemmings and Henry Condell, divided the plays into Histories, Tragedies and Comedies, and added act and scene divisions to each play. Editors preparing Shakespearean texts for modern readers therefore ask themselves hard and serious questions. Which version of the play should they default to, that is to say, use as their 'control text'? This is especially tricky with plays like *Hamlet* or *King Lear*, as different versions differ in significant ways (see the 'Texts and contexts' sections of Chapters 2 and 5 respectively). And from this first difficult decision stem many others. Should obscure passages be retained or clarified? If so, how? Is the text by moments demonstrably inaccurate, as when, for example, a speech has been seemingly misattributed? Should the lineation be changed, to tidy up the metre, or to stress a word or phrase by setting it with a half-line? If so, where should the line break take place? Editors of respected scholarly editions are always careful to justify their decisions with extensive notes. Such texts often record how their texts differ from others in small print 'collation' beneath the main text.

The main point to note, then, is that the technology and working conditions of sixteenth- and seventeenth-century printing make the Shakespearean text a deeply collaborative exercise. Producing it involves working actors, scribes, typesetters and editors, and the various distortions that may creep into this production at any stage unavoidably make editing and modernising Shakespeare's texts actively interpretative, with real decisions to be made, rather than a neutral exercise in simply making Shakespeare's words clearer to the modern reader. This book will highlight any significant variations between such versions in the 'Texts and contexts' section of each chapter.

Shakespearean performance: interpretation, not distortion

Shakespeare on stage

Performing Shakespeare's plays, on stage or on film, is another key element of how people collaborate to make Shakespeare meaningful. In the early stages of production the theatre or film director often has to make the same kinds of decisions as the editor. Which version, or 'source text' of the play should be used? Might it even be worth mixing and matching the strongest moments from several versions of the play? What overall vision for the play may justify such decisions? Critics often distinguish 'play texts' written on the page from the 'performance texts' that happen on stage or on film.

The advantage of thinking about the words on the page and onstage performance as two kinds of the same thing – a 'text' – is that they can be interrogated and analysed according to the same principles. A critic may interrogate and examine every single word of a written text to see how that text communicates as a whole. Likewise, there is no entirely meaningless element in a play or film: everything signifies in some way. Visually, we may observe the actors' positions and movements, lighting, use of stage space and depth, or costume. Aurally, we may listen out for how the actor intonates or stresses one word over another, music, songs and sound effects.

Shakespeare always shows awareness of how verbal and non-verbal expression could powerfully work together onstage. His gender-bending comedies *The Two Gentlemen of Verona*, *Twelfth Night*, *As You Like It* and *The Merchant of Venice* draw on the fact that women were not used on the stage in Shakespeare's time. Female roles were instead played by boys, because acting itself was deemed antithetical to feminine chastity. Prince Hamlet, Iago in *Othello* and Richard III all in soliloquy directly address the audience from a downstage position, called by Robert Weimann the *platea*, which is traditionally associated with Vice figures, and with the lower classes because it is closer to the 'groundlings' who had paid less for entrance and therefore had no seats (see also the relevant 'character' sections in Chapters 2, 3 and 12 respectively).

The relationship between the *platea* and its higher counterpart the *locus*, represented in the Globe by an upper-level stage, is particularly important in *Richard II*. Richard's physical descent from one space to the other ('Down, down, I come, like glistering Phaeton', III, iii, 177) anticipates and symbolises his later deposition at the hands of his rival Bolingbroke (see also Chapter 11). The theological resonances of words denoting the upper and lower stage, 'heaven' and 'hell' respectively, are activated when, say, Old Hamlet's Ghost repeatedly calls from beneath the stage trapdoor (I, v, 149–79). The positions of one actor in relation to another, or others, often form important stage pictures. In *Hamlet* the image of a man standing over a victim, ready to kill, recurs at least three times: the Player's narration of Pyrrhus slaughtering Priam (II, ii, 415–17), the enactment of Claudius's murder of Old Hamlet in dumbshow (III, ii, 128.4–6), and finally Hamlet aloft over the praying Claudius (III, iv, 74–87), each a powerful recollection of the play's concern with death and hesitation (see also Chapter 2). Editors of *King Lear* argue whether Edgar, in his first appearance as the disguised Poor Tom, is onstage at the same time as the sleeping, incarcerated Kent, which would make a powerful parallel between the downfalls of the Lear and Gloucester households (II, ii). A similar parallel is invited, albeit in a comically and magically amorous mode, between the sleeping lovers and the sleeping Titania in *A Midsummer Night's Dream* (II, ii) (see also Chapters 5 and 7).

Technical terms for analysing the positional relationships between onstage bodies include *figurenposition* and proxemics: they remind us that everything on a stage has meaning, including even the empty spaces between persons and things. Even silence can be significant. Putting a character onstage, even when he or she says nothing, can be an editorial decision, especially when the original texts do not give a stage direction. It is often an important judgement call for the director, too. It may even transform retrospectively the whole meaning of a play: does the angry Malvolio in *Twelfth Night* return to forgive those who have wronged him? Do Shylock and Jessica meet up again at the end of *The Merchant of Venice*? By subtly making thus Malvolio more or less forgiving, Shylock and Jessica more or less kind, such decisions empha-sise once more that the task of making Shakespearean texts meaningful – in textual production, in performance – is a matter of teamwork.

Shakespeare on screen

A lot of the questions, skills, and tasks mentioned above in the analysis of stage productions may also apply to film. After all, performance on stage and on film relies on the use of actors, costume, set design, lighting, colour, and often music and sound effects. But film also uses storytelling tools that are all its own. 'Reading' films of Shakespeare's work entails thinking about how close-up or panoramic shots constrain or open up space, whether the camera is fluid or static, how the shots of a film work in relation to one another. Are the 'takes' (continuous sections of film between cuts) long or short? Such questions are important: camerawork, rhythm, and use of sharp and blurred focus often relate to the characters' emotional state and relationships. One important issue that arises specifically in relation to films of Shakespeare is the use of voiceover to relay soliloquy. Voiceover tilts soliloquy away from its predominant Shakespearean use as a somewhat social, communicative storytelling device, spoken directly to Shakespeare's often illiterate audience, and makes of it instead a representation of the kind of private, silent thought associated with more modern, literate modes of individuality. But updating soliloquy thus is not the only way in which modern culture has transformed Shakespeare, and revealed some of its own key characteristics in so doing.

Bardbiz: Shakespeare's 'afterlife'

Education is often described as a 'political football'. Successive governments try to change school and even university curricula to suit their ideological ends. Consider, for example, the lively discussions in the UK about how best to teach the history of the British Empire, or in the US about whether 'Creationism' should be taught in science classes. Shakespeare is perhaps a 'cultural football'. The way he is interpreted critically, theatrically, or cinematically often reveals something of the political or social preconceptions, even prejudices, of his interpreter. In 1983 the then Chancellor Nigel Lawson (father of TV chef Nigella) declared that 'Shakespeare was a Tory' (*The Guardian* 1983). Later, and less explicitly politically, *Times* journalist Kate Maltby criticised a rehearsal preview of the 2015 Barbican production of *Hamlet* for starting with the 'To be or not to be' soliloquy (Maltby 2015). The soliloquy was soon returned to the middle of the play. The argument that Maltby's review generated in the mainstream media intermingled the small-scale question of how a single production handled an issue of plotting and character development with larger-scale ones of how Shakespearean tradition feeds into national culture. For the 400 or so years Shakespeare's plays have been produced, performed or taught, they have been intimately involved with various modes of authority.

In Shakespeare's own day Edmund Tilney, Master of the Revels, only allowed licences for plays to be performed after vetting them for seditious content. Blasphemous expletives were banned. And Shakespeare is still tied up with institutional power in various forms, be they English Literature exams or the 'Royal' Shakespeare Company. His texts played an important role in the opening and closing ceremonies of the London 2012 Olympics, presenting a certain brand of Englishness to the billion-strong global TV audience. As his long-established nicknames imply – 'The Swan of Avon', 'The Bard' – Shakespeare is *the* global byword for 'high culture' and its attendant reassurances of comfortable social respectability. Some commentators observe in this a kind of excessive Shakespeare worship, 'Bardolatry' (a term coined by the Irish playwright George Bernard Shaw in the early nineteenth century), while Shakespearean actors Sir Derek Jacobi (Cadwalladr 2010) and Christopher Eccleston (Gilbert 2015) have noted a kind of Shakespearean 'glass ceiling', where disadvantaged young people are less and less involved in drama in general, Shakespeare in particular. This may be dismissed as mere chippiness. But the original workers who had 'chips on their shoulders', eighteenth-century dockers protesting against orders to reduce the timber they were entitled to take home, helped contribute to a fairer, more equal society. By contrast, many of Shakespeare's most famous recent representatives come from a sociologically narrow group, even though Shakespeare himself apparently speaks for a universal humanity, as first and most famously praised by Ben Jonson: 'not of an age but for all time!' (*The Bodleian First Folio* n.d.: prelim p. 3). Eddie Redmayne and Tom Hiddleston both went to Eton, Benedict Cumberbatch to Harrow. The use of Shakespeare to link wealth and privilege with sensitivity and intelligence is problematic but persistent. It also marks the theory that the aristocratic Earl of Oxford not the Stratford boy Shakespeare wrote the plays, most recently put forward in the silly Roland Emmerich 2011 film *Anonymous*.

The connection of Shakespearean artistry with sociocultural conservatism helps explain the radical revisionism of productions like Heiner Müller's *Hamletmachine*, which deletes Shakespeare's text and transforms the characters and narrative entirely. But even though such productions are excellent in their own right, such an approach arguably and counter-productively strengthens the association of Shakespeare's nuanced and sophisticated theatre with conservative politics, simply because they antagonise both at once. Such iconoclastic reworkings remind us that any experience of reading or watching Shakespeare necessarily entails negotiating a dense, often contradictory, network of political, sociocultural and economic connotations, initiated before any of us were born. This is why I think it is useful to talk in terms of instances and constructions of Shakespearean meaning, variously generated from the synergy of play text, performance text and social context.

Shakespeare criticism

One important example of Shakespeare as 'cultural football', where various perspectives negotiate and clash, is of course the global industry of professional Shakespeare criticism. The university discipline of English Literature effectively arose in the early twentieth century. The Shakespearean A. C. Bradley (1851–1935) was made Oxford Professor of Poetry in 1901. Important figures or trends in subsequent Shakespeare criticism included George Wilson Knight's work on Shakespearean mythic symbolism (see the bibliography below), and Cleanth Brooks's 'New Criticism', which argued that literary works, formal artefacts in their own right, should be studied in isolation from their contexts. Still-influential critical approaches like new historicism and cultural materialism then sought in the 1980s to resituate Shakespeare's work in the historical moments of their original composition and reception. These and psychoanalytical, feminist and postcolonialist strands of criticism emerged from and engaged with Freudian or Marxist currents of thought: Sigmund Freud and Karl Marx both named Shakespeare their favourite writer. Such critical 'isms' are at heart simply ways of interrogating Shakespearean texts. I do not therefore attempt here to 'define' each approach, but rather set out the questions critics adopting them may ask, remembering all the while that Shakespeare's plays always exceed in meaning the answers that any such set of questions may yield.

Late twentieth-century critical currents
Marxism
Marxist interpreters may focus on interrelations of social classes, such as *Henry IV*'s contrasting portrayals of the court and the inns of Eastcheap, or the way *A Midsummer Night's Dream* compares Athenian aristocrats with lower-middle-class artisans. Marxist critics may also focus, as a closely related issue, on the social, societal and psychological effects of money. The Bastard in *King John* attacks money ('tickling commodity', II, i, 574 in the *Norton Shakespeare*) for undermining social

structures founded on medieval codes of chivalry and honour. In *Othello* the bitter and resentful Iago urges Roderigo to 'put money in [his] purse', as if money is the only social value that still exists (I, iii, 333–4). *As You Like It* and *King Lear* both portray younger brothers who complain their elder brothers have inherited all the family land (as was common and legal at the time). In *Lear* the blind Gloucester even imagines a world where such perceived injustices and inequalities of wealth no longer exist ('distribution undo excess / And each man have enough', IV, i, 73–4). Timon in *Timon of Athens* (reputedly Marx's favourite play) rages at how the money he has lent people has made them arrogant and ungrateful, when they fail to help him when he himself becomes poor. But perhaps the play most frequently analysed from a specifically Marxist point of view is *The Merchant of Venice*, a play which shows a world where everything, even human flesh, can be bought and sold on a market as a commodity, and where such market dynamics threaten to expose people's religious beliefs as superficial, pious and hypocritical (see also Chapter 8).

Cultural materialists and new historicists share with Marxism an interest in how socio-economic factors like class and material wealth determine people's psychologies, and especially their belief in their ability to act against existing structures of power. Cultural materialists argue that bringing out Shakespeare's plays' portrayals of subversion may overturn the idea, put forward most famously by E. M. W. Tillyard in his 1943 book *The Elizabethan World Picture*, that Shakespeare was a deep believer in rigid and unequal social hierarchies. Influenced by the ideas of Raymond Williams, who held that culture was a constant struggle between 'dominant', 'residual' and 'emergent' forces, cultural materialists examine how Shakespeare's work relates and contrasts the powerful and the seemingly powerless. New Historicism is most often associated with the work of Stephen Greenblatt, especially his 1980 book *Renaissance Self-fashioning*. Like cultural materialists, new historicists are sceptical of the idea that Shakespeare straightforwardly approved the status quo in his plays. The 'new' historicism is based on this greater emphasis on his plays' challenge to authority. While cultural materialists tend to be more optimistic than new historicists as to the possibility of subversion, the two approaches overlap in their examination of the boundaries between literary and non-literary texts. Cultural materialists often treat the category of the literary suspiciously because of its elitist connotations, analysing different texts with the same techniques. New historicists similarly juxtapose analyses of Shakespeare's plays with non-fictional texts like, say, chapters from theological tracts or eyewitness accounts from voyages to the New World. But their criticism is frequently more narrative than analytical in shape, often recounting historical anecdotes. Now over thirty years old, these approaches are still important in the way they recontextualise and repoliticise understandings of Shakespeare. New critical refractions of Marxism include the 'New Economic Criticism' (see Grav 2012).

Psychoanalytical literary criticism

Psychoanalysis has a hotly debated role in Shakespeare criticism, as it does in the modern world as a whole. New historicists have criticised it for being anachronistic. Shakespeare's characters do not of course articulate their feelings or senses of themselves in Freudian terms like superego, ego or id. Relationships within and between families were also very differently organised in Shakespearean times. But if these important terminological issues are negotiated, psychoanalytical attention to suppressed desires seething between family members, and to dream, memory and unconscious wishes, complement powerfully the Marxist-influenced critical approaches described above. Critics who take psychoanalytical approaches to Shakespeare often notice how families in the plays are rarely complete. There are no mothers, for example, in *King Lear*. Lear's and Gloucester's wives are only briefly mentioned. By contrast, Coriolanus's father is invisible, and his mother Volumnia is only too domineeringly present.

The most famous psychoanalytical reading of a Shakespeare play, however, is that by Ernest Jones on *Hamlet* (1949). Jones's discussions with Sigmund Freud in the early nineteenth century helped crystallise Freud's thinking about his most famous idea, the Oedipus complex. Freud argued that male children feel, then guiltily repress, desires to murder their father and marry their mother, terming this process the Oedipus complex after the man in the ancient myth who unwittingly kills his father Laius and marries his mother Jocasta. Jones argued that Prince Hamlet delays killing his uncle Claudius because he identifies with him. Claudius has after all achieved in Hamlet's place Hamlet's repressed desires to murder his father and have sex with his mother. Shakespeare's *Hamlet* is in Jones's reading great art because it puts its finger on something fundamental to all, or at least all male, human life.

Psychoanalytic readings of Shakespeare similarly subscribe to some extent to the Freudian conviction that psychic life, especially our sense of ourselves as men or women, is determined by these very early life events, which take place before we learn language and therefore before the mind can rationalise them consciously. Shakespeareans like Janet Adelman or Coppélia Kahn are especially interested in how childhood, parent–child relationships and dreams relate to madness and constructions of masculinity and femininity. Via, say, Ophelia, or the cross-dressing Portia, Viola or Rosalind, Shakespeare depicts the struggle to keep up a socially acceptable identity and conform to pre-established, often gendered norms.

In so far as psychoanalysis is what Sigmund Freud's patient 'Anna O' called 'a talking cure' (see Gay 1995: 68), it relates these themes of gender, sanity and social conformity to the use of language. Taking as a lead the more linguistic focus of psychoanalyst Jacques Lacan – who has written brilliantly on unfinished mourning in *Hamlet* (see Lacan 1977) – Lacanian critics focus also on the semantic density of Shakespearean language, the hidden messages tucked away in puns, poetic rhythms and rhetorical figures – to argue that language reveals more than its speaker could ever consciously comprehend. Psychoanalytical theory can therefore help us analyse Shakespeare's words, as well as the broad themes and structures of his stories.

Structuralism and post-structuralism

Lacan's intuitions about language speaking through the unconscious – an elaboration on the famous idea of a 'Freudian slip' – thus strangely reverse the relationship between speaker and speech: language speaks through its speaker, rather than the other way around. A similar reversal is fundamental to 'structuralism' and 'post-structuralism', which argue that meaning was not inherently contained 'within' signs, but emerges instead from the relationships *between* signs, their differences from each other. Such relativist currents of thought effectively work to invert long-standing relations of cause and effect. Conventional 'sources' of meaning, such as speakers and signs, are considered as mere by-products of much more powerful linguistic, unconscious and social structures. Post-structuralists thus deconstruct what seems instinctive and natural to the point where it suddenly appears as artificial, constructed and most often serving the powerful. This helps explain why psycho-analytical, post-structuralist and post-Marxist influences are especially powerful in feminist, queer and postcolonialist Shakespeare criticism, which focuses on characters marginalised and disenfranchised due to issues of gender, sexuality or race.

Marginal characters: feminism, queer, postcolonialism

Feminism

Feminist Shakespearean criticism takes a variety of overlapping forms. It may examine how Shakespearean heroines conform to or resist the social and symbolic roles set up for them, such as wife and child-bearer, idealised beloved, or, more aggressively, witch or whore. From a wider perspective, it examines the theological and socio-economic forces that compel such roles for women, and asks if Shakespeare's plays are complicit with them. As an example, feminist critics like Amy L. Smith (2002) have used sixteenth- and seventeenth-century marital tracts to contextualise plays like the infamous *The Taming of the Shrew*, where the strong, outspoken Kate ends up placing '[her] hand beneath [her] husband's foot' (V, ii, 182 in the *Norton Shakespeare*). Cross-dressing is another source of interest. Despite containing no women, the original Shakespearean performances' intermingling of sexes – boys who play girls who play boys – has been influential to feminist readings of gender. Theorists from Simone de Beauvoir (1949, newly translated 2010) to Judith Butler (2006) have argued that gender is not so much a biological fact as an acquired cultural practice, which dictates how we live in our own bodies but can be changed in and through different kinds of social roleplay. Butler terms this 'performativity'. One important strand of recent feminist thought thus examines the degrees to which men can be feminine, and women can be masculine, while asking how femininity may exert pressure on an often violently competitive modern world that coerces both men and women to adopt masculine characteristics. Seeing gender thus as a fluid continuum, rather than a straightforward opposition of man and woman, this strand of feminist criticism strongly overlaps with work influenced by 'queer theory', which deals with homosexuality, its history and its specific modes of desire.

Queer theory

Perhaps the most obvious examples of queer theory's impact on Shakespeare studies concern *Shakespeare Sonnets*. Oscar Wilde, W. H. Auden and more recently critics like Joseph Pequigney (1987) have read Sonnets 1–126, apparently to 'a lovely boy', in terms of homosexual desire. Thinkers like Michel Foucault, however, believe that, while people in Shakespeare's time indulged in same-sex acts, and were often punished violently for them, they did not self-define as 'homosexual': the category did not exist until the nineteenth century. Some critics have therefore used the word 'homosocial' to describe a variety of distinctive practices in the period involving people of the same sex, such as courtly flattery of a king or patron, Neoplatonic ideas of friendship, and a surprisingly wide legal definition of 'sodomy', which could be applied to any non-procreative sex act. Such critics argue that 'homosocial' is a better descriptor of a time where women were more marginalised, and friendships between men were correspondingly more intense. Such a context has framed discussion of, say, Shakespeare's treatment of the king and his male favourites in *Richard II* and, in *Coriolanus*, Coriolanus's rivalry with the Volscian general Aufidius, where the very energy of their martial battling seems to tip over into sexual desire. More recently Medhavi Menon has argued that 'queer' is so unsettling a force it cannot be restrained simply to issues of gender and sexuality: it is more like a deconstructive energy, questioning and subverting everything it encounters.

Postcolonialism

Postcolonial criticism of Shakespeare focuses mainly on racially marginalised characters, such as Aaron the Moor from *Titus Andronicus*, Othello and, especially, Caliban in *The Tempest*. The psychoanalyst and postcolonial theorist Octave Mannoni's 1950 study *La psychologie de la colonisation* was even translated into English in 1956 as *Prospero and Caliban*. Mannoni, and postcolonial criticism as a whole, is interested in the psychological effects on a people when another country takes theirs over, just as when Prospero takes control of Caliban's island. Theorists like Homi K. Bhabha (1994) have observed that colonised people often imitate the behaviours and speech patterns of the colonisers. This process, which he terms 'mimicry', is ambivalent in tone: it hovers uneasily between respectful homage and scornful parody. Comparable ambivalences arise in *The Tempest* when Caliban, seeking freedom from Prospero, goes straight from one ruler to another, promising to follow Stephano if their planned revolution comes to fruition. Caliban's ambivalence to authority – hatred for Prospero, love for Stephano – parallels that felt by colonised people for their colonisers' language, especially if, over time, it comes to supplant their own in their minds and communities, leaving them with no other means to talk and think. In this too Shakespeare is prescient. 'You taught me language', Caliban spits at Prospero, 'and my profit on't / Is I know how to curse' (I, ii, 364–5). The post-colonial engagement with Shakespeare is yet further complicated by the fact that the poems and plays were themselves involved in colonialism. They helped establish the sense of 'Englishness' which justified the colonial project; they were included on the curriculum as the English sought to educate ('civilise'?) large parts of the world (see also Chapter 14). This historical backdrop is important when considering 'global Shakespeares': the wide rich range of often non-English productions put on by companies across the world.

More recent developments in Shakespeare criticism

In recent years, the field of Shakespeare criticism has been taken in various new directions. The theological dimension of Shakespeare's universe is often under-examined by the relatively secular critical approaches set out above. Critical interest in the spiritual themes of Shakespeare's texts has therefore developed (see Fernie 2005b). As an interesting offshoot of this discussion, critics like Ewan Fernie (2005a) are asking if, and how, the aesthetic experience of reading and watching Shakespeare can address spiritual needs in our own era of modern scepticism and atheism. Such a 'presentist' approach argues that literary criticism must describe, even elicit, our emotional responses to Shakespeare's art. The term 'presentist' thus plays on various related senses: the critic is a subjective, self-describing 'presence', and explores the continually negotiated role of Shakespeare in our historical 'present'. Eco-criticism and disability studies are two recent related directions which avowedly use Shakespeare to historicise, justify and lend cultural weight to urgently contemporary discussions (see Egan 2006; Schaap Williams 2009), while 'new materialists' seek rather to enrich our historicised understanding of Shakespeare's text and world by focusing on material objects, such as props, costumes and furniture (see, for example, Kalas 2007, on the mirror).

Another wide-reaching critical discussion of the new(ish) millennium concerns the precise relationship between Shakespeare and our understanding of humanity. Harold Bloom (1999) famously claimed that Shakespeare invented our idea of 'the Human' by constructing, from a radically original, complex and sophisticated use of language, characters with unprecedented emotional depth. Cognitivist critics like Mary Thomas Crane (2000), Evelyn Tribble (2011), and Raphael Lyne (2014) seek to reconceptualise the ideas of character in terms of perception, mind and brain. Andy Mousley (2008) has used the term 'literary humanism' as he urges critics to locate in literature pathways to a collective, meaningful wisdom which he thinks has been forgotten in an increasingly atomised modern world. 'Posthumanist' thinkers like Stefan Herbrechter, however, explore the concept of the 'human' for its tendency to generalise and homogenise people and thus, however subtly, victimise those who do not fit readily into conformist norms (see Herbrechter 2013). They also question the very point of using the term, given that people, cyborg-like, are increasingly mediating their lives and relationships through technology.

The intellectual stakes of reading Shakespeare thus remain important in the early new millennium. 'The Bard' is often co-opted by the values and outlooks of socio-cultural elites but the plays themselves depict such power-laden processes, and the psychological consequences for people caught up in them, much more ambivalently. Perhaps this helps explain why their writer's name is now a near-synonym for the very universality of the human race. The explorations of the plays in this book seek to help students think for themselves about how these issues interrelate.

References

The Bodleian First Folio (n.d.), Digital facsimile of the First Folio of Shakespeare's plays, Bodleian Arch. G c.7, <http://firstfolio.bodleian.ox.ac.uk/> (last accessed 9 August 2016).

Cadwalladr, C. (2010), 'Derek Jacobi's King Lear: "I've always felt slightly young for the role, but now I'm 72 …"', The Observer, 28 November, <https://www.theguardian.com/culture/2010/nov/28/derek-jacobi-king-lear-interview> (last accessed 9 August 2016).

Derrida, J. (1992), 'Aphorism Countertime', in Acts of Literature, ed. D. Attridge, London/New York: Routledge, pp. 414–33.

Gilbert, G. (2015), 'Christopher Eccleston on Social Mobility: "I would stand less of a chance of success today"', Independent, 17 April, <http://www.independent.co.uk/arts-entertainment/tv/features/christopher-eccleston-on-social-mobility-its-undeniable-that-i-would-stand-less-of-a-chance-today-10181320.html> (last accessed 9 August 2016).

Greene, R. [1592] 1996, 'Greene's Groatsworth of Wit', transcribed N. Green, <http://www.oxford-shakespeare.com/Greene/Greenes_Groatsworth.pdf> (last accessed 9 August 2016).

The Guardian (1983), 'Chancellor with Shakespeare on His Side: The Terry Coleman Interview', 5 November, p. 11.

Maltby, K. (2015), 'What a Waste! It's Shakespeare for the Kids', The Times, 6 August, <http://www.thetimes.co.uk/tto/arts/stage/theatre/article4518986.ece> (last accessed 9 August 2016).

Selective critical bibliography

The World Shakespeare Bibliography (http://www.worldshakesbib.org) lists 146,670 works of scholarship and theatrical productions from 1960. To my shame I have not yet read and seen them all. I therefore offer only a very selective survey here. Useful book-length surveys of important criticism on individual plays are available in, say, the Routledge Sourcebook, Palgrave Essential Criticism and Arden State of Play, Critical Reader and Language and Writing series. Renaissance Quarterly, Shakespeare Quarterly, Shakespeare Survey and Shakespeare are good scholarly journals.

Editions

The RSC Complete Works (ed. Bate and Rasmussen, 2007) is based on the First Folio. The Norton Shakespeare (3rd edn, 2015) uses instead the Oxford text, edited by Stanley Wells and Gary Taylor. Wells and Taylor's exhaustive 650-page Textual Companion (Oxford University Press, 1988) carefully accounts for and justifies their myriad editorial decisions. The Arden, Oxford and New Cambridge series are the industry standard for single-play scholarly editions.

Shakespeare biography

Duncan-Jones, K. (2010), *Shakespeare: An Ungentle Life*, London: Methuen.

Dutton, R. (2016), *Shakespeare, Court Dramatist*, Oxford: Oxford University Press.

Enterline, L. (2012), *Shakespeare's Schoolroom*, Philadelphia: University of Pennsylvania Press.

Greenblatt, S. (2005), *Will in the World: How Shakespeare Became Shakespeare*, London: Pimlico.

Holderness, G. (2013), *Nine Lives of William Shakespeare*, London: Arden Shakespeare.

Schoenbaum, S. (1976), *Shakespeare: A Documentary Life*, Oxford: Clarendon Press.

Shapiro, J. (2005), *1599: A Year in the Life of William Shakespeare*, London: Faber and Faber.

Shapiro, J. (2015), *1606: William Shakespeare and the Year of Lear*, London: Faber and Faber.

Shakespeare on stage

The studies on individual plays in the Cambridge University Press *Shakespeare in Production* series are a good place to start. The RSC and Globe websites www.rsc.org.uk and www.shakespearesglobe.com are also attractive and informative.

Gurr, A. (2009), *The Shakespearean Stage 1574–1642*, 4th edn, Cambridge: Cambridge University Press.

Palfrey, S. and T. Stern (2007), *Shakespeare in Parts*, Oxford: Oxford University Press.

Weimann, R. (2000), *Author's Pen and Actor's Voice: Playing and Writing Shakespeare's Theatre*, Cambridge: Cambridge University Press.

Shakespeare on screen

Jackson, R. (ed.) (2007), *The Cambridge Companion to Shakespeare on Film*, Cambridge: Cambridge University Press.

Rothwell, K. (2004), *A History of Shakespeare on Screen: A Century of Film and Television*, 2nd edn, Cambridge: Cambridge University Press.

Thornton Burnett, M. (2013), *Shakespeare and World Cinema*, Cambridge: Cambridge University Press.

Thornton Burnett, M. and R. Wray (2006), *Screening Shakespeare in the Twenty-first Century*, Edinburgh: Edinburgh University Press.

Classic criticism

Barber, C. L. [1959] (2012), *Shakespeare's Festive Comedy: A Study of Dramatic Form and Its Relation to Social Custom*, Princeton: Princeton University Press.

Bradley, A. C. (1952), *Shakespearean Tragedy: Lectures on Hamlet, Othello, King Lear, Macbeth*, London/New York: Macmillan.

Brooks, C. (1949), *The Well-wrought Urn: Studies in the Structure of Poetry*, London: Dobson.

Bullough, G. (1957–75), *Narrative and Dramatic Sources of Shakespeare*, 8 vols, London: Routledge/New York: Columbia University Press.

Knight, G. W. [1930] (2001), *The Wheel of Fire: Essays in Interpretation of Shakespeare's Sombre Tragedies*, London: H. Milford.

Mahood, M. [1957] (2003), *Shakespeare's Wordplay*, London: Routledge.

Tillyard, E. M. W. (1943), *The Elizabethan World Picture*, London: Chatto and Windus.

Wright, T. (1988), *Shakespeare's Metrical Art*, Berkeley: University of California Press.

Marxist/economic criticism

Dollimore, J. (2004), *Radical Tragedy: Religion, Ideology and Power in the Drama of Shakespeare and His Contemporaries*, 3rd edn, Durham, NC: Duke University Press.

Dollimore, J. and A. Sinfield (eds) (1994), *Political Shakespeare: Essays in Cultural Materialism*, 2nd edn, Manchester: Manchester University Press.

Egan, G. (2004), *Shakespeare and Marx*, Oxford: Oxford University Press.

Grav, P. (2012), 'Taking Stock of Shakespeare and the New Economic Criticism', *Shakespeare*, 8:1, 111–36.

Greenblatt, S. [1980] (2005), *Renaissance Self-fashioning: From More to Shakespeare*, Chicago: University of Chicago Press.

Howard, J. and S. Shershow (eds) (2001), *Marxist Shakespeares*, London/New York: Routledge.

Psychoanalytical criticism and theory

Adelman, J. (1992), *Suffocating Mothers: Fantasies of Maternal Origin in Shakespeare's Plays, 'Hamlet' to 'The Tempest'*, London/New York: Routledge.

Armstrong, P. (2001), *Shakespeare in Psychoanalysis*, London/New York: Routledge.

Derrida, J. (1992), 'Aphorism Countertime', in *Acts of Literature*, ed. D. Attridge, London/New York Routledge, pp. 414–33.

Garber, M. [1987] (2010), *Shakespeare's Ghost Writers: Literature as Uncanny Causality*, London/New York: Routledge.

Gay, P. (ed.) (1995), *The Freud Reader*, London: Vintage.

Jones, E. (1949), *Hamlet and Oedipus*, London: Gollancz.

Kahn, C. (1981), *Man's Estate: Masculine Identity in Shakespeare*, Berkeley: University of California Press.

Lacan, J. (1977), 'Desire and the Interpretation of Desire in *Hamlet*', *Yale French Studies*, 55/56, 11–52.

Feminist criticism and theory

Butler, J. (2006), *Gender Trouble: Feminism and the Subversion of Identity*, London/New York: Routledge.

Callaghan, D. (1999), *Shakespeare without Women: Representing Gender and Race on the Renaissance Stage*, London/New York: Routledge.

de Beauvoir, S. (2010), *The Second Sex*, trans. C. Borde and S. Malovany-Chevallier, New York: Vintage.

Dusinberre, J. (2003), *Shakespeare and the Nature of Women*, 3rd edn, Basingstoke: Palgrave Macmillan.

Jardine, L. (1983), *Still Harping on Daughters: Women and Drama in the Age of Shakespeare*, Brighton: Harvester.

Orgel, S. (1996), *Impersonations: The Performance of Gender in Shakespeare's England*, Cambridge: Cambridge University Press.

Smith, A. L. (2002), 'Performing Marriage with a Difference: Wooing, Wedding, and Bedding in *The Taming of the Shrew*', *Comparative Drama*, 36:3–4, 289–320.

Queer criticism

Menon, M. (2011), *Shakesqueer: A Queer Companion to the Complete Works of Shakespeare*, Durham, NC/London: Duke University Press.

Pequigney, J. (1987), *Such Is My Love: A Study of Shakespeare's Sonnets*, Chicago: University of Chicago Press.

Smith, B. (1995), *Homosexual Desire in Shakespeare's England: A Cultural Poetics*, Chicago: University of Chicago Press.

Traub, V. (2002), *The Renaissance of Lesbianism in Early Modern England*, Cambridge: Cambridge University Press.

Postcolonial criticism and theory

Bhabha, H. K. (1994), *The Location of Culture*, London: Routledge.

Loomba, A. (2002), *Shakespeare, Race and Colonialism*, Oxford: Oxford University Press.

Loomba, A. and M. Orkin (eds) (1998), *Post-colonial Shakespeares*, London/New York: Routledge.

Mannoni, O. (1956), *Prospero and Caliban: The Psychology of Colonisation*, London: Methuen.

Contemporary criticism

Bate, J. [1997] (2008), *The Genius of Shakespeare*, London: Picador.

Bloom, H. (1999), *Shakespeare: The Invention of the Human*, New York: Riverhead.

Brooks, D. A., M. Biberman and J. R. Lupton (eds) (2011), *Shakespeare after 9/11: How a Social Trauma Reshapes Interpretation*, Lewiston, NY: Edwin Mellen Press.

Crane, M. (2000), *Shakespeare's Brain: Reading with Cognitive Theory*, Princeton: Princeton University Press.

Egan, G. (2006), *Green Shakespeares: From Ecopolitics to Ecocriticism*, London: Routledge.

Fernie, E. (2005a), 'Shakespeare and the Prospect of Presentism', *Shakespeare Survey*, 58, 169–84.

Fernie, E. (ed.) (2005b), *Spiritual Shakespeares*, London/New York: Routledge.

Gleyzon, F.-X. and J. Gregory (eds) (2015), *Shakespeare and the Future of Theory*, London/New York: Routledge.

Herbrechter, S. (2013), *Posthumanism: A Critical Analysis*, London: Bloomsbury Academic.

Kalas, R. (2007), *Frame, Glass, Verse: The Technology of Poetic Invention in the English Renaissance*, Ithaca, NY: Cornell University Press.

Kermode, F. (2000), *Shakespeare's Language*, London: Penguin.

Lupton, J. (2005), *Citizen Saints: Shakespeare and Political Theology*, Chicago: University of Chicago Press.

Lyne, R. (2011), *Shakespeare, Rhetoric and Cognition*, Cambridge: Cambridge University Press.

Lyne, R. (2014), 'Shakespeare, Perception and Theory of Mind', *Paragraph*, 37:1, 79–95.

McKenzie, W. and T. Papadopoulou (eds) (2012), *Shakespeare and I*, London/New York: Continuum.

Mousley, A. (2008), *Re-humanising Shakespeare: Literary Humanism, Wisdom and Modernity*, Edinburgh: Edinburgh University Press.

Ryan, K. (2015), *Shakespeare's Universality: Here's Fine Revolution*, London: Arden Shakespeare.

Schaap Williams, K. (2009), 'Enabling Richard: The Rhetoric of Disability in *Richard III*', *Disability Studies Quarterly*, 29:4, <http://dsq-sds.org/article/view/997/1181> (last accessed 29 June 2016).

Schalkwyk, D. (2008), *Shakespeare, Love, and Service*, Cambridge: Cambridge University Press.

Tribble, E. (2011), *Cognition in the Globe: Attention and Memory in Shakespeare's Time*, Basingstoke: Palgrave Macmillan.

Wilson, R. (2007), *Shakespeare in French Theory: King of Shadows*, London/New York: Routledge.

Part I. Tragedies

1 *Romeo and Juliet*

c. 1595, printed 1597, 1599

Act, scene and line references are to the 2000 Oxford edition, based on the 1599 Second Quarto (Q2), edited by Jill L. Levenson. The 2012 Arden Third Series edition, edited by René Weis, is also excellent.

Plot summary

Escalus the Prince of Verona is exasperated by frequent clashes between the feuding Montague and Capulet families, and forbids any future violence on pain of death (I, i, 93). This does not, however, stop Romeo Montague, his cousin Benvolio, and the Prince's kinsman Mercutio from provocatively sneaking into a feast at the Capulets' house (I, iv, 129). The feast has been held to introduce the young Juliet Capulet to Paris: the man to whom she has been betrothed by her parents (I, iii, 65–107). Romeo and Juliet see each other and fall in love (I, iv, 205–23), and then despite their families' wishes marry, aided by Friar Laurence (II, v, 36–7). The newly married Romeo seeks to make peace with Juliet's fierce cousin Tybalt, who has already challenged Romeo to a duel (II, iii, 8), as he threatens Benvolio and Malvolio (III, i, 55–80). But in coming between the fighters he only gives Tybalt the chance to deal a crafty, fatal blow to Mercutio (III, i, 88). The angered Romeo kills Tybalt in revenge (III, i, 131). After hearing the circumstances of the fray the Prince decides not to execute Romeo but banish him from Verona (III, i, 187). Despite Tybalt's death, Juliet's parents decide to press on with the plan of marrying her to Paris. The ceremony is arranged in a matter of days (III, v, 112–15). The desperate Juliet is rebuked by her parents for her protests (III, v, 116–203) and goes to Friar Laurence for help. Friar Laurence can see only one way for Juliet to escape from her betrothal to Paris and join her banished love: before the wedding she is to take a drug which simulates death temporarily; Friar Laurence will then instruct Romeo by letter to rescue her from the burial crypt and take her back with him to Mantua (IV, i, 89–117). Juliet performs her part of the plan (IV, iii, 57). Her lamenting family take her drugged, inert body to their crypt. Romeo, however, does not receive Friar Laurence's letter, and hears only that Juliet has died (V, i, 20). Desperate, he buys poison from an apothecary (V, i, 75) and vows to take it at her tomb. There he encounters and kills Paris, likewise mourning (V, iii, 73), and drinks down the poison, falling by Juliet's body (V, iii, 120). As Juliet awakes from her simulated death, Friar Laurence laments to her the calamitous outcome of their plan and offers to hide her in a convent (V, iii, 156–7), before fleeing some approaching watchmen (V, iii, 159). Juliet, seeing her love's dead body, fatally stabs herself (V, iii, 170). The watchmen discover the bodies and raise the alarm (V, iii, 172). Friar Laurence explains to the assembled Prince and senior members of the Montague and Capulet families Romeo and Juliet's love, marriage and plan to escape (V, iii, 229–69). The Montagues and Capulets form a truce, each agreeing to erect tributes to the victim from the other family (V, iii, 296–304).

Major characters

Juliet (I, iii; I, iv; II, i; II, iv; II, v; III, ii; III, v; IV, i; IV, ii; IV, iii; IV, iv; V, iii)

René Weis rightly calls Juliet 'one of the most demanding female parts in the canon' (ed. Weis 2012: 54). Shakespeare makes her younger than the sources, explicitly mentioning that she is thirteen years old: 'On Lammas Eve [31 July] at night shall she be fourteen' (I, iii, 23). It may be said that if an actress looks physically young enough to play Juliet, she could be too psychologically and emotionally immature to do so. The role strikes a challenging balance between innocent naïvety, shrewd awareness of Verona's ideological codes like honour and marriage, subversive stubbornness and sexual curiosity. Elements of this blend are established from Juliet's very first entry. She appears quickly when called by the Nurse in Act I, scene iii, indicating straight away a degree of obedience, but this is undercut by her wary, canny responses to her mother's questions about Paris. Significantly, her first conversation of any length is with Romeo (I, iv, 206–40). At one point their exchange takes the form of a shared sonnet, with Romeo and then Juliet taking it in turns to utter the rhymed lines, anticipating through poetic form their marital, then sexual union (I, iv, 206–19). Their kiss (I, iv, 220) would have been a bold gesture on the Elizabethan stage.

Juliet's famous speech in Act II, scene i, unwittingly observed by Romeo, comments incisively on how immaterial words, like the warring names 'Montague' and 'Capulet', frustrate material, natural desires. Romeo's name 'Montague' stops her enjoying 'any other part/Belonging to a man', lines whose sexual connotations are often brought out in performance (II, i, 84–5). This speech accentuates the tension between Juliet's love-struck idealism and the ideological pressures of the Veronese 'real world': 'a rose/By any other word [Q1 'name'] would smell as sweet' (II, i, 86–7). But Romeo's and Juliet's fates are ultimately determined by the names they bear, society and language reinforce each other, and it is simplistic to say Juliet rejects unequivocally linguistic conventions as artificial and arbitrary: her faith in the power of words marks the marriage vows she asks Romeo to exchange (II, i, 186–7).

In her next scene, her exchange with the Nurse in Act II, scene iv, her impatience to be married is enthusiastically clear. But when she actually does get married (II, v) she is surprisingly quiet, as if overawed by the occasion. This silence is especially striking given her talkativeness when next we see her in Act III, scene ii, a scene which is cut aggressively in two by news of Romeo's banishment. Before this news arrives, Juliet's impatience takes a markedly sexual turn. Her speech is full of imperatives, command verbs: she asks the night-bringing stars to 'gallop', and night multiple times to 'come' (III, ii, 10, 17, 20). Her imagery is charged with erotic energy as when she refers to her as-yet 'unmanned blood' (III, ii, 14). The surrender of her virginity will be losing 'a winning match' (III, ii, 13). And she talks of her love as a 'mansion' 'not yet enjoyed' (III, ii, 27). After the Nurse announces Romeo's exile, however, Juliet's speech becomes aggressive as never before. Noticeably in a play which is focused so tightly in a particular locale – Verona – the distressed Juliet seems to lose all sense of spatial navigation or coordination: '"Romeo is banished" –/There is no end, no limit, measure, bound,/In that word's death', and her sexual desire sinks to regret: 'death, not Romeo, take my maidenhead' (III, ii, 124–6, 137).

By Act III, scene v, however, Romeo and Juliet have consummated their marriage. Many of the features of the balcony scene are here echoed in a minor key. There is the same reluctance to say goodbye (III, v, 16, 25). Their encounter ends not with a goodbye kiss but with the Nurse ordering Romeo to flee Juliet's approaching mother, furious at Tybalt's death (III, v, 39–40). Juliet's conversation with her treads carefully between pleasing her mother and articulating her love for Romeo, as in the clever ambiguity of her wish 'To wreak the love I bore my cousin/Upon his body that hath slaughtered him' (III, v, 101–2). In Act IV, scene i Juliet encounters Paris at Friar Laurence's lodgings, whom she has already determinedly refused, defying her furious father's wish to the contrary. They exchange only single verse lines or couplets. Juliet is frustrated, tersely polite. This contrasts with her much longer speeches to Friar Laurence as Paris exits, giving a sense of desperation and confessional release. This reaches a peak of intensity in Act IV, scene i (77–88), where she articulates an upfront willingness to die and a fertile imagination of ways in which to do it.

Juliet's most powerful speech, often cut by directors to avoid Juliet dominating the play, takes place in Act IV, scene iii, just before she executes Friar Laurence's plan and drinks the death-simulating drug. 'What if this mixture do not work at all?' (IV, iii, 20). Juliet's moving anxiety is elicited by disjointed rhythms, sentences that interrupt each other, emphatic use of *anaphora* ('*And* madly play [...] *And* pluck [...] *And* in this rage [...]', IV, iii, 50–3), gruesome visions of the undead Tybalt (IV, iii, 42, 51, 56) and repeated mention of the risk she is taking. What if no one comes to rescue her? At such moments of duress, Juliet sees threat everywhere, stressing the sheer power of the rules of honour she and Romeo have transgressed. She even fears the Friar may try to kill her out of anger for performing their forbidden marriage (IV, iii, 24–5). Everyone is a potential enemy to their love. Juliet's foreboding is of course prescient.

In Act V, scene iii, Juliet's final appearance, her last word, like Romeo's, is 'die'. Her speeches here are brief, fragmented, as if overwhelmed, as if Shakespeare is letting the tragic coincidence of events, rather than Juliet's verbal eloquence, move his audience. Part of the play's tragic effect also depends on how Juliet reconciles her innocence and sensuality. She silently tests audiences' attitudes to women's sexual behaviour. Does our sympathy for Juliet depend on her innocence? If so, just how sexual is Juliet 'allowed' to be before this sympathy is tested? Indeed, the question as to whether Juliet is 'too quickly won' is one she herself poses (II, i, 128–49).

Romeo (I, i; I, iv; II, i; II, ii; II, iii; II, v; III, i; III, iii; III, v; V, i; V, iii)

Despite being named first in the title, Romeo is perhaps a less engaging and fully drawn character than Juliet. 'Compared to Juliet, Romeo is almost a cipher' (ed. Weis 2012: 7). Apart from brief (and often cut) news of his mother's death (V, iii, 210), we know little of Romeo's history or background. The play clearly focuses much more on the Capulet household and Juliet's entrapment therein. Romeo is discussed by others before he himself appears onstage, a frequent Shakespearean device to direct and increase the audience's interest towards major characters. This also distances Romeo from the fighting that starts the play, associating him from the very beginning with the lovelorn pacifism that will later lead indirectly, and tragically, to Mercutio's and Tybalt's deaths. Romeo is thus quickly set apart from his peers. Benvolio mocks the hackneyed phrasing running through Romeo's first speech of any length (I, i, 169–78) describing his love for 'Rosaline'. Rosaline, whom we never see, acts as a kind of foil against which Romeo's sudden love at first sight for Juliet (I, iv), a moment known as the 'innamoramento', may be constrasted. Via Romeo, Shakespeare establishes an analogy between a lover's passion and linguistic ingenuity. Contrasting with the vapid clichés of his earlier speeches, Romeo's very first words to Juliet initiate the sonnet they take turns to recite, as if her very sight has ushered them both irresistibly, despite themselves, into a hyper-poetic way of speaking and thinking. By the famous balcony scene, however (II, i), Romeo's language has reverted once more to tired commonplaces and clumsy requests for 'satisfaction', comically interrupted and diffused by Juliet.

The next scenes show Romeo in a more favourable light, as if to make his fall at the play's midpoint all the more tragic. In Act II, scene ii he makes good on his 'holy vow', arranging the marriage with Friar Laurence. In Act II, scene iii he responds so well to Mercutio's witty jests that Mercutio begs Benvolio for aid (63–4), and reassures Juliet's Nurse of his honourable intentions. These intentions are immediately fulfilled in the following scene's marriage ceremony. When in Act III, scene i Romeo kills Tybalt in revenge for Mercutio, it is as if he has been drawn into an eroticised violent rashness which echoes the first scene's bawdy puns on 'swords', 'heads' and 'maidenheads' (I, i, 23–5). His imagery likewise confuses fighting with sexual energy: 'O sweet Juliet,/Thy beauty hath made me effeminate,/And in my temper softened valour's steel' (III, i, 115).

The after-effects of Romeo's rashness persist throughout the rest of the play. The Friar stops him from stabbing himself, but he remains inconsolable ('Hang up philosophy!/Unless philosophy can make a Juliet', III, iii, 58–9), seeming indifferent to death even in Juliet's chamber ('Let me be ta'en, let me be put to death', III, v, 17). This is only accentuated as the play nears its close. Romeo seems calm only when he has resolved to drink the poison. His final speech (V, iii, 74–120) is carefully patterned, even dignified, seeking reconciliation with his victims Paris (whom he has just killed) and Tybalt, before addressing Juliet for the final time. Romeo dies as a serial killer, as well as Shakespeare's great lover.

Supporting characters

Mercutio (I, iv; II, i; II, iii; III, i)

Mercutio is a Shakespearean innovation: he is embellished greatly from the story's various sources. His name is apt: he is 'Mercurial' in various senses. His quick, riddling wits recall both the fleet-footed divine messenger and the ungraspable liquid metal. His is a teasing, critical, sexual voice. He is very, even pedantically, alert to the way words can refract into multiple meanings: he often turns this skill upon his poor interlocutor. He delivers his most famous speech during his first scene (I, iv, 51–93) about the Fairy Queen Mab, who causes chaos everywhere, including in lovers' brains. This long speech, often cut in performance, emphasises the links of this strange, as yet unidentified character – Romeo only names him in line 93 – with confusion and nervous energy, links that persist until his death. In his brief but charismatic entry (II, i, 4–43), Mercutio quibbles incessantly on the word 'conjure' (II, i, 6, 17, 18, 27), as if to 'conjure' back the infatuated and suddenly vanished Romeo, who has turned back to Juliet's balcony. He mocks Romeo's love frequently. Romeo retorts 'he jests at scars that never felt a wound' (II, i, 44) but this mockery is often portrayed in performance as a form of homosexual jealousy. Mercutio reduces Romeo's clichés to contemptuously bare near-monosyllables ('Romeo! Humours! Madman! Passion! Lover!', II, i, 8) and his love to bawdy body parts ('quivering thigh', II, i, 20). In Act II, scene iii, once he has learned of Romeo's meeting with Juliet, he spars with him verbally, sneering at Romeo for his 'French slop', or effeminate behaviour (II, iii, 43). The French King at the time, Henri III, surrounded himself with male favourites or *mignons* (cute ones), from which we still get the word *minions*. The word association game they then play (II, iii, 68–82), like the sonnet Romeo shares with Juliet, uses interlocking verbal structures to signal reciprocal amity. Their punning play on often bawdy words like 'pink', 'pump', 'goose', 'sauce', 'bitter', 'ell' and 'cheverel', emphasises Mercutio's genuine affection for Romeo. This makes more credible, and tragic, their later sacrifices for each other. Mercutio's love for Romeo might also explain the aggressiveness of his jests to the arriving Nurse, his rival Juliet's companion, whom he insults for her age ('hide her face', II, iii, 101) and stupidity, calling her 'an old hare', an animal associated with lasciviousness, and a 'hoar' (white with age, homophone with 'whore', II, iii, 125). In his final scene, Act III, scene i, Romeo's observation that Mercutio 'never felt a wound' (II, i, 44) is disproved with grim literalness. The brawl scene is artfully structured. Mercutio ironically characterises the peaceful Benvolio as a violent troublestarter, introducing even before Tybalt's entry ominous themes of quarrelling and unprovoked violence (III, i, 15–29). When Tybalt does appear, Mercutio continues his habit of mockingly transforming his interlocutors' words. Tybalt accuses Mercutio of consorting with Romeo. Mercutio mockingly takes 'consort' to mean 'play music together' (III, i, 45–9). Tybalt is therefore already half-provoked even before Romeo's appearance finally sets him off. Mercutio's near-final words 'A plague a both your houses' (III, i, 106) anticipate and set in motion the tragic themes of the play's second movement.

Tybalt (I, i; I, iv; III, i)

Tybalt's nickname 'Prince of Cats' derives from his near-namesake Tybalt/Tibault – the Prince of Cats in the medieval folklore collection *Reynard the Fox*. It says much of his athletic, aristocratic aggressiveness, and perhaps alludes to his feline, fatal swipe on Mercutio under Romeo's arm. His violent appearances are brief, but always meaningful: he reminds us of the sheer hatred between the Montague and Capulet clans, especially between their youngest generations. Juliet's mother's grief at Tybalt's death has sometimes been performed as a sign of a long-lasting love affair between them. In Act V, scene iii he lies in the crypt with Juliet: 'Tybalt, liest thou there in thy bloody sheet?' (V, iii, 97). This staging stresses Juliet's close, even claustrophobic, adhesion to the Capulet family, but most directors cut it, stressing instead Romeo and Juliet's isolation as young lovers.

Friar Laurence (II, ii; II, v; III, iii; IV, i; IV, iv; V, ii; V, iii)

Friar Laurence, like Benvolio, offers a moderate voice. As a holy man he is trusted and respected by all the warring factions and the audience cannot therefore help but side with him. Like Mercutio, but much more gently, he mocks Romeo's amorous excesses ('Thy love did read by rote, that could not spell', II, ii, 87) and counsels calmness even in his most desperate moments: 'Wisely and slow; they stumble that run fast' (II, ii, 94). This approach also comes through when he advises Paris against hasty marriage (IV, i, 1). As the deviser and key agent in Juliet's plan to escape with Romeo to Mantua, he also has an important expository function, keeping the story moving (e.g. V, ii).

Benvolio (I, i; I, ii; I, iv; II, i; II, iii; III, i) / 'Balthazar' (V, i; V, iii)

'Ben-voglio' means 'good will'. Benvolio is gentle, sensible and peacemaking. He sometimes gets caught up in the jesting (especially against Juliet's Nurse), but mainly he reminds the audience of the continual danger his friends run. 'You know not what you do' (I, i, 60–1), 'thou wilt anger him' (II, i, 24), 'now, these hot days, is the mad blood stirring' (III, i, 4). It is repeatedly left to him to explain violent situations to the visiting authorities (I, i, 102–11; III, i, 152–75). He announces Mercutio's death to Romeo (III, i, 116). The role of Romeo's companion after his banishment to Mantua is taken over by 'Balthazar' in scenes i and iii of Act V. Benvolio does not seem to leave Verona. But for practical staging purposes though this role could be doubled. The two roles share similar temperaments, so I have included them together here.

Nurse (I, iii; II, iii; II, iv; III, ii; III, iii; III, v; IV, ii; IV, iv)

The Nurse and the higher-born Mercutio antagonise each other: she calls him a 'saucy merchant' full of gallows-worthy 'ropery' (II, iii, 134–5), but her relation with Juliet arguably parallels his with Romeo. Like Mercutio, the Nurse is an energetic, linguistically adventurous, often bawdy companion, telling Juliet 'You shall bear the burden soon at night' (II, iv, 75) and 'you shall rest but little' (IV, iv, 33). Also like Mercutio, the Nurse can often be oddly conformist when it comes to gendered behaviour. Mercutio can be phallically bawdy, stressing a masculine sexuality; he prefers Romeo when he is comically verbally combative and engages with his rhythmically strident and thrustingly alliterative jests ('now art thou sociable, now art thou Romeo', II, iii, 84). Likewise, Juliet's Nurse is often uneasy when Juliet transgresses feminine 'ideals' of chastity and obedience, as when she sides with Paris as 'the properer man' (II, iii, 192). Her absence from the final scenes makes Juliet's isolation in the crypt, away from all social norms and protection, all the more acute. We learn early on that she only has four teeth (I, iii, 15) and was once herself a mother: her dead daughter 'Susan' echoes the name of Shakespeare's own, Susannah (I, iii, 20, 22). In her first scenes, the Nurse immediately seems talkative and verbally playful, playing on Juliet's age 'not fourteen' and the word 'teen' as trouble or pain (I, iii, 14).

In Act II, scene iii she spars with Mercutio, and voices concern to Romeo about Juliet, while setting up the clandestine marriage. As well as go-between or 'drudge' (II, iv, 74), the Nurse is Juliet's messenger, breaking the sad news of Tybalt's death and Romeo's banishment (III, ii, 37–70); her lookout, warning the lovers of Juliet's mother's arrival (III, v, 39–40); and confidante, comforting and consoling Juliet in dark times (e.g. III, ii, 138–9). She is also brave enough, or familiar enough, to interrupt Capulet as he rebukes his daughter, even splitting his verse line in two (III, v, 167–8). But her relative reticence in Act IV, scene ii – just a few, short lines – shows the lasting after-effects of her lord's rebuke. She seems relieved as Juliet 'agrees' to marry Paris. The Nurse's chatty grasp of language seems completely eliminated by the discovery of Juliet's 'dead' body, the last time we see her. Her almost comically excessive repetitions 'O woe! O woeful, woeful, woeful day' are near-meaningless: mere sad sound (IV, iv, 75–80).

Capulet (I, ii; I, iv; III, i (silent); III, iv; III, v; IV, ii; IV, iv; V, iii)

In terms of sheer line count Juliet's father is surprisingly prominent. He has the fourth-largest role. He is important also in the ways in which our sympathies are guided towards Romeo and Juliet. His first lines, added in Q2, strike a surprisingly conciliatory tone (''tis not hard, I think,/For men as old as we to keep the peace', I, ii, 3–4). This might be dismissed as politically astute manoeuvring to please the Duke, but otherwise this shifts the responsibility of the violence to the younger members of the families. *Romeo and Juliet* is less about conflicts between generations, then, than conflicts between members of the same generation. The sense of Capulet being a moderate, reasonable man continues in Act I, scene iv when he upbraids Tybalt during the feast for threatening Romeo. We next see him in Act III, scene i after the deaths of Tybalt and Mercutio – the stage directions are unambiguous – but he says nothing. He seems even dismissive of Tybalt's death soon after ('Well, we were born to die', III, iv, 4), less concerned by the feud with the Montagues than by public appearances. His main concern is not to trivialise Tybalt's death by holding the wedding too soon after ('Wednesday is too soon', III, iv, 19).

His undoubted rage in Act III, scene v and Act IV, scene ii at Juliet's stubborn refusal to marry Paris could at least partly be down to social pressures: 'Day, night […] work, play […] still my care hath been / To have her matched' (III, v, 176–8). This rage is fearsome enough to quiet the otherwise talkative Nurse. But Capulet is quick to forgive Juliet, who has of course by now hatched her plan with Friar Laurence, when she pretends to him that she has accepted Paris's hand. He seems genuinely affectionate for his daughter, even as he of course treats her as a marital bargaining chip. His desperation as he discovers Juliet's 'death' (IV, iv, 57–8, 60, 85–90) recalls the reason why he negotiated so carefully with Paris: 'Earth hath swallowed all my hopes but she' (I, ii, 14). The sense of a quick-tempered, frightening, but well-meaning man comes through in the final scene as Capulet makes the first move towards reconciliation ('O brother Montague, give me thy hand', V, iii, 296).

Capulet's wife (I, iii; I, iv (silent); III, v; IV, ii; IV, iii; IV, iv; V, iii)

Juliet's mother (who has no name of her own) was a teenage mother: 'I was your mother much upon these years / That you are now a maid' (I, iii, 74–5). She is sometimes portrayed in performance as a trophy wife, much closer in age to Tybalt than to her husband, and therefore perhaps attracted to Tybalt. Indeed, a good proportion of her lines are taken up complaining about Tybalt's death. She addresses far fewer words than the Nurse to her daughter. Her defence of Juliet against her father's rage (III, v, 174) is short-lived, even half-hearted, dismissively concluding 'I have done with thee' (III, v, 203). Her complaints following Juliet's simulated death (IV, iv, 44–6) and actual death (V, iii, 206–8, her final lines) could in performance come across as simulated, reflecting perhaps a jealous, frustrated ambivalence towards her child.

Paris (I, ii; III, iv; IV, i; V, iii)

Like Tybalt, Paris has relatively few lines but his role is structurally important. There is a major opportunity in Act IV, scene i, where Paris and Juliet talk together in brief, clipped manner, for the actor to portray Paris sympathetically or predatorily. This helps guide the audience's attitudes to Juliet, and especially Romeo, who of course kills him.

Play structure

Romeo and Juliet has been described as a kind of 'hybrid' where themes of young love, traditionally associated with comedy, give way to tragedy. The comedy goes wrong.

Indeed, the motifs of fairy and folklore raised by Mercutio's Queen Mab speech have strong affinities with *A Midsummer Night's Dream*, written at around the same time. This 'hybrid' may thus be seen as an experiment in tragic form, where comedic themes struggle against tragic destiny, the crossed stars described in the Prologue. Shakespeare's story is more symmetrically structured than his sources to accentuate a narrative arc of rise and fall, thus bringing out the passage from comedy to tragedy. The play starts with a Prologue, ends with an Epilogue, and a Chorus comments on the action near the middle of the play. This symmetrical comi-tragic structure is strengthened by Friar Laurence's regular appearances, alternating his meetings with Romeo (II, ii; III, iii) and Juliet (the wedding in II, v; IV, i), and by mirroring motifs like day and night. Before their wedding Romeo urges the sunlike Juliet to kill the envious moon (II, i, 47), but afterwards the lovers urge their wedding night to live forever (III, v, 1–35). The play's final words 'Juliet and her Romeo' symmetrically reverse the order of the lovers' names in the title. Such symmetries guide our attention to the play's central 'fulcrum point', which is densely packed with incident. Romeo kills Tybalt in the scene immediately after his marriage (II, v; III, i). Romeo later says they had only been married 'an hour' (III, iii, 66). Fate is cruel indeed. The intensity of the narrative pacing makes the audience feel the unremitting pressure the young lovers are under. The fact that the play's viewpoint only leaves Verona briefly and rarely, once Romeo is banished, supports his complaint that 'There is no world without Verona walls' (III, iii, 17). We therefore feel something of Romeo's disorientation when he leaves his city for the first time. Correspondingly, the fact we do not see Romeo for the whole of Act IV makes us feel something like Juliet's loss.

Language

As well as experimenting with tragic structure, *Romeo and Juliet* also deals with the relation between infatuation, poetic creation and uses of language. It draws on and comments on various conventions of love poetry like the 'aubade' where lovers complain of the approaching dawn (III, v, 1–35), the 'epithalamium' or marriage poem (III, ii, 1–31), and the clichéd images which recur in such genres as love's arrow (I, i, 205) and blind Cupid (II, i, 33). The play and its characters are self-conscious about the inadequacy of such conventional language to relay love, that most spontane-ous, authentic and unique of experiences. Juliet gently chides Romeo for kissing 'by th' book' (I, iv, 223). Friar Laurence likewise mocks Romeo for loving Rosaline 'by rote' (II, ii, 88). Much of the play's energy comes from the various ways it tries to do justice to love linguistically, refreshing these conventions anew to reflect love's shocking novelty. As seen above, Romeo's very first words to Juliet initiate a sonnet, embedded within the dialogue, which they take turns to recite.

This novel fusion of different verse forms is perhaps the most explicit example of the play's engagement with the Petrarchan sonnet tradition. Francesco Petrarch (1304–74), the most celebrated early sonneteer, wrote 366 poems to his love Laura. Around the time of *Romeo and Juliet*'s first performances, the English courtier poet Sir Philip Sidney had written a popular sonnet sequence *Astrophil and Stella*, replicating Petrarchan forms and themes of unrequited love. Mercutio sneers, however, that for Romeo 'Laura to his lady was a kitchen-wench' (II, iii, 38), and the play scrutinises Petrarchan strategies for writing about love. For example, Romeo's use of Petrarchan antithesis — Petrarch calls love a 'freezing fire', for example — is hopelessly banal when describing Rosalind: 'I live dead, that live to tell it now' (I, i, 220). But Juliet's densely antithetical descriptions of Romeo after his banishment are movingly frustrated and urgent: 'Beautiful tyrant, fiend angelical / Dove-feathered raven, wolvish-ravening lamb' (III, ii, 73–85). One variant on the play's exploration of Petrarchism and conventional love poetry consists of bodily descriptions and depictions of sexuality. The 'blazon', for example, visualises the beloved lady's body as an itemised, praised, catalogue of distinct parts. Mercutio parodies this convention explicitly, by mocking Romeo's exaggerated descriptions of Rosaline's 'fine foot', 'straight leg' and 'quivering thigh' (I, i, 20) and, more generally, via near-continual sexual innuendo, as if to highlight the carnal desire that lurks beneath the hypocrisy of poetic idealisation. He implies such poets are victims of syphilis ('their bones, their bones', II, iii, 34) and that Romeo's beloved is sexually voracious. Mercutio's reference to a 'medlar tree' (II, i, 35) plays on 'meddler' as lascivious woman and the medlar fruit, which has a large eye known colloquially as an 'open arse' (II, i, 39). His reference to Romeo's love as a 'popp'rin' pear' (II, i, 39) plays not only on the fruit's origin, the Flemish town of Poperinghe but also on 'pop her in' (II, i, 41). Romeo is weakened by the 'blind bow-boys butt-shaft' (II, iii, 15), whose phallic connotations are clear, and is 'fishified' by his love (II, iii, 36).

Mercutio even uses sexual language to Juliet's Nurse when she asks the time: 'the bawdy hand of the dial is now upon the prick of noon' (II, iii, 106). The urge to eroticise language is irresistible, irrepressible. Indeed, the very energy with which Mercutio and Romeo find further innuendo in already suggestive words like 'curtsy', 'pink' and 'pump' threatens to take on its own, independent force. Running through the play is a sexually confrontational energy, rife amongst the Veronese youth, which symbolises and ignites verbal and physical conflict. The brawl at the start of the play is full of quibbles on 'heads' and 'maidenheads' and the constant reference to swords and spears has clear phallic connotations. The overall atmosphere of threatening restlessness comes through in the frequent use of quick dialogue (e.g. II, iii, 66 or IV, i, 18–38) and the jumpy, often repetitious verse rhythms. Mercutio, Romeo and Juliet all repeat themselves. Mercutio uses repetition to stress his bawdy puns, like the orifice-like shape of 'O' in 'O Romeo O that she were, that she were' (II, i, 38). Repetition also stresses the confusingly punned meanings of repeated homophones (e.g. 'soul' and 'sole'), as when Romeo jests with Mercutio 'O single-soled jest, solely singular for the singleness' (II, iii, 63). Chiefly, however, repetition signals impatience or frustration. Juliet's speech is exuberant almost to bursting as she repeats 'out of breath' and 'Good or bad?' (II, iv, 30, 31, 34, 36). And in sadder circumstances Romeo repeats obsessively the dread words 'banishment' and 'banishèd', as if striving hopelessly to gain some kind of grasp and control over the situation (III, iii, 12, 20, 21, 40, 42, 46, 51, 53, 57).

This youthful linguistic restlessness also comes through via the busily metaphorical way Romeo and Juliet recreate each other in their imaginations. Romeo fears his bewitching night with Juliet is little more than a dream, but then concedes this dream is better than reality: 'Too flattering sweet [Q1 'true'] to be substantial' (II, i, 184). Such dreamy transformations, and the night, are frequently invoked. Against the backdrop of night Juliet becomes a 'rich jewel' (I, iv, 159) and 'snowy dove' (I, iv, 161). Juliet desperately wills the creative (and sexual) fantasies that night allows to continue, pretends 'it was the nightingale, and not the lark' that is singing (III, v, 2). Perhaps the play's grandest association of night with fantasy, however, is Juliet begging the night on her death to 'Take' Romeo 'and cut him out in little stars / And he will make the face of heaven so fine, / That all the world will be in love with night, / And pay no worship to the garish sun' (III, ii, 22–5). Such transformations are beautifully transgressive. Veronese language and law restrain the symbolic values of human bodies, restricting them to mere 'Montagues' or 'Capulets'. The transformative way Romeo and Juliet lovingly look at each other opens these symbolic values back up. Strengthened by Romeo's love, Juliet glimpses a sense of herself as infinite: 'my bounty is as boundless as the sea' (II, i, 176). In many ways, not least in Juliet's frustration with names and Mercutio's dizzyingly polyvalent use of puns, *Romeo and Juliet* expresses an urge to free words and persons from their semantic limits.

Themes

Youth, subversion and suicide

The tension between authority and youthful subversion runs throughout *Romeo and Juliet*. It is a key text in the history of thinking about the 'transitional phase' from childhood to adulthood (see ed. Levenson 2000: 16–30), generational conflict and freedom. The social structure of Verona is so tautly upheld, by young and old alike, that the only way out for Romeo and Juliet is feigned or actual suicide. The implied relationship between suicide and freedom, already troubling, is made more so as it is weighed against its danger as a sin with grave consequences for the soul in the afterlife. Juliet, alone, about to drink the potion, hints at such fears when she sees 'my cousin's ghost / Seeking out Romeo' (IV, iii, 54–6). The play's superhuman, supernatural dimension includes themes of fate, fortune and predestination. The Chorus famously invokes 'star-crossed lovers' (Prologue, 6), and Romeo fears early on 'Some consequence yet hanging in the stars' before even seeing Juliet (I, iv, 105). Juliet has a similarly dark inkling of their tragic future just as Romeo leaves her bed, warning 'Methinks I see thee now [...] As one dead in the bottom of the tomb' (III, v, 54–8), and complaining of fickle fortune (III, v, 60–5). Romeo screams 'I am fortune's fool' as Tybalt falls (III, i, 136). Sometimes even words flip from comic to tragic use, as if subject to fortune's cruelty: Mercutio jests with his friends about the duelling move the *passado* (II, iii, 25), a word that fatally goads his future killer: 'Come, sir, your *passado*' (III, i, 83).

'O woeful time' (IV, iv, 56)

Time therefore appears as the means through which fortune fatally unfolds its pre-destined ends. But the play's treatment of time also strengthens its oppositions of hatred and repression, and freedom and love. The story takes place within a fixed temporal framework: a Sunday to a Thursday in mid-July, about two weeks before Juliet's birthday on 'Lammas Eve' or 31 July (I, iii, 19). The play is structured and scheduled around Juliet's proposed wedding to Paris, a timeframe which shrinks as the play draws on, Capulet originally suggesting another 'two summers' (I, ii, 10), then the following Thursday (III, iv, 20), then the following day (IV, ii, 23). The play thus associates with repression such 'countable', pre-scheduled time, while linking with love a subjective sense of time that is looser, freer, subject to its own mysteri-ous mode of measurement. 'Love's heralds should be thoughts, / Which ten times faster glides than the sun's beams' (II, iv, 4–5), drawn by 'nimble-pinioned doves' or 'wind-swift Cupid wings' (II, iv, 7, 8); 'In a minute there are many days' (III, v, 45). This swift sense of love, entirely associated with the young, contrasts radically with older people's much slower sensations of time. Friar Laurence consistently counsels patience and care: 'Wisely and slow; they stumble that run fast' (II, ii, 94) and Capulet rues with his cousin that 'you and I are past our dancing days' (I, iv, 144). It would seem that *Romeo and Juliet*, subtly and cumulatively, implies that the older a person gets, the more a body 'absorbs' time, the more its feelings of time mutate. This is at least partially why young and old cannot empathise with each other. The play depicts the 'generation gap' as a radical difference in perceptions of time, perceptions which themselves alter as time goes on.

Texts and contexts

Texts

Romeo and Juliet exists in two main versions: 'Q1', the 'bad' Quarto of 1597, whose publication was not officially recorded and is thought by some to be a pirated version; and 'Q2', the longer version which has since become the basis of the play now familiar to us. Jill Levenson's Oxford edition offers the text of Q1 as an appendix for students interested in comparing the differences.

Contexts

The connection of love with death – Romeo and Juliet both die with a kiss – is a long-standing and powerful literary tradition. In tragic myths of antiquity, like those of Pyramus and Thisbe or Hero and Leander, lovers strive and fail to surmount insurmountable obstacles. Wagner's term *Liebestod*, or love-death, has since been used as a generic term for such stories, where the erotic charge is inseparable from the thrill of subversion and mortal risk.

There are, however, more specific source texts for Shakespeare's *Romeo and Juliet*. The main two are Arthur Brooke's 1562 verse translation of Pierre Boaistuau's 1559 novella *The Tragicall Historye of Romeus and Juliet*, and William Painter's 1567 prose translation of Boaistuau, *The Goodly Hystory of Rhomeo and Julietta*. Boaistuau himself derived his story from earlier versions by Matteo Bandello and Luigi da Porto, the first to set out the names and key narrative incidents. The story would have been familiar to at least some members of Shakespeare's early audiences. Shakespeare's version reduces the age of Juliet (in the other versions she ranges from sixteen to eighteen) and alludes more frequently to classical *Liebestod* myths like Phaethon, Echo and Proserpina.

The play in performance

Early performances made clever use of the Globe's upper and lower levels, and perhaps the trapdoor, tracing a literal 'descent' from the 'heights' of the lovers' infatuation – the famous balcony scene – to the 'depths' of their destiny in the crypt. *Romeo and Juliet* has, of course, proved popular up until the present day, but it is not without recurrent challenges for actors and directors. Casting the play remains difficult. More experienced actors are better able to understand the verse but look too old onstage, while younger actors often 'flatten' the roles' emotional contradictions. Other challenges consist in staging Romeo's killing of Paris while retaining enough sympathy for him to make his own death tragic, and the decision to retain or not Juliet's 'potion' speech. Franco Zeffirelli cut it in his 1968 film because he did not want to distract attention from the rest of the ensemble, but for generations of viewers this has greatly reduced Juliet's psychological complexity, intelligence and capacity to act. Notable twentieth-century productions include Peter Brook's of 1947, which omitted the reconciliation between the Montagues and the Capulets; Terry Hands's of 1973, which implied a homoerotic relationship between Romeo and Mercutio; and Daniel Mesguich's inventive, even iconoclastic, 1985 reinvention, setting the play in a gigantic library peopled by characters from other stories. *Romeo and Juliet*'s emphasis on youth and the 'generation gap' perhaps encourages more than other Shakespeare plays such rebellious staging and modernisation. *Romeo and Juliet* taps into – and perhaps helped accelerate – a cultural appetite for young people rebelling against parental authority. It is perhaps more than coincidence that the most influential film version came out in 1968, a year famous for youth culture and political unrest. Michael Bogdanov's 1986/7 production updated Verona to a Thatcherite Britain where greed was good and the Montague–Capulet rivalry was based on snobbish, consumerist one-upmanship, extending even to the ostentatious statues set up in their dead children's honour. This production was also praised for the plausible, even touching, way it managed to integrate the long, often confusing Queen Mab speech. Mercutio recited it as kind of spoken-word lullaby to the drowsy Romeo. Twenty-first-century productions of *Romeo and Juliet* like Rupert Goold's (RSC 2011) still, twenty years on, reference Baz Luhrmann's 1996 film version.

Like *West Side Story*, Luhrmann updates the tale to a fictionalised American-Latino gangland ('Verona Beach'), where youths pop pills and 'sword' is a name for a brand of gun. Luhrmann also resurrects a much older stage tradition, dating back to the eighteenth-century actor-director David Garrick: Romeo (Leonardo DiCaprio) dies, but only just, after Juliet (Claire Danes) awakes, sharing a tragically brief reunion.

Critical reception

The critical reception of *Romeo and Juliet* is wide, incorporating adaptations such as *West Side Story* as well as scholarly articles. Gillian Woods's 2013 book in the Palgrave *Essential Criticism* series anthologises landmark essays by, among others, A. C. Bradley, Caroline Spurgeon, Kiernan Ryan, Hugh Grady, and Coppélia Kahn. Catherine Belsey's recent student guide (2014) is also helpfully cogent and accessible. Harry Levin (1960) offers a sensitive, still useful analysis of linguistic and structural symmetry. Julia Kristeva (1987) argues that Juliet's 'my only love, sprung from my only hate' parallels psychoanalytical theories about childhood eroticism and subsequent human attachments. Jonathan Goldberg (1994) explores how the play's language is subversive in its polysemous playfulness. Introducing a strong and varied special issue of *Shakespeare Survey* ('*Romeo and Juliet* and its Afterlife') Stanley Wells (1996) examines the difficulties modern directors face in bringing the play to the stage, such as disparities between Quarto texts, half-forgotten poetic traditions, and centuries of mediation and adaptation in a variety of genres. Wells's essay also offers a succinct performance history from the 1660s to the 1990s. Julia Lupton and C. J. Gordon (2013) draw our attention to Romeo and Juliet's material universe, a playworld of gloves, stools and letters, using 'affordance theory' to posit that these 'inanimate' items and others energise each other:

> the uncanny resonances in the larks' inverted evensong allows us to attend to the ecological disruptions that wrinkle Verona's various communicative systems, pushing the play towards considerations of urbanism as a network of flows among several species and forms of traffic. (Lupton and Gordon 2013: 264)

Matthew Spellberg (2013) sees by contrast how *Romeo and Juliet*'s language develops its own, dream-eliciting momentum, spinning away from such materiality.

Discussion questions

* Is amorous Romeo's sudden, murderous anger with Tybalt (III, i) believable? If so, how does its build-up make it believable?

* Generations of readers and playgoers have found Juliet charming, but does Juliet's 'charm' subtly uphold a patriarchal ideal, which tempers female sexuality with non-threatening, male-defined interpretations of 'innocence'?

Bibliography and further reading

Editions

Shakespeare, W. (2000), *Romeo and Juliet*, ed. J. Levenson, Oxford: Oxford University Press.
Shakespeare, W. (2012), *Romeo and Juliet*, ed. R. Weis, London: Arden Shakespeare.

Critical response

Belsey, C. (2014), *Romeo and Juliet: Language and Writing*, London: Arden Shakespeare.
Goldberg, J. (1994), '*Romeo and Juliet*'s Open Rs', in J. Goldberg (ed.), *Queering the Renaissance*, Durham, NC: Duke University Press, pp. 218–35.
Kristeva, J. (1987), '*Romeo and Juliet*: Love-hatred in the Couple', in *Tales of Love*, trans. Leon S. Roudiez, New York: Columbia University Press, pp. 209–33.
Levin, H. (1960), 'Form and Formality in *Romeo and Juliet*', *Shakespeare Quarterly*, 11, 3–11.
Lupton, J. and C. Gordon (2013), 'Shakespeare by Design: A Flight of Concepts', *English Studies*, 94:3, 259–77.
Spellberg, M. (2013), 'Feeling Dreams in *Romeo and Juliet*', *English Literary Renaissance*, 43:1, 62–85.
Wells, S. (1996), 'The Challenges of *Romeo and Juliet*', *Shakespeare Survey*, 49, 1–14.
Woods, G. (2013), *Romeo and Juliet: A Reader's Guide to Essential Criticism*, Basingstoke: Palgrave Macmillan.

2 *Hamlet*

c. 1600, First Quarto printed 1603, Second Quarto printed 1604

Act, scene and line references are to the 2006 Arden Third Series edition of the Second Quarto (Q2) text, edited by Ann Thompson and Neil Taylor. Additional Folio-only passages are discussed in the 'Texts and contexts' section.

Plot summary

The Danish court at Elsinore is under threat from the Norwegian King Fortinbras. King Hamlet is dead and his Queen Gertrude has remarried with his brother Claudius. Claudius and Gertrude now rule Denmark. But a Ghost resembling the dead King haunts the castle battlements (I, i). Prince Hamlet, the son of Gertrude and dead King Hamlet, is urged by his friend Horatio to see his father's Ghost for himself (I, ii). That night the Ghost tells his son that Claudius murdered him to gain the crown. The Prince must now 'avenge' and 'remember' his father (I, v). The Prince vows to do so, and adopts an 'antic disposition' to subvert the court of his murderous uncle, whom he hates for marrying his mother, and to appear harmless as he confirms for himself his Father's Ghost's shocking news (I, v, 70). He taunts first Claudius's main courtier Polonius (II, ii, 65–356; III, ii, 367–77) and Polonius's daughter Ophelia (II, i, 71–97; III, i, 90–187), with whom the Prince once shared tenderness, even love. A worried Claudius, who has been spying on his stepson throughout, recruits Prince Hamlet's university friends Rosencrantz and Guilden-stern to assist this surveillance (II, ii, 1–40). A troupe of actors come to court (II, ii, 358). Prince Hamlet hatches a plan to stage a performance of the murder and remarriage, and observe any guilty reactions from Claudius (II, ii, 471–4, 523–40). After the dumbshow Prologue, and as the play proper is performed, Claudius panics and flees (III, ii, 258): Prince Hamlet is now in no doubt that Claudius is guilty (III, ii, 278–80). Perturbed, Claudius resolves to send Hamlet to England, with letters requesting his stepson's execution, accompanied by Rosencrantz and Guildenstern for security (III, iii, 1–27): this plan is not, however, set in motion before Act IV, scene iv. Shortly after Claudius, alone, prays for forgiveness. Hamlet sneaks up on him and has the chance to kill him there and then but he prefers not to. Claudius's prayers might help him in the afterlife. Hamlet vows therefore to kill his enemy as he is 'about some act / That has no relish of salvation in't' (III, iii, 91–2). Gertrude suddenly and sternly requests her son's presence. Polonius once more spies on the encounter (III, iv). As Hamlet attacks Gertrude for remarrying, and with her ex-husband's brother and murderer to boot, Hamlet mistakes the hidden Polonius for Claudius, fatally stabbing him through the curtain where he was hiding (III, iv, 28). The Ghost reappears (to Hamlet alone), berating him for inaction (III, iv, 106–11). Polonius's death affects deeply Ophelia and her brother Laertes, returning from France. Ophelia grows mad (IV, v) then dies (IV, vii, 164–81). A furious Laertes seeks revenge on his father's murderer (IV, vii, 134–5). This is an opportunity for Claudius, because the original plan to kill Hamlet has failed. Hamlet explains later to Horatio that he read then rewrote the death warrant, so as to have Rosencrantz and Guildenstern executed in his place (V, ii, 17–56). The infuriated Claudius thus plots with Laertes to fight a mock duel with Hamlet when he returns to Denmark. Laertes' sword will be sharpened and dipped in venom, and a poisoned drink will be on hand in case Laertes is unable to kill Hamlet himself (IV, vii, 1–160). On his return, the Prince is shocked to discover Ophelia's funeral procession: he clashes with Laertes in her open grave (V, i). The disturbance is broken up. The arranged duel takes place (V, ii). The swords change places during the fighting (V, ii, 85) and both fighters are stabbed by the poisoned blade. Toasting the fighters, Gertrude drinks from the poisoned cup (V, ii, 273). As she swoons away, the dying Laertes confesses to Hamlet the plot on his life (V, ii, 298–305). Hamlet stabs Claudius and forces him to drink down the rest of the poison (V, ii, 306–10). Claudius, then Laertes die a matter of lines later, before Hamlet too succumbs (V, ii, 342). After this savagely swift bloodbath Horatio is the only main character left to confront the incoming invader Fortinbras, who takes the Danish crown.

Characters

Hamlet (I, ii; I, iv; I, v; II, ii; III, i; III, ii; III, iii; III, iv; IV, ii; IV, iii; IV, iv; V, i; V, ii)

Hamlet is more obsessed than any other play with just one person. Hamlet has the longest role of all Shakespeare's works, and even when he is offstage people talk of little else but him. Critics have long tried to rationalise this most complex and contradictory character, or, as Hamlet himself puts it, pierce 'the heart of my mystery' (III, ii, 356–7) or 'that within which passeth show' (I, ii, 85). But attributing such a singular, consistent personality to Hamlet is difficult because he seems constructed from a patchwork of different Renaissance roles: what Ophelia lists as 'courtier', 'soldier', 'scholar' (III, i, 150). Hamlet acts like a soldier when approaching the Ghost of his father, threatening to 'make a Ghost of anyone who lets [stops] me' (I, iv, 60), like a prince when he imperiously shows little remorse for killing Polonius (III, iv, 20), and like a university wit in his jests with Horatio (I, ii, 179–80). Sometimes he even acts like a court jester, mocking Claudius through riddles, caustically but cryptically spitting truth to power (IV, iii, 49–50). Throughout he is elusive and contradictory, alternating excitably, pedantically quick wit with crippling melancholy. As if this were not complicated enough, everything Hamlet does is tinged with an element of self-conscious theatricality. He is after all an enthusiastic amateur actor. Perhaps this is a comment on the way courtiers of Shakespearean times adopted and maintained calculated poses, on how fashioning fashionable identities was often essential for survival.

From Hamlet's first appearance we already see his contempt for Claudius, pointedly speaking to his mother and snubbing his uncle ('I shall in all my best obey *you*, Madam', I, ii, 120, my emphasis). His famous first soliloquy (I, ii, 129–58), an outpouring of disgust and confusion, is full of self-interruption and repellent imagery. The world is a corrupted Eden: 'an unweeded garden / That grows to seed' (I, ii, 135–6), women are mere 'frailty' (I, ii, 146), his mother who has deserted his dead father a 'beast' (I, ii, 150). This immediately sets up the dramatic conflicts that will run through the rest of the play and sets the emotional tone. As on his friend's Horatio's advice he encounters the Ghost of his father, he proclaims 'I hold not my life at a pin's fee' (I, iv, 65). He has nothing left to lose. When the Ghost reveals from the hereafter that Claudius is a murderer, whose victim is to be avenged, Hamlet hits on a tactic that has confused viewers and readers for generations. Rather than simply kill the man who killed his father and have done with it, Hamlet confides in his allies that he will 'put an antic disposition on' (I, v, 170), that is, pretend to be mad. Amleth in Shakespeare's source tale does likewise. But for Shakespeare's Hamlet this tactic is sudden, semi-improvised and uncertain; even he is unsure he will actually carry it out, as his word 'perchance' suggests (I, v, 169). It seems he feigns madness to buy time while his lingering doubts about the Ghost are resolved. He suspects later 'the spirit that I have seen / May be a de'il' (II, ii, 533–4). But Hamlet's famous inaction taps into wider, cultural anxieties in Shakespeare's time, about Ghosts and the afterlife, and the legitimacy of revenge: a question explored throughout the whole 'revenge tragedy' genre.

Hamlet's 'antic disposition' is reported to us by an 'affrighted' Ophelia, who tells her father that his dress is in disarray, he stares at her continuously, and utters a sigh 'so piteous and profound [...] it did seem to shatter all his bulk / And end his being' (II, i, 91–3). We the audience do not see him next, however, until Act II, scene ii – the play's longest scene – which sees a sequence of encounters between Hamlet and various members of or visitors to the court. Throughout, Hamlet expresses his joy in, and talent for, second-guessing and frustrating others' theories and interpretations of his behaviour. Polonius is mocked as a 'fishmonger' and a 'tedious old fool' (II, ii, 171, 214) and receives enigmatic warnings about Ophelia's blossoming sexuality. Rosencrantz and Guildenstern follow with such suddenness on Polonius's departure as to suggest the whole court is working together to keep Hamlet under surveillance. Hamlet sees straight through his old friends, now working for his enemy uncle. As if to confuse them, he varies his responses from angry scepticism ('you were sent for', II, ii, 244) to sudden amnesia ('you are welcome to Elsinore', II, ii, 306), and yokes together images and ideas with unexpected, striking strangeness: 'O God, I could be bounded in a nutshell and count myself a king of infinite space – were it not that I have bad dreams' (F only, II, ii, 254–7). Hamlet's tone suddenly changes to joy, however, with the arrival of the players (announced II, ii, 283; entry II, ii, 359), reminiscing to the Player King about his own theatrical career and even embarking on a speech he once recited (II, ii, 436). This speech, perhaps ominously, concerns a young man killing an old man (Pyrrhus and Priam), but who is suspended in inaction (II, ii, 471–3). These motifs resurface in the long, pivotal soliloquy 'O what a rogue and peasant slave am I', the first since Hamlet's encounter with the Ghost (II, ii, 485–540). This speech sees Hamlet applying his often sharply cruel intelligence to himself, putting himself like a paranoiac in the place of those who would criticise and persecute him ('Am I a coward?'). It then stresses the argument, implied throughout, that theatre can strike people 'to the soul'. By using the play to 'catch the conscience of the king', Hamlet plans to use theatrical simulation to reveal political dissimulation, to use acting as a form of action.

Analogies between the political and the theatrical stage grow stronger from this point on. The most famous speech in world literature, 'To be or not to be' (III, i, 55–89), often misnamed a soliloquy, is not in fact delivered alone. The hidden, spying Claudius and Polonius are, like us, a kind of audience. As is well known, this speech continues the near-suicidal strand of Hamlet's imagery introduced near the beginning of the first soliloquy ('O [...] that the Everlasting had not fixed/His canon 'gainst self-slaughter', I, ii, 132). Its enduring celebrity lies at least partially in the enigmatically dense way it articulates the choice to live or die: the only truly serious philosophical problem, to paraphrase Albert Camus's statement on suicide. It has also been cited to support the argument that Hamlet is the first character to articulate a 'modern' self-conscious individuality. But it contains no first-person singular pronouns, no 'I', no 'we': if Hamlet is talking about himself, he is only doing so via general, even universal, questions. Doubts about the afterlife may lead to paralysing fear. Such observations are surely, if obscurely, influenced by Hamlet's continued scepticism about the Ghost, and by extension about the purgatorial suffering he claims to have endured. Like both of Hamlet's previous long soliloquies, this pseudo-soliloquy's fluidly run-on versification gives the impression of improvised, real-time thinking in speech. Hamlet's thinking, however, is interrupted by the entrance of Ophelia.

Hamlet's cruelty to Ophelia in III, i, 89–160 is, of course, often debated in feminist criticism. Stage business can often play a part in directing audience sympathies, especially if Hamlet is seen to have overheard Ophelia planning the encounter with Claudius and her father beforehand. Nonetheless, Hamlet's rage, as well as Polonius's death, is often seen actively to contribute to Ophelia's tragic end. Critics like *Hamlet*'s Oxford editor George Hibbard suggest that, in ordering Ophelia to live a life of chastity ('Get thee to a nunnery'), and insisting 'God has given you one face and you make yourselves another', Hamlet is scapegoating her for Gertrude's sexual transgressions (ed. Hibbard 1987: 51). Hamlet has after all already made telling generalisations about female sexuality, for example warning Polonius not to let Ophelia 'walk in th'sun' (II, ii, 181, 'sun' playing on conceiving a 'son' and walking dangerously alone). He will later make bawdy puns on Ophelia's 'cunt' ('did you think I meant country matters? [...] That's a fair thought to lie between maid's legs', III, ii, 110–12). Arguably, however, Hamlet is as cruel with himself as he is with her, his lacerating self-description ('I am proud, revengeful, ambitious …', III, i, 123–4) warning her to keep away from him for her own safety. This reading, that Hamlet is being 'cruel only to be kind' (III, iv, 176) might be corroborated by his repeated 'farewell' (III, i, 132, 139). Despite everything, he finds it difficult to leave Ophelia. Ophelia's distress on Hamlet's departure is, likewise, evident. Apart from brief, terse, even sulky, exchanges before *The Mousetrap*, the lovers will not see each other again.

Hamlet in the next scene like a director advises the players how best to deliver the lines with which he hopes to trap Claudius. His speech has been read as a valuable historical record of acting technique at the time, and taken as Shakespeare's own views on such matters. Hamlet makes no mention here of his quarrel with Ophelia. As she and the other courtiers arrive, he is nervous, impatient, eager for his theatrical plan to unfold: 'Begin … Begin' (III, ii, 245–6). As Claudius rises, panicked at seeing the onstage replication of his crime, Hamlet cannot resist another sly dig: 'What, frighted with false fire?' (F only, after III, ii, 258). He is elated at the outcome, all doubts about the Ghost's story finally allayed ('I'll take the Ghost's word for a thousand pound', III, ii, 278–9). He then attacks Rosencrantz and Guildenstern ('Do you think I am easier to played on than a pipe?', III, ii, 361–3) and tricks Polonius, when he begs Hamlet to come and see Gertrude, into absurdly admitting he can see 'a cloud' shaped like a 'camel', 'weasel' and a 'whale' (III, ii, 369–73). Suddenly alone, he expresses in soliloquy his newfound resolve ('Now could I drink hot blood/And do such business as the bitter day/Would quake to look on', III, ii, 380–2) but, perhaps recalling the Ghost's command not to 'contrive/Against thy mother' (I, v, 86), decides, mingling anger and self-possession, 'I will speak daggers to her but use none' (III, ii, 386).

This newly assured, ascendant Hamlet blurs strength and cruelty. In a scene the eighteenth-century writer, critic, editor and lexicographer Samuel Johnson called 'too horrible to be read or uttered' Hamlet decides not to kill the praying Claudius, despite opportunity to do so, because he does not want his uncle's soul to be saved (III, iii, 87). Ethical problems likewise attend Hamlet's casual, unrepentant manslaughter of the 'rash intruding fool' Polonius and sustained verbal attack on Gertrude (III, iv). Making good his early, ominous promise to show his mother 'a glass/Where you may see the inmost part of you' (III, iv, 18–19), Hamlet tells Gertrude that Claudius killed her ex-husband (III, iv, 27) and presents two portraits, one of Claudius, one of Old Hamlet, as if to make their contrast all the more evident. The exchange becomes fragmented and fraught; Gertrude complains 'these words like daggers enter in my ears' (III, iv, 93). In some recent performances Hamlet is physically violent to his mother: David Tennant, for example, grabs her over the marital bed. But he is interrupted by the reappearance of the Ghost. Whereas before the Ghost was visible to everyone, this time only Hamlet can see him: Gertrude confirms she sees and hears 'nothing at all' (III, iv, 129). Again, the play silently asks questions it stubbornly refuses to answer. Is this second visitation a mere hallucination in Hamlet's mind, and if so are we the audience who also see the ghost 'as mad as he' (V, i, 146)? Is the visitation a kind of punishment for Polonius's murder? Alternatively, does the Ghost have some kind of celestial, supernatural control as to who or what can see him? The dramatic action does not let us pause over these questions. Hamlet begs Gertrude to visit Claudius's bed no longer ('assume a virtue if you have it not', III, iv, 158), confessing his madness has been an act all along. Gertrude seems to side with her son, vowing to keep secrets from Claudius, as Hamlet leaves, dragging Polonius's body behind him.

The play's final third grows increasingly chaotic. Hamlet has hidden Polonius's body somewhere in court, preventing a dignified burial. As Rosencrantz and Guildenstern ask where the body is, he calls them sycophantic 'sponges' who 'soak up the king's countenance'. When Claudius intervenes – the first time Hamlet and the King have confronted each other since the first act – Hamlet publicly humiliates him, calling him his 'mother' on the basis that 'man and wife is one flesh' (III, iv, 50). Sent to England, Hamlet on his journey regrets 'How all occasions do inform against me' (Q2 only, IV, iv, 30–65). By the time Hamlet returns to Elsinore, during which time he has discovered Claudius's plot on his life and arranged the execution of Rosencrantz and Guildenstern in retaliation, Ophelia has grown mad and died, and Laertes has sworn to kill Hamlet in revenge. The mounting body count suggests the tragedy is nearing its close.

The stage tableau opening the final act – the clown digging Ophelia's grave – illustrates vividly this increasing morbidity. But the Gravedigger's mordant humour is contagious, as when he quibbles with Hamlet on the multiple sense of 'lie' (fib, lie down) and the use of the past or present tense when talking of the dead (V, i, 127). Hamlet returns to his thought that life and death somehow continue each other – our bodies after all in the grave feed worms – when he sees his jester Yorick's skull. 'Alexander returneth to dust, the dust is earth, of earth we make loam, and why of that loam whereto he was converted might they not stop a beer-barrel?' (V, i, 198–200). These meditations are interrupted by Ophelia's funeral and Hamlet's brawl with Laertes in her grave. Hamlet's cry 'I loved Ophelia!' (V, i, 258) seems in these morbid circumstances naïve, even duplicitous. The fight is broken up. We do not see Hamlet again until the next scene, when he recounts how he arranged the deaths of Rosencrantz and Guildenstern, and prepares for the arranged duel with Laertes, mocking the foppish messenger Osric. Hamlet seems at once resigned to and reconciled to his fate: 'There is special providence in the fall of a sparrow [...] The readiness is all [...] Let be' (V, ii, 197–202). The duel itself sees the rapid deaths of Gertrude, Laertes and Claudius. As Hamlet himself dies, he tells Horatio Fortinbras has his 'dying voice' (V, ii, 340). 'Voice' here tropes 'vote' or 'nomination', but Hamlet's 'dying voice' is not only the voice of a dying person, nor even just a voice that is itself dying, but also something like the voice of mortality itself. Hamlet is poisoned and is fully aware he cannot be saved. Hamlet's story ends, as it started, with a voice spoken from the ambiguous, Ghost-like space between life and death.

Ghost (I, i; I, iv; I, v; III, iv)

The Ghost is more important than mere line count or number of appearances might suggest. He (it?) sets the revenge story in motion. The mysteries as to quite what kind of being he is contribute to the play's explorations of time, duty and the afterlife. He says he is Hamlet's 'father's spirit/Doomed for a certain term to walk the night [...] Till the foul crimes done in my days of nature/Are burnt and *purged* away' (I, v, 9–13, my emphasis). He therefore alludes, dangerously, to the forbidden Catholic concept of Purgatory, but – prudently for Shakespeare – does not actually mention its name itself. The Ghost finds himself thus between heaven and hell because he is murdered 'even in the blossoms of [his] sin' (I, v, 76): the Ghost, impossibly, is able to tell the story of his own murder from a distanced vantage point. The Ghost uneasily blends this supernatural power with a cruel sense of being enslaved: he is 'forbid' to divulge his situation fully to Hamlet (I, v, 13), and the laws thus dictating him are never fully elucidated or explained. This confuses of course the theological basis for the Ghost's commands, such as 'let not thy soul contrive/Against thy mother aught' (I, v, 85–6) or to swear secrecy (I, v, 149, 155, 160). The problem as to how precisely Hamlet should fulfil his filial duty is not only abstractly spiritual, however; it is also implicit in the vague way the Ghost formulates his commands: his final words to the Prince are 'Remember me', which may or may not be limited to the act of killing Claudius (I, v, 91). This might even mean, presumably, that Hamlet must not just kill Claudius but also think only of his father for the rest of his life. This extreme might seem absurd, but it does raise the question of just what such 'remembering' entails. The perhaps cruel ambiguity of the Ghost's command explains why he could be seen as allegorising the conscience, or its more modern, psychoanalytical equivalent the superego. If the internal compulsion to be good has no clear objective then a potentially limitless and debilitating guilt may result. 'Conscience does make cowards' (Q2, III, i, 82; F adds 'of us all'). The painful haziness of just what the Ghost is, let alone of his requests, is sometimes brought out in performance. In a recent RSC production, Patrick Stewart played Claudius and the Ghost, a 'conceptual doubling' that helped explain Hamlet's frequent, semi-conscious bewilderment. Which twin to kill? Which to obey?

Claudius ('King') (I, ii; II, ii; III, i; III, ii; III, iii; IV, ii; IV, iii; IV, iv; V, i; V, ii)

Claudius's first speech establishes him as a tough-minded political operator. He uses Denmark's conflict with Norway to justify his quick marriage to Gertrude (I, ii, 1–39). In this speech, and that to Hamlet just after, he uses mellifluous, balanced phrasing to establish himself as a reasonable man ('mirth in funeral and dirge in marriage', 'that father lost, lost his'). Unlike his dead, warrior-like brother, Claudius duplicitously conceals secret motives behind this superficial charm. He repeatedly hides and spies on people and asks others like Rosencrantz and Guildenstern to do likewise. He is wary and sly, intelligently dismissing Polonius's straightforward diagnosis of Hamlet's feigned madness as unrequited love, and keeping his cool even when, in the dumbshow preceding *The Mousetrap*, his crime is played out before the entire court. Ophelia's observation that 'the King rises' (III, ii, 257) is only made when Hamlet says that the onstage murderer 'gets the love of Gonzago's wife', rather than during the onstage events themselves. The precise moment when Claudius knows that Hamlet knows that he is a murderer is for directors and actors to arrange. But it is clear that Claudius is transformed by the experience, growing tougher and acting more urgently, hatching the plan quickly afterwards to send Hamlet to England (III, iii, 4), entering immediately after Gertrude's interview to find out what has gone on (IV, iv), and improvising to extract the maximum political advantage from Laertes' anger by deflecting it onto Hamlet (IV, v, 120–50). But, as a strange variation on the conflict between Claudius's outward actions and inward ambition, this busy activity conceals a guilty fear. In an aside he reveals a lashed conscience (III, i, 49), and confesses in soliloquy that his 'offence is rank ...' and that he has a 'bosom black as death' (III, iii, 36, 67). He contrasts 'above', where justice is holy and unimpeachable, with the 'corrupted currents of this world', where 'Offences gilded hand may shove by justice', that is, where everyone has their price (III, iii, 58–9). This cynical outlook on the world is exposed, however, with his final words. His call for help – 'O, yet defend me, friends, I am but hurt' – is completely ignored by the court he has helped to corrupt (V, ii, 308).

Gertrude ('Queen') (I, ii; II, ii; III, i; III, ii; III, iv; IV, i; IV, v; IV, vii; V, i; V, ii)

Near-despised by her son throughout the play, Gertrude's first appearance is near-silent, passively obedient to her new husband's wishes, only conceding later that her remarriage was 'oerhasty' (II, ii, 55). She is reticent, polite, but often cold, showing tenderness mainly to Ophelia, confiding 'I do wish / That your good beauties be the happy cause / Of Hamlet's wildness' (III, i, 37–9), and describing Ophelia's death respectfully (IV, vii, 164–81). Gertrude speaks only once during the performance of the dumbshow and *The Mousetrap* – her famous verdict that 'the lady doth protest too much' (III, ii, 224) – and says little even as her new husband rises in panic. Some actresses have portrayed Gertrude as genuinely and innocently unaware even here, others have played her as suspicious for some time. The text starts to indicate subtle gradations in her behaviour during and after her interview with Hamlet, which Hibbard calls the 'play's emotional centre' (ed. Hibbard 1987: 276). A lot rides, for example, on whether an actress delivers Gertrude's response to Hamlet's insinuated accusations ('as kill a King?') with shock or scepticism (III, iv, 27). Her sympathies seem to tilt more towards her son from this point. Claudius has to repeat his request to accompany him, as if there is some reluctance on her part (IV, i, 38, 44). But she remains a politically canny survivor, protecting her husband as Laertes accuses him of murder (IV, v, 128), and expressing fury at Laertes' attempted rebellion ('You false Danish dogs!', IV, v, 110). Reading Gertrude thus, caring more for her kingdom than her son, makes of her death a mere accident, not a guilt-laden suicide. She realises only too late 'I am poisoned' (V, i, 295).

Ophelia (I, iii; II, i; III, i; III, ii; IV, v)

Ophelia is not named as one of the characters present onstage for the first collective court scene. She appears only in the following scene, as if innocently distanced from the aggressive political world. Here she responds civilly but spiritedly to her brother's advice about Hamlet's love: Polonius's family seems a happy, honest contrast to the secret and dysfunctional goings-on in Hamlet's. Laertes' concern is, however, borne out when Hamlet focuses his mad anger on her, the young lady he later claims to love, rather than Gertrude, the chief target of his rage in his first soliloquy. Ophelia emerges early in the play as the innocent pawn of the (broadly male) power dynamics that surround her. She is the first victim of Hamlet's 'antic disposition', while for her father and her king she is little more than bait to trap him. Ophelia is clearly loyal to Polonius. Even in her madness, she laments 'I cannot choose but weep to think they should lay him i'th' cold ground' (IV, v, 69–70). But Polonius and Claudius exploit this when asking her to show them Hamlet's love gift, a ring inscribed with a poem (II, ii, 114–21). This prop is sometimes used to justify Hamlet's attack on Ophelia as revenge for what he sees as an act of treachery, but this completely and unfairly ignores Ophelia's lack of control over the situation. Actors sometimes imply Ophelia's madness stems from this encounter, but her later, vigorous responses to Hamlet during *The Mousetrap* ('you are naught') suggest she is still clear-minded and assertive (III, ii, 140). Ophelia's madness is thus predominantly if not entirely caused by Hamlet's murder of her father. Laertes rightly observes that Ophelia's 'distracted' speech contains 'thoughts and remembrance fitted' (IV, v, 172–3). There are indeed faint, scrambled memories of Ophelia's sane life, singing 'he is dead and gone' in mourning reference to Polonius, or 'By Cock they are to blame': an oblique retort, perhaps, to Hamlet's sexual insults (IV, v, 29–30, 61). The flowers she obliviously gives to people she once recognised parodically and prophetically anticipate the 'garlands' she makes as she drowns (IV, vii, 166), and the 'sweets to the sweet' Gertrude strews upon her coffin (V, i, 232). Ophelia's enduring association with water – 'mermaid like' in dying, she is 'like a creature native and endued to that element' – adds to the sense that her increasingly watery, pawn-like passivity was somehow tragically predestined (IV, vii, 174–8). As part of Ophelia's incredibly important cultural afterlife, the French philosopher Gaston Bachelard has coined the term 'Ophelia complex' to describe a recurrent metaphorical link between women, water and death, where female power emerges only at the price of martyrdom (see ed. Thompson and Taylor 2006: 26).

Polonius (I, ii; I, iii; II, i; II, ii; III, i; III, ii; III, iii; III, iv)

Gertrude impatiently complains 'more matter with less art' midway through one of Polonius's many overlong speeches. Polonius is frequently pompous, self-obsessed and boring, and a duplicitous, often cowardly spy, fatally hiding behind Gertrude's curtain, even asking his son's friend to spy on him in France (II, i, 6–71). He is also demonstrably simple-minded about human behaviour and psychology. He thinks, for example, that the Prince's strange behaviour is due to his refusal to let Ophelia and Hamlet see each other (II, i, 100; II, ii, 140). This is arguably a projection of Polonius's own personality: he admits in aside that he similarly 'suffered much extremity for love as a youth' (II, ii, 186–7), and shares Hamlet's youthful enthusiasm for the stage. His revelation that he once played Julius Caesar (Shakespeare wrote his *Julius Caesar* at around the same time as Hamlet) ironically, metatheatrically, predicts his own death (III, ii, 99–100).

Laertes (I, ii; I, iii; IV, v; IV, vii; V, i; V, ii)

Laertes has little in common with his circumspect, dissembling father, except his protective attitude to his sister: he is brave and impulsive. When he angrily re-appears in Act IV, scene v, his situation, as son of a murdered father, clearly parallels Hamlet's. But these parallels only highlight differences between the two young men: Laertes does not feign madness but threatens Claudius without delay. His boldness persists when he attacks the priest who judges Ophelia's death harshly, and when he embraces her in the grave. During the duel that will kill him and Hamlet, however, Laertes undergoes a profound change. Before the duel he coldly pretends to accept Hamlet's apology, but afterwards he turns against Claudius, just as he dies, poignantly echoing his father's verbal tic 'springes [traps] to catch woodcocks' to denounce his 'own treachery' (V, ii, 291–2).

Horatio (I, i; I, ii; I, iv; I, v; III, ii; IV, v; IV, vii; V, i; V, ii)

Horatio functions chiefly as Hamlet's confidant and has little independent exist-ence. He helps bring out the tone of certain scenes. His fear stresses the strange and frightening nature of the Ghost, and his scholarly discussions with Hamlet and the guards allude to the climate of philosophical scepticism popular in learning institutions at the turn of the sixteenth century. Hamlet's affectionate speech to him before *The Mousetrap* likewise taps into cultural norms concerning friendship amongst aristocratic men (III, ii, 50–70). As an interestingly metatheatrical develop-ment towards the end, Horatio promises to 'tell [Hamlet's] story' after his death (V, ii, 333). Nobody else is alive to do so. The dying Hamlet desperately knocks the poisoned cup from his hand to stop him committing suicide (V, ii, 325–7). Horatio the survivor thus embodies the play we have just been watching, almost as if he is the play's own ghost.

Play structure

Hamlet is one of Shakespeare's most claustrophobic plays. Despite the story's length, our gaze leaves the Court of Elsinore only once and briefly (IV, iv). The outside world is only fleetingly even mentioned, as when Claudius refers to the 'distracted multi-tude' (IV, iii, 4). This spatial restriction is perhaps a nod to the seventeenth-century revival of classical ideas, especially Aristotle's recommendation in the *Poetics* that tragedies should work around a single event, and be set in a certain location. But while *Hamlet* broadly keeps to a 'unity of place' it does not obey Aristotle's equivalent rule about time. Aristotle thought tragedies were more movingly and therapeutically realistic if they depicted a period lasting no longer than twenty-four hours. Any longer would be too unbelievable a stretch in relation to time elapsed onstage. But *Hamlet* has become perhaps the most important tragedy ever written, even though its three large 'movements' stretch stage time much more emphatically. The first act portrays events taking place within a timeframe of thirty hours. Then elapses a long break: Ophelia mentions 'twice two months' since King Hamlet died (III, ii, 119), the first such temporal marker, which may come as a shock. The rest of the play deals with events of about two days, during which Polonius is killed, Hamlet leaves Denmark, encounters pirates and returns, Ophelia grows mad and dies, and the final, fatal duel takes place. The implausible rapidity of these events is often forgotten in the dramatic excitement. *The Mousetrap* and its aftermath occupy the play's central 'movement', strengthening the sense of theatre and politics being nestled within each other, and contributing to the strange sense of *Hamlet* being not only a play of three distinct time periods, but also a play of two halves. There is a very clear sense of 'before' and 'after' the play-within-the-play, affirmed by Laertes' symmetrical departure and return, and emphasising the deathly acceleration that races the play to its end. The subtly disorienting blurring of triangular and dualistic structures – three movements, two halves – also marks the play's doubled comparisons of its three young men. Hamlet is contrasted with Fortinbras because they are both princes, and with Laertes because they are both bereaved, avenging sons. The play's blurring of binary and triangular timeframes thus confuses our temporal navigation in the story; but it also provokes a more ethical form of navigation: we are silently challenged to judge these three young male characters against each other, and thus perhaps thereby question the bases on which our evaluations of masculinity are made.

Language

Hamlet is extremely inventive. It contains more than 600 words used for the first time in Shakespeare's works, and about 170 new to the whole English language, like 'avouch' (I, i, 56), 'blastments' (I, iii, 41) and 'strewments' (V, i, 222). This linguistic struggle against existing norms reflects Hamlet's intellectual and ethical engagements with his father's command, and his play's challenge to the clichés of the revenge tragedy genre. Hamlet frequently connects ideas in innovative, unexpected ways, as when, say, he compares himself to a 'pipe' with Rosencrantz and Guildenstern (III, ii, 362). But this linguistic originality clashes with a more backward-looking preoccupation with repetition, as if Hamlet cannot quite let words go. He has comparable trouble saying goodbye to women, as signalled by his repetition of 'farewell' to Ophelia (III, i, 137, 139) or 'goodnight' to Gertrude (III, iv, 211, 214). The question of letting the past go also of course haunts Hamlet in the ghostly shape of his father.

Echoing his earlier, soliloquised 'Heaven and earth, must I remember?' (I, ii, 141), Hamlet repeats to himself over and over the Ghost's final command 'Remember me' just after it disappears (I, v, 95, 98, 110). Hamlet's famous, seemingly 'modern' sense of psychological distinctiveness or individual 'personality' thus seems constructed from various linguistic strategies, tics and quirks. But the play also makes extensive use of sixteenth- and seventeenth-century vocabularies of introspection, which differ greatly from ours. The 'soul' is a powerful preoccupation, unsurprisingly given the Ghost's vivid and visible proof of the terrors of the afterlife. In early performances the below-stage space is not only the grave where Ophelia is buried, it is also the purgatorial space from where the Ghost repeatedly calls to 'Swear' (I, v, 149, 155, 160, 179). The space implies an unsettling link between death and purgatorial torture, and this fear is pervasive. Gertrude complains Hamlet's accusations turn 'my very eyes into my soul' (III, iv, 87); Claudius, unable in his distraction fully to pray, panics about his soul 'struggling to be free' (III, iii, 68).

Conscience is a similarly important word. In one sense it refers to an interior indicator that distinguishes acts worthy from salvation from those that are not. Hamlet unrepentantly says Rosencrantz's and Guildenstern's deaths are 'not near' his conscience, and defiantly asks Horatio: 'Is't not perfect conscience' to kill Claudius (V, ii, 64, 71). The word's positive value is, however, complicated by the 'To be or not to be' speech, in which Hamlet perhaps surprisingly links conscience with cowardice (III, i, 82). Conscience forces people to carry on living, rather than brave the unknown (and unknowable) torments of the afterlife: Hamlet's speech grammatically and syntactically aligns 'conscience' with 'dread' which 'puzzles the will' (III, i, 79), and with the 'pale cast of thought' that prevents not only suicide but 'enterprises of great pitch and moment' (III, i, 84). From the flow of Hamlet's thoughts here emerges the (contradictory) idea that suicidal action is the microcosm of action itself. If you are brave enough to kill yourself then you can do anything; but you would of course no longer be alive enough to do so. This logic groups the 'will' on one side and, on the other, conscience, the survival instinct and thought: it transfers 'conscience' from ethical and theological contexts to more intellectual ones of reason, prudence, even sanity. Two conclusions, which feed powerfully into our understanding of the key themes of play, might be drawn from this. First, the 'will', if left to its own devices (i.e. if is not 'puzzled'), functions very much like madness. Second, Hamlet links such 'willful' madness with bravery and with death. Perhaps, then, according Hamlet's own reasoning, the suicidal Ophelia becomes the heroine Hamlet always wanted to be?

Themes

Baroque melancholia

Hamlet's doubts about death and suicide might be related to the emergence in European literature near the beginning of the seventeenth century of a 'baroque sensibility', where consciously elaborate language relayed a strange blend of morbid imagery and gallows humour. *Hamlet* adopts a similarly inquisitive, sceptical approach to death, as the awestruck seriousness of the Ghost gives way progressively to a more comic, even disrespectful, tone. No one in *Hamlet* is buried properly. Yorick's stinking skull is dug up and uncaringly tossed around by the Gravedigger. Ophelia receives only minimal rites due to her 'doubtful' death. Polonius's body is hauled around the castle, even as Hamlet satirically, gloomily alludes to 'politic worms' and fattening 'ourselves for maggots' (IV, iii, 20). The play's closing wordplays also imply that death, that universal leveller, mocks indifferently all human pretension. 'Union' means not just the poisoned pearl which kills Gertrude and Claudius, nor even just their 'union' in death; it also predicts the collective 'silence' that will also engulf Hamlet a mere matter of lines later (V, ii, 310). The long groan added to the F text notwithstanding, Hamlet's final words are 'the rest is silence' (V, ii, 343). 'Rest' may mean 'repose', as when Horatio says 'Goodnight, sweet prince / And flights of angels sing thee to thy *rest*' (V, ii, 343–4, my emphasis). Hamlet might understandably hope his death will be more silent and restful than his father's. But 'rest' can also mean 'remainder', inviting a reading more in keeping with Hamlet's restless inquisitiveness. The 'rest is silence' because no one has told us, nor can tell us, about the mysterious 'silence' which greets the moment of death, and will persist for the 'rest' of time.

The 'time of death'

Read thus, Hamlet's last words recall 'the undiscovered country from whose bourn / No traveller returns' in the 'To be or not to be' speech (III, i, 78–9). The play's most famous moment argues all fundamental questions boil down to the decision to kill oneself or not: 'To be or not to be' is of course '*the* question' (III, i, 55, my emphasis). Doubts and fears surrounding suicide were of course powerfully influenced by contemporary authorities: as terms like 'self-murder' and 'self-slaughter' remind us, suicide was in Shakespearean times no less a crime or sin than homicide. Failed suicides were treated as attempted murders. But the precise boundaries or definitions of suicide were up for debate. The gravedigger compares Ophelia's drowning to a recent law case: *Hales v. Petit* (1554). The lawyers argued whether a self-slaughterer could in fact be held legally responsible for his act. After all, the doer and the deed cannot co-exist in time: the act of suicide has not legally been accomplished while its actor is still alive to accomplish it. To sort out the problem, lawmen had to break down artificially the moment of death into three separate stages, during one of which the accused became guilty. The gravedigger concludes for Ophelia: 'an act hath three branches, to do, to act, to perform. Argal [Ergo], she drowned herself wittingly' (V, i, 12–13). As well as being a formidably difficult existentialist and ethical test case – debates rage even today over the Dignitas clinic in Switzerland or mercy killings – suicide also calls into question time and temporal sequence. Time is irreducibly fluid – it can be broken down infinitely into smaller and smaller units of measurement – but the passage from life to death has no such fluidity: there is only one or the other. Doctors might record a 'time of death', but time and death seem mutually exclusive.

'The time is out of joint'

Hamlet therefore explores various ways of experiencing time, which may or may not harmonise with each other. Hamlet complains 'The time is out of joint' after the Ghost departs (I, v, 186). Priests thought sinners atoned in Purgatory for thousands of years: the near-eternal, purgatorial time the Ghost endures and represents clashes with the recognisable mortal time of Elsinore and the condensed real time of onstage performance. By juxtaposing such wildly different time perceptions, the play scrutinises time as a fixed and singular system which somehow guides and controls the events that occur within it. Hamlet himself reaches no single conclusion about these questions of free will and predestination, first bitterly resisting Claudius's and Gertrude's casual fatalism about King Hamlet's death, then coming to believe 'There's a divinity that shapes our ends' and 'a special providence in the fall of a sparrow' (V, ii, 197–8). He concludes, just before the final bloodbath, with the relaxed ambivalence about unanswerable questions that sceptical philosophers of the time called *ataraxia*: 'The readiness is all [...] Let be' (V, ii, 201–2). The question of whether time is a continuum, of whether the present is simply a mere continuation of the past, is obviously relevant to the Ghost's desire for past acts to be repeated, re-venged, re-membered. The repetition in the biblical formulation 'an eye for an eye, a tooth for a tooth' suggests revenge restores to time a symmetry that the revenged transgression had disturbed. But for Hamlet, who in his famous delay seems to suspect almost despite himself that two wrongs do not make a right, past, present and future never slot together so harmoniously. This comes through especially in the very confusing moment when he only hits upon the idea of putting on *The Mousetrap after* he has already suggested it to the Player King (II, ii, 524–31).

Doubts about death, suicide, time and revenge thus ripple through this play, part of a critical scepticism also illustrated in the ways it inverts 'serious' politics and 'trivial' theatre. The spying Claudius and Polonius see unseen, like a theatre audience. *The Mousetrap* makes Claudius break down with guilt, as if the play has turned its gaze on its viewer. Similar skills are key to political and theatrical success alike: the sobbing Player King and the 'mad' Hamlet convince others through powerful, willed, interior self-belief in the role they play. And the boundary between authentic and simulated behaviour is hazy indeed: the longer Gertrude abstains from having sex with Claudius, Hamlet tells her, the easier it will get, 'For use almost can change the stamp of nature' (Q2 only, III, iv, 166). But by thus suggesting genuine behaviour is 'almost' reducible to changeable, adaptable habits, Hamlet implies a certain flexibility, susceptibility, even vulnerability, at the heart of sanity. The 'antic disposition' he promises merely to act perhaps becomes genuine madness when he, and only he, sees the Ghost; Hamlet undermines madness and sanity as stable categories, veering with perilous melancholy from one to the other. The play frequently links mental distress to sexuality, as in the surprising bawdiness of Ophelia's mad songs: 'Young men will to't if they come to't / By cock they are to blame' (IV, v, 62); and in his lowest moments Hamlet often attacks what he sees as his mother's insatiable sexual appetite: 'incestuous sheets' (I, ii, 157), 'making love / Over the nasty sty' (III, iv, 92) or the rank materiality of the human bodies generated by such appetite: 'Why may not imagination trace the noble dust of Alexander till 'a find it stopping a bung-hole?' (V, i, 193–4). Hamlet also debunks Renaissance humanist idealism in the speech containing perhaps his most famously melancholic declaration: 'I have of late, and wherefore I know not, lost all my mirth' (II, ii, 262); 'What piece of work is a man [...] this quintessence of dust?' (II, ii, 269, 275). Hamlet has perhaps of all literary characters considered these questions the most searchingly and articulately.

Texts and contexts

Texts

There are two accepted early versions of *Hamlet*: that published in the Second Quarto, first published in 1604 (Q2), and that of the 1623 Folio (F). Either individually or conflated, these early texts form the basis of all editions used in university or A-Level courses. I do not therefore cover here the First Quarto (Q1), published in 1603 and informally called the 'bad Quarto', which places the 'To be or not to be' speech much earlier (II, ii). Readers interested in Q1 may, however, consult the 2006 Arden Third Series edition. F is shorter than Q2. F does not contain about 230 of the lines of Q2; Q2 does not contain about 70 of F's lines. The major differences include Horatio's speech about ill omens following Julius Caesar's death (I, i, in Q2, not F); Hamlet's soliloquy 'How all occasions do conspire against me' (IV, iv, in Q2, not F); the exchange between Hamlet, Rosencrantz and Guildenstern about Denmark being a 'prison' (II, ii, in F, not Q2); and the allusion to child actors or 'Little Eyases' (II, ii, in F, not Q2). There are also differences between passages contained in both texts: only 6 per cent of the lines common to both versions are identical. The first line of Hamlet's first soliloquy, for example, reads in Q2 'sallied flesh' and in F 'solid flesh': actors have to decide whether to stress the former's implied feelings of disgust, or the latter's of entrapment. As another problem for the modern editorial or onstage interpreter, some passages in the original versions are quite simply near-impossible fully to understand, as in Hamlet's 'dram of eale' speech about drunkenness (Q2 only, I, iv, 13–38), which the eighteenth-century editor Lewis Theobald called the most baffling in all Shakespeare's works. There is, therefore, no 'pure', unadulterated version of *Hamlet*; it demands active, interpretative decision-making from all those who edit it, direct it, act in it, read it or watch it.

Contexts

Shakespeare did not invent the story of *Hamlet*. The first known written record of this old Nordic tale is in Latin, by Saxo Grammaticus, and dated to about AD 1200. The main character's name is Amleth, which means 'stupid'. This is perhaps an early influence on Hamlet's frustration with his own perceived inactivity, as well as his feigned madness: Amleth similarly pretends to be mad as part of a plan to kill his uncle in revenge for his father's murder. There is also a version of the tale in François de Belleforest's 1570 *Histoires tragiques*, which adds the idea that Hamlet is melancholic. Shakespeare's version contains less misogynistic moralising than his sources, and adds the roles of Laertes and the Ghost and the story of Ophelia's madness, while implying more strongly that the murder is unknown to everyone in the court except the murderer.

The play in performance

Hamlet is of course one of the world's most-performed plays. H. L. Mencken quipped, 'Hamlet has been played by five thousand actors. No wonder he's crazy' (quoted in Esar 1995: 365). Since the start of the twentieth century, influential portrayals of the prince in the theatre include those by John Gielgud (six productions, 1930–45), Laurence Olivier (1937), David Warner (1965), Jonathan Pryce (1980) and Simon Russell Beale (2000), and, on film, by Olivier again (1948), Derek Jacobi (1980), Kenneth Branagh (1996) and Ethan Hawke (2000), whose Hamlet, heir to 'Denmark Inc.', struggles in an era of omnipresently globalised capitalism.

Every production of *Hamlet* explores the tension between the political and the psychological. Jonathan Pryce played both Hamlet and the Ghost, as if his father's spirit had taken possession of him, implying that Claudius's murder was the only way to exorcise it. Olivier's staged and film productions are perhaps the most famous 'modern' examples of a tradition, started by Edmund Kean, which focuses on the prince as a case study of inactivity, 'someone who couldn't make up their mind', perhaps caused by Oedipal tensions with Gertrude. Olivier's film version stressed Gertrude's desirability by casting an actress, Eileen Herlie, who was over ten years *younger* than the man playing her 'son'(!). Branagh's four-hour uncut film version of Q2 was seen by many reviewers as an attempt to rival Olivier's.

Feminist critics like Carol Chillington Rutter have lamented an egotistical focus on the titular role at the expense of the women characters. Many recent productions of *Hamlet* seem predominantly star vehicles, weakening any sense of *Hamlet* being an ensemble piece, as when the role is taken by film stars like Jude Law (2009) or Benedict Cumberbatch (2015). The lukewarm reviews for this most recent production perhaps suggest a certain fatigue with 'celebrity Hamlet'. But recent productions with David Tennant (2009), John Simm (2010) and Michael Sheen (2011, set in a mental institution) have delivered fresh, accessible Danes. Radical, even non-Shakespearean, retellings of the story such as Charles Marowitz's trilogy of theatrical collages (1965–72), Heiner Müller's *Hamletmachine* (1990) and Sulayman Al-Bassam's *The Al-Hamlet Summit* (2006) testify to the text's inexhaustibly stimulating creative energy.

Critical reception

From 1990–2006 there have been on average of 400 publications every *year* on *Hamlet*. There is even a scholarly journal dedicated wholly to the play, *Hamlet Studies*: the only text by Shakespeare to be so honoured. A quick Google search for 'Shakespeare Hamlet' yields over 15 million hits. David Bevington's *Murder Most Foul* (2011), however, recently surveys this enormous cultural influence and Sean McEvoy's Routledge *Sourcebook* (2006) usefully anthologises some important essays. Terence Hawkes (1986) recaps valuable early twentieth-century criticism and illuminatingly interprets the play's peculiar, topsy-turvy narrative sequencing. Jacques Lacan (1977), Francis Barker (1984) and Karin S. Coddon (1989) offer classic examples of, respectively, psychoanalytical, cultural materialist and new historicist approaches. Stephen Greenblatt (2013) relates the play to anxieties arising from Reformation transformations of mourning ritual, John Gillies (2013) to those surrounding original sin. Rhodri Lewis (2012) explores Aristotelian ideas of the mind to historicise the play's treatment of memory and 'remembrance' while Jonathan Baldo (2014) examines the idea of 'distraction'. John Lee (2000) surveys the historical debate as to whether Hamlet is the first literary work to articulate modern individuality, and Douglas Bruster (2007) reads extremely closely Hamlet's most famous soliloquy. Jacques Derrida (1994) has greatly influenced much modern criticism. Derrida argues the Ghost's unexpected entry yields a strange form of hope. The future is no mere continuation of the past and present: it is its own category. Life can be made unpredictably meaningful at any moment. Recent essays by, say, John F. DeCarlo (2013) and Johann Gregory (2013), explore the ethical, existential and psychological stakes of such ideas.

Discussion question

＊ What, if anything, is 'modern' about *Hamlet*?

Bibliography and further reading

Editions

Shakespeare, W. (1987), *Hamlet*, ed. G. Hibbard, Oxford: Oxford University Press.
Shakespeare, W. (2006), *Hamlet*, ed. A. Thompson and N. Taylor, London: Arden Shakespeare.

Critical response

Baldo, J. (2014), 'Shakespeare's Art of Distraction', *Shakespeare*, 10:2, 138–57.

Barker, F. (1984), *The Tremulous Private Body: Essays on Subjection*, London: Methuen.

Bevington, D. (2011), *Murder Most Foul:* Hamlet *Through the Ages*, Oxford: Oxford University Press.

Bruster, D. (2007), *To Be Or Not To Be*, London: Continuum.

Coddon K. (1989), '"Suche strange desygns": Madness, Subjectivity and Treason in *Hamlet* and Elizabethan Culture', *Renaissance Drama*, 20, 51–7.

DeCarlo, J. (2013), 'Hamlet and the Ghost: A Joint Sense of Time', *Philosophy and Literature*, 37:1, 1–19.

Derrida, J. (1994), *Spectres of Marx: The State of the Debt, The Work of Mourning and the New International*, trans. P. Kamuf, New York/London: Routledge.

Esar, E. (1995), *20,000 Quips and Quotes: A Treasury of Witty Remarks, Comic Proverbs, Wisecracks and Epigrams*, New York: Barnes and Noble.

Gillies, J. (2013), 'The Question of Original Sin in *Hamlet*', *Shakespeare Quarterly*, 64:4, 396–424.

Greenblatt, S. [2001] (2013), *Hamlet in Purgatory*, Princeton: Princeton University Press.

Gregory, J. (2013), 'Wordplay in Shakespeare's *Hamlet* and the Accusation of Derrida's "Logical Phallusies"', *English Studies*, 94:3, 313–30.

Hawkes, T. (1986), '*Telmah*', in *That Shakespeherian Rag: Essays on a Critical Process*, London/New York: Methuen University Paperbacks, pp. 92–119.

Kerrigan, J. (1996), *Revenge Tragedy: Aeschylus to Armageddon*, Oxford: Clarendon Press.

Lacan, J. (1977), 'Desire and the Interpretation of Desire in *Hamlet*', *Yale French Studies*, 55/56, 11–52.

Lee, J. (2000), *Shakespeare's* Hamlet *and the Controversies of Self*, Oxford: Oxford University Press.

Lewis, R. (2012), 'Hamlet, Metaphor, and Memory', *Studies in Philology*, 109:5, 609–41.

McEvoy, S. (ed.) (2006), *Shakespeare's 'Hamlet': A Sourcebook*, London/New York: Routledge.

3 *Othello*

c. 1603, first performance 1604, first printed 1622

Act, scene and line references are to the 2006 Oxford edition, edited by Michael Neill, whose excellent introduction has been very helpful for this chapter.

Plot summary

The scene is Venice, at war with Turkey over Cyprus. Soldier Iago vows to help his friend Roderigo woo Desdemona, daughter to the Venetian noble Brabantio, and husband to Othello, a soldier and Moor (see I, i, 96–9). Iago resents Othello promoting the Florentine Cassio instead of him (I, i, 7–32). This anger only grows more mysteriously intense as the play progresses. Under cover of night Iago and Roderigo shout up to Brabantio's chamber that Othello has abducted Desdemona and they are having sex (I, i, 88–9). Brabantio, discovering Desdemona missing, raises the alarm (I, i, 140, 166). He and his guards confront Othello, and the two competing parties put forward their cases to the arriving Duke (I, iii, 48–208). The Duke sides with Othello due to his eloquence, his tested service as a soldier, Desdemona's own loving testimony, and the pressing matter of the Cyprus wars (I, iii, 1–12, 220–1). The scene passes to Cyprus, where it is reported a storm has done away with the Turkish fleet (II, i, 1–30; II, ii). The arriving Venetians celebrate the happy news. Iago notes that Cassio offers Desdemona great courtesy during the celebrations (II, i, 165) and plots to convince Othello they are having an affair (II, i, 276). He knows Cassio has 'poor and unhappy brains for drinking' (II, iii, 30–1) so gets him to drink more than he should. Roderigo assists Iago by provoking the drunk Cassio to fight (II, iii, 135). In the scuffle Montano the Governor of Cyprus is seriously wounded (II, iii, 149), and as punishment Othello strips Cassio of his officership (II, iii, 239–40). Iago suggests Cassio should approach Desdemona, who could then ask, or beg, her husband for Cassio's reinstatement (II, iii, 305–6). Iago then asks his wife Emilia to get Desdemona to give Cassio's requests a sympathetic ear (II, iii, 368–9). Having thus established contact between Desdemona and Cassio, and engineered a situation where they are required to confer often alone, Iago implies to Othello this relationship is sexual. Cassio's departure from Desdemona after their first meeting is 'guilty-like' (III, iii, 38). Desdemona's glowing defence of Cassio (III, iii, 93) is thus already coloured for Othello with suspicion. Iago's lies steadily exacerbate Othello's mistrust of Desdemona and Cassio. The opportunity for Iago to back up his accusations with 'ocular proof' (III, iii, 362) arises when Desdemona drops her handkerchief (III, iii, 291). Emilia picks it up and gives it to her husband (III, iii, 315). Iago in turn leaves the handkerchief in Cassio's house for him to discover (III, iii, 323–4), and mentions to Othello that he had seen it in Cassio's possession (III, iii, 433–42). The handkerchief thus becomes the ultimate test of Othello's wife's fidelity. When she cannot find it he flies into a jealous rage (III, iv, 76–95). He later has a fit (IV, i, 41). Cassio by now has discovered the planted handkerchief at his home and asks his lover, a prostitute Bianca, to have it copied (III, iv, 174). Bianca at first refuses – she too reads it as a sign of infidelity – but ultimately agrees (III, iv, 196). Iago arranges to meet with Cassio and asks Othello to observe the encounter, unseen to all (IV, i, 70). Iago asks Cassio about his lover Bianca, and Othello mistakes Cassio's dismissive, bawdy responses as insults to Desdemona (IV, i, 107–14). When Bianca angrily comes on scene, contemptuously throwing the handkerchief to the ground (IV, i, 143–9), the hidden onlooker Othello's mind is made up. There is now no doubt for him that Desdemona is unfaithful. He attacks her in full view of the Duke's dignitaries visiting from Venice, who want Othello to return from Cyprus (IV, i, 229–34). Roderigo grows impatient with Iago for not securing him the promised love of, or at least sex with, Desdemona (IV, ii, 173). Iago thinks Roderigo should kill his rival Cassio (IV, ii, 227–30). So, that night, Roderigo attacks Cassio, who flees wounded (V, i, 24–7). In the ensuing commotion Iago kills off Roderigo, who has of course been accomplice and witness to his scheming (V, i, 63). Othello meanwhile suffocates his wife (V, ii, 84, 91), too soon for Emilia to reveal to him the full story about Iago's deceit (V, ii, 130–220). Iago, who has just arrived on the scene, threatens her (V, ii, 222). But Emilia will not remain silent, so Iago kills her (V, ii, 233). Realising he murdered without cause the woman he loved, Othello kills himself (V, iii, 355).

Characters

Iago (I, i; I, ii; I, iii; II, i; II, iii; III, i; III, ii; III, iii; III, iv; IV, i; IV, ii; V, i; V, ii)

Like *King Lear*'s Goneril, Regan and Edmond, or like Richard III (see Chapters 5 and 12 respectively), Iago is central to discussions of Shakespearean villainy. But these other villains have a relatively clear political motive for their foul deeds. Iago refuses, even at the end, to say why he has convinced Othello to kill his wife. 'Demand me nothing: what you know, you know;/From this time forth I never will speak word' (V, ii, 301–2). Samuel Taylor Coleridge argued that Iago exhibited 'motive-less malignity' (see Foakes 1989: 15, 113). Perhaps this makes Iago more genuinely evil than Shakespeare's other villains: only Iago is bad purely for badness's sake, shoulder-shruggingly seeing his cruelty as mere reflections of the social injustice and ingratitude he sees everywhere around him. Of the play's characters I discuss him first, before the play's title character Othello, because he is in the play from the very first scene and is the prime mover of the play's tragic action.

Iago's advice to Roderigo to 'put money' in his 'purse', repeated eight times in a speech of just over twenty lines, is an early indicator of his priorities and cynicism (I, iii, 329–54). By moments the phrase seems metaphorically to mean 'cheer up': Iago is after all convincing Roderigo not to give up on his hope to have sex with Desdemona. But it also recalls Iago's suspicions from his first speech that old honourable codes of loyalty – the 'old gradation' – no longer apply (I, i, 36). Cash is now the only reality. Iago repeating 'Put money in thy purse' also has a more practical function, semi-hypnotising Roderigo into liquidating his assets. Roderigo promises soon after to sell his land (I, iii, 370) and later complains he has run out of cash (IV, ii, 187). Iago's claim that he has made this 'fool' his 'purse' (I, iii, 372) suggests the money from Roderigo's sale has benefitted him personally: 'He calls me to a restitution large / Of gold, and jewels, that I bobbed from him' (V, i, 16–17).

Like certain tabloid newspapers, then, Iago interweaves macho sexual desire (for Desdemona) with fear and prejudice (against the stereotyped, nameless 'Moor') to pretend to help his fellow man. But he is really only advancing his own, very different interests. Iago draws on these duplicitously blokey techniques to reach wider male audiences. At twenty-eight (I, iii, 307–8) Iago is younger than frequently supposed, but he is at a good age to appeal to older and younger soldiers alike, as when he gets the soldiers to exert the necessary peer pressure on Cassio to drink ('they are our friends!', II, iii, 33). After the brawl he appeals to casual sexism ('our general's wife is now the general', II, iii, 302–3) to set up the meetings between Cassio and Desdemona, meetings which help make plausible Iago's tales of adultery to Othello. Iago is thus demonstrably expert at guiding to his ends these avowedly masculine codes of thinking and feeling, even before he talks to Othello directly. In the second half of the play Iago is much more mobile and physically active. Like a stage director he busily coordinates observers and the unwitting observed. And he rides his luck. The eavesdropping Othello thinks Desdemona is cheating on him only because Cassio never mentions Bianca by name (IV, i, 90–164). He is only found out when his wife exposes him with perhaps implausible slowness. The Duke vows to punish Iago but we do not see him die. Could his luck even hold after the play's final words are uttered? … Iago couldn't *escape*, could he?

Othello (I, ii; I, iii; II, i; II, iii; III, ii; III, iii; III, iv; IV, i; IV, ii; IV, iii; V, i; V, ii)

Enemies like Iago, Brabantio and Roderigo only rarely use Othello's name. They prefer the coldly dismissive generalisation 'the Moor'. Insults like 'thick-lips' (I, i, 66) and 'sooty bosom' (I, ii, 70) suggest Othello is a Black African, as he has most often been portrayed onstage. Iago calls Othello 'black' (II, iii, 29), and Othello sadly wonders if Desdemona is unfaithful 'for I am black' (III, iii, 265). But it is also worth remembering that both 'Moor' and 'black' were semantically wide in the early seventeenth century: 'Moor' could refer even to a Caucasian if he or she was from another country and 'black' was often a moral term as well as, even rather than, a descriptor of skin colour. Othello has therefore been played as a person from a wide range of different nationalities.

The play emphasises Othello's decline by accentuating his strength at the beginning. Just before he dies he scorns the service he has done the state ('no more of that', V, ii, 339), but when we first meet him his pride in integrating Venice through such service, and his converted Christianity, helps him fearlessly counter Brabantio's threats and accusations (I, ii). The tension of grandeur and wretchedness haunts Othello throughout: he was originally of 'royal siege' (I, ii, 22), 'sold to slavery' (I, iii, 138), then freed again. His experience of slavery proves his love for Desdemona: only she has since been able to 'confine' his 'unhousèd free condition' (I, ii, 26). While praising Desdemona, Othello nonetheless sees marriage and slavery as comparable, implying a continuum of love, desire and violence that Iago is so capable of exploiting. Sex is also linked to fighting when Othello supports Desdemona's request to the Duke to go with her husband to Cyprus (I, iii, 262–72). Othello's first thought here is to reassure the Duke that sex with his wife – 'appetite' and 'satisfaction' – will not exhaust his ability to perform his soldierly duties, dismissing 'feathered Cupid' in surprisingly harsh terms ('corrupt and taint my business', I, iii, 269). Even here, early on in the play, women and sexuality rival a macho, soldierly community and set of values.

The sense of Othello struggling with a latent eroticised violence persists throughout the play. In soliloquy he confesses: 'I am abused, and my relief / Must be to loathe her' (III, iii, 270–1). These struggles may surface psychosomatically, as in his fit in Act IV, scene i, or when the doomed Desdemona ominously observes 'you're fatal [...] When your eyes roll so' (V, ii, 36–7). They also lead to some of the play's most moving and dramatic moments, as when Othello, sobbing, strives in vain to forgive ('I should have found in some place of my soul / A drop of patience', IV, ii, 46–64). Othello's final soliloquy ('It is the cause, it is the cause', V, ii, 1–22), while calmer in tone, gives no hint at resolution. He does not name the all-important 'cause', suggesting not that he has resolved to kill his wife, but that he is merely trying to convince himself of such resolve. In 1861 the actor Edward Pechter looked in a mirror, as if to blame his skin colour. This speech is punctuated with kisses and fearful descriptions of death's irrevocability ('I know not where is that Promethean heat / That can thy light relume', V, ii, 12–13), relying simply on scraps of the masculine solidarity Iago manipulates so adeptly ('she'll betray more men', V, ii, 6).

Othello's final speeches, made after he has killed Desdemona, contain discontinuous, almost delirious moments, recalling his distress before his fit: 'Ha! No more moving? / Still as the grave. Shall she come in? Were't good? / I think she stirs again – no. What's best to do?' (V, ii, 95–7). His delusion extends to thinking Desdemona's death should cause 'a huge eclipse / Of sun and moon' (V, ii, 101–2), and once Emilia has told the truth of Iago's betrayal, he asks bewilderedly 'where should Othello go?', his third person hinting at a distance he now feels from himself (V, ii, 270). Motifs of futile self-escape also mark his final speech. As he stabs himself Othello roleplays one of his previous victims, 'a turbaned Turk', a 'circumcisèd dog' (V, ii, 352, 354). And as he does so he becomes again the very slave he has sought to banish from himself all play long. With his final act, he internalises Iago's xenophobic standpoint, punishing his own alienated body.

Desdemona (I, iii; II, i; III, iii; III, iv; IV, i; IV, ii; IV, iii; V, ii)

Desdemona's name appropriately derives from the Greek for 'unfortunate'. She is much younger than her husband, a factor Iago exploits to make plausible his stories of adultery, but she is not a helpless pawn. Her opinion on Othello's travelling tales is forthright ('strange, 'twas passing strange, / 'Twas pitiful, 'twas wondrous pitiful', I, iii, 160–1) and her first speech testifies to her bold audaciousness in marrying a Moor and fleeing her father. Weighing up her 'divided duty' (I, iii, 180), she sides with her husband, much as her own mother sided with Brabantio. On her arrival in Cyprus, she is deeply troubled by her husband's absence but is civil enough to feign jollity with Iago. This, however, enables Iago to make jests on words like 'black', 'witty' and 'foul', all of which are readily applicable to adulterers (II, i, 121–64). Yet more ominously, Desdemona frankly promises Cassio she will make Othello's 'bed a school' (III, iii, 24), implying she will deprive Othello of sex until Cassio is re-instated. Regardless of Iago's lies, then, Cassio already virtually replaces Othello in Desdemona's marriage bed.

By the 'brothel scene' (IV, ii), any half-jokes about Cassio's or Othello's role in Desdemona's bed have become deadly serious. Othello strikes Desdemona and whizzes her around, foreshadowing the violence of the suffocation scene. But even when Othello calls Desdemona a 'strumpet' and 'whore' and strikes her, she remains defiant: 'By heaven you do me wrong' (IV, ii, 81–9). After he leaves enraged, however, Desdemona promises later to Emilia she 'ever will [...] love him dearly' (IV, ii, 158). Her famous 'Willow song' – Othello says Desdemona will 'sing the savageness out of a bear' (IV, i, 184–5) – echoes her sad causeless guilt ('let nobody blame him, his scorn I approve'). Desdemona, even in dying, blames herself for Othello's violence. She desperately begs for her life, and struggles for a distressingly long time: Othello has to attack her twice (V, ii, 84, 91), and she twice briefly comes to (V, ii, 118, 124–5). But at the last she says her death was down to 'I myself' (V, ii, 124). This is an especially brave, even shocking, deathbed confession for early audiences, for whom suicide was so criminalised.

Cassio (I, ii; I, iii (silent); II, i; II, iii; III, i; III, iii; III, iv; IV, i; V, i; V, ii)

Conveniently forgetting his own name's Spanish roots, Iago attacks Cassio as a foreign 'Florentine' (I, i, 19). Single ('*Almost* damned in a fair wife', I, i, 20) and threateningly attractive, with 'a daily beauty in his life that makes [Iago] ugly' (V, i, 19–20), Cassio is a credible victim of Othello's jealousy. He is also susceptible to the ambition and casual misogyny that characterises the Venetian army. He drunkenly boasts his higher rank will confer on him more heavenly favour than Iago ('the lieutenant is to be saved before the ensign', II, iii, 101–2), and guardedly confesses he thinks Desdemona has 'an inviting eye' (II, iii, 23). Sober, he remains contemptuous of Bianca, thinking a woman's mere proximity could threaten his masculine image: 'I think it no addition nor any wish / To have him see me womaned' (III, iv, 189), and pressurises Desdemona to continue to ask Othello's forgiveness on his behalf, even though he has only just finished jealously rebuking her (III, iv, 106–17). Roderigo stabs Cassio in Act V, scene i, tragically distancing him from the action and preventing him corroborating Desdemona's pleas of innocence. It is not until the final act that it is thought he will pull through and survive.

Emilia (I, iii (present but silent?); II, i; III, i; III, iii; III, iv; IV, i (present but silent?); IV, ii; IV, iii; V, i; V, ii)

In Shakespeare's source text, the story by Cinthio, the villain's wife is terrified of her husband. Shakespeare's equivalent, Emilia, is much more argumentative. She stands up frequently to Iago, and protests, on her own volition, Desdemona's innocence to Othello (e.g. V, ii, 224–8). Critics have thus attributed to sheer slow-wittedness her failure to confess her theft of the handkerchief, even when Desdemona asks for its whereabouts (III, iv, 22), or when its disappearance sparks a genuine argument between Desdemona and Othello (III, iv, 85–95). Her confession only comes terribly late, in Act V, scene ii. Different actors will respond to this challenge in different ways. Perhaps she confesses out of fear now she has a death on her conscience; perhaps earlier she merely thinks lying and marital conflict are routine, so fatigued, brutalised and battle-hardened is she by being Iago's wife. Plausibly in this earlier scene Emilia could be just offstage, out of earshot. The way this scene is played and directed determines our interpretation and judgement of Emilia. Perhaps she lies to Desdemona out of loyalty to, even desire for, her husband. We might also argue that she cannot know just how fatal the loss of this 'trifle' (III, iii, 324) will turn out to be. Continually withholding the truth from Desdemona, however, and her vicious attacks on Bianca (V, i, 119) surely cloud the proto-feminist message Emilia voices elsewhere. One such statement, that husbands always 'belch' their wives 'when they are full' (III, iv, 101–2), pointedly changes the topic when Desdemona asks about the handkerchief. Talking at least as much about her own situation as Desdemona's, Emilia distracts attention from the handkerchief (and thus her theft) by alluding guiltily and resentfully back to Iago's brutality. Emilia is perhaps less a feminist than a feminist issue. To what degree is a woman's wrongdoing to women compelled by the misogyny around her? Her attack on double standards of infidelity for men and women (IV, iii, 79–97), justifying wives' adultery when husbands are neglectful, raises similar questions. More than a simple revenge fantasy on her own husband, the speech may also be read as Emilia's frustration with herself, at the misguided loyalty to her husband that stops her from telling Desdemona the truth, with the gender norms she has thus internalised, and their roots in the misogynist 'serpent's curse' on Eve and all women since (IV, ii, 16). This enforced passivity helps explain why she shifts responsibility and blame when Desdemona dies onto Othello: 'O gull, O dolt / As ignorant as dirt' (V, ii, 161–2); 'O dull Moor' (V, ii, 224). Emilia makes no moral judgement, however, about her own action, neutrally stating she found the handkerchief 'by fortune, and did give my husband' (V, ii, 225). Like her husband, Emilia illustrates the tragic results when people absorb the negative expectations about them, and thus claim no responsibility when acting according to those expectations.

Bianca (III, iv; IV, i; V, i)

Bianca's name means 'white', playing ironically on her role as a courtesan. But her complaint that Cassio has not been with her for eight days implies she feels more for him than for her other companions (Iago observes such a 'strumpet' may 'beguile many, and be beguiled by one', IV, i 93). As another irony of her name, 'Bianca' as 'white' woman, like Othello the 'black' Moor, is furiously jealous of the handkerchief's owner. Her attacks on this 'minx' and 'hobby-horse' unwittingly condemn her to the eavesdropping Othello (IV, i, 147–8). Iago and Emilia later scapegoat her for Roderigo's death (V, i, 115). In some productions she is even raped by Iago's men at the end of the scene as punishment.

Roderigo (I, i; I, iii; II, i; II, iii; IV, ii; V, i)

Roderigo is an indispensable assistant for Iago's schemes, especially provoking and framing the drunk Cassio. He is often caricatured as a useable idiot, conveniently and pitilessly dispatched when Iago has no further use for him, but recently, and interestingly, he has been portrayed as menacing and violent, a social striver who voices complaints common among minor courtiers of the time. Brabantio's decision not to marry his daughter to Roderigo perhaps exposes unfair and rigid Venetian class distinctions.

Brabantio (I, i; I, ii; I, iii)

Desdemona's father's complaints highlight from the start of the play the preconceptions and prejudices that empower Iago's insinuations and filter into Othello's self-doubt: perhaps this 'black ram' is not good enough for his daughter after all (I, i, 88). Brabantio does not come to Cyprus. His absence isolates Desdemona and symbolises patriarchal disapproval. His death is reported near the end of the play (V, ii, 202).

Play structure

The most famous discussion about the structure of *Othello* concerns its 'double time scheme'. Bianca's complaint that Cassio has neglected her for a whole week (III, iv, 168–71), Othello's accusation that Emilia has cheated on him 'a thousand times' (V, ii, 209–10) or the message travelling back to Venice of the Turk's defeat, seem to suggest a longer duration than the quick run of events required by Iago's plot. These continuity problems can, however, be explained in terms of characters exaggerating for their own ends, as when Othello suddenly 'remembers' the handkerchief's backstory, it is plausible that Othello, suspecting his wife of lying, makes up a story off the cuff to make her feel guilty. Other inconsistencies can be explained as misguided soldierly camaraderie or mind-clouded jealousy, as when Othello never tells

Desdemona that Iago has been slandering her, despite ample opportunity to do so (e.g. IV, ii) or sheer tragic coincidence, as when Desdemona lets pass unheard Emilia's suspicious confession that Iago once suspected her of sleeping with Othello. Critical attention to inconsistencies and 'double time scheme' coincided with the rise of neo-classical perspectives which upheld the Aristotelian unities of time, action and place: the play should depict events lasting no longer than twenty-four hours, originating from a single root cause, occurring in a single location, to make the stage and play imitate reality more believably. But perhaps *Othello* is more like a fable than an exact record. There are tricky discrepancies which may well have crept in unnoticed during the drafting and printing process, like Cassio expressing ignorance of Othello's marriage, even when Desdemona later says Cassio helped Othello woo her. But these are often forgotten in performance, simply because the stage action is so fluid. The stage is only rarely cleared, so there are relatively few scenes, as if to emphasise the easiness of Iago's destructive movements within this interconnected, claustrophobic community.

Despite the play's fluid rapidity, however, two distinct, but interlocking halves can be identified. In the first, before Iago frames Cassio, *Othello* displays comedic aspects: two lovers happily defy the patriarchy to marry. The Venetians' war is quickly won without visible, onstage bloodshed. But then, in the second, Cassio's demotion, Iago's first successful action, forces him into closer proximity with Desdemona, and Iago gets closer to Othello. Iago and Othello share only a few lines in the first half of the play. They share entire long scenes in the second. How precisely does Iago make Othello believe here that his wife is unfaithful? Many intermingling factors are in play. As well as distorting the 'ocular proof' (III, iii, 362), Iago focuses generalised cultural prejudice against women on Desdemona in particular, capitalises on his reputation as 'Honest Iago', and exploits Othello's latent anxieties, demonstrably shared by other men, about the possession of women, a sign amongst men of successfully upheld masculinity. Indeed, there comes a kind of tipping point where Iago no longer needs to do very much and can simply let jealousy, often associated in the Renaissance with irrational passion, follow its own self-destructive momentum: jealousy is after all 'Begot upon itself, born on itself' (III, iv, 157).

Arguably the play's dramatic centrepoint is Iago and Othello's exchange in Act III, scene iii, which itself may be divided into two sections: before and after Iago gains possession of the handkerchief (III, iii, 290). In the first section Iago prepares the ground, saying Cassio, leaving Desdemona, looks 'guilty', as if he has something to hide, conferring suspicion even at this early stage on Desdemona's mistimed insistence on Cassio's suit, intensifying Othello's dissatisfaction with him. Othello later expressly mentions multiple times where Iago expresses scepticism subtly, even wordlessly, about his wife's relationship with Cassio: 'I like not that' (III, iii, 32); his raised eyebrow (III, iii, 116); his ironic 'indeed' (III, iii, 103–4); and the fact that Iago actually decides to ask about Cassio in the first place. To minimise suspicion that he has any vested interests in Othello's situation, Iago hides behind clichéd generalities about the importance of 'good name' and warnings about 'jealousy' (III, iii, 159, 168). He nonetheless advises Othello 'Look to your wife', as if he is acting in Othello's best interest and Desdemona has already done enough wrong to deserve surveillance (III, iii, 200). This subtly and destructively echoes Brabantio's imperative 'Look to her, Moor, if thou hast eyes to see ...' (I, iii, 290), continuing and intensifying Brabantio's doubts that a 'foul Moor' could not have married someone like Desdemona on his own merits, without the use of the witchcraft Shakespeare's contemporaries took so seriously.

Even before Iago gets the handkerchief, then, doubt is established: in his gloomy soliloquy (III, iii, 261–81) Othello seems practically convinced his wife is unfaithful ('she's gone'). Once Iago has the 'napkin' he alternates feigned sympathy ('I am sorry to hear this', III, iii, 346) with a more strident, aggressive tone, as if to disorient his victim. At points, stressing his reputation for 'honesty', he accuses Othello of ingratitude, like a master rebuking the pupil (III, iii, 375–82), a position of authority which strengthens his provisos about the handkerchief. The pure 'ocular proof' Othello craves is impossible. Unless he were actually to see Desdemona being 'tupped', the handkerchief will have to suffice as proof (III, iii, 397). It is only at this point that Iago (falsely reluctantly) explicitly accuses Cassio of boasting of his conquests in his sleep (an accusation Cassio cannot knowingly deny) and wiping his beard with Desdemona's handkerchief, careful all the while to appear even-handed and honest by conceding the handkerchief would only be one of 'other proofs' (III, iii, 431, 442). Othello and Iago's diabolical parody of a 'wedding', where they, kneeling, pledge lifelong engagement to each other before 'ever-burning lights' (III, iii, 463–79) displays, and intensifies, Othello's near-complete commitment to Iago's story.

Language

George Wilson Knight wrote an essay called 'The Othello Music' ([1930] 2005: 109–35). Othello's mellifluous, round, singable vowels are especially prominent in the tale which wins Desdemona and impresses the Duke. But his grandiloquence also indicates a kind of defensiveness, as if he strives to compensate through language for his otherness; its occasional bombastic emptiness hints at the latent vulnerability of the man uttering it. Othello's main use of prose is when he suffers the epileptic fit (IV, i, 32–40). Verse is perhaps, then, a self-conscious effort.

As a variant on this exploration of full and empty linguistic expression, and as frequently in Shakespeare's plays, *Othello* explores the possible effects of repetition. Emilia, dying on Desdemona's marriage bed, echoes briefly Desdemona's 'Willow song', linking her lady yet more strongly to the song's sad story, implying its validity to the tragic wives here and perhaps for centuries to come. Othello's gruff insult to Desdemona, 'Goats and monkeys!' (IV, i, 255), echoes Iago's similes about feminine lasciviousness: 'were they as prime as goats, as hot as monkeys' (III, iii, 405). 'Will' can mean desire, pleasure, delight, sex drive or aggressive determination ('the power and corrigible authority of this lies in our wills', I, iii, 321). Keywords like 'honest', 'virtue' and 'monster' are repeated through the play. The frequent and often ironic repetitions of 'honest' question the very honesty of the word 'honesty' itself: it means different things each time it is used. This semantic flexibility perhaps comments on, and even helps develop, the word's cultural shift, observed by the editor of the Oxford text Michael Neill, from contexts of 'honourable' nobility to 'trustworthy servants': perhaps 'honest Iago' is not only purely ironic but a sign of the social condescension Iago jealously and violently seeks to revenge (ed. Neill 2006: 160–1).

'Virtue' likewise shifts in gendered meaning from feminine chastity, as when Cassio asks 'the virtuous Desdemona to undertake for me' (II, iii), to masculine, martial valour, as when an agitated Othello bids 'farewell' 'to the big wars/That make ambition virtue' (III, iii, 351–2). 'Monster' parallels such agitation, referring not only to jealousy, as in Iago's famous 'green-eyed monster which doth mock/The meat it feeds on' (III, iii, 170–1), but also to the cuckoldry the jealous man is so afraid of. 'A hornèd man's a monster and a beast' (IV, i, 58). 'Monster' sometimes has no clear meaning at all; indeed, it is associated with the very ambiguity of words. This is especially clear when Othello grows annoyed at Iago's tendency to repeat his own words back at him, as if to doubt them. 'By heaven, thou echo'st me,/As if there were some *monster* in thy thought/Too hideous to be shown' (III, iii, 109–11, my emphasis). Repetition clearly bothers Othello. He screams 'What needs this iterance, woman?' (V, ii, 147) when Emilia similarly repeats his words sceptically. The weird tendency of excessively repeated words to become their own opposites mirrors linguistically Desdemona's transition from virtuous wife to adulterous monster. Othello, for example, seizes on the word 'committed' when Desdemona asks 'Alas, what ignorant sin have I committed' (IV, ii, 70), parodying what he sees as Desdemona's lack of 'commitment' to the marriage (IV, ii, 72, 73, 76, 81). He similarly spins Ludovico's word 'obedient' (IV, i, 240) when describing Desdemona ('she's obedient, as you say, obedient./Very obedient', IV, i, 247–8). Differing in their outward appearances and actual uses, words, and perhaps language itself, emerge as inherently dissimulating, even Machiavellian.

Themes

Machiavellianism

Machiavellianism is one of *Othello*'s key themes. Iago's famous confession to Roderigo 'I am not what I am' (I, i, 65) echoes Machiavelli's advice in chapter 18 of *The Prince*, first printed in 1532: 'to *appear* merciful, faithful, humane, religious, upright, and to be so, but with a mind so framed that should you require not to be so, *you may be able and know how to change to the opposite*' (Machiavelli 2005: 61, my emphasis). But while Iago is clearly the play's most violently enthusiastic Machiavellian, more virtuous characters also selectively communicate to their own advantage: Desdemona 'deceived' Brabantio (I, iii, 291); Othello 'beguiles' Desdemona and the Duke with his 'tale' of 'most disastrous chances' (I, iii, 156, 91, 133). The play thus seems to explore Machiavellianism as a spectrum: Iago's brutally harmful untruths at one end, Othello's and Desdemona's amorously motivated semi-truths at the other. It also explores evil, frequently expressed via Christian imagery of demons or devils, as behaviour lying outside this spectrum. Attempts by, say, Orson Welles to explain away Iago's behaviour in terms of impotence miss perhaps something fundamental about this Shakespearean exploration of evil as something fearsomely inexplicable to mortal minds: 'motiveless malignity' (see Foakes 1989: 15, 113). Unlike Machiavellians, evildoers have no motivation, political or otherwise, for the harm they do. Iago never gives a single, clear reason for destroying others' lives, alluding only briefly and confusedly to a frustrated desire for Desdemona (II, i, 282–4), racial hatred (I, i, 88), or paranoid jealousy about being cuckolded by Cassio (V, i, 19) or Othello (II, i, 290; IV, ii, 146–7). He even confesses 'I know not' if Othello has slept with his wife (I, iii, 375). The only thing we know for sure is that he 'hate[s] the Moor'. In Iago's mind hatred is its own self-perpetuating reason.

Machismo and 'trifles'

The Venetian culture that dictates that husbands should be jealously possessive of their wives is, therefore, not really the concrete reason for Iago's aggressiveness; it is more a tool he can use to exploit and harm Othello. The play depicts a butch, military world which makes tragedies like Othello's only too possible: it is perhaps more than coincidence that Iago continually urges his victims Othello and Roderigo 'Be a man' (I, iii, 330). And in this macho world women are merely status symbols. Othello often uses metaphors to describe Desdemona that juxtapose value with purity ('chrysolite', V, ii, 143; 'pearl', V, ii, 346) while Cassio dismisses Bianca as a 'bauble' (IV, i, 130). The reduction of women to signs, of which the meaning is insecure and can be reinterpreted, contributes to the wider sense that Othello depicts a disorienting social transition where things are no longer what they seem. At the very beginning of the play Iago, passed over for promotion by Cassio, laments the disintegration of the 'old gradation, where each second / Stood heir to th'first' (I, i, 36–7). The implication is that when Iago reinvents the legible world to suit his purposes, as when he persuades Othello to see the handkerchief as harmful, or Cassio to see drink as harmless, he is simply exploiting a pervasive social instability he himself hates. After all, when Cassio drunkenly attacks Montano he falls victim to the very process Iago condemns, being quickly 'cashiered' (dismissed) by his general (I, i, 48).

The constant danger of such victimisation explains an anxious stress on place-holding ('lieu-tenant') in both military and marital senses ("twixt my sheets / He's done my office', I, iii, 377), and on 'reputation' (see ed. Neill 2006: 32). Cassio complains to Iago after his disgrace that 'I have lost the immortal part of myself, and what remains is bestial' (II, iii, 254–5). Iago significantly changes his mind about reputation depending on his interlocutor and the potential advantage of the situation, reassuring Cassio that reputation is 'an idle and most false imposition' (II, iii, 259–60) but warning Othello that 'he who filches from me my good name [...] makes me poor indeed' (III, iii, 163–5). Othello's early assurance of his good standing ('My parts, my title and my perfect soul/Shall manifest me rightly', I, ii, 32) is replaced in his final speech by an almost desperate plea to the shocked nobles to 'Speak of me as I am' (V, ii, 341). Reputation is a form of social legibility. It is all the more important in this play world where the symbolic values of men, women (and handkerchiefs) can change or be made to change unpredictably.

'Blackness' and theological fears

The protagonists' self-consciousness about being read or misread by others has a theological dimension. The 'demi-devil' Iago (V, ii, 299) seems indifferent to salvation, even cackling about the 'divinity of Hell' (II, iii, 335), but the afterlife looms heavy for the others. Cassio and Desdemona both stress their desire to be 'saved' (II, iii, 99; IV, ii, 86). Othello begs Desdemona to atone for her sins before he kills her (V, ii, 26–8), only to realise that it is he who will be damned for killing an innocent woman: 'When we shall meet at count,/This look of thine will hurl my soul from heaven/And fiends will snatch at it': he sees these 'fiends' so vividly that he addresses them (V, ii, 272–80). It is not for nothing that he says Iago has 'ensnared' his 'soul' as well as his 'body' (V, ii, 300).

Othello's Christianity is an important, but vulnerable, part of his integration into the Venetian state. Condemning Cassio's drunken violence, for example, he reaches instantly for Christian morals: 'Are we turned Turks, and to ourselves do that/Which Heaven hath forbid the Ottomites?/For Christian shame, put by this barbarous brawl!' (II, iii, 161–3). By identifying himself with the 'we' of Christian Venice against the 'Turks', Othello attempts to make people forget his own Moorish otherness. But this attempt ends of course in tragic failure. The play's ironically antithetical subtitle 'the Moor of Venice' reminds us of Othello's outlandish situation, hinting at how his 'blackness' – a word used infrequently but significantly – becomes a focal point for Venetian cultural anxieties. As well as a straightforward target of Iago's and Roderigo's prejudice, Othello's blackness also explores more subtly how such prejudice may develop psychologically and culturally. In Shakespeare's time and ours, a whole range of metaphors link light to knowledge ('clarity', 'enlightened') and darkness to ignorance ('obscurity', 'in the dark'). And *Othello* sees this epistemological value system transferred with disturbing ease to human skin. As seen above, Iago's macho Venice is almost paranoid about the structures of social legibility through which knowledge may be established, but Othello's 'blackness' resists these structures. He is both Christian *and* Moor, an explorer accused of witchcraft and a former slave. Indeed, it is precisely this exotically unreadable ownership of multiple, contradictory roles that seems so to tantalise Desdemona, and the Duke who hears Othello's life story.

This helps explain why this outsider is ultimately confused by his own blackness, which affects his own social role as a husband: 'Haply [Perhaps] because I am black [...] she's gone' (III, iii, 266–70). The play's interrogation of marriage is a key element of its wider exploration of the psychological impact of changing social structures and symbolisms. Weddings are twice aggressively parodied: first, when Iago and Othello kneel and exchange vows, and second, when Desdemona is murdered in the marriage bed Iago says 'she hath contaminated' (IV, i, 200). In parallel, Othello's marital jealousy is presented as the result and mirror image of Iago's. Iago vows to 'put the Moor [...] into a jealousy so strong/That judgement cannot cure' (II, i, 291–3). Jealousy, this 'green-eyed monster' which seems to take on a life and momentum of its own in the increasingly frantic second half, emerges weirdly as both cause and effect of a macho world struggling with its own inwardly destructive rivalries.

Texts and contexts

There are two known early versions of Othello: a Quarto text printed in 1622 (Q), and that printed in the 1623 Folio (F). There are some major differences between the two. F adds a seven-line speech by Othello ('Never, Iago: Like to the Pontic sea ...', III, iii, 453–62) and the 'Willow song' (IV, iii, 29–48). In F Othello describes Desdemona more sexually, as she gives him before they marry a 'world of kisses' rather than a 'world of sighs' (Q, adopted for the Oxford text I, iii, 159). This sensuality may contribute to the plausibility of Iago's slanders. Othello kills an 'Indian' in Q and the Second Folio, and a 'Iudean' (Judean?) in F (cf. V, ii, 346). Perhaps this is a misprint, but discussions as to the probability of one reading or another have led to detailed research into early modern political relationships between Venice, India and Judea. The story of the play is based on Story Seven, Third Decade, in *Gli Hecatommithi* (*One Hundred Tales*) by Giovanni Battista Giraldi Cinthio (1504–73). This is a relatively basic morality tale about the danger of mixed-race relationships. Shakespeare condenses the timeframe radically and makes the central character more sympathetic.

The play in performance

Othello's performance history indicates changing attitudes to race and race relations. The German philosopher and critic August Wilhelm Schlegel (1767–1845) read the play as the story of a fundamentally barbaric character whose superficial 'civility' dissipates under pressure (see Orkin 1987: 182–3, n. 38). Victorian audiences were often scandalised by Othello and Desdemona's marriage as an example of miscegenation, or 'mixing' of races. Critics condescendingly praised early twentieth-century black actors playing Othello like Ira Aldridge or Paul Robeson for their 'natural simplicity' while white actors used 'black-face' make-up to play the role, recalling unfortunate memories of the 'nigger minstrel' genre. Since the mid-twentieth century non-white actors have tended to play Othello. Notable stage productions include Laurence Olivier's 1964 production, Janet Suzman's 1987 South African anti-apartheid interpretation of the play and Patrick Stewart's 1997 'photo-negative' version, where he, as Othello, was the only white member of the cast. Sam Mendes in 1997 cast Simon Russell Beale as a psychotic, unpredictable and short-fused Iago, obsessively picking things up in case they may serve for later stratagems (as of course the handkerchief does). Michael Grandage's 2007 Donmar production was highly praised, and in 2009 the black UK comic Lenny Henry played Othello in Whitehall in London. On film, Welles's expressionist, high-contrast 1952 black and white version attributed Iago's jealous anger to sexual impotence. Radical retellings of the Shakespearean original include Charles Marowitz, *An Othello* and Paula Vogel, *Desdemona: A Play about a Handkerchief*. It is important to note that the play's performance history has been an important indicator of, and influence on, changing attitudes to gender as well as race. Desdemona's role was cut in the eighteenth century, because she was judged to be more tragic and sympathetic the meeker and more obedient she was. But since pivotal performances by Sarah Stephenson and Lisa Harrow (1971), and Felicity Kendal (1980), coincidental with the 1970s highpoint of feminism, Desdemona has been played increasingly as an assertive, self-possessed, spirited and intelligent young woman.

Critical reception

Like the play's performance history, the play's critical history witnesses its historical influence on cultural and political issues of race and gender. Martin Orkin (1987) traces 'how racist mythology inscribes cultural responses to the play'. Ania Loomba (2002) and Poonam Trivedi (2003) have since offered notable postcolonial interventions. Michael Bristol (1990) examines uses of comic and carnival convention, while Stephen Greenblatt [1980] (2005) and Hugh Grady (1996) offer classic studies of Iago's Machiavellian use of empathy: how he sees things from others' perspectives so as better to dominate them. Timothy Turner (2015) has revived this question in relation to early modern histories of psychological torture, while Paul Cefalu (2013) argues that this question of Iago as 'mind-reader' necessitates and helps justify a critical method that supplements cognitivist with psychoanalytical theory. Cefalu thus joins a powerful tradition of psychoanalytical essays on *Othello*. Christopher Pye (2009) brings Lacanian and Marxist theory together to read the play as genuinely 'early modern' in its newly aesthetic portrayals of psychological and social 'groundlessness'. Joel Altman's *The Improbability of Othello* (2010) is an important recent book-length study, which over 450 pages traces the play's engagement with categories from Renaissance logical and rhetorical training.

Discussion questions

＊ Are there ways of staging the play that could make us sympathise – or at least empathise – with Iago?

＊ Does the play critique feminine meekness? Is it Desdemona's fault that she lets herself be killed?

Bibliography and further reading

Edition

Shakespeare, W. (2006), *Othello*, ed. M. Neill, Oxford: Oxford University Press.

Critical response

Altman, J. (2010), *The Improbability of Othello: Rhetorical Anthropology and Shakespearean Selfhood*, Chicago: Chicago University Press.

Bristol, M. (1990), 'Charivari and the Comedy of Abjection in *Othello*', *Renaissance Drama*, 21, 3–21.

Cefalu, P. (2013), 'The Burdens of Mind Reading in Shakespeare's *Othello*: A Critical Psychoanalytic Approach to Iago's Theory of Mind', *Shakespeare Quarterly*, 64:3, 265–94.

Foakes, R. (ed.) (1989), *Coleridge's Criticism of Shakespeare: A Selection*, London: The Athlone Press.

Grady, H. (1996), *Shakespeare's Universal Wolf: Essays in Reification*, Oxford: Oxford University Press.

Greenblatt, S. [1980] (2005), *Renaissance Self-fashioning: From More to Shakespeare*, Chicago: University of Chicago Press.

Knight, G. W. [1930] (2005), *The Wheel of Fire: Interpretations of Shakespearean Tragedy*, London/New York: Routledge.

Loomba, A. (2002), *Shakespeare, Race and Colonialism*, Oxford: Oxford University Press.

Machiavelli, N. (2005), *The Prince*, trans. and ed. P. Bondanella, Oxford: Oxford University Press.

Orkin, M. (1987), '*Othello* and the "Plain Face" of Racism', *Shakespeare Quarterly*, 38, 166–88.

Pye, C. (2009),'"To throw out our eyes for brave Othello": Shakespeare and Aesthetic Ideology', *Shakespeare Quarterly*, 60:4, 425–47.

Trivedi, P. (2003), 'Reading "Other Shakespeares"', in P. Aebischer, N. Wheale and Ed Esche (eds), *Remaking Shakespeare: Performance across Media, Genres, and Cultures*, Basingstoke: Palgrave Macmillan, pp. 56–73.

Turner, T. (2015), 'Othello on the Rack', *Journal for Early Modern Cultural Studies*, 15:3, 102–36.

4 Macbeth

c. 1606, first recorded performance 1611

Act, scene and line references are to the 2015 Arden Third Series edition, edited by
Sandra Clark and Pamela Mason.

Plot summary

Three Witches resolve to meet with Macbeth (I, i), a Thane (Scottish Earl) and
captain in the army of King Duncan. Duncan is told that Macbeth has helped him
see off a rebellion. Unknown to Macbeth, Duncan makes him Thane of Cawdor to
reward his help and replace an executed rebel (I, ii). The Witches meet as predicted
with Macbeth, joined by his fellow Thane and soldier Banquo. They prophesy that
Macbeth will be Thane of Cawdor and then King, and that Banquo will never be king
himself but will father a long line of kings. When Macbeth learns he has been made
Thane of Cawdor, he takes this as a sign that the rest of the Witches' prophesies
will come true (I, iii). He tells his wife by letter of the meeting and his hopeful
interpretations. When Macbeth arrives home his wife urges him to kill King Duncan
when he visits their house. Macbeth may then reign in his stead (I, v). Macbeth
murders Duncan (II, i–ii). The King's body is discovered and Macbeth says the responsibility lies with drunken guards, whom Macbeth then kills as punishment. The
other Thanes, such as Macduff and Lennox, remain unconvinced, however. Luckily
for Macbeth, Duncan's sons Malcolm and Donalbain, fearful for their own lives, flee
the country (II, iii). Suspicion therefore falls on them (II, iv) giving Macbeth breath-
ing space and a power vacuum that justifies his taking the throne. The Witches'
prophecy has come true (III, i). But Macbeth knows Banquo, the prophesy's only
other witness, suspects foul play (III, i, 2–3, 47–8). Macbeth therefore has Banquo
killed to silence him. But Banquo's son Fleance escapes (III, i–iii). Macbeth learns
of Fleance's survival just before a feast with the other Thanes, held presumably
to cement their allegiance. He panics. Fleance alive affirms the Witches' predic-
tion: Banquo's descendants will indeed found a great and enduring royal dynasty.
As Macbeth joins the dinner table, shaken, Banquo's Ghost appears to him but
nobody else. Macbeth barks out to it defiant allusions to murder. A flustered Lady
Macbeth quickly breaks up the dinner, and the Thanes grow even more suspicious
(III, iv). Macduff goes to England to join Malcolm and mount an army, seeking to

return the line of Duncan to the throne (III, vi). A worried Macbeth returns to the Witches to learn more about his future; their 'apparitions' warn him to 'beware Macduff' (IV, i, 70). But they also state 'none of woman born/Shall harm Macbeth' (IV, i, 79–80) and 'Macbeth shall never vanquished be, until/Great Birnham Wood to high Dunsinane Hill/Shall come against him' (IV, i, 91–3). Macbeth takes arrogant reassurance from this. He grows displeased, though, when the Witches show him Banquo's long dynastic line of kingly sons (IV, i, 111–23). He resolves to kill Macduff following the Witches' warning. But in Macduff's absence Macbeth's soldiers massacre Macduff's wife and children instead (IV, ii). News of the massacre inspires Macduff and a formerly unwilling Malcolm to return to Scotland and try to wrest the throne back from the tyrant (IV, iii). The scene shifts abruptly to Lady Macbeth who since the dinner party has gone mad. She sleepwalks with eyes open, ignores other human beings, washes her hands obsessively as if to cleanse them of blood and alludes to the traumatic sight of the murdered Duncan (V, i). We hear later of her offstage death (V, v, 16), rumoured to be suicide (V, ix, 37). The play's last scenes depict the final battle between Macbeth and the forces led by Macduff and Malcolm. The arrogant reassurance Macbeth took from the Witches' prophecies is ultimately futile. Great Birnham Wood does indeed come to Dunsinane Hill because Malcolm's soldiers had been wearing parts of it as camouflage. And Macduff was not 'of woman born' but 'untimely ripped' (V, viii, 16): pre-modern obstetrics often involved saving children by extracting them from their dead mothers. Realising the Witches deceived him in their reassuring prophesies Macbeth loses hope, but fights on. The play ends with the victorious Macduff bearing the decapitated Macbeth's 'cursed head' (V, ix, 21). Malcolm announces his coronation. Thanes are now to be called Earls, hinting at a unification of England with Scotland.

Characters

Macbeth (I, iii; I, iv; I, v; I, vii; II, i; II, ii; II, iii; III, i; III, ii; III, iv; IV, i; V, iii; V, v; V, vii; V, viii)

The audience does not see Macbeth until Act I, scene iii, but hears about him almost immediately. He is mentioned first by the Witches (I, i), then by the 'bloody' sergeant, who describes him as a 'brave' and skilled soldier (I, ii, 16). When Macbeth first appears, however, he is unsettled. While capable of slitting men 'from the nave to th'chops' (I, ii, 22) he hesitates before the mystically androgynous 'weïrd sisters' (I, v, 8). Macbeth's problems with women or woman-like creatures also mark his fraught but erotically charged rivalry with his wife. His first letter to her, telling her of the Sisters' prophecy (I, v, 1–14), is arguably a call for help, asking her to make his wavering mind up for him, even to scapegoat her for Duncan's murder. Macbeth's soliloquies, or lengthy asides if people are near earshot (Banquo in I, iii, the Thanes in I, vii) help illustrate this turmoil. His first such speech runs as follows:

This supernatural soliciting
Cannot be ill; cannot be good. If ill,
Why hath it given me earnest of success,
Commencing in a truth? I am Thane of Cawdor.
If good, why do I yield to that suggestion
Whose horrid image doth unfix my hair,
And make my seated heart knock at my ribs,
Against the use of nature? Present fears
Are less than horrible imaginings.
My thought, whose murder yet is but fantastical,
Shakes so my single state of man
That function is smothered in surmise,
And nothing is, but what is not.
(I, iii, 132–44)

The opening lines' balanced structure suggests at first a busily strategising, calculat-
ing mind. The contrasting options 'cannot be ill, cannot be good' are each developed
with a semi-rhetorical question of roughly equal length. But the options are not
neatly opposed. Macbeth starts logically, projecting his recent promotion as a sign
that the Sisters' other prophecies will come true as well. As King he shall be 'the
state of man'. But this thought 'shakes' Macbeth at the very moment of thinking it.
The soliloquy seems then at its mid-point to gain in momentum. Increasingly fluid,
run-on lines predominate as mere 'fears' give way to 'horrible imaginings'. Macbeth
cannot even bring himself to associate the word 'murder' directly with Duncan,
guiltily internalising it to his own 'thought'. While seeking to disavow it as merely
'fantastical', he cannot quite shake it. It lingers on in his head, a kind of residue of
bewilderment: 'Nothing is, but what is not'. Later, following coy but resonant conversations with his wife, another soliloquy sees him crystallising his resolve to kill
Duncan. Nevertheless, the broad pattern from resolution to doubt seems to recur:

If it were done, when 'tis done, then 'twere well
It were done quickly. If th'assassination
Could trammel up the consequence, and catch
With his surcease, success: but that this blow
Might be the be-all and the end-all, here,
But here, upon this bank and shoal of time,
We'd jump the life to come. But in these cases,
We still have judgement here, that we but teach
Bloody instructions, which being taught, return
To plague the inventor. This even-handed justice
Commends th'ingredience of our poisoned chalice
To our own lips. [...] This Duncan
Hath borne his faculties so meek, hath been
So clear in his great office, that his virtues
Will plead like angels, trumpet-tongued, against
The deep damnation of his taking off;
And pity, like a naked new-born babe,
Striding the blast, or heaven's cherubin, horsed
Upon the sightless couriers of the air,

Shall blow the horrid deed in every eye,
That tears shall drown the wind. I have no spur
To prick the sides of my intent, but only
Vaulting ambition, which o'erleaps itself,
And falls on th'other
    [it appears Macbeth is about to say 'side', but his wife's entry interrupts]
(I, vii, 1–28)

This speech contains some of the most hotly debated phrases in the whole of Shakespeare. The sentences run over or abruptly interrupt the iambic pentameter line and, syntactically, are as tortuous and confused as indecisive real-time thought. Broadly speaking Macbeth is again weighing up winning the crown (note the prominent word 'success' in both speeches) against the need to murder. But this speech adds an other-worldly dimension to Macbeth's fear. The references to 'angels' and 'heaven's cherubin' suggest a concern, comparable to Hamlet's, with punishments that might befall a sinner or criminal in 'the life to come'. And even were the issue of the after-life not enough, Macbeth seems to be saying, the worldly political consequences would be dire. He would ultimately be discovered ('blow the horrid deed in every eye'), disgraced and killed, bringing the 'poisoned chalice [...] to his own lips'. And Macbeth even thinks this is fair: such justice is 'even-handed'.

But subtler implications intermingle with this apparent message. The speech also deals with the radical difference between imagining a deed and actually doing it. Many verbs here hover between indicative and subjunctive moods (ed. Clark and Mason 2015: 73). And 'here' is repeated with mysterious intensity, as if Macbeth wants the deed already over and done with in the 'here' and now (Edmund Kean, who played Macbeth as a villain, thumped his heart at this point). The moment when imagination passes into action seems also to be a strange temporal experience. 'This bank and shoal of time', describing time as river-like linear flow, gives way to the yet more abrupt monosyllables of the 'be-all and the end-all', a phrase so naturalised into the English language it has sadly lost much of its linguistically innovative and context-based force. It is implied that the moment of action somehow exists outside normal perceptions of time. The murderous blow could 'jump the life to come' (my emphasis). The murderer must likewise leap out of his nervous hyper-self-consciousness to actually do the deed. Macbeth's final chain of imagery suggests a bounding horse ('spur', 'prick the sides', 'vaulting', 'o'erleaps'), and is interrupted mid-flow by his wife's entrance.

Murderous action is thus presented as a suspension or interruption of time and the consciousness which unfolds within it. You are conscious of it only in retrospect. This is emphasised just before Duncan's murder when Macbeth hallucinates a blood-dripping, 'air-drawn dagger' (II, i, 30–64) which he fails physically to grasp. This famous speech is full of tensions between material and mystical existence: 'I have thee not, and yet I see thee still' (II, i, 35) and Macbeth frets the earth will echo his earlier footsteps between his and Duncan's chambers, revealing his guilt. Unlike the earlier speeches this is a true soliloquy: 'Now o'er the one half world / Nature seems dead' (II, i, 50). Everyone else is asleep, channelling and emphasising Macbeth's isolation.

This isolation grows after Duncan's murder, perhaps more so than for any other Shakespearean tragic protagonist. His wife madly melts away from the action and then dies, and his enemies gradually close in. The relatively lucid calculations of the first soliloquy gradually disappear. His speech to the murderers comparing men to dogs already hints at an awkwardness with his new kingly title (III, i, 93–108). His panicky desire for spiritual atonement ('Will all great Neptune's ocean wash this blood/Clean from my hand?', II, ii, 61–2) is increasingly interspersed with strange, then brutally desensitised behaviour. The world seems to him more and more frightening: 'Light thickens,/And the crow makes wing to th'rooky wood./Good things of day begin to droop and drowse,/Whiles night's black agents to their preys do rouse' (III, ii, 51–5). Alongside, his attitude to violence becomes chillingly casual and resigned: 'I am in blood/Stepped in so far, that should I wade no more,/Returning were as tedious as go o'er' (III, iv, 134–6). The unconsciousness of fierce acts has now become Macbeth's predominant psychological mode: 'the firstlings of my heart shall be the firstlings of my hand' (IV, i, 146–7).

The perceptible momentum of this development makes plausible his complete metamorphosis into a mad tyrant by the time we next see him in Act V, scene iii. The oscillations and modulations in tone are correspondingly more intense. His final speeches can be glumly embittered, as illustrated by two famous examples:

> I have lived long enough: my way of life
> Is fallen into the sere, the yellow leaf,
> And that which should accompany old age,
> As honour, love, obedience, troops of friends,
> I must not look to have.
> (V, iii, 22–6)

> Life's but a walking shadow, a poor player,
> That struts and frets his hour upon the stage,
> And then is heard no more. It is a tale
> Told by an idiot, full of sound and fury
> Signifying nothing.
> (V, v, 16–27)

But precisely because Macbeth has 'nothing' to lose, his melancholy can instantly switch to resigned fury, especially as, with his last words, he realises that despite the Witches' riddling assurances, he has been vulnerable to Macduff all along:

> Yet I will try the last. Before my body
> I throw my warlike shield. Lay on, Macduff,
> And damned be him, that first cries, 'Hold, enough'.
> (V, viii, 32–4)

Lady Macbeth ('Lady') (I, v; I, vi; I, vii; II, ii; II, iii; III, i; III, ii; III, iv; V, i)

We first meet Lady Macbeth in Act I, scene V. She delivers two soliloquies very close together, interrupted only by a messenger. The first (I, v, 15–29) instantly establishes her murderous, ambitious contrast with her husband, whom she thinks 'too full of the milk of human kindness'. The second (I, v, 38–54) is intensified by the messenger's news that Duncan is coming. If the King is to be murdered, it must be that very night. She therefore prays for aid to 'those spirits / That tend on mortal thoughts' (I, v, 39–40), and who ominously seem to resemble the Weïrd Sisters. The Sisters have 'beards' (I, iii, 46) and the Lady seeks likewise to grow more masculine ('unsex me here', I, v, 41) and violent ('make thick my blood', 'take my milk for gall', I, v, 43, 48). Macbeth praises her 'undaunted mettle' (I, vii, 74). Arguably patriarchal culture not only frustrates her but also forces her to channel and live out her fantasies through her husband. Like him, she seems aware of the peculiar unconsciousness of action: the idea that doers are only conscious of their deeds after the event, that action must necessarily take over the consciousness at the moment of its enactment. When she asks 'that my keen knife see not the wound it makes' (I, v, 52), she imagines the guilty act projected to the personified blade, and blinded by intensely pure concentration.

This semi-conscious, intuitive rapidity seems to characterise the Lady in the first half of the play. Such transports are often associated with sexual desire, especially in performance ('When you durst do it, then you were a man', I, vii, 49) and may even foreshadow the way she slips from sanity and sleepwalks to her death. She is busily, even impulsively, resourceful on her husband's return, coming up with the plan and the logistics (I, vii, 60–73), laying out the daggers for Macbeth to use (II, ii, 12–13), fainting to distract an awkward line of questioning ('Help me hence, ho', II, iii, 120), and trying to bluff it out to her guests as her distressed husband talks of men of blood and gory locks (III, iv, 50–5). Her soldierly eye for a good plan appeals to Macbeth's military side, but Lady Macbeth's persuasive techniques are also cannily and cunningly psychological. She rivals and thus makes vulnerable her husband's sense of manhood through a violent, and famous, relinquishing of maternal duty.

> [...] I have given suck, and know
> How tender 'tis to love the babe that milks me.
> I would, while it was smiling in my face,
> Have plucked the nipple from the boneless gums,
> And dashed the brains out, had I so sworn
> As you have done to this
> (I, vii, 54–9)

The precise effect the wife has here on her husband depends on whether the Macbeths 'really' had children or not. 'I have' is readable as a subjunctive, shorthand for mere hypotheses like 'I would have' or 'might have', especially given the mood of the text that follows. And the degree to which readers or viewers should even give real-world backstories to fictional constructs like Lady Macbeth is a moot point. The critic L. C. Knights famously scorned scholars who scoured the text for evidence (Knights 1933). The actor Simon Russell Beale recently pointed out, however, that every production must somehow deal with the issue to make the characters coherent and believably relatable (BBC Radio 4, December 2015). Justin Kurzel's 2015 film even starts with the children's funeral.

The Macbeths' marital tussles may be especially intense in this famous exchange about infanticide, but they never quite go away. Immediately after Duncan's murder the Lady's rebukes become only more fearsome, tutting 'Consider it not so deeply' when Macbeth bawls about the blood upon him (II, ii, 31). She then snaps 'Infirm of purpose / Give *me* the daggers' and carries away the blades that, seeing not the wounds they make, will permanently stain her with traumatically invisible blood (II, ii, 53–4, emphasis added). From this pivotal moment follows a kind of 'chiasmus' effect. Macbeth rises in force as the Lady wanes. Macbeth had closely consulted his wife over Duncan's murder, less so with Banquo's ('Be innocent of the knowledge, dearest chuck, / 'Till thou applaud the deed', III, ii, 46–7). Likewise, the Lady's dialogues after the catastrophic feast are noticeably curt, indicating in different actors irritation with her husband, mute resignation, even signs of encroaching madness. We do not see her again for more than another act, until the famous 'sleepwalking' scene. Her madness is perhaps intimated as early as Act II ('Had he not resembled / My father as he slept, I had done't', II, ii, 13–14). This appearance, the Lady's last, is marked by hypnotic repetitions ('to bed, to bed', obsessive handwashing), unconscious confession of the murder ('do you mark that?' gasps the doctor) and hallucinations of supernatural retribution ('Cannot come out of his grave', V, i, 63–4). Just before she dies, then, she echoes her husband's half-mad fear of Banquo's Ghost.

Banquo/Banquo's Ghost (alive, I, iii; I, iv; I, vi; II, i; II, iii; III, i; III, iii; III, v) (as ghost, IV, i) (as apparition, onstage appearance optional)

Banquo, who is told 'Thou shalt get kings, though thou be none' (I, iii, 67), was thought an ancestor of Shakespeare's King, James I. He is portrayed as a sacrificial victim of Macbeth's tyrannous butchery. But he is nobody's fool, suspecting Macbeth played 'most foully' for Duncan's crown (III, i, 3). He is also ambitious. His soliloquy in Act III, scene i against Macbeth is arguably based on personal rivalry rather than concern for the state: 'May they not be my oracles as well / And set me up in hope?' (III, i, 10). Banquo's Ghost is a key staging issue. Sometimes directors put him onstage, sometimes not. This guides how the audience sees through Macbeth's eyes and empathises with him.

The Witches/Weird Sisters (I, i; I, iii; III, v; IV, i)

Like Banquo's Ghost, the staging of the Witches – whom Terry Eagleton called the 'heroines' of the play – is a big question for directors (Eagleton 1986: 1–2). Do they appear more often than the text dictates, stressing their grip on these puppet-like mortals? They sometimes appear at the end of some productions (ed. Clark and Mason 2015: 81, 102), suggesting ominously that Malcolm's reign will similarly be manipulated: Raphael Holinshed's *Chronicles* state that Donalbain later attacks his brother. Simply by being a trio, the Witches dimly echo mythological characters, like the three Fates or three Furies. Perhaps they are a perverted and degraded version of the Three Graces. The Witches either control the action themselves or act as agents for more powerful forces, 'our masters' (IV, i, 62), or 'Hecate', in a scene often cut in performance and attributed to Middleton. They are the play's most mysterious creatures, resisting singular interpretation. They 'palter [...] in a double sense' (V, viii, 20).

Macduff (I, vi; II, iii; II, iv; IV, iii; V, iv; V, vi; V, vii; V, viii; V, ix)

Macduff grows into the play. His silent first appearance (I, vi) indicates nothing of his later importance, though he does surface at significant moments. He knocks just as Macbeth and his wife hurriedly discuss what to do after killing Duncan, and discovers the body ('horror, horror, horror', II, iii, 64): he is already a kind of voice for justice and normality. In Act II, scene iv he pointedly goes back to his homestead of Fife rather than see Macbeth crowned, distancing himself from Ross and the rest of the Thanes. His central scene, however, is Act IV, scene iii, which signals a shift in the power balance for the whole play. He urges Malcolm to become King, but Malcolm only agrees when a disconsolate Macduff hears of his wife's and children's deaths. Macduff ' must feel' his pain 'like a man' (IV, iii, 224): a provocative and interesting association of masculinity with emotional susceptibility. The only character to appear in all four of the last scenes, his movement into the play coincides with an increase in momentum, until he slays Macbeth at the play's climax.

Duncan (I, ii; I, iv; I, vi) and his sons

Citing Macdonwald's rebellion as evidence, some productions have implied Duncan is a tyrannous ruler, further complicating our already complex sympathies with Macbeth. But, as even his murderer himself admits, Duncan seems a good king, endowed with Christ-like, piteous mildness. His son **Donalbain (I, ii; I, iv; I, vi; II, iii)** has a relatively minor part, but **Malcolm (I, ii; I, iv; I, vi; II, iii; IV, iii; V, iv; V, vi; V, vii; V, ix)**, voices many of the concerns of Jacobean audiences as to the personal attributes of good kings and tyrants, especially when he lists the qualities he lacks (IV, iii, 91–4) and worries to Macduff about 'the cistern of [his] lust' (IV, iii, 63).

The Porter (II, iii, doubled sometimes with a murderer and/or Seyton)

Often dismissed as mere 'comic relief', the Porter's address to the audience shifts tone abruptly and seemingly confounds conventional narrative sequencing, just after a moment of high dramatic suspense. There is, however, a continuation between the politicised violence of Macbeth's murder and the Porter's pithy observations of contemporary politics: his play on the word 'equivocation' alludes to justified lying under torture, permitted by certain religious moralists.

Thanes

Apart from Macduff, the Thanes (and a nameless 'Lord') are largely there to move the story along and relay necessary information. Ross, Angus and Lennox are initially loyal to if suspicious of Macbeth, and progressively join Macduff's cause. Lennox even calls Macbeth a 'tyrant' in Act III, scene iv. Some directors individuate the Thanes, but most often the same actor delivers these largely interchangeable roles' lines. Menteith and Caithness, recruits to Macduff's cause, join the play in the later stages and make the battle scenes more grandly populous.

Play structure

The shortest of Shakespeare's tragedies, *Macbeth* has also been called the 'most circular of the plays' (ed. Clark and Mason 2015: 81): its beginning, middle and end all depict attempted or actual regicide. The play accentuates these parallels. Duncan's and Macbeth's deaths both take place offstage, as if encouraging the audience to suffer 'horrible imaginings' (I, iii, 140), nor does either character have a dying speech. The circular structure is also stressed by recollections between what might be called the play's three 'movements': before Duncan's murder, then between Duncan's and Banquo's murders, and Macbeth's decline after Banquo's death. A supernatural apparition heralds each transition from one movement to the next: the airborne dagger, Banquo's Ghost, and the royal line of Banquo's descendants. Macbeth meets with the Witches in the first and third movements. Such recollections help emphasise larger-scale patternings in the story, like the sense of increasing chaos and paranoid tyrannical overcompensation, figured in miniature by Macbeth's declining mental state, and Macbeth's falling while Macduff rises, concluded by the rapid, fragmented final act which oscillates feverishly between the camps.

Language

Macbeth is mainly in verse, except for the prose used for Macbeth's letter to his wife, the Porter's speeches and the Lady's speeches while mad. The play is second only to *Richard II* in its characteristically Shakespearean use of rhyme to conclude scenes or speeches, especially Macbeth's. It is almost as if Macbeth has absorbed the Witches' darkly contagious influence: their 'supernatural soliciting', most often set in alliterative tetrameter, is also heavily rhymed ('double, double, toil and trouble / Fire burn, and cauldron bubble', IV, i, 35–6). The strangeness of the Witches and their realm seeps into the play's language via curious neologisms like 'unsex' (I, v, 40), the first recorded use of the noun 'assassination' (I, vii, 2), and exotically Scottish terms like 'kerns and galloglasses' to denote soldiers (I, i, 13). 'Bloody instructions' bleed into the play's imagery (I, vii, 9). Were *Macbeth* a colour it would be a very dark red, so prevalent are its motifs of blood, night and sleep. The play's very first line after the Witches' Prologue, 'What bloody man is that?' sets its dark and violent tone, just as 'who's there?' commences the introspective mysteries of *Hamlet* (I, ii, 1). Banquo's Ghost shakes his 'gory locks' at Macbeth (III, iv, 48). Macbeth later frets 'Blood will have blood' (III, iv, 120) and fears the 'secret'st man of blood' (III, iv, 124).

Macbeth's tyranny makes Macduff lament 'Bleed, bleed poor country' (IV, iii, 31). Much of the play takes place at night. Ross is surprised that 'by th'clock 'tis day,/And yet dark night strangles the travelling lamp' (II, iv, 6–7). The idea that this night is magically powerful explains Lady Macbeth's prayers that it transform her (I, v, 52) and the frequently repeated motif of enchanted sleeplessness. 'The owl scream[s] and the cricket cri[es]' (II, ii, 17). No one sleeps soundly. 'Macbeth doth murder sleep' (II, ii, 36–41) and while the Lady, mad, insistently commands 'to bed, to bed, to bed' (V, i, 66, 68), we never see her rest.

The play's portrayal of bloody and beastly acts plays on Renaissance ideas that man was tensely poised between angel and animal: 'what beast was't then/That made you break this enterprise to me?' (I, vii, 47–8). The bloody sergeant compares Macbeth and Banquo to a 'lion' and 'eagle' (I, ii, 35), but these conventionally noble creatures gradually give way to ravens and owls (I, v, 38; IV, ii, 11). Macbeth's horrified prayer to 'seeling night' (III, ii, 47) darkens terms usually linked to aristocratic falconry. 'Seeling' meant sewing a falcon's eyes closed to train it. Night itself now seems to hunt its prey. Macduff refers to his wife and children as devoured 'chickens' (IV, iii, 221). His bewildered reiterations 'All [...] did you say all? [...] All?' (IV, iii, 219–20) illustrate the play's frequent association of violence, trauma and repetition, illustrated most famously by Lady Macbeth's frantic handwashing and echo-laden speeches, but also present in the sly wordplay 'Seyton/Satan', the increasingly demonic tyrant's violent assistant. The Witches' homophonic language filters deeply into that of their mortal victims.

Themes

Fatal supernaturalism

Macbeth is, as is well known, the play that dare not speak its name: superstitious stagehands instead call it 'the Scottish play' to ward off its curses (ed. Clark and Mason 2015: 2), as if in awed respect for its portrayal of the uncannily supernatural and eerily unknowable. As well as the bearded Weïrd Sisters, a disputed scene, containing a song also in Middleton's *The Witch*, sees appear the goddess of the underworld herself, Hecate (IV, i, 39–43). Hallucinations like Banquo's Ghost, or the Lady's flashback of Duncan's body, hover at the brink of the protagonists' consciousness, mirrored by how productions may reveal or not to the audience the actors playing these victims.

One such hallucination, the 'air-drawn dagger' as the Lady scoffingly and contemptuously calls it (III, iv, 59), is a 'fatal vision' (II, i, 36). The adjective is important. It plays on a relatively obvious sense – the dagger is *lethal* to Duncan – and a slightly subtler one: *fated*. The sense of predestination is clear from the Witches' predictions, from the Lady's vow that Duncan 'never shall sun that morrow see' (I, v, 60), and from Macbeth's despair that 'tomorrow, and tomorrow, and tomorrow' will always creep 'in this petty pace from day to day,/To the last syllable of recorded time' (V, v, 18–20). The play's tight, claustrophobic structure also compels us to ask if Macbeth's, and our, actions are ever truly free. *How* did the dagger appear to Macbeth? Where did it come from? And does it affect his choice and desire to murder? If so, the dagger seems to signal an irresistible collusion between the Weïrd Sisters, who tantalise him with the prospect of being King, and his wife, who forces him to act on this ambition. The Lady links the Sisters to 'fate and metaphysical aid' (I, vi, 29) and Duncan unexpectedly, and conveniently, visits the Macbeths that very night …

Irreversible action

Duncan's surprise arrival, at the perfect moment to kill him, shows how willingly *Macbeth* sacrifices plausibility (Aristotle's tragic 'verisimilitude') for dramatic action. Macbeth complains 'Time, thou anticipat'st my dread exploits' (IV, i, 143). The artful compression of stage time seems almost to trap him, keeping him under constant pressure, harrying, hurrying and refusing considered decisions (see ed. Clark and Mason 2015: 72–4). The Lady interrupts just before Macbeth can finish his soliloquised thoughts ('falls on th'other [side]') (I, vii, 28) and urges him 'To beguile the time/Look like the time' (I, v, 63). Their exchanges before and after Duncan's murder are similarly rapid, disjointed, staccato (II, ii, 15–20). And, as the Porter laments, the door knocks incessantly just as Duncan is slain (II, ii, 58, 66, 69, 74; II, iii).

In such a feverish atmosphere, Duncan's death is a stab in the dark in more ways than one. The play implies repeatedly that rationality disappears at the moment of action: a person has to 'forget' himself or herself to stop self-consciousness getting in the way. Persons do not 'act' as such; they only project future deeds or remember past ones. At the moment of action itself, they have to become weirdly automatic, a kind of puppet to their own bodies. Macbeth frets about deeds 'acted, ere they may be scanned' (III, iv, 138); the Lady gasps 'I feel now/The future in the instant' (I, v, 57–8). Action troubles conventional distinctions of past, present and future. Macbeth and his wife thus struggle to come to terms with the sheer radical difference between the present, now Duncan is dead, and the past, when he was alive. Past and present are no longer subsets of the same category (i.e. time): Duncan's death has split them into completely separate categories. 'What's done cannot be undone' (V, i, 66–7).

One of the subtler, craftier wordplays in *Macbeth* echoes 'done', the irrevocable pastness of death, with 'dun', Scottish word for 'dark', as when Lady Macbeth says 'dunnest smoke of hell' (I, v, 51). The drama between the Macbeths is intensified by their half-repressed sense that hellishly 'dun' punishments will follow the 'done' deed. The mad Lady fearfully gasps 'hell is murky' as if she at that very moment gazes deep into the sulphurous pit (V, i, 36). Famously, Macbeth cannot utter 'Amen': '"Amen"/Stuck in my throat' (II, ii, 33–4). The murder seems to have subjected the Macbeths to incurable, irreversible holy truth. Even the Lady's seemingly polite speech to Duncan is full of words like 'service' and 'business', codewords she and her husband have established for murder, as if she is struggling to keep the plot under wraps (I, vi, 14, 16).

Secrecy and equivocation

Secrecy – to others, to oneself – is thus another key theme of *Macbeth*: 'nothing is that is not' (I, iii, 144). The Lady complains 'We must lave [wash] / Our honours in these flattering streams' (III, ii, 33–4) and a grimly comic interlude between Lady Macduff and her son hints at the lack of honest men in the kingdom (IV, ii, 46–65). The play, moreover, refers repeatedly to 'equivocation', the practice sanctioned by the Catholic Church of withholding the truth under torture: 'that could swear in both the scales against either scale' as the Porter puts it (II, iii, 8–9). Macbeth's reign compels such secretive practices. He is often portrayed in modern-dress productions as a harbinger of state surveillance and tyrannical paranoia. Successful kingship is never too far from the surface in *Macbeth*. Malcolm's list of good kingly qualities (e.g. 'Bounty, perseverance, mercy, lowliness, / Devotion, patience, courage, fortitude', IV, iii, 93–4) chimes with precepts from many contemporary rulebooks.

Texts and contexts

The earliest printed text of *Macbeth* is that in the 1623 Folio. Shakespeare seems to have drawn on Holinshed's *Chronicles*, which depict Duncan as a 'negligent' king with 'small skill in warlike affairs'. Shakespeare tones this down to bring out the Macbeths' ambitious aggression. Topical allusions to the 1605 Gunpowder Plot have been found in the Porter's mention of a 'farmer that hanged himself on th'expectation of plenty' (II, iii, 4–5): the mastermind of the Plot, Father Garnet, used 'Farmer' as an alias (see ed. Clark and Mason 2015: 17–18). The play seems also strongly to commend James I by sympathising with his alleged ancestor Banquo.

The play in performance

Macbeth is an unlucky play but this has not stopped a flow of productions. In the eighteenth century two rival traditions emerged for portraying Macbeth: the 'noble' or 'evil' murderer. The first was advocated by David Garrick and John Philip Kemble, who would somewhat egocentrically invent dying speeches for Macbeth to encourage the audience's sympathy. This 'noble Macbeth' tradition was later exemplified by William Charles Macready, John Gielgud and Simon Russell Beale, who played Macbeth as so isolated and piteous that his death becomes a kind of assisted suicide, a mercy killing (see ed. Clark and Mason 2015: 118).

In contrast to this tradition, where Macbeth is tragically, well-meaningly torn, some actors have portrayed him as straightforwardly and demonically evil. In this reading Macbeth wants Duncan dead from the very beginning: the Witches' predictions are nothing but a pretext: actors in this tradition include Edmund Kean and have continued up to Patrick Stewart's Stalinesque tyrant. In the early twentieth century productions start to drop the Hecate scenes as inauthentic, and modernist versions of the story start to appear, such as *Macbett* and the proto-surrealist Alfred Jarry's *Ubu roi*. Increasingly the story is read to allegorise militarised state tyranny and totalitarianism, as when, in the 1992 Bogdanov production, 'God Save the Queen' drowns out 'Flower of Scotland' or Rupert Goold quotes heavily from Cold War-era costume, music and spliced film footage (2007–8, see ed. Clark and Mason 2015: 106).

Film versions have absorbed and innovated these varied strands of performance tradition. *Macbeth on the Estate* (BBC 2 1997) translates questions of tyranny to small-town gangland violence. In Trevor Nunn's gloomily lightless 1978 production Judi Dench's Lady is obsessed with Ian McKellen's Macbeth, who starts progressively to cast her aside. Orson Welles's 1948 film deploys the high-contrast black and white filmic style of his *Citizen Kane* and quotes from fetishism and voodoo iconography in his depiction of the Witches. Akira Kurosawa's excellent 1957 *Throne of Blood*, as *Ran* does with *King Lear*, transfers the action to Samurai Japan. The 1983 BBC film, with Jane Lapotaire and Nicol Williamson, like Roman Polanski's bloodily allusive 1971 tribute to his murdered wife Sharon Tate, uses a traditional setting with gloomy Scottish heaths, and dressing the characters in animal skins. This aesthetic also marks the 2015 Justin Kerzel film with Michael Fassbinder and Marion Cotillard.

Critical reception

Recent criticism of Macbeth has focused on how its treatment of political violence resonates with our own age of terror. Graham Holderness and Brian Loughrey (2011) argue that Macbeth '*is* himself the Gunpowder Plot' (emphasis in original), and an emblem of what Jean Baudrillard theorised, even before the terrorist attacks of 11 September 2001, as 'the terrorist imagination': 'a will to power, a demand to "authenticate the potency of the self" through violence, and an "apocalyptic" urgency' (see Appelbaum 2015: 32). Peter C. Herman usefully categorises 'groups' of *Macbeth* critics, suggesting a majority reads the play 'as a straightforward endorsement of Jacobean absolutism' (2014: 121). But Herman himself argues that '*Macbeth*'s engagement with the Gunpowder Plot [...] overlaps with the play's anti-absolutist critique of Stuart origins' (2014: 121): Banquo's lineage up to James is after all prophesied by 'hags'. Ellen Spolsky (2011) examines questions of perception, like Macbeth's of the air-drawn dagger, in terms of the cognitive paradigms that have influenced much new Shakespeare criticism. Howard Marchitello (2013) examines the play's distinctive treatment of temporality, while Stephanie Chamberlain (2005) relates Lady Macbeth to early modern depictions of the murdering mother, a feminist, revisionist response to the kinds of questions debated by A. C. Bradley and L. C. Knights. Older Macbeth criticism is ably anthologised in Alexander Leggatt's 2006 *Sourcebook*.

Discussion questions

＊ Why do you think Shakespeare hides Duncan's death from the spectator's view (unlike, say, Macbeth's visible killing of Young Siward)?

＊ Is Macbeth a terrorist? Or a tragic hero?

Bibliography and further reading

Edition

Shakespeare, W. (2015), *Macbeth*, ed. S. Clark and P. Mason, London: Arden Shakespeare.

Critical response

Appelbaum, R. (2015), 'Shakespeare and Terrorism', *Criticism*, 57:1, 23–45.

Chamberlain, S. (2005), 'Fantasising Infanticide: Lady Macbeth and the Murdering Mother in Early Modern England', *College Literature*, 32:3, 72–91.

Eagleton, T. (1986), *William Shakespeare*, London: John Wiley & Sons.

Herman, P. (2014), '"A deed without a name": Macbeth, the Gunpowder Plot, and Terrorism', *Journal for Cultural Research*, 18:2, 114–31.

Holderness, G. and B. Loughrey (2011), 'Shakespeare and Terror', in D. A. Brooks, M. Biberman and J. R. Lupton (eds), *Shakespeare after 9/11: How a Social Trauma Reshapes Interpretation*, Lewiston, NY: Edwin Mellen Press, pp. 23–56.

Knights, L. C. (1933), *How Many Children Had Lady Macbeth? An Essay in the Theory and Practice of Criticism*, Cambridge: Minority Press.

Marchitello, M. (2013), 'Speed and the Problem of Real Time in *Macbeth*', *Shakespeare Quarterly*, 64:4, 425–48.

Spolsky, E. (2011), 'An Embodied View of Misunderstanding in *Macbeth*', *Poetics Today*, 32:3, 489–520.

5   *King Lear*

c. 1605–6, first performance 1606–7, first printed 1608

Act, scene and line references are to the 1997 Arden Third Series edition, edited by R. A. Foakes. Scenes given in quotation marks refer to Foakes's decision to see Edgar's entry/soliloquy (II, ii, 172–92) as an entirely distinct scene, thus splitting Act II, scene ii in three. Textual variations are discussed in the 'Texts and contexts' section.

Plot summary

King Lear plans to divide his kingdom equally among his three daughters. Goneril is married to the Duke of Albany; Regan is married to the Duke of Cornwall; and Cordelia is as yet unmarried but set to be betrothed to either the King of France or the Duke of Burgundy. As a kind of test to earn their share of the kingdom, Lear asks his daughters to tell him how much they love him. Goneril and Regan perform this task and are duly awarded in return their equal thirds. Cordelia, however, says nothing. Lear, enraged, refuses her a dowry and banishes her as well as Kent, a noble who comes to her aid. The French King marries Cordelia anyway and they leave for France (I, i). Kent, however, remains in Britain in disguise as 'Caius' (I, iv). Meanwhile, Edmund, the illegitimate son of high-ranking courtier the Earl of Gloucester, plots against his father and legitimate brother Edgar, apparently to get the family land (I, ii). He forges letters incriminating Edgar in an assassination attempt on Gloucester, and Edgar is forced to flee (II, i). To aid his escape Edgar disguises himself and acts as Poor Tom, a mad beggar (II, ii/'II, iii'). Lear, accompanied by his Fool, is now lodged at Goneril's castle. Scuffles occur between Lear's entourage, including 'Caius' who is now in Lear's service, and Goneril's servants, including her arrogant steward Oswald. Goneril orders Lear to discharge fifty knights. A furious Lear refuses and leaves to visit Regan (I, iv; I, v). Regan and Cornwall are lodging at Gloucester's castle. Kent attacks Oswald there and despite Gloucester's protests is put in the stocks by Cornwall. When Lear discovers his servant thus imprisoned his rage only increases, and he appeals to Regan against her sister's cruelty. But Regan takes Goneril's side. Goneril arrives at Gloucester's castle. The sisters take each other's hands in solidarity against their father and ask him to discharge every single one of his knights. Lear, apoplectic, flees into the countryside, 'abjur[ing] all roofs', just as a storm breaks (II, ii/'II, iv'). He, 'Caius' and his Fool take refuge in a hovel. Edgar/Poor Tom, desperate for shelter from the storm, joins them (III, i;/'III, ii'). Gloucester is appalled by Lear's daughters' behaviour and sides with Lear. But he mistakenly confides in Edmund that he has received word from Cordelia and the French forces (III, iii). Gloucester helps Lear to food and better shelter (III, iv, 148–9), and helps him escape to Dover. Edmund denounces his father to Cornwall (III, v). Gloucester is interrogated for treason and Cornwall and Regan, on Goneril's suggestion, pull out Gloucester's eyes. Gloucester's servants retaliate and Cornwall is fatally wounded in the fray (III, vii). Cast out, Gloucester encounters Edgar, still in disguise. Gloucester asks his new 'friend' to guide him to a cliff-edge so that he may fall to his death. But Edgar only pretends to accept, leading his father to solid ground instead. Gloucester leaps forward, but falls only on his face. Edgar convinces him he survived the 'fall' by being saved by an angel (IV, i; IV, vi). Meanwhile, Albany attacks his wife Goneril for her cruelty (IV, ii), and Cordelia and her French soldiers start to arrive in Britain (III, i; IV, iii). Lear's anger has by now transformed fully to madness. He has taken to running along the beach, wearing a crown of flowers (IV, iv), and discussing despairing thoughts with the equally desperate Gloucester (IV, vi). Lear can, however, dimly and fleetingly recognise Cordelia as his daughter (IV, vii). Before the war between the British and French forces, the recently widowed Regan and her sister develop a rivalry over Edmund (IV, ii, 24–8; IV, v, 32–4). Goneril fatally poisons Regan out of jealousy (V, iii, 97), but kills herself (V, iii, 225) when Edmund is fatally wounded by his masked brother in a duel. Edgar only reveals his identity as Edmund lies dying, telling him also their father has died (V, iii, 64–200). Despite Edgar's victory, Lear and the French forces are beaten. Lear and Cordelia are taken prisoner (V, iii, 1–17). The dying, regretful Edmund decides to countermand his earlier order to hang them (V, iii, 35, 249). But this countermand comes too late. Cordelia is hanged, and Lear kills her hangman too late to save her. The dying Lear howls over his daughter's body before his heart finally breaks. Lear dies (V, iii, 255–309). Albany decides that Edgar and Kent should share the crown (V, iii, 319). Kent refuses, hints at suicide and exits (V, iii, 321). The survivors who remain survey the carnage in bewilderment.

Characters

Lear (I, i; I, iv; I, v; II, ii/'II, iv'; III, ii; III, iv; III, vi; IV, vi; IV, vii; V, iii)

King Lear is a darkly ironic title. For most of the play Lear is not really a King. He lacks any meaningful power, retaining 'name' and 'addition' only (I, i, 137). And even this 'addition' is stripped away before the play is halfway over, because Goneril and Regan dismiss his hundred knights. Lear's anger at this dismissal clearly, ironically, reverses his banishment of Cordelia after his love test in the first scene. This test, asking his daughters 'which of you shall we say doth love us most' (I, i, 51), is emotionally manipulative but also presupposes a woefully simplistic exchange-rate mechanism. Lear thinks love may be unproblematically converted to words, which may then be exchanged for quantifiable land. Cordelia's refusal to speak ('Nothing, my lord', I, i, 87) rejects not so much Lear's request for love as his reduction of love to such a drily measurable system. Lear's behaviour in this scene is a crucial discussion issue for actors and directors. Goneril and Regan observe that their father 'hath but ever slenderly known himself' (I, i, 294–5) and that 'The best and soundest of his time hath been but rash' (I, i, 296–7). But does the actor playing Lear support these observations? If Lear comes across as strong and confident then Goneril's and Regan's comments on his sanity are exposed as self-justifying lies, and his tragic mental decline becomes more directly attributable to their actions. If, however, he already seems weak, eccentric or doddery then Goneril's and Regan's seizure of power becomes more justifiable in offering the kingdom stronger (but crueller) leadership. We next see Lear in Act I, scene iv, where signs of his mental decline are starting to emerge. His conversations with the Fool develop an ominously eccentric turn of phrase, and he rages at Goneril (I, iv, 254–81). Again, the staging of this exchange helps direct the audience's judgement. If Lear's hundred knights are genuine vandals (as they are in Brook's RSC production), then Goneril is at least somewhat justified in her complaints, making Lear's near-the-knuckle verbal violence yet more unpalatable. He calls Goneril a 'detested kite' and asks the gods to 'dry up in her the organs of increase' (I, iv, 271). 'If she must teem,/Create her child of spleen, that it may live/And be a thwart disnatured torment to her' (I, iv, 273–5). Harsher still, perhaps, than Cordelia's banishment (Frances Barber's Goneril in Trevor Nunn's film production burst into tears), this is a key moment in the audience's developing judgement of Lear, and Goneril's increasingly violent vengeance upon him and his allies.

Lear's rage intensifies with Regan and Cornwall at Gloucester's castle ('who put my man i'the stocks'?, II, ii, 371) and when Goneril and Regan take each other's hands against him (II, ii, 318–475). It is dramatically important that the storm coincides with this first full recognition of the daughters' betrayal. The moment seems to evoke the idea of the King's 'Two Bodies', the post-medieval belief that the King's physical body symbolises the hierarchical 'body-politic' of his kingdom. The storm that batters Britain is a clear analogy of Lear's psychological upheaval. Lear's repressed despair ('You think I'll weep/No I'll not weep', II, ii, 471–2) finds a cosmic outlet. Nature sympathises with Lear's rage even as it unsettles his wits. The affinity between Lear's anger and the storm, including the gradual waning of both, is sustained throughout the central scenes. In its sheer ferocity Lear's famous speech 'Blow winds, and crack your cheeks' both praises and imitates the storm (III, ii, 1–9). Then, as Lear, Kent and the Fool find shelter, making the storm's force less immediate, observers start to notice that 'his wits are gone' (III, vi, 84). The mock 'trial' of Goneril and Regan (III, vi, 35–81), where Lear attacks his daughters as if they are really present, which the Fool lightly mocks, demonstrates Lear's 'unsettle[d]' wits visibly to the audience (III, iv, 157). Others report the dismaying speed of Lear's decline as he himself remains offstage for about one whole act. Cordelia describes him as he flees his own troops as 'mad as the vexed sea' (IV, iv, 2). The Quarto version stage directions (see 'Texts and contexts' section) confirm on his next entry that he is 'mad' (stage direction after IV, vi, 79). Lear's crown of weeds sadly parodies his former glories as well as, perhaps, Christ's crown of thorns.

His speech in this act, like Ophelia's in *Hamlet*, consists of 'Reason and impertinency mixed' (IV, vi): a favourite Shakespearean contradiction. Lear grandly reverts to regal verse as soon as he hears Gloucester's voice: 'Ay, every inch a King' (IV, vi, 106), and his conversations with Gloucester deliriously alternate shrewd political verse commentary ('Robes and furred gowns hide all', IV, vi, 161) with fearful paranoia, in prose, about women and female sexuality: 'there's hell, there's darkness, there is the sulphury pit' (IV, vi, 123–4). The famous 'recognition' scene with Cordelia signals perhaps the final quenching of Lear's inner storm: 'the great rage/You see is killed in him' (IV, vii, 78–9). Lear's speeches are from this point predominantly melancholy and resigned. He counsels the defeated Cordelia 'let's away to prison' (V, iii, 8–16) as if reconciled with the falseness of the world, only enraged again when confronted with Cordelia's dead body: 'I might have saved her' (V, iii, 268). Lear dies exhausted by the 'tough world' (V, iii, 313) and the stormy mess of contradictions that raged within him.

Cordelia (I, i; IV, iv; IV, vi; IV, vii; V, iii)

'Cor' comes from the Latin word for 'heart', and 'delia', as Samuel Daniel's 1592 poem sequence of that name suggests, is an anagram of 'ideal'. Lear calls her 'our joy' (I, i, 82) before crying in disappointment 'I loved her most' (I, i, 124). The etymology of Cordelia's name implies that she is less a psychologically consistent character than an allegory for the play's powerful, even fairy-tale, morality. Her response to Lear's love test contains perhaps the most mysterious word possible. 'Nothing, my lord' (I, i, 86). She explains that 'love' should include husbands as well as fathers (I, i, 99–100), but her appeal to nothingness also undermines Lear's idea that 'love' is straightforwardly measurable, quantifiable and rewardable. Despite Lear's rage and Burgundy's rejection (I, i, 250), Cordelia persists in attacking the exploitable falseness of Lear's idea that love can directly translate to words as well as land, rebuking her sisters for lying (I, i, 270–7). It is not surprising that the famously 'plain-spoken' Kent, who unflinchingly tells Lear when exiling Cordelia 'thou dost evil' (I, i, 171), sides with her unconditionally. Cordelia's largely monosyllabic speeches to her father in the 'recognition' scene are similarly simple, straightforward and kind (IV, vii, 30–42).

Edmund (I, i; I, ii; II, i; III, iii; III, v; IV, ii; V, i; V, iii)

Like Iago and Richard III (see Chapters 3 and 12 respectively), Edmund is a violent, aggressive, vice-like 'malcontent' who enjoys addressing the audience directly. And like Iago passed over for promotion, and Richard III insulted for his hunchback, Edmund has at least some grounds for feeling jealous. As a bastard born outside wedlock he is deprived of the landowning rights his brother enjoys. When Edmund is contemptuously dismissed by his father as a 'whoreson' (I, i, 22) and ignored as he cuts himself ('Look sir, I bleed', II, i, 40), Shakespeare goads his audience to pity Edmund's resentment, and ask at what point his cruelty, especially his role in Gloucester's blinding, exhausts this pity. Edmund shares Iago's central philosophy. Life is unfair so rely on yourself. 'Well, then,/Legitimate Edgar, I must have your land' (I, ii, 4). Edmund mocks his father's astrological fatalism as 'the excellent foppery of the world' (I, i, 118), prizing instead quick-wittedness and decisive action ('men are as the time', V, iii, 30–1). He suggests he gained this 'fierce quality' by being conceived in the exciting, extra-marital 'lusty stealth of nature' (I, ii, 11–12): his father concedes 'there was good sport at [Edmund's] making' (I, i, 22). His gentler brother Edgar was only begot in the dutiful confines of aristocratic marriage (between 'a sleep and wake', I, ii, 15). Edmund thus reconceives bastardy as a positive quality. In this he demonstrates the wilful, enterprising resourcefulness he attributes to bastardy in the first place, and for which Goneril and Regan both desire him (V, i, 56–70). Edmund mingles sexual charisma with Machiavellian murderousness, lying to his father (II, i 29–85) and trying to cover up Cordelia's death as suicide (V, iii, 252–3). It is therefore perhaps surprising that at the end of the play he tries to repeal his command, even though all is lost for him: 'Some good I hope to do/Despite of mine own nature' (V, iii, 241–2). This may, somewhat cynically, be interpreted as a plot device: it after all helps get to the stage the elements and characters required for the play's finale, but it also hints at the kind of person Edmund might have become were he not compelled by social forces to 'Stand up for bastards!' (I, ii, 22).

Gloucester (I, i; I, ii; II, i; II, ii/'II, iv'; III, iii; III, iv; III, vi; III, vii; IV, i; IV, vi; V, ii)

Gloucester establishes straight away the hierarchical system that sets sons 'by order of law' like Edgar above bastards like Edmund, whose 'breeding' is merely 'at my charge' (I, i, 8). He also links such familial hierarchies to political and cosmic ones, thinking Edgar's alleged plot to kill him and Lear's banishing Cordelia have damaged all at once: 'These late eclipses in the sun and moon portend no good to us [...] We have seen the best of our time. Machinations, hollowness, treachery and all ruinous disorders follow us disquietly to our graves' (I, ii, 103–14). Gloucester continues a moderate, peacemaking voice throughout the central acts, protesting as Kent is put in the stocks (II, i, 46), helping the homeless Lear to shelter (III, vi) and then facilitating his escape to Dover (III, vi, 88–9). In this, as a kind of counterpoint, Gloucester illustrates Cornwall, Goneril and Regan's growing power and cruelty, culminating of course in his blinding: the literal, perhaps emotional, centre of the play (III, vii, 70–84). After Gloucester's blinding his hope for another, better world is more egalitarian, less hierarchical: 'Distribution should undo excess/And each man have enough' (IV, i, 73–4). But this hope is fragile and melancholic at best, tinged with frequent desires to die. His 'survival' of his suicide attempt at Dover Cliff, engineered by the disguised Edgar, one of the most troubling moments in this saddest of plays, helps him to 'bear/Affliction till it do cry out itself/"Enough, enough" and die' (IV, vi, 76–7). But then his conversation with Lear makes him almost jealous of Lear's madness: 'So should my thoughts be severed from my griefs' (IV, vi, 277). But like Lear, Gloucester too succumbs to contradictory emotions. The blind old man's heart 'burst[s] smilingly', Edgar reports to Edmund, just as he joyously rediscovers his lost legitimate son (V, iii, 198).

Edgar (I, ii; II, i; 'II, iii'; III, iv; III, vi; IV, i; IV, vi; V, ii; V, iii)

Edgar has no lines in the opening scene. His probable absence contributes to an early sense of him being adrift from Lear's court, anticipating his later banishment. Edgar is Gloucester's legitimate son, of course, but the play seems almost to mock his birth-given identity by putting him through several rebirths. On his exile, he emerges from grime and filth – grimly parodying the maternal blood that covers the newborn – with a new name, 'Poor Tom' (II, ii, 191). On meeting his father again he plays a peasant (IV, v), and in disguise represents Albany as he kills Edmund (V, iii, 115). He is then nominated King of Britain as the play ends (V, iii, 319). In his shifting identities Edgar becomes a powerful symbol for the play's key ideas. The maddening Lear calls 'Tom' a 'philosopher', seeing in this 'naked fellow' something like pure human truth: 'the thing itself' (III, iv, 150; IV, i, 42; III, iv, 104, 107). Lear thus tries to imitate him, likewise trying to strip himself from vain material possessions: 'unbutton here' (III, iv, 107), a strange pre-echo of Lear's near-final words 'Pray you undo this button' (V, iii, 308). Edgar/Tom also functions as a kind of mouthpiece. His shrill, often meaningless cries relay something of the play's unremitting bleakness. And, in his own voice, Edgar despairs at the dreadfully uncertain recognition that though 'I'm worse now than 'e'er I was [….,] worse I may be yet' (IV, i, 28–30). Even hope is its own form of cruelty. This idea underscores the Dover Cliff scene. The very fact Edgar justifies his actions to the audience ('Why I do trifle thus with his despair / Is done to cure it', IV, vi, 33) implies he thinks it might have been better just to put the poor blind old man out of his misery. The play's final gesture towards hope, attributed to Edgar in the Folio version, urging to 'Speak what we feel, not what we ought to say' (V, iii, 323), likewise seems hollow. Did not Cordelia do precisely this, and did this not indirectly cause this death and ruin? Perhaps mad Poor Tom, not sane King Edgar, voices the play's deepest truths.

Lear's Fool (I, iv; I, v; II, ii; III, ii; III, iv; III, vi)

Like Edgar/Poor Tom and the mad Lear's political commentary, Lear's Fool contributes to the sense that madness and sanity are not black and white opposites. The flattery-ridden autocratic court makes it hard for anybody to speak sense to a King, unless it is cloaked in 'foolishness'. Granted, the Fool complains he is 'whipped for speaking true [...] whipped for lying, and sometimes I am whipped for holding my peace' (I, iv, 174–6) and Lear does indeed threaten him with 'the whip' (I, iv, 108), but Goneril's grudging description of him as 'all-licensed' remains broadly true (I, iv, 191). Seemingly without punishment the Fool snubs Lear, 'pin[ing] away' after

Cordelia's banishment (I, iv, 71). He then criticises him repeatedly for giving away his kingdom to his daughters (e.g. I, iv, 177–9). Cordelia and the Fool share no scenes so the same actor may play both roles. Lear seems to confuse them when he says over Cordelia's dead body 'my poor fool is hanged' (V, iii, 304), suggesting Cordelia and the Fool are mirror images of the same truth-telling presence. Regan thinks 'Jesters do oft prove prophets' (V, iii, 72) and in the Folio text the Fool prophesies, not unreasonably given the play's subsequent events, that 'shall the realm of Albion / Come to great confusion' (III, ii, 91–2).

But the rhyming or riddling way in which the Fool prophesises or counsels, as when he sings of prudence and prosperity ('Leave thy drink and thy whore / And keep in-a-door / And thou shalt have more / Than two tens to a score', I, iv, 116–25), implies that truth itself has an element of madness and chaos. This perhaps explains why the Fool fades away in the storm scenes. The storm ushers in a new, even more aggressive reality to which the Fool's eccentrically folklorish wisdom no longer applies, and for which the devil-ridden screaming of Poor Tom is the new herald. Poor Tom is Lear's new Fool: the new voice of truth. The Fool disappears entirely into the new, stormy regime of Goneril and Regan in Act III, scene vi, just before Gloucester's blinding.

Goneril (I, i; I, iii; I, iv; II, ii; 'II, iv'; III, vii; IV, ii; V, i; V, iii)

Goneril is Lear's 'eldest born' (I, i, 54). She speaks first to Lear in the love test, and is the first to house and then expel her father. At a telling moment, Lear attacks Goneril for the reduction of his retinue, even though Regan initiates the suggestion (II, ii, 396–405). This implies that Goneril is the habitual recipient of Lear's 'rash mood': she wearily observes that Lear 'always loved our sister most' (I, i, 292). Lear calls Goneril a 'degenerate bastard' and hopes 'that she may feel / How sharper than a serpent's tooth it is / To have a thankless child' (I, iv, 245, 279–81). As with Edmund, then, Shakespeare carefully balances parental mistreatment against the child's vengeful aggression, constructing thereby a compellingly complex ethical situation. Does Goneril's anger with her father justify her idea to 'pluck out' Gloucester's eyes? In the second half she becomes increasingly intoxicated with Edmund, who displays a militaristic virility she frustratedly has never been able to perform. But she proves herself the shrewder tactician, stressing the stupidity of fighting the unnecessary, ultimately fatal duel with the champion who turns out to be Edgar (V, iii, 149–51). Goneril also skilfully engineers the poisoning of her sister (V, iii, 97), showing not only her love for Edmund, the direct cause of her suicide, but also her loveless, aggressive, ultimately solitary upbringing.

Regan (I, i; II, i; II, ii; 'II, iv'; III, vii; IV, v; V, i; V, iii)

Regan is Goneril's rivalrous younger sister. She is second to speak in Lear's test, exploiting the situation by waspishly superseding her sister's protestation of love: 'she comes too short' (I, i, 72). Regan thus blends aggression with an insecure fear of acting alone. This marks her bitingly dismissive but often brief retorts to her father: 'sir, to the purpose' (II, ii, 370), 'you are old / Nature in you stands on the very verge / Of her confine' (II, ii, 335–7), 'Return you to my sister' (II, ii, 347), 'Being weak, seem so' (II, ii, 390). One such retort, famous for its tight-lipped pithiness, hints at a lifetime of frustration that we never get to see:

> Lear: I gave you all –
> Regan: And in good time you gave it.
> (II, ii, 439)

This mixture of frustration and fear characterises her attraction to the brutal Cornwall, who effectively replaces Goneril as Regan's prop. In performance Regan is often played like a cowardly rodent who peeps out, bites and then retreats to a position of safety. For example, she lets Cornwall take the lead in putting Kent/'Caius' in the stocks, stepping in only to increase the punishment: 'all night too' (II, ii, 132). Regan's desire to outdo her elder sister, and even her husband, arguably leads to Gloucester's blinding. Goneril suggests the deed but Regan actually does it. The audience is often understandably appalled by Gloucester's first eye being put out but Regan seems only encouraged, killing a servant and urging Cornwall on as he seems to waver (III, vii, 70–81). As Cornwall dies Regan's self-preservation instinct kicks in and her sisterly rivalry now revolves around Edmund. In her behind-the-scenes negotiations with Oswald, Regan seems cold and determined: 'more convenient is [Edmund] for my hand / Than for your lady's' (IV, v, 33–4). The implication is that Regan dies only because she was not fast enough to kill Goneril.

Kent/'Caius' (I, i; I, iv; II, ii; 'II, iii'; 'II, iv'; III, i; III, iv; III, vi; IV, iii; IV, vii; V, iii)

Ridiculed by Cornwall for his 'saucy boldness', Kent personifies a kind of faith in stability and traditionalism. Like Cordelia, whom he defends, he believes in 'bonds' (I, i, 93). Words should relay meanings; servants should obey masters. With forty-eight years 'on [his] back' (I, iv, 38–9), this member of the older generation emphasises a change to Goneril and Regan's new, Machiavellian, self-interested regime. Kent puts his principles far above his personal advancement. Despite Lear punishing him, he still, disguised, serves his King, praising his 'Authority' (I, iv, 30) and vowing 'services' (I, iv, 31). His fight with Goneril's steward Oswald functions as a kind of theatrical shorthand for the larger tensions between Goneril's staff and Lear's hundred knights (II, ii, 14–23), and his arrest and punishment by Regan and Cornwall likewise symbolises and ignites long-standing tensions between Lear and his eldest daughters. Kent is less present in the second half of the play, but he engineers the return of Cordelia's army and like a Greek chorus laments the final scene's tragedies. He refuses Albany's offer to rule the kingdom, gloomily hinting at a suicide-like 'journey [...] shortly to go' (V, iii, 320) near the play's very end.

Albany (I, i; I, iv; IV, ii; V, i; V, iii)

Albany is understandably appalled at Lear's eldest daughters' worst excesses: 'Gloucester, I live/To thank thee for the love thou showd'st the King/And to revenge thine eyes' (IV, ii, 97). But he is ultimately too gentle to be effectual in this roughest of plays. During their argument Goneril cuts him off in mid-sentence, mocking his 'manhood' (IV, ii, 69). And despite his passionate misgivings, Albany fights on his wife's side. 'It touches us as France invades our land' (V, i, 25). Likewise, even though he declares a duel with Edmund over Goneril's supposed infidelity (V, iii, 83–9), it is ultimately Edgar who does the fighting.

Cornwall (I, i; II, i; II, ii; 'II, iv'; III, v; III, vii)

Gloucester's description of Cornwall as the 'fiery' Duke (II, ii, 281) is borne out by later events. Cornwall takes the lead with Kent's punishment, mocking 'Caius' contemptuously (II, ii, 93–102). He is also merciless with Gloucester, siding with Edmund politically and temperamentally. It is not surprising Regan replaces Cornwall with Edmund so seamlessly in her affections when Cornwall dies.

Play structure

Even as it foregrounds madness and chaos, King Lear is, in both Quarto and Folio versions, carefully patterned and structured. The first two scenes present in careful alternation Lear's and Gloucester's families, accentuating the parallels between them. Both families are motherless, Lear's wife receives only brief mention (II, iii, 320), and contain clearly differentiated loyal and disloyal children. Lear has only daughters, Gloucester only sons. This, and the way certain scenes are staged, strengthens the idea that Lear's and Gloucester's declines mirror each other. In Act II, scene iii Lear's servant Kent in the stocks and Edgar, both banished, disguised and lost, share the stage, quite unaware of the other's presence. This stage image stresses the sudden shift from their respective former positions of power. Poor Tom stabbing himself with 'pins, wooden pricks' (II, ii, 187) subtly echoes Edmund's self-stabbing to 'beget opinion/Of [his] more fierce endeavour' (II, i, 33–4), further linking Edmund's plotting with its devastating consequences, while accentuating the difference between the half-brothers.

Not only is Lear organised 'spatially' by thus comparing the two families and their members, it is also loosely organised sequentially. Three broad movements may be discerned: the mounting of familial tensions, their explosion with the Storm and Gloucester's blinding, and an aftermath with Lear's madness and war. Again, the play's use of echoes and parallels provokes the audience to find continuities and contrasts between these movements. Cordelia leaves in the first movement and returns in the third. Edgar takes over from the Fool as the play's choric truth-teller. The mad Lear's mock trial of his daughters (III, iv, Q only) parodies his early love test, much as his crown of weeds symbolises his delusion that he is still 'every inch a King' (IV, vi, 106).

These structural repetitions and variations correspond with the play's frequent imagery of wheels. Lear sees himself, like the punished Greek criminal Ixion, trapped upon a 'wheel of fire' (IV, vii, 46). Kent and Edmund appeal to a similarly inescapable 'wheel of Fortune': 'Fortune [...] turn thy wheel' (Kent, II, ii, 171); 'The wheel is come full circle' (Edmund, V, iii, 172). The wheel is of obvious importance in a play about forgiveness and reconciliation, madness and sanity, loss and recognition, kingship and penury, and the relationship between younger and older generations. The idea that children become their parents' parents is strong in *King Lear*: 'Old fools are babes again' (Goneril, I, iii, 20); 'The younger rises when the old doth fall' (Edmund, III, iii, 24); 'Thou mad'st thy daughters thy mothers' (the Fool, I, iv, 163). Lear even once calls his madness his 'mother' ('O, how this mother swells up toward my heart/*Hysterica passio*, down', II, ii, 246–7), as if he realises it will make a kind of child of him. Thus turning old men back to children, nature, like fortune, seems to impose a circular, not linear shape on time. But this is not the only way the play interrogates nature.

Language

'Nature', including its cognates 'natural' and 'unnatural', is one of several keywords that rumble ominously through the play. It often relates to familial duties and relationships. Goneril and Regan are 'unnatural hags' (II, ii, 467): their behaviour sinisterly implies that nature, in this familial sense, can be unnatural, denatured, inherently cruel. Edmund invokes Nature as a 'goddess' when praying that the quickest, strongest and most ruthless (i.e. he) may prevail (I, ii, 1). There is no singular idea of nature in *King Lear*. Those who first see it as a benevolent and maternal presence often end up seeing it as red in tooth and claw: 'Mother Nature' gives way to the law of the jungle. The Fool and his disappearance help trace this development. In Shakespeare's time, a 'Natural' was a slang term for a Fool, as when Lear complains 'I am the natural fool of fortune' (IV, vi, 187). And the wisdom of Lear's wise 'natural' 'Fool' is often based on observing the patterns or behaviours of the natural world. Lear is like an 'egg', a 'sparrow', an 'oyster', a 'snail', an 'ant', or an 'eel' (I, iv, 151; I, iv, 206; I, v, 25; I, v, 27; II, ii, 257; II, ii, 314). Conversely, the Fool and others compare the daughters to wolves, vultures, boars and tigers (I, iv, 300; II, ii, 324; III, vii, 57; IV, ii, 41). The implication is that animals and birds guide us toward right ways of thinking and acting. But when Lear flees Gloucester's castle to live with 'the wolf and owl' during the storm (II, ii, 399), the Fool is noticeably discomfited. His understanding of nature is entirely undermined. Nature tells the truth not in its firm structures of good and bad, but in its frightening unpredictability. The storm brings Poor Tom, who makes Gloucester think 'man a worm' (IV, i, 35), echoing Lear's fear that 'Man's life's as cheap as beasts' (II, ii, 456). Tom's naked body, like Lear's a mere 'frame of nature' (I, iv, 260), is 'the thing itself' (III, iv, 104).

Tom is thus a 'philosopher', who knows 'the cause of thunder' (III, iv, 150–1): only he is closest to nature at its rawest. But if Tom thus somehow personifies nature, then his repeated allusions to 'Flibbertigibbet' and the Prince of Darkness (III, iv, 113) hint of the monster at its very heart.

'Monster', another keyword, further illustrates how *King Lear* scrutinises attempts like the Fool's to use the natural world as a guide to truth. Lear's eldest daughters are repeatedly called 'monstrous' ('Monster ingratitude!', Lear, I, v, 37), as well as 'unnatural'. Albany clearly has Goneril in mind when he groans 'Humanity must [...] prey upon itself,/Like monsters of the deep' (IV, ii, 50–1; see also IV, ii, 64). Monsters hover ambivalently at the edge of conventional truth categories, confusing the ways we organise phenomena into concepts. Similar mysteries attend the play's polytheistic, non-Christian theological universe. Gods are mentioned in the plural. Characters swear by a range of pagan and invented deities, like 'the sun', 'Hecate' (I, i, 110–11), 'Jupiter' (I, i, 179) and Edmund's 'Nature' (I, ii, 1). It is as if the victims trapped on this hellish stage are groping for a god to swear by, desperate to gain their approval. But the blinded Gloucester bitterly doubts any such relationship can exist. 'As flies to wanton boys are we to th'gods/They kill us for their sport' (IV, i, 38–9). Edmund echoes such doubts when he mocks his father's reliance on portents (I, ii, 118), as do Kent and Edgar when they ask 'Is this the promised end?' 'Or image of that horror?' (V, iii, 261–2). In this near-godless context Edgar's affirmation to Gloucester – 'thy life's a miracle' – is desperately moving in its falseness and futility (IV, vi, 55).

The eerie echoes of the words 'nothing' and 'never' emphasise the suspicion that there is no god, no ultimately meaningful code to live by. Lear's line 'Never never never never never' (V, iii, 307) expresses the desolation of Cordelia's death in the simple absence of any other word. At the start of the play Cordelia of course has 'nothing' to say to her father's request for love (I, i, 88). Her father's threatening reply 'Nothing will come from nothing. Speak again' (I, i, 90) subtly reminds her that she would not have existed were it not for him: he expects a grateful speech in exchange. When Cordelia remains reticent Lear swears he will give 'Nothing' as dowry to her and France (I, i, 247). Later, the Fool mocks Lear for foolishly reducing himself to 'nothing' (I, iv, 129), while Lear calls the Fool's most riddling speeches 'nothing' (I, iv, 126). Lear's repetition of the Aristotelian maxim 'Nothing can be made out of nothing' to the Fool (I, iv, 128) invites the audience to somehow recollect Lear's argument with Cordelia. But the precise connection between these two exchanges is obscure. 'Nothing' is explained to the audience. Perhaps this is apt because the difficulty of making connections and establishing meaning is a key element of Lear's increasing confusion and madness, subtly developed as the play continues. Lear's 'Let me not be mad, sweet heaven' (I, v, 45) and 'O fool, I shall go mad' (II, ii, 475) are movingly lucid recognitions of an increasingly patchy mental state.

Themes

Necessity

One of *King Lear*'s main themes is necessity. Lear's and Gloucester's experiences with the naked 'thing itself' Poor Tom, and the kingdom's poor, force them to question what people need and how kingdoms might meet those needs. During the storm Lear curses his arrogance ('Take physic, pomp', III, iv, 33) and praises the 'poor naked wretches' of whom he has taken so little care (III, iv, 23–36). The blinded Gloucester asks 'Distribution' to 'undo excess' so that 'each man' may 'have enough' (IV, i, 73–4). The question of 'true need' is raised with searing clarity in Lear's 'Reason not the need' speech (II, ii, 453–75). At its most gloomily nihilistic, insisting on 'nothing', cruelty and death, the play arguably suggests nothing is necessary at all: as Lear puts it, even 'basest beggars' are 'in the poorest thing superfluous' (II, ii, 453–4). But if even the poorest, who by definition use least resources, are surplus to requirements, then what does that say about the rest of us? Something like this chilling recognition strikes Lear when he grumbles 'Age is unnecessary' (II, iv, 344). Paradoxically, the natural necessity of ageing makes us progressively less necessary, more burdensome, for the Gonerils and Regans who will ultimately look after us.

Generations

A world where 'age' genuinely was 'unnecessary' would of course indeed be cruel and recall the bitterest social-cleansing experiments of the most fascistic governments. But by staging a worst-case scenario – Goneril and Regan do indeed set 'a plot of death' upon their father (III, vi, 86) – *King Lear* silently examines just why, ethically, societies do not exterminate the old, however 'unnecessary' they become. Is our care of the old based on an altruistic love for humanity for its own sake, or, more cynically, on a perpetual, self-interested, inter-generational 'deal', where parents give their children life and care, just so their children will look after them as they get old? *Lear* seems to probe intensely the issues arising from this 'deal', such as whether children should be forever dependently grateful for a gift of life they never requested, and the problems of converting emotional terms like love and gratitude into numerically measureable care-giving, and gifts like land and money. Lear's belief in a perfect exchangeability of love and wealth is clear in the love test. Lear gives 'thirds' of his kingdom to his eldest daughters while Cordelia's 'price is fallen' when she fails to declare her love (I, i, 198); he also thinks Regan is 'twice' Goneril's 'love' simply because she gives him fifty knights instead of twenty-five (II, ii, 448). But this rigid belief makes Lear vulnerable to 'Monster ingratitude' (I, v, 37): Goneril and Regan easily and woundingly show their father their increasing contempt simply by gradually counting down the number of knights he is allowed to have.

Lear's zero-sum system of 'gratitude' or 'ingratitude' is, however, unable to compute forgiveness, like Cordelia's, which is by definition superabundant.

Forgiveness ascends and breaks the logic through which one wrong is straight-forwardly, vengefully 'exchanged' for another.

> Lear: If you have poison for me, I will drink it.
> I know you do not love me, [...]
> You have some cause [...]
> Cordelia: No cause, no cause.
> (IV, vii, 71–5)

Cordelia, showing Lear the misguidedness of his rigidly held outlook in her very gentleness, develops the themes of blindness and sight, which are sustained through-out the play. Goneril says Lear is 'dearer than eyesight' (I, i, 56), alluding with subtle disdain to his figurative blindness and foreshadowing her attack on Gloucester. Kent begs Lear to 'see better' when he banishes Cordelia (I, i, 159). The blind Gloucester, regretting his faith in Edmund, 'stumbled as he saw' (IV, i, 21). When Lear asks 'who is it that can tell me who I am?' the Fool responds 'Lear's shadow' (I, iv, 221–2). Jesters do oft prove prophets. It is only when Lear becomes a 'shadow' of his former self that he can see himself, or at least his love for Cordelia, clearly, as in a mirror. 'Shadow' was for the Elizabethans another word for reflection. More sadly, Lear becomes his own shadow in death: the shade or 'ghost' that Kent urges not to be 'vexed' (V, iii, 312).

Texts and contexts

There are two early versions of *King Lear*: the 1609 Quarto *'The True Chroni-cle Historie of King LEAR'* ('Q') and the 1623 Folio *The Tragedy of King Lear* ('F'). Performances and scholarly editions often conflate these two versions. The main differences between them are as follows. The Fool is portrayed differently via an accumulation of small individual differences, especially the mysterious prophecy (F only), that he says he will utter 'before [he] go[es]' (III, iii, 81–94). The play's final speech – identical in both versions – is uttered by Albany in Q, Edgar in F. Such changes, including also the excision of a moving reported depiction of Cordelia (IV, iii), arguably indicate a conscious decision to minimise confusion with the 'romance' genre and make the play more definitively a tragedy.

The sources of *King Lear* range from broadly folkloric to the more specifically historical. It shares key themes and images with the 'meat loves salt' and 'coat o'rushes' folktales. In the former a king banishes his daughter for saying she only loves him as much as 'meat loves salt', but realises his error, and how powerful his daughter's love is, when she removes the salt from his feast. In the latter the banished daughter disguises herself in a 'coat o'rushes'. A story in Philip Sidney's 1590 *Arcadia* (Book Two, chapter ten) shares the broad lines of the Gloucester subplot: a blind old Prince, who wishes to die after being usurped and cast out by his bastard son but is helped by his good son Leonatus (see Sidney 2002: 253–8). More specific historical sources include accounts like Geoffrey of Monmouth's or Raphael Holinshed's, which variously situate the story in AD 969 or 800 BC, and John Higgins's additions to the sixteenth-century didactic work *The Mirror for Magistrates* (1574). The Lear story is also told in miniature in Edmund Spenser's epic 1596 poem *The Faerie Queene* (Book Two, Canto ten, verses 27–8). Perhaps Shakespeare's clearest source, however, is the play *The True Chronicle History of King LEIR, and his three daughters* (1605). Shakespeare minimises the presence of Lear's Queen (whom in the *Chronicle* Lear has just buried) and introduces the plot of Edgar and Poor Tom, whose speeches contain many lexical echoes of Samuel Harsnett's *Declaration of Egregious Popish Impostures* (1603). The historical context of *Lear's* first performances is also important. Fundamentally the tragedy warns of the consequences of a divided kingdom. James I sought to unite his new kingdom, England, with his old one, Scotland.

The play in performance

Directors have to make serious decisions about the contexts and backstories of *King Lear*: just how present or absent is Lear's wife? (Are there portraits of her, for example?) Does Lear show signs of mental weakness from the very beginning, as he is dividing up the kingdom? ('He hath but *ever* slenderly known himself'..., I, i, 294–5, emphasis added) Are Edgar and the Fool present in this first scene? The staging can, as ever, tilt an audience's sympathies one way or another. And the emotional stakes are high because *King Lear* is perhaps the most brutal of Shakespeare's tragedies. The eighteenth-century editor Samuel Johnson was 'so shocked by Cordelia's death that I did not know whether I ever endured to read again the last scenes of the play till I undertook to revise them as an editor' (quoted in Tomarken 2009: 89). From 1681 Nahum Tate's version, with a happy ending, was popular.

In the late twentieth century however, the play's brutality has chimed with historical meditations of war, torture and genocide. Peter Brook's production, filmed in the late 1970s, showed a world completely without pity, as did a Granada TV 1983 production, with Laurence Olivier as Lear, stressing a pagan world stripped of Christian charity (a word deriving from the Latin *caritas* – universal love). Akira Kurosawa's excellent film *Ran* (1985) transfers the story to contexts of samurai codes of honour. Innovative *King Lears* since then have seen Lear in a wheelchair (Brian Cox, directed by Deborah Warner, NT 1990) and as a hobo (directed by Nicholas Hytner, RST 1990). Derek Jacobi's Lear (directed by Michael Grandage, Donmar Warehouse 2010), was praised for its moving depiction of a retreat into senility. One of the most recent high-profile filmed versions of the play (Trevor Nunn, RSC 2008), with Ian McKellen as Lear, cast as Regan the actress Monica Dolan, who later played real-life serial murderess Rosemary West in the mini-series *Appropriate Adult*.

Critical reception

Influential early critical accounts, like those of A. C. Bradley, read Lear in providential, even strangely happy, terms: Lear 'loses the world but gains his soul' (ed.

Foakes 1997: 14). Indeed, in speeches like 'Let's away to prison' (V, iii, 8–19), Lear, reconciled with Cordelia, seems to strike a contented note despite the desperateness of the situation. The 1980s, however, saw a sustained attack on this position. Jonathan Dollimore [1984] (2003), for example, critiqued the implications of such providential readings, arguing they justified social inequalities as preordained and thus unchangeable. Stephen Greenblatt (1988) then focused on the play's relation with Harsnett's *Popish Impostures* as twinned forms of 'demonic theatre'. Margreta de Grazia (1996) examines the play's related portrayals of primogeniture, zero-sum economies and claustrophobic human relationships. More recently the play has been read as a kind of figurehead for cognitive criticism and eco-criticism. Raphael Lyne (2014) reads the play in terms of 'social cognition' and 'theory of mind', while Andrew Bozio (2015) takes as a starting point Gloucester's phrase 'I see it feelingly' to explore cognition, even synaesthesia, in Renaissance terms of humoral physiology. James Kearney examines the relationship between cognition, consciousness and the play's depiction of re-cognition, arguing that 'a world of ethical promise seems to lie beneath or behind the tragic world of *Lear*' (Kearney 2012: 465). This utopianism marks also Robert B. Pierce's revisionist reading of Gloucester's blindness (2012), and a recent eco-critical turn in *Lear* criticism. In an influential essay Laurie Shannon (2009) explores uses of the word 'beast', the cultural influence of Pliny the Elder's *Natural History*, emerging sciences of zoology and animal analogies in political writing. Stuart Elden (2013) reads *Lear* as a geopolitical meditation on the differences between 'territory, 'land' and 'earth', and Julián Heffernan (2015) reads Tom as an embodied way for audiences then and now to think through the 'human–animal divide' and the relationship of *bios* (practical life) with *zoe* (animal life). Such themes implicitly underlie Simon Palfrey's stylistically daring recent essay (2014) and book (2015) on Tom, whose voice 'supplies a rhythm that is intuited infinitesimally before semantics, before volitional or witnessed actions' (Palfrey 2014: 7).

Discussion questions

* The play shows an eighty-year-old man with no wife and three daughters of marriageable age. Is the play therefore strictly plausible? If not, how can we explain the power of *King Lear*?

* How does the play work as a meditation on the clichéd phrase 'giving the gift of life'? Is it really a gift if the person is not yet alive to ask for it? Do gifts always necessitate gratitude? If so, is there really any such thing as a 'pure' gift?

* 'I am a man more sinned against than sinning!' Is this fair, or just self-pitying?

→

✳ 'Speak what we feel, not what we ought to say' – is this not a strange conclusion to the play, given that this is precisely what Cordelia did at the beginning, thus setting the tragic events in motion?

✳ What does *King Lear* say about 'the human condition' in so far as we only live as humans on the 'condition' that our parents created us?

Bibliography and further reading

Editions

Shakespeare, W. (1997), *King Lear*, ed. R. A. Foakes, London: Arden Shakespeare.
Sidney, P. (2002), *Sir Philip Sidney: The Major Works, Including* Astrophil and Stella, ed. K. Duncan-Jones, Oxford: Oxford University Press.

Critical response

Bozio, A. (2015), 'Embodied Thought and the Perception of Place in *King Lear*', *Studies in English Literature*, 55:2, 263–84.
de Grazia, M. (1996), 'The Ideology of Superfluous Things: *King Lear* as Period Piece', in M. de Grazia, M. Quilligan and P. Stallybrass (eds), *Subject and Object in Renaissance Culture*, Cambridge: Cambridge University Press, pp. 17–42.
Dollimore, J. [1984] (2003), *Radical Tragedy: Religion, Ideology and Power in the Drama of Shakespeare and His Contemporaries*, Basingstoke: Palgrave Macmillan.
Elden, S. (2013), 'The Geopolitics of King Lear: Territory, Land, Earth', *Law and Literature*, 25:2, 147–65.
Greenblatt, S. (1988), 'Shakespeare and the Exorcists', in *Shakespearean Negotiations: The Circulation of Social Energy in Renaissance England*, Berkeley: University of California Press, pp. 94–128.
Heffernan, J. (2015), '"The Naked Fellow": Performing Feral Reversion in *King Lear*', *Comparative Drama*, 49:2, 133–62.
Kearney, J. (2012), '"This is above all strangeness": King Lear, Ethics, and the Phenomenology of Recognition', *Criticism*, 54:3, 455–67.
Lyne, R. (2014), 'Shakespeare, Perception and Theory of Mind', *Paragraph*, 37:1, 79–95.
Palfrey, S. (2014), 'Attending to Tom', *Shakespeare Quarterly*, 65:1, 1–21.
Palfrey, S. (2015), *Poor Tom: Living 'King Lear'*, Oxford: Oxford University Press.
Pierce, R. (2012), '"I Stumbled When I Saw": Interpreting Gloucester's Blindness in *King Lear*', *Philosophy and Literature*, 36:1, 153–65.
Shannon, L. (2009), 'Poor, Bare, Forked: Animal Sovereignty, Human Negative Exceptionalism, and the Natural History of *King Lear*', *Shakespeare Quarterly*, 60:2, 168–96.
Tomarken, E. (2009), *Samuel Johnson on Shakespeare: The Discipline of Criticism*, Athens, GA/London: University of Georgia Press.

6   *Anthony and Cleopatra*

Composition and first performance c. 1606–7

Act, scene and line references are to the 1994 Oxford edition, edited by Michael Neill. I base my spelling 'Anthony' on his.

Plot summary

Shakespeare's 1599 play *Julius Caesar*, a kind of prequel to *Anthony and Cleopatra*, had shown Brutus and Cassius assassinating Julius Caesar, and Julius's adopted son/ nephew Octavius Caesar beating down this rebellion with the help of the patrician Lepidus and (Mark) Anthony. These three men now share the Empire equally among them as a triumvirate, although they have fought with each other in the past. The balance of power is shaky. As *Anthony and Cleopatra* begins, Anthony is in Roman-occupied Alexandria, Egypt. Behind Anthony's back Romans accuse Cleopatra of distracting him from military and political duty (I, i, 1–13). This suspicion is shared by Octavius (I, iv, 1–10), whose distrust lasts throughout the play. Nonetheless, when Anthony hears his wife Fulvia has died (I, ii, 118), that Parthian forces have invaded Empire territory in Syria (I, ii, 99–101), and that 'Pompey', son of Julius Caesar's vanquished enemy of the same name, angrily wants to avenge his father (I, ii, 182–4), he defies Cleopatra's complaints and returns to Rome (I, iii). Pompey takes news of Anthony's return as a sign that he is being taken seriously: he should therefore step up battle preparations with co-rebels Menecrates and Menas (II, i). The first meeting in the play between Octavius and Anthony (II, ii) hints at their long-standing grievances and stresses Lepidus's efforts as peacemaker. Octavius reminds Anthony that Fulvia attacked him, and accuses him of ignoring his messages (II, ii, 46–7, 77). Octavius's follower Agrippa thinks the best way to resolve these issues, to cement allegiance between Octavius's and Anthony's families and to cooperate against the threat of Pompey, is to get the newly widowed Anthony to marry Octavius's sister Octavia (II, ii, 133–4). The triumvirs agree this course of action (II, ii, 56). But Anthony's follower Enobarbus privately doubts to his peers that Anthony will ever leave Cleopatra (II, ii, 240–6). Cleopatra physically attacks the messenger who tells her that Anthony and Octavia are married (I, v, 62; II, ii, 65). Meanwhile, Pompey negotiates with the triumvirs. They offer him Sicily and Sardinia on the condition he rids them of pirates and ceases his rebellion (II, vi, 34–8). After a brief initial exchange of threats – Pompey is stronger by sea, the triumvirs by land – the negotiators grow more accommodating. Anthony thanks Pompey, for example, for sheltering his mother during the Perusine wars. A deal is struck (II, vi, 58–62). But the boozy feast held to celebrate the agreement in no way calms deep-rooted political rivalries: Menas thinks Pompey should murder the triumvirs while he has the chance (II, vii, 73), and angrily deserts him when he refuses (II, vii, 82). Menas turns out to be right. Octavius renews war on Pompey (III, iv, 4), defeats and kills him (III, vi, 18), and has Lepidus arrested for siding with the enemy (III, v, 8–9). The victory over the Parthians (III, i) has not stabilised the Triumvirate. Anthony is angry at Octavius's single-minded bid for power, and Octavius is angry because Anthony has insultingly neglected his sister in private and in public. Anthony has publicly crowned Cleopatra as his queen (III, vi, 5), and is reuniting Eastern territories against the Romans (III, vi, 15). This simmering anger comes to a head at the sea battle of Actium (III, viii–xi). Cleopatra's ships flee (III, xi, 55) and Octavius defeats Anthony. Anthony's allies Enobarbus, Scarrus and Camidius had warned that fighting by sea was a tactical error (III, vii, 35–66). Octavius asks Cleopatra via his arrogant messenger Thidias to leave Anthony 'And put yourself under his shroud' (III, xiii, 71). Cleopatra seems to accept Octavius's offer, gushing 'He is a god' (III, xiii, 60) and letting Thidias kiss her hand. The furious, humiliated Anthony quarrels with Cleopatra (III, xiii, 105–32) and flogs Thidias, sending him back to Octavius in disgrace, taunting his fellow triumvir (III, xiii, 135–53). Octavius responds and another battle ensues, this time by land (IV, iii–xiii). Enobarbus had been worried by Anthony's change of fortune (III, xiii, 41–6, 195–201) and deserts him for Octavius (IV, v, 9). But when Anthony sends through the treasure Enobarbus left behind with 'overplus', as if to forgive him (IV, vi, 20–1), Enobarbus kills himself for shame and so as not to fight his old friend, captain and benefactor (IV, x, 23). Anthony scores minor victories (IV, ix, 1) but is let down by the surrender of Cleopatra's forces (IV, xiii, 10) and so loses this battle too. Cleopatra, ashamed and fearful of Anthony's rage, sends word that she is dead (IV, xiv, 7). Anthony stabs himself from despair at losing his love and the battle (IV, xv, 103). Anthony is brought before Cleopatra (IV, xvi) before he dies (IV, xvi, 65). Rather than suffer the humiliation of being Octavius's prisoner, Cleopatra too kills herself by letting poisonous snakes bite her breast (V, ii, 310). Octavius vows to bury the dead lovers honourably together.

Characters

Cleopatra (I, i; I, ii; I, iii; I, v; II, v; III, iii; III, vii; III, xi; III, xiii; IV, ii; IV, iv; IV, ix; IV, xiii; IV, xiv; IV, xvi; V, ii)

Shakespeare's Cleopatra is a complicated blend of uncertainty, neediness and calculation. These three attributes come through clearly from her very first line ('If it be love indeed, tell me how much', I, i, 14). She is uncertain about Anthony's fidelity ('*if* it be love'), needs reassurance ('*tell* me') and sees this reassurance in measurable terms ('how much'). She is jealous from the beginning of Anthony's legal wives Fulvia ('the married woman', I, iii, 20) and then Octavia, about whom she interrogates and berates her messenger, and she is near-obsessively voyeuristic. Her sense of frailty helps explain her adroit psychological manipulation. She often deploys reverse psychology as a key element of her calculated strategising. As Enobarbus famously says, 'she makes hungry/Where most she satisfies' (II, ii, 244–5). The play shows repeatedly Cleopatra's ability to somehow 'satisfy' her lovers precisely by frustrating them. Near the beginning she plots to distance herself tantalisingly from her lover: 'If you find him sad,/Say I am dancing; if in mirth, report/That I am sudden sick' (I, iii, 3–5). She then rebukes her lady who counsels obedience: 'Thou teachest like a fool – the way to lose him' (I, iii, 10). She also berates Anthony for not crying when Fulvia dies: 'Now I see, I see/In Fulvia's death how mine received shall be' (I, iii, 64–5), a kind of histrionically martyristic guilt-tripping which also ironically fore-shadows the tragic misunderstanding that kills them both. Her self-interest persists even when she awkwardly lifts up the dying Anthony: 'Hast thou no care of *me*?' (IV, xvi, 62, emphasis added).

Cleopatra's manipulative neediness intertwines with her more political manoeuv-ring, learnt over long experience and in part compensating for her lack of military skill and physical strength. Indeed, it is difficult to know where political strategising stops and sexuality begins. Anthony alludes, often angrily, to her love affairs with in-fluential Romans like Gnaeus Pompey and Julius Caesar (I, v, 28–34; III, xiii, 117–20). This seductive skill is visible onstage when she charms an angry Anthony ('If I be [cold-hearted]/From my cold heart let heaven engender hail', III, xiii, 159–68), or praises a victorious Caesar ('He is a god', II, vi, 108). Conversely, she is an incom-petent warrior, fleeing at Actium and Alexandria ('triple-turned whore!', IV, xiii, 13), struggling to fit Anthony's armour (IV, iv, 7) and not killing herself in acceptably virtuous, stoical ways. Octavius sneers: 'She hath pursued conclusions infinite/Of easy ways to die' (V, ii, 352–4).

The militarily weak Cleopatra has therefore to adopt a mode of governance which is uniquely hers, uniquely feminine, and based on public image and spectacle. She is always in the public eye, having no soliloquies, and hardly ever away from her women and eunuchs, Charmian, Iras and Mardian, with whom she has frequently tender, even bawdy, conversations. Cleopatra dies one of the most self-consciously spectacular deaths in all Shakespeare (V, ii, 49–62), carefully stage-managing the suicide and interspersing her death with defiant speeches. It is precisely this politics of spectacle to which Anthony is amorously subjected. He too is displayed, made theatrically visible and thus continually subject to the opinion of any 'common liar' (I, ii, 62).

Anthony (I, i; I, ii; I, iii; II, ii; II, iii; II, vi; II, vii; III, ii; III, iv; III, vii; III, ix; III, xi; III, xiii; IV, ii; IV, iv; IV, v; IV, viii; IV, ix; IV, xi; IV, xiii; IV, xv; IV, xvi)

Anthony's transition from hard-headed Roman soldier to 'strumpet's fool' (I, i, 13) is accentuated from the play's very first speech. His first entrance seems to support this criticism. He refuses Octavius's messenger, seeking instead 'some pleasure now' (I, i, 49). The play does, however, offer glimpses of the adept negotiator, soldier and strategist portrayed in *Julius Caesar*. In negotiations he stands his ground against Octavius's inability to 'lend me arms' (II, ii, 93), countering that he was able but unconcerned ('neglected, rather', II, ii, 94). He cultivates advantageous political relationships with, say, Pompey (II, vii) and, despite his love for Cleopatra, accepts without much quibbling the political necessity of marrying Octavia (II, ii, 151–6). Octavius speaks admiringly of Anthony surviving hard battles by drinking horse's 'stale' (urine) (I, iv, 62), but the defeat at Actium forces Anthony to look back gloomily at his earlier victories, a decisive shift in his character (III, xi, 8–24, 135–53). His battle speech to his soldiers before a later conflict is morose and defeatist ('perchance tomorrow/You'll serve another master' IV, ii, 24–33); he only revises it in more positive terms reluctantly, on Enobarbus's urging, and with unconvincing curtness ('I hope well of tomorrow', IV, ii, 42). His second defeat (IV, xiii, 32–48) echoes the first at the end of Act III, but here Anthony is visibly more animated and even angrier at Cleopatra ('Triple-turned whore!', IV, xiii, 13). He struggles to reconcile past and present versions of himself ('here I am Anthony,/Yet cannot hold this visible shape', IV, xv, 13–14). This intensifies in two important scenes for Anthony, Act IV, scenes xv and xvi, where his grandiose comparison with mythological figures, appeals to former glories, and fantasies of stoic nobility contrast with his haphazard and near-botched suicide (IV, xvi, 60).

(Octavius) Caesar (I, iv; II, ii; II, iii; II, vi; II, vii; III, ii; III, vi; III, viii; III, xii; IV, i; IV, vi; IV, xii; V, i; V, ii)

Octavius is the cold-hearted counterpart to Anthony and Cleopatra. He dismisses anyone who is 'too indulgent' to Anthony (I, iv, 16), growing angrier yet with him when hearing of Pompey's progress ('Anthony/Leave thy lascivious wassails', I, iv, 55–6). He sternly disapproves of the revelling during the peace-making party on Pompey's galley ('our graver business/Frowns on this levity', II, vii, 119–20). This tough-mindedness comes through when he sets the soldiers who betrayed Anthony at the front of his ranks, endangering them in the process, 'That Antony may seem to spend his fury/Upon himself' (IV, vi, 6–10). He also adapts advantageously to changing circumstances, calling Cleopatra a 'whore' in life (III, vi, 67) but praising her in death ('No grave upon the earth shall clip in it/A pair so famous', V, ii, 357–8) He likewise cries when Anthony dies: 'the gods rebuke me, but it is tidings/To wash the eyes of Kings' (V, i, 26–7) and makes a long tribute speech (V, i, 35–51). Octavius's changeable opinions, and undoubted political ambition, cast doubt on his victorious promises not to parade Cleopatra in triumph before the Roman people (V, i, 59–66), especially as he threatens Cleopatra's children if she kills herself to escape captivity (V, ii, 131–3).

Enobarbus (I, ii; II, ii; II, vi; II, vii; III, ii; III, v; III, vii; III, x; III, xiii; IV, ii; IV, vi; IV, x)

Enobarbus functions as a kind of 'chorus', charting Anthony's success and decline, and accurately foretelling that Anthony will not leave Cleopatra for Octavia. Initially loyal to Anthony, he quarrels with Cleopatra about military tactics, accentuating her lack of skill in such matters (III, vii, 1–19). As Anthony suffers defeat, he resolves to 'seek some way to leave him' (III, xiii, 200–1). He then finds, though, that Octavius is a dishonourable captain, executing even those who have turned to him (IV, vi, 11–19). This helps explain why, when Enobarbus receives gold from Anthony despite his betrayal, he kills himself from shame, careful above all for his posthumous reputation (IV, x, 12–23). Like Anthony, Enobarbus voices worrying vulnerabilities in thought and identity, which he perceives to be lost when he forgoes Anthony's friendship: his 'heart', 'dried with grief, will break to powder' (IV, x, 15–17).

Pompey (II, i; II, vi; II, vii)

Pompey only has a relatively minor role in terms of line count but he is structurally important. He reveals how the latent tensions between Anthony and Octavius are now beginning to surface. His refusal to kill the triumvirs when he has the chance, even as Menas urges him to strike, proves fatal (III, vi, 18). This reveals the new, merciless politics initiated and symbolised by Octavius.

Lepidus (I, iv; II, ii; II, iv; II, vi; II, vii)

Lepidus means 'fine one' in Latin (III, ii, 7), and, like Pompey, he illustrates how fine, upstanding actions lead in Octavius's empire only to defeat. The warnings are already in place when Octavius says he is 'too indulgent' to Anthony (I, iv, 16). He tries very hard to broker a peacekeeping deal between Anthony and Octavius, but is only mocked for it (II, vi; 'he is their beetle', III, ii, 19). Lepidus's misguided trust in his fellows is evident when he grows comically, idiotically drunk during Pompey's feast (II, vii, 24–48). We do not see him again. His downfall is soon reported: '[Octavius] accuses him of letters he had formerly wrote to Pompey [...] his poor third is up, till death enlarge his confine' (III, iv, 6–11). In Shakespeare's sources Lepidus is much crueller. By portraying him as an occasionally bumbling politician who wants peace, his offstage imprisonment shows further Octavius's ruthlessness, contributing to the darkening atmosphere.

Octavia (II, iii; III, ii; III, iv; III, vi)

Octavia illustrates the rivalry between her husband Anthony and brother Octavius, but she herself is most often silent. When she is 'given away' to Anthony she whispers brief thoughts in Octavius's ear (III, ii, 46). She does, however, later make brave, doomed attempts to broker peace between Anthony and Octavius: 'Wars 'twixt you twain would be/As if the world would cleave [...] slain men/Should solder up the rift' (III, iv, 30–2).

Play structure

Anthony and Cleopatra is tragedy on a grand scale. Aristotle said tragedies must have a single setting but this play sprawls over whole continents, from Rome to Egypt and back again, telescoping a fourteen-year love affair into four hours. Tonal shifts correspond to the geographical ones. The languorous early scenes with Cleopatra and her women (e.g. I, v; II, v, 1–23) are counterbalanced, during the chaotic battle episodes, with rapid, frequent scene clearances, resulting in some of the shortest scenes in all Shakespeare. Act III, scene ix, for example, is only four lines long.

The play's thematic and narrative centre is the battle of Actium (III, viii–xi). Anthony and Cleopatra decline rapidly thereafter. Caesar is less visible in the fourth act, as if his rise is slowly leaving the tragic lovers behind. The third and fourth acts both end with Cleopatra's bad decisions leading to the downfall of their armies, but Cleopatra's ability to win Anthony back round progressively wanes. By Act IV Anthony's rage is such that Cleopatra is compelled to escape and send false word that she has killed herself: 'The last she spake/Was "Anthony, most noble Anthony"' (IV, xv, 29–30). The structure and staging of *Anthony and Cleopatra* is often radical and innovative. Anthony dies with more than an act to go ('the crown of the earth doth melt', IV, xvi, 64). The 'Monument' scene, where Cleopatra's women haul the dying Anthony to the top of the stage, makes real physical demands of the actors: 'How heavy weighs my lord!' (IV, xvi, 34).

Language

Enobarbus delivers *Anthony and Cleopatra*'s most famous speech, describing the Egyptian Queen's victory procession 'upon the River of Cydnus' (II, ii, 194). Heavily indebted to Thomas North's translation of the Greek historian Plutarch, this speech lavishly describes luxurious sensual pleasure. 'The barge she sat in, like a burnished throne/Burned on the water' (II, ii, 198–9). The winds are 'lovesick' with Cleopatra's 'perfumèd' sails (II, ii, 200–1), as are the waters with the silver oars' strokes, beating in time to the rhythm of flutes (II, ii, 201–4). Juxtaposed with these delights are hints of unattainable desire. Cleopatra makes a 'gap in nature' (II, ii, 224), which may presumably never be quite filled. Moreover, when describing the boys who seem to grow red and hot as they blow cooling winds, Enobarbus says 'what they undid did' (II, ii, 212). Cleopatra's boys emblematise her tantalising contradictions because they undo precisely as they do, rather than (as would be more logical and sequential) do and then undo. The very strangeness of this paradox seems akin to the 'infinite variety' Enobarbus ascribes to Cleopatra. The mellifluous versification of Enobarbus's speech regularly marks Cleopatra's use of language, too. She often uses drowsily long vowels: 'Give me to drink mandragora [...] That I might sleep out this great gap of time / My Anthony is away' (I, v, 3, 5–6). Her sharper, often paranoid utterances, even occasional violence, such as against her messenger, come through all the stronger when set against such languorous verbal melody. Enobarbus's watery imagery also surfaces elsewhere in the play. Images of melting are especially frequent, linked to political and individual instability. Cleopatra cursing Anthony's marriage to Octavia ('Melt Egypt into Nile!', II, v, 79) parodies Anthony's false dismissal of Rome to stay with her ('let Rome in Tiber melt', I, i, 35). Anthony later complains 'Authority *melts* from me' (III, xiii, 90), grimly anticipating the last word the 'dolphin like' former triumvir hears before he dies 'The crown of the earth doth *melt*' (IV, xvi, 64; V, ii, 88–9).

Cleopatra's Egypt is thus related to natural, fluid elements, contrasting with Octavius's, cold-blooded, man-made, solid Roman Empire. For Anthony, Cleopatra is the 'serpent of old Nile' (I, v, 25), nuancing somewhat Enobarbus's association of the queen with mystery and 'infinite variety'. The Nile's 'dungy earth' (I, i, 37) was famously fertile, generating beasts like the crocodile, new and strange to Roman eyes, with confusing speed and copiousness (II, vii, 40). When transposed to treasure and reward, this markedly anti-Roman generative generosity kills Enobarbus with guilt ('O Anthony, / Thou mine of bounty', IV, vi, 30–1). The 'aspics' that kill Cleopatra also gave close links to the Egyptian river, famous for leaving slime 'Upon the caves of Nile' (V, ii, 351). It is as if the differences between Rome and Egypt are too great for individual human bodies to bear.

Themes

Duty and pleasure

Perhaps the key theme of *Anthony and Cleopatra* is the opposition of duty and pleasure. Anthony is poised between Octavius/Octavia and Cleopatra, between Rome and Egypt. Shakespeare makes this a more clearly dualist structure by, say, not giving Anthony's first wife Fulvia an onstage role and never staging him with Octavius and Cleopatra at once. Anthony seems to oscillate between these two poles, flowing mercurially, like the Nile, between stoicism and sensuality. His relationship with Cleopatra blurs genuine with fantasised identities, as if people fall less in love with people than with their own *ideas* of other people. Anthony says early on of the dead Fulvia, 'she's good, being gone' (I, ii, 126), interestingly paralleling in eroticised mode Octavius's political observations about how rulers make their subjects love them: 'deared, by being lacked' (I, iv, 44). Anthony and Cleopatra are erotically and politically potent figures, so it is not surprising the fantasy elicited by absence plays an important role in their love. Cleopatra is only onstage with Anthony for about one-third of the total scenes. At least as often she is idealising, imagining and fanta-sising her lover, with only her maids and eunuch for company: 'O happy horse, to bear the weight of Anthony' (I, v, 21). Cleopatra can imagine Anthony as everything from the grandest godlike 'demi-Atlas' (I, v, 23) to the tiniest 'tawny-fine fish': 'I'll think them every one an Anthony/And say "Ah, ha! You're caught"' (II, v, 12, 14). It is perhaps impossible for any actor in the role, as a physical, mortal human being, fully to replicate this rich variety of fantasised identities.

Reputation, reality and anti-climax

Cleopatra's fantasising illustrates a wider tension in the play between the human bodies we see onstage and their symbolic, regal or heroic reputations. The surrounding cast speaks of little else but Anthony, Cleopatra or the pair of them (e.g. I, i, 1–13; II, i, 19–27; II, ii, 178–252). The cultural pressures they have to live up to are enormous. As if to convince each other of their soaring reputations, they wear each other's clothing, a kind of reciprocal narcissism that binds them together away from the rest of the world: 'I [...] put my tires and mantles on him, whilst/I wore his sword Philippan' (II, v, 23–4). This sense of grandiosity is arguably furthered by the soothsayer scenes and the vision of Hercules deserting Anthony's camp (I, ii, 5–56; II, iii, 9–30; IV, iii, 14–15): the lovers are struggling against not only Octavius but destiny itself.

But the play consistently punctures these bubble-like self-images. Anthony is conspicuously absent from the crisis at Actium (ed. Neill 1994: 76), blaming Cleopatra's flight: 'My heart was to thy rudder tied by th'strings' (III, xi, 56). His protests that 'I am Anthony yet' (III, xiii, 92–3) ring increasingly hollow with each defeat. The fear of shameful disparity between past glory and present reputation haunts him throughout ('I have fled myself', III, xi, 7). For her part, Cleopatra fears being put to public show as a defeated victim in Rome (IV, xv, 72; V, i, 55–6), even implying this very play is a kind of humiliation: 'I shall see/Some squeaking Cleopatra boy my greatness/I' the posture of a whore' (V, ii, 219–21). Shakespeare's play subjects these great heroes to subtle but sustained scrutiny. Important historical details, like Anthony sending the soldier to the Parthians or Octavius's attack, are brushed over with surprising and dismissive speed (III, i, 9; III, viii, 4), while Anthony's botched suicide and undignified hauling of his expiring body to the monument are uncomfortably long (IV, xv, 44–141; IV, xvi, 1–64). Octavius thinks news of Anthony's death is strangely anti-climactic: 'The breaking of so great a thing should make/A greater crack' (V, i, 14–15). And Cleopatra dies before the end of her dying speech: her sentence 'What should I stay' has to be completed by Charmian (V, ii, 312).

Rivalries of love and death

The lovers' desire to die with the kind of grandeur their reputations deserve almost becomes a strange rivalry. They seek to 'out-die' each other as if, paradoxically, to be the lover who presents the more loving homage or tribute. This idea of death as a kind of loving gift helps explain a strand of imagery that runs throughout. Enobarbus sneers that Cleopatra has 'a celerity in dying' (I, ii, 143), playing both on her histrionic threats to kill herself ('I will make death love me', III, xiii, 193) and on her sexual appetite for orgasms, for which 'death' was a commonplace euphemism. Anthony says he 'will be a bridesgroom in my death, and run into't as to a lover's bed' (IV, xv, 100–1). The squire he asks to stab him is suggestively called Eros. Cleopatra's death scene, elaborately costumed ('Give me my robe, put on my crown', V, ii, 279), with care taken to make sure that her diadem is in place (V, ii, 340–1), is as self-consciously theatrical as sensual, even frankly sexual. The Clown's speeches about the poisonous 'worm' stress its phallic connotations, nuancing Cleopatra's delirious idea she is stoically hard or 'marble constant' (V, ii, 240) and her insistence that 'the stroke of death is as a lover's pinch' (V, ii, 294). Just before Cleopatra's death Anthony comes as if in a dream ('*Husband* I come', V, ii, 286), and the cluster of motifs of sleep, childbirth, conception and death implied as Cleopatra calls the asp 'baby at my breast, / That sucks the nurse asleep' (V, ii, 308–9) are given material actuality in performance when she dies on her 'bed' (V, ii, 354), rather than her throne, an emendation dating from John Dryden's 1677 adaptation *All for Love*.

Texts and contexts

The only early text of *Anthony and Cleopatra* is in the 1623 Folio. Shakespeare's main source for the stories is Thomas North's 1579 translation of Plutarch's *The Lives of the Noble Grecians and Romans*. Plutarch, as a Greek, wrote a subtler, more contradictory portrayal of Anthony and Cleopatra. Roman historians tended rather to attack them for their shared dereliction of duty (see ed. Neill 1994: 10). Shakespeare further nuances the story by making Lepidus less cruel, silently deleting his tortures and executions. Likewise, Shakespeare softens some of Anthony's more Machiavellian acts to strengthen a binary contrast between him and Octavius.

The play in performance

Anthony and Cleopatra has had a limited stage history. In performance it is a logistical nightmare. Practitioners have found it near-impossible to strike a balance between its grandiose, overblown spectacle and the need to squeeze the action into a manageable timeframe. Stanley Wells has wondered if this is a play 'which can be fully realised only in the theatre of the mind' (quoted in ed. Neill 1994: 69). Early to mid-twentieth-century productions have arguably been guilty of a stereotyped 'Orientalism'. There were no Egyptian or black Cleopatras in the 'big' English productions. Michael Benthall's production, for example, featured Laurence Olivier and Vivien Leigh, stressing the glamour of the love story (St James's Theatre 1951) Responding to a perceived Shakespearean scepticism to the great reputations of his heroes, however, successful Cleopatras have often cast against type. The Orientalist stereotype of a languid, sensual Cleopatra was rejected by Janet Suzman's performance (directed by Trevor Nunn, Stratford 1971, London 1973, televised 1975). This production accentuated the Romans' political pressure, stressing Cleopatra's 'regality' by dying on a throne and not her bed. Tony Richardson directed a modern-dress production (Bankside Globe 1973) while Glenda Jackson's 1978 RST performance (directed by Peter Brook) hinted via its claustrophobic lighting at political entrapment rather than sensuous expansiveness. Keith Hack in his Young Vic production (1983) sought to restore the play's heroism: Keith Baxter's pathos-laden Anthony was a real success. Octavius has developed from the conventionally dry politician by implying an illicit, taboo sexuality, hinting at homoerotic desire for Anthony, as with Jonathan Hyde for Adrian Noble's production (1982), or even incestuous desire for Octavia, as with Tim Piggott-Smith for Peter Hall's (1987). Patrick Stewart and Harriet Walter played the roles in Greg Doran's much-praised RSC 2006 production, Anthony hopelessly enthralled by Cleopatra.

Critical reception

George Wilson Knight influentially praised *Anthony and Cleopatra* for setting passion transcendentally above mere politics: 'the high metaphysic of love [...] melts life and death into a final oneness' (Knight [1931] 2002: 262). Janet Adelman's classic study (1973) argues, however, that the play does not reconcile its structural para-doxes so easily. The 'common liar' is in fact proven 'true' by Anthony's debauchery and decline. Cleopatra's use of her treasure seems by moments mysterious, even crafty, in her final negotiations with Caesar, implying perhaps she planned to outlive Anthony all along. Adelman thus sees the play as a critique to relatively straight-forward Virgilian, Chaucerian and Marlovian dichotomies between Rome and the East. Linda Charnes (1993), like Adelman, notes the proliferation of messengers and go-betweens in *Anthony and Cleopatra*. The resulting 'Chinese whispers' effect parallels for Charnes Cleopatra's metatheatrical anxiety about her own story being relayed correctly to future audiences, and not distorted in the 'posture of a whore'. Politicised identity emerges as a question of careful negotiation, even stage manage-ment. David Lucking (2015) has similarly recently read the play in topical contexts of media manipulation.

Jonathan Gil Harris (1994) deconstructs the play's apparent opposition of Roman stoicism and Eastern 'delight' with reference to early modern interpretations and imitations of the myth of Narcissus, hopelessly enthralled by his own mirror image. Eric Langley (2009) takes up Harris's arguments about self-reflexivity by focusing closely on repetitious rhetorical figures. David Hillman incisively brings to bear psychoanalytic dynamics of transference to the play's use of the word and concept of 'love', which he deems 'insufficiently examined' and 'vague' (Hillman 2013: 302). David Schalkwyk (2011) likewise urges renewed critical attention to this most ap-parently natural emotion, testing 'love' in the play against historical frameworks of the 'passions' and more recent, cognitive debates about what precisely constitutes an 'emotion'. Mary Thomas Crane (2009) historicises cognitive theory to explore how the Romans link Egypt with nature and femininity to useful ideological and im-perialist ends. William Junker (2015) relates the temporality of imperialist ambition, as in Octavius's dream of being 'eternal in our triumph', to the play's allusions to the Book of Revelation. Adrian Streete (2008) likewise focuses on these biblical echoes, arguing that the play puts forward theologically and theatrically charged near-allegory for early modern anxieties about Christian time and doomsday. The clear, full Aristotelian, biblical, Stoic and Neoplatonic contexts that Sofie Kluge assembles for the play (2008) include comparisons of Cleopatra with Revelation's 'Whore of Babylon' (Revelation 17: 1–2).

Discussion questions

✻ Does *Anthony and Cleopatra* conform to or challenge conventional ideas of tragedy?

✻ How does the play establish oppositions between Rome and Egypt? And does it only do so in order then to undermine them?

✻ 'It's a wonderful part. But just remember, all you future Anthonys, one little word of advice: Cleopatra's got you firmly by the balls' (Laurence Olivier). Is this true? If so, how does Cleopatra achieve such mastery?

Bibliography and further reading

Edition

Shakespeare, W. (1994), *Anthony and Cleopatra*, ed. Michael Neill, Oxford: Oxford University Press.

Critical response

Adelman, J. (1973), *The Common Liar: An Essay on Antony and Cleopatra*, New Haven, CT/London: Yale University Press.
Charnes, L. (1993), *Notorious Identity: Materialising the Subject in Shakespeare*, Cambridge, MA/London: Harvard University Press.
Crane, M. (2009), 'Roman World, Egyptian Earth: Cognitive Difference and Empire in Shakespeare's *Antony and Cleopatra*', *Comparative Drama*, 43:1, 1–17.
Gil Harris, J. (1994), '"Narcissus in thy face"', *Shakespeare Quarterly*, 45:4, 408–25.
Hillman, D. (2013), '"If it be love indeed": Transference, Love, and *Anthony and Cleopatra*', *Shakespeare Quarterly*, 64:3, 301–33.
Junker, W. (2015), 'The Image of Both Theaters: Empire and Revelation in Shakespeare's *Antony and Cleopatra*', *Shakespeare Quarterly*, 66:2, 167–87.
Kluge, S. (2008), 'An Apology for Antony: Morality and Pathos in Shakespeare's *Antony and Cleopatra*', *Orbis Litterarum*, 63:4, 304–34.

Knight, G. W. [1931] (2002), *The Imperial Theme: Further Interpretations of Shakespeare's Tragedies Including the Roman Plays*, London/New York: Routledge.

Langley, E. (2009), *Narcissism and Suicide in Shakespeare and His Contemporaries*, Oxford: Oxford University Press.

Lucking, D. (2015), 'Bad News: Medium as Message in *Antony and Cleopatra*', *English Studies*, 96:6, 619–35.

Schalkwyk, D. (2011), 'Is Love an Emotion? Shakespeare's *Twelfth Night* and *Antony and Cleopatra*', *Symplokē*, 18:1–2, 99–130.

Streete, A. (2008), 'The Politics of Ethical Presentism: Appropriation, Spirituality and the Case of *Antony and Cleopatra*', *Textual Practice*, 22:3, 405–21.

Part II. Comedies

7 A Midsummer Night's Dream

Composition and first performance c. 1595–6, first printed 1600

Act, scene and line references are to the 1994 Oxford edition, edited by Peter Holland.

Plot summary

Theseus, Duke of Athens, is to marry Hippolyta. Preparations are in full swing. The celebrations are to include a performance of the mythological story *Pyramus and Thisbe* put on by 'rude mechanicals', that is, local craftsmen (III, ii, 9). A lord, Egeus, complains to Theseus that the youth Lysander has 'bewitched' his daughter Hermia (I, i, 27), whom he had betrothed to Demetrius. Theseus rules in Egeus's favour. Hermia must 'fit [her] fancies to [her] father's will', and marry the man she does not love (I, i, 118). Meanwhile Hermia's friend Helena jealously laments her own, unrequited, love for Demetrius (I, i, 181–93, 226–51). An important pattern is thus established. Lysander and Demetrius both love Hermia, Hermia loves only Lysander, Helena loves only Demetrius, and nobody loves Helena. Hermia and Lysander decide to flee the cruel dukedom that obstructs their love (I, i, 213). They take refuge in a forest, where they sleep (II, ii, 71). Demetrius searches for them, followed despite his complaints by an obsessed Helena (II, i, 188–244). Sprites and fairies inhabit this forest. Their King and Queen, Oberon and Titania, argue over a 'little changeling boy' (II, i, 120). Titania refuses to hand him over, so Oberon vows revenge by slipping into her eyes as she sleeps a love drug. This will make her fall in love with the 'next thing [...] she waking looks upon' (II, i, 182). Oberon then spies unseen Helena and Demetrius's arguments. He pities 'the sweet Athenian lady' and asks his sprite-servant Robin Goodfellow ('Puck') to drug 'the disdainful youth' so that her love may be requited (II, i, 260–3). Puck is to recognise Demetrius by his 'Athenian garments' (II, i, 264). Oberon meanwhile drugs Titania (II, ii, 32). Puck gets his assignment wrong. He confuses Demetrius with the sleeping Lysander, who also wears Athenian clothing. He slips the love drug into Lysander's eyes (II, ii, 85) and Lysander wakes just as Helena, tired from chasing Demetrius, stops close by to rest. The love drug strikes and Lysander falls instantly in love with Helena. '[R]un through fire I will for thy sweet sake' (II, ii, 109). He chases Helena as she flees through the forest (II, ii, 140). Meanwhile, the 'rude mechanicals' continue in the same forest their rehearsals for *Pyramus and Thisbe*. This story, albeit more tragically, also deals with mistaken identity. Pyramus, seeing some bloodstained clothing on the ground, thinks his lover Thisbe has been devoured by a lion and stabs himself. Thisbe then stabs herself from grief. During the rehearsal Puck decides to bewitch one of the actors, the weaver Bottom, who plays Pyramus. Puck replaces Bottom's head with that of an ass (III, i, 96). The other actors flee from fear and Bottom is left alone, lost, in the forest (III, i, 114). Titania awakes and, love-drugged, grows comically 'enamoured' with the braying, ass-headed weaver (III, i, 122). The story returns to the Athenian lovers, only this time shifting from Helena and Lysander to Hermia and Demetrius. Demetrius begs Hermia to love him ('why rebuke you him that loves you so?', III, ii, 43) but Hermia storms off, distressed at Lysander's disappearance ('hast thou killed him sleeping?', III, ii, 70, exit 81). A resigned Demetrius falls asleep (III, ii, 86). Oberon is distressed that his plan to reconcile two lovers has so spectacularly misfired (III, ii, 88). Puck recognises he has 'mistaken quite' (III, ii, 88), seeing the difference between Demetrius, whom he had never seen before, and Lysander, whom he had love-drugged earlier (III, ii, 42). Puck is therefore sent off to find and bring back Helena, while Oberon love-drugs the sleeping Demetrius, who was after all the drug's original target (III, ii, 104). Helena returns to the scene, alarmed and pursued by the love-drugged Lysander (III, ii, 121). As Demetrius awakes he, too, under the influence of the drug, falls in love with Helena ('goddess, nymph, perfect, divine!', III, ii, 137). Neither man had loved Helena at the beginning; now both are smitten. Helena takes this as a cruel joke: 'I see you all are bent/To set against me for your merriment' (III, ii, 145–6); 'they have conjoined all three/To fashion this false sport in spite of me' (III, ii, 194). Hermia now returns, finally finding Lysander (III, ii, 175). But Lysander, still hopelessly enthralled by the magic drug, now rejects her bitterly ('Why seek'st thou me?', III, ii, 189). Hermia thus attacks Helena in jealous rage ('you juggler, you canker blossom,/You thief of love', III, ii, 282). Helena flees (III, ii, 343). Oberon and Puck, seeing the chaos they have caused, vow to make amends: 'When they next wake, all this derision/Shall seem a dream and fruitless vision' (III, ii, 370–1). Puck, either by magic or by imitating the lovers' voices, guides the four youths to the same spot, where they fall asleep (III, ii, 396–447). Puck casts a spell: 'Jack shall have Jill/Naught will go ill' (III, ii, 461–2). Egeus, Theseus and Hippolyta, who are hunting in the forest, conveniently appear just as the lovers awake (IV, i, 101). Lysander is cured of his earlier infatuation with Helena and loves Hermia again. But Demetrius happily still bears some sign of his own infatuation, because he still loves Helena: 'my love to Hermia/Melted as the snow, seems to me now/As the remembrance of an idle gaud' (IV, i, 164–6). Demetrius therefore asks to withdraw his betrothal to Hermia and Theseus approves: 'Fair lovers, you are fortunately met [...] Egeus I will overbear your will' (IV, i, 176–8). Harmony is also restored in the fairy realm. Oberon is no longer angry with Titania ('Her dotage now I do begin to pity', IV, i, 45). He breaks the spells on her and Bottom (IV, i, 69, 82). Bottom gets his real head back again. Theseus and Hippolyta, Hermia and Lysander, and Helena and Demetrius all marry in the same ceremony, commemorated by the performance by the 'rude mechanicals' of Pyramus and Thisbe (V, i). The Epilogue falls to Puck, who begs the audience's indulgence.

Characters

Helena (I, i; II, i; II, ii; III, ii; IV, i; V, i)

Helena is the last of the lovers to be introduced and, like Rosalind and Celia in *As You Like It*, needs to be played by an actress taller than that playing Hermia: 'My legs are longer, though, to run away' (III, ii, 343). Helena's first speech signals a deep jealousy of Demetrius's love for Hermia. She even wants to be 'translated', transformed, into her childhood friend (I, i, 191). In her next, similarly sad soliloquy (I, i, 226–51), she seems progressively to decide to 'go tell' Demetrius of 'fair Hermia's flight', so desperate is she to please her beloved. Helena is often self-scorning and melancholy. 'I am as ugly as a bear' (II, ii, 100). While the play's fairy-filled, magical context and self-consciously poetic, idealising language suspends disbelief, mollifying Helena's evident distress, some questions arise. Demetrius near the end of the play does not receive Puck's antidote. Perhaps, then, he is only in love with Helena because he remains drugged. And neither she nor Hermia utters a single word during the whole of Act V, implying that the happiness of the play's happy ending is predominantly patriarchal.

Hermia (I, i; II, ii; III, ii; IV, i; V, i)

The play's motif of patriarchy is clearly introduced via Hermia. Hermia is spoken for by her father Egeus to the 'renownèd duke' Theseus (I, i, 20) long before she speaks herself. Her first utterances are, moreover, brief and interrupted (I, i, 52, 56). Egeus dismisses her as an 'unhardened youth' (I, i, 35). Her longer speeches, however, show a transgressive spirit, insisting on her love for Lysander despite the Athenian law's threat of death or banishment to a convent (I, i, 53, 56). Hermia is self-willed. She similarly resists Lysander's sexual advances after escaping together into the forest ('Lie further off, in human modesty', II, ii, 63): her later dream of a 'serpent' who 'ate my heart away' has been read phallically as an expression of Renaissance anxieties about feminine chastity (II, ii, 151–62). Hermia's clear-minded determination also comes through in her surprisingly aggressive language to Demetrius, whom she suspects of killing Lysander ('cur', 'worm', 'adder', III, ii, 45–81), and to Helena during their argument (III, ii, 282–344). Her final full lines, 'Methinks I see these things with parted eye,/When everything seems double' (IV, i, 188–9), not only signal the play's successful resolution, aligning the lovers into 'doubled' couples, but also recall Demetrius's and Lysander's 'doubleness' when they forgo her for Helena.

Lysander (I, i; II, ii; III, ii; IV, i; V, i)

The two young men are less clearly differentiated than Helena and Hermia. Broadly speaking, though, Lysander seems nicer than the often priggish and arrogant Demetrius. He determinedly defends his love against Hermia's father (I, i, 99–110) and accepts Hermia's refusal to grant him 'bed-room' (II, ii, 57) with good grace:

'end life when I end loyalty' (II, ii, 69). Utterer of one of the play's most famous lines ('The course of true love never did run smooth', I, i, 134), he displays noble boldness in the ensuing comic chaos, especially as he bravely chases Puck imitating Demetrius ('I followed fast, but faster he did fly', III, ii, 416). But these conventionally aristocratic qualities may seem in retrospect somewhat snobbish when he mocks the performance of *Pyramus and Thisbe*. The decidedly non-frightening lion is, for example, 'a very fox for his valour' (V, i, 238).

Demetrius (I, i; II, i; II, ii; III, ii; IV, i; V, i)

Lysander early on calls Demetrius 'spotted and inconstant' (I, i, 110). Arguably the love drug accentuates, even punishes, a fickleness that is there all along. According to Lysander, who of course has his own agenda, Demetrius had 'made love to' (flirted with) Helena but, having 'won her soul', spurned her as soon as Egeus agreed to marry Hermia to him (I, i, 107–8). We may ask, therefore, what Helena sees in Demetrius. But we may also suggest, somewhat troublingly, that Helena's way of loving seems tied up with melancholy and suffering. Cruelty does little to put her off but she is suspicious of adoration. Demetrius is aggressive with Helena ('I am sick when I do look on thee', II, i, 212) and promises to 'slay' Lysander (II, i, 190). In the final act, however, he joins Lysander in joyously, even cruelly, laughing at *Pyramus and Thisbe*: the bizarrely talking wall is for him 'the wittiest partition that I ever heard discourse' (V, i, 165–6).

Titania (II, i; II, ii; III, i; IV, i)

Titania is daughter of Titan, whose story, like that of Pyramus and Thisbe, comes from Ovid's *Metamorphoses*. The relationship is apt: Titan is linked to Diana, the goddess of the moon (*Metamorphoses* 3.173), and Circe, whose drink causes the drinker to change shape (*Metamorphoses* 14.382). The parallel motif of jealousy in fairy and Athenian realms is introduced when Titania complains of Oberon's love for 'amorous Phillida' and 'the bouncing Amazon' Hippolyta (II, i, 70). She refuses to give up the little 'changeling' to Oberon even though their 'brawls' cause 'contagious fogs', make 'the green corn' rot and 'hoary-headed frosts / Fall in the fresh lap of the crimson rose' (II, i, 87, 90, 108).

Oberon (II, i; II, ii; III, ii; IV, i)

Oberon, the King of the Fairies, plans to 'drop the liquor' of the 'love in idleness' in Titania's eyes almost immediately after their quarrel and his unsuccessful attempt to convince her to give up the child (II, i, 178, 168). His instant decision to love-drug Demetrius after his stubborn refusal to accept Helena's love is thus, arguably, a kind of deflected anger towards Titania (II, i, 257–64), an attempt to gain at least some measure of control over the situation. But his impish companion Robin Goodfellow, Puck, comically undermines any such control.

Robin Goodfellow ('Puck') (II, i; II, ii; III, i; III, ii; IV, i; Epilogue)

'Puck' echoes the 'Pouke', a sprite of old wives' tale or fairy-tale, mentioned in line 341 of Spenser's wedding celebration poem *Epithalamion: 'Ne* [Nor] *let the pouke, nor other evill sprights* [...] *Fray us with things that be not'*. 'Puck's' different names hint more generally at the more pervasive spirit of metamorphosis that he brings to the enchanted forest. He is the most actively mischievous of the fairy realm, standing out amongst the often kind and benevolent servants of Titania. His first dialogue reveals that he is a kind of farmyard 'gremlin' who 'frights the maidens of the villag'ry', stops milk turning into butter and makes beer 'bear no barm' or frothy head, drink spill, and even 'wisest aunt' 'topple' over (II, i, 35–57). In the play itself he demonstrates this mischievous desire in contexts of love. Puck is a kind of Shakespearean equivalent of Cupid, more wilful than the 'blind Cupid' of legend, who 'translates' (i.e. transforms) Bottom in order to make an absurd love object for the drugged Titania (III, i, 106–13), and who turns invisible, imitating others' voices to cause confusion amongst the Athenian lovers ('up and down, up and down,/I will lead them up and down', III, ii, 396–447). Puck is very closely associated with Oberon throughout, speaking in his own voice either to him or to himself except for a brief conversation with Titania's fairy (II, i, 1–57), and the Epilogue.

Bottom (I, ii; III, i; IV, I; IV, ii; V, i)

Bottom, like Falstaff (see Chapter 11), is one of Shakespeare's gloriously unapologetic egocentrists. When first we meet him, during the tradesmen's first rehearsal, he instantly takes command, boasting of this rhetorical prowess ('I will move storms', I, ii, 22–3) and almost transforming the play into a one-man show: 'Let me play Thisbe too' (I, i, 45); 'Let me play the lion too' (I, i, 63). He even wants a prologue that mentions his name (III, i, 19–20), under the pretext that revealing the names of the actors will prevent the spectators from being scared by the gory events (and the lion). By Act III, scene i he has effectively, and amusingly, taken over from Quince the direction of the play. Directors and actors have to decide whether Bottom is distressed or not by his transformation into an ass, but in Act IV, scene i he is clearly friendly and respectful towards the fairies, seemingly unbothered by his 'translation' and calling for 'sweet hay' (IV, i, 32–3). His triumphant return to his fellow amateur dramatists (IV, ii, 23–40) is one of the play's most cheering moments. His natural irrepressibility comes through especially in the final act when, as he performs, he talks back to the Duke himself, good-naturedly concerned by Theseus's ironic incomprehension. 'No, in truth, sir [...] [Thisbe] is to enter now, and I am to spy her through the wall. You shall see, it will fall pat [exactly] as I told you' (V, i, 182–5).

Quince (I, ii; III, i; IV, ii; V, i)

Quince, the nominal director of *Pyramus and Thisbe,* is sometimes played as a skittish, nervous control freak. Worried that a bad performance would be 'enough to hang us all' (I, ii, 68), he is frequently, comically exasperated by Bottom's continued attempts to interrupt. After sternly affirming 'You can play no part but Pyramus' (I, ii, 76), however, he then changes his tone straight away, overselling Bottom's part as if the *prima donna* weaver has flown into a huff. 'Pyramus is a sweet-faced man; a proper man as one shall see in a summer's day; a most lovely, gentlemanlike man' (I, ii, 76–8). Trying to keep his cast under control, he sometimes takes refuge in dry wit, alluding, for example, to syphilis when he retorts to Bottom about wigs and false beards: 'some of your French crowns have no hair at all', I, ii, 87).

Snug (I, ii; III, i; IV, ii; V, i)

'Snug the joiner' (I, ii, 56) has few lines, especially because he plays the lion, which is 'nothing but roaring' (I, ii, 61–2). Snug is 'slow of study' (I, ii, 60) but comments incisively on the relationship between theatre and social elevation. The 'rude mechanicals' can be 'made men' with a royal income for the rest of their lives, if their play pleases the king (IV, ii, 17). Flute agrees, repeatedly stressing that Bottom in the star role would earn 'sixpence a day during his life', the average daily wage for tradesmen (IV, ii, 18–22).

Flute (I, ii; III, i; IV, ii; V, i)

'Francis Flute, the bellows-mender' (I, ii, 36) is conventionally the youngest of the tradesman-actors. He has 'a beard coming' (I, ii, 42) and plays *Pyramus and Thisbe*'s only female role. In performance Flute sometimes plays Thisbe's final death scene (V, i, 318–41) with real tragic force despite the intentional badness of the verse, demonstrating a genuine talent he never knew he had.

Theseus (I, i; IV, i; V, i)

Theseus is one of the great figures of Greek myth. His story, which includes the slaying of the Minotaur and the rescue of Ariadne, is told at length in book eight of Ovid's *Metamorphoses*. Shakespeare, however, gives him a relatively minor role. Actors have to decide how apologetic, or pompous, Theseus is when he tells Hippolyta 'I wooed thee with my sword [...] But I will wed thee in another key' (I, i, 16–18), when he tells a recalcitrant Hermia that 'To you your father should be as a god' (I, i, 47) or when, conversely, and much later, he 'overbear[s]' Egeus's 'will' (IV, i, 178). After hearing from the youths about the magical episodes of the forest, Theseus becomes in a famous speech a doubting voice of 'reason', telling Hippolyta:

> [...] I never may believe
> These antique fables, nor these fairy toys.
> Lovers and madmen have such seething brains,
> Such shaping fantasies, that apprehend
> More than cool reason ever comprehends.
> The lunatic, the lover, and the poet

Are of imagination all compact.
One sees more devils than vast hell can hold:
That is the madman. The lover, all as frantic,
Sees Helen's beauty in a brow of Egypt.
The poet's eye, in a fine frenzy rolling,
Doth glance from heaven to earth, from earth to heaven,
And as imagination bodies forth
The forms of things unknown, the poet's pen
Turns them to shapes, and gives to airy nothing
A local habitation and a name.
Such tricks hath strong imagination
That if it would but apprehend some joy
It comprehends some bringer of that joy;
Or in the night, imagining some fear,
How easy is a bush supposed a bear!
(V, i, 2–22)

Theseus's breakdown of 'imagination' into that of the 'madman', 'love' and 'poet' recalls Plato's ancient idea, recounted by Socrates in the *Phaedrus*, that there are four furies [*mania*]: prophecy, mystic rites, poetic inspiration and love (244a–245c). But Socrates, unlike Theseus, believes these forms of madness offer a portal into truths which are much truer than the mere material 'reality' we sense every day. While hotly debated by critics, Theseus's scoffing disbelief of 'imagination' surely seems ironic: a mythological hero is dismissing 'antique fables' and, more importantly, what we the audience have witnessed and imaginatively invested in. This dreamiest of plays seems energetically and everywhere to challenge Theseus's 'cool reason', even as it gives it a voice. Hippolyta is much more sympathetic to the lovers' adventure: 'the story of the night told over [...] More witnesseth than fancy's images' (V, i, 23–5).

Hippolyta (I, i; IV, i; V, i)

Hippolyta is in myth an Amazon, a fearsome warrior woman, but in this play she has few lines. Theseus 'wooed [her] with [his] sword' (I, i, 16). She may be meek or grudging in defeat. She is present but silent when Hermia and Egeus argue over Hermia's 'virgin patent' (I, i, 80). Her reactions to a man deciding a woman's fate could indicate much about her character, especially if (as often occurs) her role is doubled with Titania. She eventually joins the wider spirit of comedic reconciliation, though, evidently enjoying *Pyramus and Thisbe*, laughingly dismissing it as 'the silliest stuff that ever I heard' (V, i, 209). After Bottom's dying speech she even confesses: 'Beshrew my heart, but I pity the man' (V, i, 284).

Play structure

The play's timeframe is set out near the beginning. Theseus informs Hippolyta their wedding will take place in four days. And these four days elapse in a languid, appropriately dreamy style. The stage is only rarely completely cleared. The scenes thus smoothly overlap: a powerful contrast with, say, the rapid changes of scene in *Anthony and Cleopatra*. *A Midsummer Night's Dream* is 'ensemble-minded'. The most important scenes all portray group interaction. The Athenians form a kind of 'erotic quadrilateral', accentuated by the ladies' similar-sounding names, the young men's similarly headstrong characters, and the two men turning comically from Hermia to Helena. The rare soliloquies, such as Helena's (I, i, 226–51), or Hermia's (II, ii, 151–62), express a desire *not* to be alone. The play introduces its three main 'ensembles', the lovers, the artisans and the fairies, in each of the first three scenes, suggesting parallels between them. But they are kept largely separate. Titania never meets the Athenian lovers, for example. The rare encounters between them, like Puck's with the Athenians, or Bottom's with Titania, are thus emphasised all the more.

The staging implies analogies and symmetries within and between the play's three main groups. For example, Titania sleeps as Hermia and Lysander sleep (II, ii, 30, 71). They are ignorant of each other's situations but their shared staging predicts their common enthralment to the love drug. Likewise the lovers and Bottom both awake, near the end of the fourth act, in similar states of confused rapture after their 'dreams'. Connections between Athens and the fairy world are often strengthened, as frequently happens in performance, when Theseus is doubled with Oberon and Hippolyta with Titania. The question of representation, and how it relates to what is being represented, is one of the play's major preoccupations. It after all closes with a play-within-a-play. Puck's direct address to the audience similarly stretches the conventional boundaries of comedy, which ordinarily ends once lovers are happily reconciled.

Language

A Midsummer Night's Dream displays characteristic Shakespearean fascination with and richness of language. Perhaps the play's predominant linguistic feature is the repeated and variously metaphorical invocation of the moon. We are after all dealing with a midsummer *night's* dream. Near the beginning the moon is associated with sterility. This 'pale companion' (I, i, 15) is 'cold' and 'fruitless' (I, i, 73), 'sealing day' between Theseus and Hippolyta (I, i, 84). But by moments the personified moon seems more sympathetic to love. Titania fears that the (feminised) moon, 'lamenting some enforcèd chastity' has angrily changed all the seasons (III, ii, 190). And, like the kindly aunt to whom Lysander and Hermia seek to flee (I, i, 157), the moon is compared to a 'dowager', a widow who has inherited property from her late husband (I, i, 5): the aunt-moon-dowager seems to protect lost young lovers. More concretely, the 'chaste beams of the wat'ry moon' change the direction of Cupid's fiery arrow so that its erotic force is absorbed into the flower Oberon calls 'love in idleness' (II, i, 161–8). This quasi-magnetic power recalls Helena's use of 'lode-stars' and 'adamant' (II, i, 195) to describe her love, as well as the idea the moon somehow attracts people to their destiny. A fairy boasts to be 'swifter than the moonë's sphere', as if struggling against its predictable, predestined cycle (II, i, 7). But the panicking artisans rely on this cycle, consulting an almanac to predict the future: 'find out moonshine' (III, i, 49). The moon must shine on the night of their performance because, just like Titania and Oberon (II, i, 60), 'Pyramus and Thisbe meet by moonlight' (III, i, 45).

The themes of loving togetherness and overarching order, intimated by the metaphorical use of the moon and reflected by the play's overall narrative shape, are replicated phonetically via extensive and variedly patterned use of rhyme. Some of the play's most famous passages, like Oberon's luscious description of Titania's fairy bed (II, i, 248–67) and the incantatory dropping of the 'love in idleness' in various victims' eyes (e.g. II, ii, 33–40), are entirely in (tetrametric) rhyme. As with the Witches in *Macbeth*, rhythm and rhyme contribute to the spell. But, unlike *Macbeth*, magic meets via rhyme with love. Lost in the forest, Hermia and Lysander talk in rhyme as if lovingly to ward off their fear (II, ii, 33–40), while Titania's love for Bottom is signalled through rhyming couplets (III, i, 143–54), triplets (III, i, 156–8), even quintuplets (III, i, 160–5). Rhyme is also continually used as the love-drugged Lysander falls in love with Helena, and Helena complains of mockery (II, ii, 94–162).

Rhyme can thus betoken frustrated as well as reciprocated love, giving ordinarily discordant conversations a melodic and rhythmical harmony that hints at the enchanted setting and magical events. Act III, scene ii, the longest and most complicated scene in the play, moves between rhymed and blank verse. These transitions are themselves meaningful. Rhyme markedly stops at the moment Helena shifts from melancholy to anger ('Injurious Hermia!', III, ii, 195) and does not return until just before the four lovers leave the stage and Puck and Oberon decide to make amends (III, ii, 340–4). Lysander and Demetrius's angry exchange with Puck (impersonating their voices as situation dictates) is once more in rhyme, reminding us of Puck's tricksiness, while suggesting reassuringly that it is only a matter of time before Puck and Oberon restore harmony (III, ii, 401–41). The association of rhyme with harmony is strengthened through the fourth act. Helena's sestet before she sleeps is a cross-rhymed quatrain and concluding couplet, like the final six lines of a Shakespearean sonnet (III, ii, 442–7), and Puck's final spell over the lovers is a very simple mixture of two-beat and four-beat lines, like a slowing heartbeat, bringing everything to rest: 'all shall be well' (III, ii, 448–64). Oberon's spell releasing Titania from her earlier spell is in rhyme (IV, i, 70–3), as is the dialogue that signals their reconciliation (IV, i, 74–101). Puck's reassuring Epilogue to the audience is in the rhyming tetrameter that has throughout the play increasingly signified spells, magic and enchantment. This works to link further the onstage protagonists' magical experiences with the audience's own feelings of enjoyment.

The tradesmen use rhyme in a more forthrightly comical way, as when Flute/Thisbe rhymes 'cowslip cheeks' with the decidedly non-tragic simile 'His eyes were green as leeks' (V, i, 326–9). Their persistent misuses of other poetic techniques similarly, humorously, bring together incongruous ideas. Malapropisms include 'odious' for 'odours' (III, i, 77–8). Strange antitheses, mocked by the aristocrats, include *Lamentable comedy* (Shakespeare's own *Lamentable Tragedy of Romeo and*

Juliet was written at about the same time) and 'sweet moon, I thank thee for thy sunny beams' (V, i, 266). Over-repetition ('O night, O night, alack alack alack', V, i, 170) and excessive alliteration are also frequent, especially in Bottom/Pyramus's dying speech: 'dreadful dole', 'O dainty duck, O dear!', 'Quail, crush, conclude and quell' (V, i, 272, 275, 281).

The interest in words' sonorous qualities, harmonies or absurd extremities extends readily to the play's extensive use of songs and music. Bottom's songs, sung to ward off invaders and his own fear, make Titania's ear magically 'enamoured' (III, i, 131), while the fairies' 'Lulla, lulla lullaby' form together a protective, but fragile, barrier over the sleeping Titania (II, ii, 15). In this play 'translation', familiar to us from more linguistic contexts, also means magical transformation: 'Bottom, thou art translated' (III, i, 113). The night's and the moon's transformative capacities are ultimately inseparable from those of language and theatre. Theseus (V, i, 210) and Puck (Epilogue/V, i, 414) call actors 'shadows', bringing stagecraft, spirits, shades, and the night into delicious contact together.

Themes

Nature and enchantment

A central idea in *A Midsummer Night's Dream* is that the natural world and its cyclical seasonal rhythms of fertility are enchanted. The Fairy's opening speech to Puck (II, i, 7), by noting they 'creep into acorn cups' (II, i, 31), implies there is a 'fairy-soul' in all created trees and flowers. Titania reinforces this idea when she calls to the fairies to protect the realm from blight, bats and owls (II, ii, 1–9) and says the winds, fogs and rains are vengefully angry at her discord with Oberon (II, i, 87). Oberon's mini-history of the love-drug 'love in idleness' is set within a densely, richly mythologised natural landscape: the drug is 'purple with love's wound' (II, i, 167). This alludes to the myth of the anemone flower in Venus and Adonis, a myth, like that of Pyramus and Thisbe, recounted in Ovid's *Metamorphoses* and the basis of Shakespeare's 1592 mythological poem of the same name. The anemone thus bridges myth, nature and sexuality, metamorphosing metamorphosis itself. Through it, the mythological metamorphosis, from Adonis's blood to the anemone, is itself transformed, into the Athenian lovers' metamorphosis from cold-heartedness to panting desire. Bottom's transformation into an ass likewise arguably echoes older traditions: in ancient fertility rituals the donkey was a phallic symbol. In some performances Bottom-as-ass simulates sex with Titania.

Violence and sexuality

The midsummer element of the play likewise keys into festive traditions of May-rites, which are associated with sex. Hermia's dream evokes the phallic and biblical symbolism of the serpent. Theseus's marriage to a woman he once conquered similarly suggests a certain continuum between sexuality and violence: Hippolyta is often silent, allowing an actor the possibility of building a certain simmering resentment into the role. Helena's wretched self-hatred similarly hints that sexual desire and violence are intertwined. She condemns herself as Demetrius's mere 'spaniel' ('The more you beat me I will fawn on you', II, i, 204–5), and serves as scapegoat for Hermia's jealous rage (III, ii, 282–4), even though Lysander would more fairly be its recipient.

Theatre, transformation and dream

Themes of power and powerlessness mark also, of course, class-based distinctions between the Athenian nobles and the tradesmen, for whom Puck's contemptuous epithet 'rude mechanicals' (III, ii, 9) has been perhaps been a little too readily adopted by a predominantly middle- or upper-middle-class literary-critical community. The workmen may bumble in their language but they are skilled artisans, keen for social advancement. The theatre thus offers possibilities for societal as well as psychological transformation. Snug and Flute dream of earning their 'sixpence a day' for achieving royal favour for their performance (IV, ii, 18–22). And these transformative possibilities are invested with fairy-like magic: Bottom changes into Pyramus soon after having been changed into an ass. Perhaps via this constant appeal to the power of theatre to transform, A Midsummer Night's Dream makes to its audience an implicit, but progressively powerful plea to undergo a comparable journey towards a new receptiveness, away from a Theseus-like scepticism. This culminates in Puck's Epilogue, which begs the audience to view in retrospect the play they have just seen as 'no more yielding than a dream' (V, i, 419), and the fairies' final arrival, which only the audience sees because Theseus and the other Athenians have now left the stage forever (V, i, 362–429). In terms of pure stage time and stage presence, magic has 'outlived' the voice of reason, in a final metatheatrical *coup de théâtre*.

Texts and contexts

The text of A Midsummer Night's Dream 'does not leave the editor tearing out his/her hair in anguish' (ed. Holland 1994: 119). There are, however, some variations between the Quarto of 1595, the play's first printing, and the version printed in the 1623 Folio, especially in the final act, where in the Folio a character called 'Philostrate' announces Pyramus and Thisbe to the assembled, celebrating Athenian nobles. Jonathan Bate (2016) has called A Midsummer Night's Dream Shakespeare's 'most Ovidian play but also his most Shakespearean'. Ovid's Metamorphoses, a compilation of mythological tales of transformation, powerfully influences Shakespeare throughout his career, but especially during the 1590s. Oberon's suggestion that Titania guides Theseus through his military and amorous adventures, almost in love with him, inventively fuses Ovidian myth with English folktale, faery tradition (II, i, 74–80). It therefore arguably echoes Arthur Golding's incorporation of fairies into his 'Englished' version of the *Metamorphoses*. Bottom's transformation into an ass likewise creatively assimilates originally distinct traditions, parodying antique myths of the Minotaur and foolishly avaricious King Midas's ass's ears, while alluding also to the animal masks of medieval theatre, and tapping into the Erasmian tradition of the paradoxical 'mock encomium' as exemplified by the 'Praise of Folly'. Erasmus's personified, feminised Folly echoes, like Bottom (IV, i, 207–10), the famous passage from Paul's First Letter to the Corinthians 2: 9: 'Eye hath not seen, nor ear heard, neither have entered into the heart of man, the things which God hath prepared for them that love him.' Faith, like folly, differs from reason. Perhaps both are superior to it.

The play in performance

A Midsummer Night's Dream has been adapted for ballet (George Balanchine 1962; Frederick Ashton 1964), opera (Benjamin Britten 1960) and film (Max Reinhardt 1935; Michael Hoffman 1999). Felix Mendelssohn's 1842 musical score is still famously used at weddings to signal the bride's arrival. *The World Shakespeare Bibliography* states that *Dream* is now Shakespeare's most often performed play, with 2,058 professional productions between 1959 and 2015. The most influential version, however, probably remains Peter Brook's (RSC 1970), which featured abstractly bare staging, druid-like brightly coloured robes and trapezes to show fairy flight. Bill Alexander (1986) doubled Titania's and Hippolyta's roles but not Theseus's and Oberon's, implying the play's underlying ethos was somehow female. Alexandru Darie's production (Comedy Theatre of Bucharest 1991) innovatively featured a sexually rapacious Hermia, only just able to keep her clothes on. Michael Boyd (RSC 1999) stressed the play's kinship with fertility rites, giving Titania and the fairies sensual ritual dances. Greg Doran (RSC 2005, 2008) placed a huge moon over the set, while the 'changeling' boy was a life-size puppet. Tim Supple (RSC 2006) set the play in India, performing the text in six Indian languages as well as English. Irina Brook, Peter's daughter, adapted the script: the six 'mechanicals' (stage technicians) had to play all the roles because the other actors had been held up by an airport strike (Bouffes du Nord, Paris 2008).

Critical reception

Christopher Thurman (2015) elaborates on the Platonic heritage of Theseus's speech. Adam Rzepka (2015) looks at the historical influences, such as Aristotle's *De Anima*, of Theseus's terms 'imagination', 'apprehension' (i.e. sense impression) and 'comprehension' (i.e. computing that sense data to get a sense of the world). Lee Oser (2014) explores 'imagination' again in Aristotelian terms but also brings in more theological contexts, like the Jesuit Ignatius Loyola's *Spiritual Exercises*. Jesse M. Lander (2012) examines how the play stretches the limits of belief and disbelief, and Wendy Wall argues that 'Fairylore becomes a channel through which Shakespearian

drama grapples with [...] class-specific practices [and] debates about English community in the late sixteenth and early seventeenth centuries' (Wall 2001: 68). Peter
Herman (2014) takes this more avowedly politicised direction further, seeing the
play as an innovatively comic meditation on tyranny. Jonathan Bate traces in the
play 'different kinds of theatrical imitation' of Ovid (Bate 1993: 132), based on Renaissance classroom exercises like *translatio* and *imitatio*. In a valuable collection of
essays on Shakespeare's Ovidian influence in general, Niall Rudd (2000) compares
Shakespearean and Ovidian treatments of *Pyramus and Thisbe*. A. B. Taylor (2004)
offers a close comparative reading of the play and its Ovidian subtexts in terms of
'sexual marginality'. And Hugh Grady's subtle, sophisticated account argues that the
play's self-conscious theatricality, engagingly fragmented and uneven ('some parts of
it are more aesthetic than others'), yields conceptions of beauty that are more alive,
perhaps more ideologically tolerant, than those which value merely harmoniously
unified form (Grady 2008: 281).

Discussion questions

* Does reading *A Midsummer Night's Dream* in political terms weaken its
   ability to delight?

* Can we analyse aesthetic pleasure, or does such pleasure disappear at the
   moment of analysis?

Bibliography and further reading

Editions

Ovid (2002), *Ovid's Metamorphoses*, trans. Arthur Golding, ed. M. Forey, London/New
   York: Penguin.
Shakespeare, W. (1994), *A Midsummer Night's Dream*, ed. P. Holland, Oxford: Oxford
   University Press.

Critical response

Bate, J. (1993), *Shakespeare and Ovid*, Oxford: Oxford University Press.
Bate, J. (2016), 'Shakespeare: Who Put those Thoughts in His Head?', *The Guardian*,
   20 April, <https://www.theguardian.com/culture/2016/apr/20/shakespeare-thinking-
   philosophy-jonanthan-bate> (last accessed 30 June 2016).
Grady, H. (2008), 'Shakespeare and Impure Aesthetics: The Case of *A Midsummer
   Night's Dream*', *Shakespeare Quarterly*, 59:3, 274–302.
Herman, P. (2014), 'Equity and the Problem of Theseus in *A Midsummer Night's Dream*:
   Or, the Ancient Constitution in Ancient Athens', *Journal for Early Modern Cultural
   Studies*, 14:1, 4–31.

Lander, J. (2012), 'Thinking with Fairies: *A Midsummer Night's Dream* and the Problem of Belief', *Shakespeare Survey*, 65, 42–57.

Oser, L. (2014), 'Imagination, Judgement, and Belief in *A Midsummer Night's Dream*', *Literary Imagination*, 16:1, 39–55.

Plato (1997), 'Phaedrus', trans. Alexander Nehamas and Paul Woodruff, in *Complete Works*, ed. J. M. Cooper and D. S. Hutchinson, Indianapolis: Hackett Publishing, pp. 506–56.

Rudd, N. (2000), 'Pyramus and Thisbe in Shakespeare and Ovid', in A. B. Taylor (ed.), *Shakespeare's Ovid: The* Metamorphoses *in the Plays and Poems*, Cambridge: Cambridge University Press, pp. 113–25.

Rzepka, A. (2015), '"How easy is a bush supposed a bear?": Differentiating Imaginative Production in *A Midsummer Night's Dream*', *Shakespeare Quarterly*, 66:3, 308–28.

Taylor, A. B. (2004), 'Ovid's Myths and the Unsmooth Course of Love in *A Midsummer Night's Dream*', in C. Martindale and A. B. Taylor (eds), *Shakespeare and the Classics*, Cambridge: Cambridge University Press, pp. 49–65.

Thurman, C. (2015), 'Fine Frenzies: Theseus, Shakespeare and the Politics of Their Poets', *Shakespeare*, 11:2, 115–34.

Wall, W. (2001), 'Why Does Puck Sweep?: Fairylore, *Merry Wives*, and Social Struggle', *Shakespeare Quarterly*, 52:1, 67–106.

8 *The Merchant of Venice*

Composition and first performance 1596–7, first printed 1600

Act, scene and line references are to the 2010 Arden Third Series edition, edited by John Drakakis.

Plot summary

Bassanio seeks to marry Portia, a lady from 'Belmont' (maybe a town in Southern Italy, Belmonte Calabro, but no such association is made in the text). He asks his friend, Antonio, a Merchant of Venice, for the money he requires for the voyage (and dowry). Antonio, however, lacks ready cash because he has spent it all on goods currently at sea (I, i, 176–9). He therefore approaches a Jew, Shylock, to lend him 'three thousand ducats' (I, iii, 1). Shylock agrees, on the condition that if the money is not paid back, a pound of Antonio's flesh is to be 'cut off and taken / In what part of your body pleaseth me' (I, iii, 146–8). Two plot strands intertwine with this. In one, Shylock's daughter Jessica flees the family home to marry Antonio's friend Lorenzo and become thus a Christian (II, iii; II, vi; II, viii). In the other, Portia's father has set up a riddle to test his daughter's suitors. There are three caskets – one of gold, one of silver, one of lead – and the suitor who chooses the casket that contains Portia's picture can marry her. The challenge carries a hard condition: 'swear [...] if you choose wrong / Never to speak to lady afterward / In way of marriage' (II, i, 40–2). The Prince of Morocco chooses gold and fails (II, vii). The Prince of Aragon chooses silver and fails (II, ix). Bassanio chooses lead and succeeds (III, ii). Portia rewards him with a ring (III, ii, 171). Bassanio's friend Graziano also 'got a promise' from Portia's gentlewoman Nerissa 'to have her love' (III, ii, 206–8). But the couples' joy is short-lived. Bassanio receives word that Antonio's ships have hit 'merchant-marring rocks': they and his fortune have sunk (III, ii, 249–69). Antonio therefore cannot raise the money to pay back the bond in time, and Shylock is plying 'the Duke at morning and at night' for it to be paid back in flesh (III, ii, 313–19). A trial is to be held. Unbeknownst to their husbands, Portia and Nerissa plot to help Antonio and his friends by disguising themselves, 'accoutred like young men' (III, iv, 60–78). During the trial scene (IV, i) – one of the tensest in all Shakespeare – it looks like Antonio will be killed onstage. Shylock raises the sharpened knife to Antonio's chest, ready to cut 'nearest the merchant's heart' (IV, i, 229). But Portia, disguised as the lawyer

'Doctor Balthazar' dramatically interrupts: 'Tarry a little, there is something else' (IV, i, 301). The law, 'Balthazar' explains, forbids Shylock from shedding 'one drop of Christian blood' (IV, i, 306). Shylock is thus in an impossible position. He cannot cut Antonio's flesh away without shedding blood, but he cannot accept the money offered in lieu of the flesh, either: he has just repeatedly 'refused it in the open court' (IV, i, 334). To make matters worse for Shylock, Portia reminds him that if any 'alien' (IV, i, 345) attempts to kill a Venetian citizen, the wronged party receives half the goods, the state the other, and the 'alien's' life remains 'in the mercy / Of the Duke only' (IV, i, 348–52). Antonio waives his right to receive half Shylock's goods, requesting that they should pass to Lorenzo and Jessica on Shylock's death (IV, i, 380–1). But he does compel Shylock to 'presently become a Christian' (IV, i, 383). The trial concludes. A relieved Bassanio thanks 'Doctor Balthazar' and offers a reward. 'He' responds 'I'll take this ring from you' (IV, i, 423). Bassanio is embarrassed by losing his wife's gift but has no choice. Graziano, no less embarrassed, gives away his wedding ring to Nerissa, disguised as Portia's clerk (IV, ii, 13). When they hear their rings have been given away, Portia and Nerissa scold their husbands for infidelity (V, i, 147–208). They then reveal possession of the rings but do not let their husbands off the hook, teasingly confessing they earned them back from the Doctor and his assistant by having sex with them (V, i, 259, 262). The teasing over, they reveal to their amazed husbands that it was in fact they, in disguise, who saved Antonio (V, i, 269–70).

Characters

Shylock ('Jew') (I, iii; II, v; III, i; III, iii; IV, i)

The play's title refers of course to Antonio but Shylock is the play's towering figure. That said, Shylock appears in surprisingly few scenes. The Christians refer only rarely to Shylock by name, preferring the dismissive epithet 'Jew' (the word also used, incidentally, for Shylock's speech prefixes in early printed editions of the play). His first scene accents with grim curtness the conflict between Jews and Christians. His first aside signals an absolute refusal to share anything with Christians except the strictest of business dealings (I, iii, 31–6). The second ('How like a fawning publican [tax-collector] he looks', I, iii, 37–48) grows in aggression and disdain. He clearly 'hate[s]' Christians for lending 'out money gratis [interest-free]', thus bringing down the overall rate of the market (I, iii, 40). His early conversations with Antonio are wary, barbed. We know Antonio has 'spit' in the past at him (I, iii, 108). This lends a bitter edge to their discussion of the biblical origins of usury, or lending money for interest (I, iii, 65–92). Shylock seems to joy in the power that his loan gives him over his Christian enemy, using terms that denote apparently specifically Christian virtues like 'patience' and 'suffrance' (I, iii, 105–6). The play works to elicit some sympathy for Shylock, however, distinguishing him from more caricatured Jewish vice figures like Barabas in Marlowe's The Jew of Malta. In Act II, scene v, for example, when he loses Jessica, his avarice seems down to the fact that money is now all he has. Jews could not after all legally hold land. He associates Jessica with his wealth closely and repeatedly ('my daughter my ducats', II, viii, 12–24). The Jessica–Lorenzo subplot thus suggests Shylock insists so murderously for Antonio's pound of flesh (III, iii, 4–17) as payback for his own, his daughter. This context explains the furious literalism of perhaps Shylock's most famous speech, 'Hath not a Jew eyes' (III, i, 53–66), which echoes Talion law as expressed, say, in Deuteronomy 19: 21 ('eye for eye, tooth for tooth') and extends it to 'hands, organs, dimensions, senses, affec-tions, passions' (III, i, 47). Often read as a plea for tolerance between religions, the impatient rhythms seem rather to urge vengeance ('shall we not revenge?', III, i, 60, 62), and competitively, too: 'I will better the instruction' (III, i, 65–6). For Shylock, Antonio's mutilation will weaken symbolically Christian arrogation to moral superiority. This engagement with Christian morals is especially acute in the trial scene, the play's dramatic climax. The Duke's call to Shylock to be 'gentle' (IV, i, 33), anticipating Portia's famous speech about 'the quality of mercy', is undercut by the suspicion that if Shylock mercifully relinquished his grip over Antonio, the Christians would instantly destroy him.

Antonio (I, i; I, iii; III, iii; IV, i; V, i)

The eponymous Merchant of Venice starts the play with glum monosyllables. He knows not why he is so sad. His colleagues suggest he is worried about his good-bearing ships, out at sea (I, i, 7–39), or even in love (I, i, 45), but Antonio rejects both ideas. A Marxian line of argument suggests that Antonio is semi-consciously – and only semi-consciously – aware of the difficulty of reconciling his mercantile activity with the Christian ethos on which his self-esteem/happiness is primordially founded. Another hypothesis, often accentuated in performance, is that he loves Bassanio. He doth protest too much, perhaps, at suggestions of love ('fie fie', I, i, 46) and offers instantly to help Bassanio financially, even though he himself has no ready cash and Bassanio admits 'that which I owe you is lost' (I, i, 147). Tellingly, just as Shylock is about to strike, Antonio begs Bassanio to tell his wife about him: 'bid her be judge/Whether Bassanio had not once a love' (IV, i, 272–3). Antonio's ongoing, bitter conflict with Shylock is of course a key strand: 'I am as like […] to spit on thee again', he snarls (I, iii, 125–6). But in the fifth act, once Shylock's threat to him has been vanquished, Antonio is more peripheral: the story centres more on the three young couples, leaving him to apologise 'I am th'unhappy subject of these quarrels' (V, i, 229).

Portia (I, ii; II, i; II, vii; II, ix; III, ii; III, iv; IV, i; V, i)

Like Antonio in Venice, Portia in Belmont is initially melancholic: 'my little body is aweary of this great world' (I, ii, 1–2). She protests to Nerissa that she is not to marry whom she chooses and uses this as a pretext to attack her various suitors. The Neapolitan prince, County Palatine, M. Le Bon, the Englishman, the German and the Scot all seem to play up to certain commonly received stereotypes, fore-shadowing key themes of identity, community and prejudice. In contrast to these nincompoops she indicates an inclination for Bassanio, agreeing with Nerissa that he is 'worthy of thy praise' (I, ii, 114–15). This becomes progressively more explicit as Morocco and Arragon fail and Bassanio is the final suitor left. Before Bassanio chooses his casket she implies strongly that she wants him to win. 'One half of me is yours' (III, ii, 16–19). The song that plays while Bassanio chooses helps him: its first stanza's rhyme sound 'ed' (bred/head/nourishèd) of course also rhymes with lead (III, ii, 63–5). But Portia's aside as Bassanio chooses correctly, 'I feel *too much* thy blessing' (III, ii, 108–13, emphasis added), foretells the problems to come. On hearing Bassanio's bad news about the capsizing of Antonio's ships, the decision for her and Nerissa to dress as men is almost instantaneous, accompanied by a description of the masculine universe, which is affectionate but astutely observant about their 'lies' and 'frays' (III, iv, 68–9). When Portia re-enters during the trial scene as Balthazar (taking the name of her own messenger, III, iv, 45), she pointedly knows Shylock's name but does not use it, referring to him only as 'Jew' (IV, i, 178, 93). This echoes, uneasily, her earlier stereotyping of her hapless failed suitors, perhaps therefore casting a doubtful light on her most famous speech 'The quality of mercy is not strained' (IV, i, 180–201). Note too that Portia/Balthazar refuses to let Shylock off the hook even once Antonio's life is safe, urging state repossession of his goods (IV, i, 342–59). Portia again orchestrates proceedings in Act V. The ring episode continues, in a much more relaxed and comedic mode, themes of revenge, forgiveness and the exchange of goods with flesh, as when the wives pretend to have given their bodies to the lawmen to win back their husbands' wedding rings.

Bassanio (I, i; I, iii; II, ii; III, ii; IV, i; V, i)

Some critics accuse Bassanio of being a 'self-aggrandising opportunist' (ed. Halio 1993: 32). Note how in his first major speech he stresses to Antonio Portia's money (she is 'richly left'), before her 'fair' beauty or 'wondrous virtues' (I, i, 161–3). It is also he, not Antonio, who first approaches Shylock for the loan: Antonio only enters later (I, i, 35). Granted, when Shylock sets out the condition about the pound of flesh Bassanio baulks: 'I'll rather dwell in my necessity' (I, iii, 151), but in perfor-mance this is often mere lip-service. He has by his own admission carelessly lost Antonio money in the past (I, i, 146–7), and is still in debt ('worse than nothing', III, ii, 258). His and his wife's future happiness may therefore be vulnerable, as perfor-mances of the closing scenes occasionally imply.

Jessica (II, iii; II, v; II, vi; III, v; V, i)

Jessica's first entrance clearly establishes sympathy between her and her 'merry devil', clown and servant Lancelot Gobbo. The soliloquy that follows reveals her inner dilemma: 'what heinous sin is it in me/To be ashamed to be my father's child! [...] though I am a daughter to his blood/I am not to his manners' (II, iii, 15–17).

These dilemmas are perhaps never fully resolved. Like Portia, Jessica dresses as a boy: her desire to escape displays a degree of agency and self-determination (II, vi, 26). But there are hints that Lorenzo is just using poor Jessica, as when she promises 'I will gild myself/With some more ducats, and be with you straight' (II, vi, 49–50). Jessica is, markedly, absent from the trial scene, as if, despite everything, seeing her father's aggression and ultimately disgrace is too much for her to bear. Irene Middleton (2015) focuses usefully on Jessica as torn between 'Jew daughter' and 'Christian wife'.

Lorenzo (I, i; II, 4; II, vi; III, iv; III, v; V, i)

Lorenzo is absent when Shylock makes his 'bond' with Antonio (I, iii), and from the trial scene (IV, i), as if to segregate Antonio's and Lorenzo's respective conflicts with Shylock from each other. His conversation with Jessica about their loving night together, full of loaded mythological allusions to fleeing lovers (V, i, 1–22), signals a radical tonal shift from the high drama of the court scene to more languorous lyricism.

Graziano (I, i; II, ii; II, iv; II, vi; III, ii; IV, i; V, i)

Graziano is the most vocal of the three young Venetian lovers. Like Romeo's friend Mercutio in *Romeo and Juliet* he 'speaks an infinite deal of nothing' (Bassanio, I, i, 115) and is 'too wild, too rude and bold of voice' (II, ii, 173). He seems a little calmer as Bassanio wins Portia's hand, quietly and wholly content to marry Nerissa in parallel, but soon reverts to his talkative ways in the trial scene, contributing fully to the near-persecutory noise, and even saying at one point that Shylock is enough to break his faith and become a 'Pythagorean' (IV, i, 130). Pythagoreans believed souls travelled eternally from one body to the next.

Nerissa (I, ii; II, i; II, ix; III, iv; IV, i; IV, ii; V, i)

Nerissa, Portia's confidante, hardly ever leaves her lady's side. She has a chiefly narrative function, justifying Portia's father's decision to marry Portia off to the winner of the contest, explaining for the audience's benefit the contest's rules, and describing the past suitors whom we never see.

Lancelot Gobbo/Lancelet Giobbe ('Clown') (II, ii; II, iii; II, v; III, v)

Lancelot's name echoes that of the Arthurian knight, evoking the peculiar chivalric, mythological element of Belmont. It also plays, as John Drakakis points out, on 'lancelet' a surgical instrument that may be used to circumcise Jewish baby boys (ed. Drakakis 2010: 166). As Shylock's man, the question arises as to whether he is Jewish himself. His first speech anticipates themes of flight from Shylock and the guilt that may result, themes developed via Jessica. Despite the odd malapropism like 'the very defect of the matter' (II, ii, **136**), his direct appeals to the audience are not inarticulate about frustrations and poverty. He seems ambitiously keen to be called a 'master': he at least tries to get his blind father, who does not recognise him, to address him as such (II, ii, 43–60). Such clownish confusions, which also entail faking his own death, hint at a sad son desperate for his father's attention. This melancholy is consistent with his gentleness with Jessica, with whom he often shares stage space (II, iii; III, v), and his astute analogies between the current situation and wider biblical narratives, such as 'the sins of the father are to be laid on the children' (III, v, 1–2, echoing Jeremiah 31: 29–30). He argues frustratedly with Lorenzo and Jessica, clearly upset by their betrothal and flight ('less than an honest woman', III, v, 38). The play's detailed attention to Lancelot and his father, poor, uneducated, disabled, blind and ultimately deserted, arguably silently accuses the more fortuned, fortunate, characters' flippancy.

Morocco (II, i; II, vii)

Portia's failed suitors form an especially vivid counterpoint to the world of the Gobbos. Morocco boasts of his 'birth', 'graces' and 'qualities' (II, vii, 32–3) and his speeches are conspicuously overlong. He, however, raises interesting questions about racial prejudice, self-consciously asking Portia 'Mislike me not for my complexion' (II, i, 1) and appearance more generally, ironically and wrongly reasoning: 'Is't like that lead contains her? 'Twere damnation / To think so base a thought' (II, vii, 49–50).

Arragon (II, ix)

Arragon, whose name of course plays on 'arrogant', unlike Morocco does not want to choose 'what many men desire. [...] I will not jump with the common spirits / and rank me with the common multitudes' (II, ix, 31–2). He is also somewhat mean, refusing to choose lead because he does not want to 'hasard all he hath' (II, ix, 20). He therefore chooses silver: 'I will assume desert' (II, ix, 50), but not before offering a thoughtful, incisive meditation on how 'purchased' 'estates, degrees and offices' may be 'derived corruptly', distorting 'merit' and 'the true seed of honour' (II, ix, 40–6).

Salarino, Salerio and Salanio (I, i; II, viii; III, i)

The characters that have come to be known as the 'three sallies' are broadly interchangeable. Swapping lines among the roles is rarely noticed in performance, as they play mainly an expository function. The three of them do, however, contribute to the size of Antonio's cohort and by contrast accentuate Shylock's isolation. Shylock only has Tubal, especially when Lancelot and his daughter desert him.

Play structure

In the first half, before news of Antonio's ruin (III, i, 2–3; III, ii, 242), the play seems to contrast its 'fairy-tale' element, with far-off princesses and love tests, with the hard-and-fast commercial realm of Venice, full of 'bonds' and 'interest'. If this reading is accepted, then Portia's intervention may be read as a kind of comedic *deus ex machina*. The ring episode, often seen as an anti-climax after the court scene's dramatic intensity, thus emerges metatheatrically as the victory of theatre itself, in its most magical mode the romance, over the dreary pragmatism of the commercial 'real world'. Indeed, the beginning of the play seems precisely to emphasise such a contrast. At the beginning Antonio meets many friends and business partners in a blurry rush: one set of friends arrives as another departs (I, i, 57–68). Antonio's friends urge him to overcome his melancholy, as if to get back to business. In the next scene, by contrast, Nerissa sympathises with Portia's weariness. Happiness is not easy: 'they are as sick that surfeit with too much as they that starve with nothing' (I, ii, 5–6).

Venice's commercial energy, as if indifferent to human emotion, soon spills over into conflict. The first time Antonio and Shylock share a scene (I, iii) they attack each other in asides (either to the audience or to friends like Bassanio). The exchange for 'an equal point of your fair flesh' (I, iii, 147) comes after a heated argument. Shylock's protestations of 'love' and a 'merry bond' (I, iii, 166, 169) are false, naïve. Jew and Christian will of course refuse to back down, and this scene ironically foreshadows the outcome: Shylock's later compelled conversion. 'The Hebrew will turn Christian' (I, iii, 174). The play thus subtly internalises Judeo-Christian narratives of predestination.

Act II, at least in the middle scenes, is rapid and urgent. It busily intertwines Portia's 'three-casket' narrative with Jessica's flight from Shylock. Events are starting to wind their way up. Act III starts with the despairing news that Antonio's ship has been wrecked. This is the thematic and structural mid-point of the play, from which latent continuations and parallels between Belmont and Venice become more and more explicit. The three young couples connect the two realms in a literal way: representatives of the one are now betrothed to those of the other. But they share symbolic resonances, too. Jessica gives Lorenzo a 'casket' (II, vi, 34), echoing Portia's contest and by extension the thematic continuity of love with wealth. Likewise Jessica's theft of the ring that belonged to Shylock's dead wife Leah (III, i, 107–10) parallels and anticipates Bassanio's and Graziano's thefts. Correspondingly, directors often subvert the play's comedic closure to show the persistence of religious conflict and greed. Jessica is, for example, rejected by the Venetians, or reconciles with Shylock, or Shylock undergoes violently forced baptism. So, while the play may be read as a simple triumph of fantasy over mercantile reality, it also has potential to be read ambivalently, a problem play, rather than a comedy.

Language

The play's plays on words enact in miniature some of its key themes. That on 'purse' and 'person' (I, i, 138) suggests your wealth dictates your identity. That on 'thrive' and 'thrift' (I, iii, 85–6) ascribes success to a particular economic attitude. 'Fiend' and 'friendly' (II, ii, 28) hints at the diabolical duplicity that perhaps lurks in any close relationship. An extended such play echoes 'Jew' with 'ewe' and with 'jewel'. 'Ewe' alludes to a biblical example of usury (Genesis 27: 13–23) where lent sheep were returned to the lender with some newborn lambs as a form of interest (I, iii, 76). 'Jewel' implies links to Leah's, Portia's and Nerissa's rings (see III, i, 79–80) and thence to Elizabethan figurative uses of 'jewel' and 'ring' as genitals, virginity or chastity.

The way these homophones blur various understandings of value, replicating almost the very dynamic of exchange itself, contributes linguistically to the sense that the play explores the possibility of a 'universal equivalent'. Theoretically, quantity x of any object can be measured in terms of, exchanged for, quantity y of any other object. The main way the play tests this idea is of course the exchange of Antonio's 'credit' with his flesh. Credit, from the Latin *credere*, to believe, is Shylock's 'trust' that he can pay back the loan. And this immaterial 'trust' is made material in the most intimate way possible, exchangeable for the flesh nearest the heart. Wealth can consist of actual organic, living matter, be it 'ewes and rams' (I, iii, 91) or 'purchased slave[s]' (IV, i, 89). Via Antonio's mutilation the 'wolvish' Shylock (IV, i, 137) seeks perhaps to hijack Eucharistic symbolism, the physical eating of Christ's body whose 'real presence' inheres in the consecrated host. In performance Antonio is often in a Christ-like pose as he is about to be stabbed. The play 'bonds' together the most distant things in the most terrifying ways.

The word 'bond', of course, thuds through the play. In the 'I'll have my bond' exchange (especially III, iii, 12–17), Shylock overwhelms Antonio's pleas in one of the most repetitious passages in all Shakespeare. Shylock's tendency to repeat himself plays on theological stereotypes. Jews were associated with Battalogia or 'tedious babbling' at least partially because Battalogia replicates linguistically the usuriously 'empty' generation of something from nothing (see ed. Drakakis 2010: 85). But such repetition is completely absent from Shylock's final lines ('I pray you, give me leave to go from hence ...', IV, i, 391–3), whose heavy monosyllables echo Antonio's first ('In sooth I know not why I am so sad', I, i, 1). Antonio's pain seems somehow transferred to his Jewish nemesis.

The start of the fifth act is perceptibly more lyrical, however. Lorenzo and Jessica competitively compare themselves to famous lovers of antiquity whom Shakespeare sometimes returns to in other plays: Troilus and Cressida, Dido and Aeneas, Pyramus and Thisbe, and Jason and Medea (V, i, 4–22). This exchange strikes a tone that is never quite replicated elsewhere in the play. Inscribing themselves into mythological tradition, Lorenzo and Jessica become literary characters who are aware of themselves as such. The magic of their magical night is inseparable from a kind of dizzying metatheatrical self-consciousness, remarkable in its distinctiveness from the surrounding events.

Themes

'Fortune'

Perhaps the key theme of *The Merchant of Venice* is fortune. The play interrogates the word's various senses – money, luck, destiny, chance, randomness – and the ways they can coalesce. Morocco chooses the golden casket, the clearest sign of a financial fortune, but un-fortunately fails. Antonio's bad fortune destroys his fortune when his ships capsize. Via the motif of fortune, then, these examples also probe the question as to whether value is only ever contingent and temporary. 'Even now worth this / And now worth nothing' (I, i, 34–5). Exchange rates and value fluctuations are repeatedly mentioned. Lancelot drily observes 'this making of Christians will raise the price of hogs' (III, v, 21–2): Jessica, as now a Christian who can eat pork, will increase demand for pigs, and therefore their price. Conversely, Shylock scowls that Antonio 'lends out money gratis' (I, iii, 40) because this will undercut his own interest rates. Value, then, is not defined inherently or internally but conditioned unpredictably by what others are doing. It 'toss[es] on the ocean' like Antonio's ships (I, i, 7). This uncertainty perhaps explains motifs like emptiness ('I know not why I am so sad', I, i, 1) and blindness, illustrated by Lancelot's 'sand-blind' father (II, ii, 32).

Money, commodity and love

The play even links fluctuating market value with the fluttery feeling of love. Bassanio, who of course needs Antonio's money to visit Portia, cashes in quite literally on the 'love' Antonio bears him. As he finds in the leaden casket Portia's 'counterfeit' or miniature portrait, an Elizabethan status symbol, he takes possession of Portia herself (III, ii, 115). Portia likewise makes herself interchangeable with material commodities when she declares: 'This house, these servants *and this same myself,* / Are yours, my lord'. I give them with this ring' (III, ii, 172, emphasis added). The ring episode in Act V is not therefore a tacked-on episode after the high drama of Shylock's disgrace: its comically problematic circulations logically extend this thematic exploration of commodities, persons, bonds and values.

Compulsion, mercy and justice

The *Merchant of Venice* also probes, however, the limits of universal exchangeability, chiefly in its treatment of 'mercy' (Portia's word) versus 'compulsion' (Shylock's) and 'justice' as some kind of ideal legal-theological balance between the two. When Shylock asks rhetorically 'whose compulsion' forces him to spare Antonio he implicitly deems justice a simple question of exchange. But Portia famously appeals to the 'quality of mercy' as precisely that which confounds such a zero-sum economy: 'It is twice blest: / It blesses him that gives and him that takes' (IV, i, 182–3). This idea that Christian 'mercy' is grander than tit-for-tat Talion 'justice' is, however, compromised by its context. Despite Portia's fine contrasts, it is worth remember-ing the Venetians demanded high taxes from the Jews and thus got rich from the very practices they sought to condemn (ed. Drakakis 2010: 60). Portia cannot simply void Shylock's contract because "'Twill be recorded for a precedent' (IV, i, 216) and Shylock pointedly observes: 'If you deny [me justice] let the danger light/Upon your charter and your city's freedom' (IV, i, 36). Trade's theological, moral and legal frameworks are hard to define and establish.

Texts and contexts

The Merchant of Venice was first printed in Quarto form in 1600, a relatively clean text, which served as the basis for the version included in the 1623 First Folio: we know this because both versions share the odd error and idiosyncrasy. John Drakakis's introduction to the play in the Arden Third Series edition is excellent on the play's contexts and influences. Not surprisingly, many of the play's key subtexts are biblical. Portia's last-minute salvation of Antonio recalls Abraham's near-sacrifice of Isaac in Genesis 22. There is perhaps a clownish echo of the Book of Job in the older spelling of 'Gobbe', especially given Lancelot's frequent expressions of suffer-ing. The motif of blindness in Lancelot's relationship with his father, and Shylock's allusion to generation of rams and sheep, are shared by the story of Esau and Jacob (Genesis 27: 34–40). There is also something also of the 'prodigal son' (Luke 15: 11–32) in Bassanio's use of Antonio's money. Ideas and motifs from myth inter-mingle with these faint biblical allusions. The 'three-casket' theme, with its male chooser and eroticised stakes, echoes Paris's choice between the three goddesses, which leads ultimately to the Trojan War. The Jessica–Lorenzo subplot resembles that of Abigail from Marlowe's *The Jew of Malta*, and recalls also Rachel, Leah's sister, who likewise steals from her family (Genesis 31: 19).

Echoes from other texts thus contribute to the play's mixture of mythical sym-bolism with a forthright engagement with Judeo-Christian ethics: an interesting framework for the play's near-bloody exploration of usury. As Walter Cohen notes, *The Merchant of Venice* strikes a newly violent note. The sources do not refer, for example, to 'any prior enmity between merchant and usurer' (quoted in ed. Drakakis 2010: 59). Usury, then and now, was a hot topic. Long before Shakespeare's time Aristotle had distinguished money made available for agricultural production from profit. But the German Protestant Reformer Martin Luther attacked 'the practice of one person becoming surety [financial benefit] for another' as a 'presumptuous en-croachment upon the work of God' (quoted in ed. Drakakis 2010: 10). Distinctions began to form between 'interest', a justifiable reward for the risk of moneylending, and 'usury', which was relatively risk-free. A Usury Act, passed into English law in 1571, tolerated interest rates of up to 10 per cent (Korda 2009: 132)

Discussions about the ethics of lending money were often used as pretexts to attack Jews. Jews, the traditional race of exile and Exodus, and forced through lack of property into usury, were said to 'skin and fleece' Christians (ed. Drakakis 2010:

18). It is fair to say though that anti-Semitism was based more on psychological projections than real-world experience of Jewish people. Jews had officially been banned from England since 1292: Jews inhabited England only illegally, converted Jews ('Marranos') only rarely. But lack of actual contact with Jewish people did not stop a significant outpouring of English anti-Semitic feeling in 1594 with the trial and execution of Roderigo Lopez, a Portuguese Jew, accused of plotting to poison the Queen. Shakespeare's Venice may be seen as a testing space, safely distanced from England herself, to explore the economic and religious causes and effects that intermingle in this aggressively anti-Semitic scapegoating. The play in part shows an economic and 'religious community' (Anderson, quoted in ed. Drakakis 2010: 27) responding to fears of exile and rootlessness that Judaism has historically and culturally represented.

Venice's reputation at the time for economic freedom and (often uneasy) religious co-existence let Shakespeare's early English audiences see the play after the Lopez affair as a kind of case study for their own preoccupations. Venice had grown rich due to her geographically and economically advantageous position, which allowed access to the rich markets of Turkey and the Eastern Mediterranean. She therefore used commerce, rather than expensive fighting, to secure allies and gain political advantage. This required cashflow, however, and therefore the kind of moneylending services that only Jews could unproblematically supply. Our word 'bank' comes from 'banco', the benches on which moneylenders sat, while 'ghetto' comes from the word for the Venetian Jewish quarter, named after the nearby foundry. Contemporary moralisers argued the free flow of liquid money was as unstable as the watery, marshy land on which the city was built, and that economic liberty encouraged sexual licence. Venice's reputational and cultural significations help establish links therefore between the predominantly religious and political themes of first four acts, and the change in focus in the fifth to the young couples' love.

The play in performance

The first 'sympathetic' Shylock, to dispense with the caricatured red beard and stereotyped gestures, was Edmund Kean. The play has never made for entirely comfortable viewing, and generations of productions have used it to explore ever-developing issues of conscious or unconscious prejudice, Jewishness, money and commodification. In some respects *The Merchant of Venice* is incredibly topical, as we pick over the economic and political debris of the 2008 financial crash, but it is a difficult play to stage because of its treatment of Jewish characters. In 1910 Oscar Asche played Shylock with a Whitechapel-Yiddish accent, clearly echoing the East European Jewish community of London's East End (ed. Drakakis 2010: 121). Theodore Komisarjevsky's 1932 production stressed the play's inner tensions: its sets were deliberately discordant, based on cubist art, while Morocco was made look like a dancer from 'The Black and White Minstrel Show', projecting Portia's implicit scorn. The play has been performed in Yiddish (e.g. 1901, 1903) and Hebrew

(1972). The Holocaust inevitably in some way conditions more recent viewers' responses to the play. Some productions make Shylock and Jessica wear yellow stars, echoing how Nazis identified Jews. In 1985–6 East Berlin Deutsches Theater cast the Holocaust survivor Fred Düren as Shylock. He appeared at the trial scene in an Auschwitz uniform. Yet the Nazis themselves staged the play only once, thinking the play showed too much sympathy for Jews, especially Jessica.

The most sophisticated productions, like the play itself, situate its anti-Semitism sensitively within swirling economies of greed, finance and desire. The 1985–6 East Berlin production compared Shylock's ghetto to the Berlin Wall, over which Jessica would climb to get the latest consumer goods. Jonathan Miller's 1970 production set the play in the high-capitalist Victorian era, cutting the text to guide audience sympathies toward Shylock, and stressing that Jessica was not welcome in Belmont. Peter Zadek's German-language production, which toured and ran intermittently from 1988–95, costumed Shylock similarly to his Christian counterparts to stress the universality of moneymaking, and portrayed Portia as the kind of ironic, indifferent and aggressive youth generated by such a culture. David Thacker in 1993 updated the set with clear reference to contemporary stock markets, complete with the latest technology, while in 1999 Trevor Nunn set the story in the 'Roaring Twenties': the decadent boom preceding the Wall Street Crash of 1929 and the Second World War. Shylock emerges in this world as the 'voice of reason' against such wasteful expenditure. Michael Bogdanov's 2003 production similarly portrayed the Venetians as braying yuppies; Shylock takes refuge in religion when Jessica leaves. Bill Alexander's RSC 1987 production, which used motifs of carnival and *commedia dell'arte* for its costume and setting, also offered one of the strongest condemnations of commodification, supporting Shylock's protests about Christian Venetian hypocrisy by peopling the trial scene with black slaves. Most recently the play has been set in a blingy, glitzy, modern Las Vegas (Rupert Goold, RSC 2011, Almeida 2014).

Some productions have not shied away from negative portrayals of Shylock. Patrick Stewart, playing the role in John Barton's 1978 RSC production, called Shylock 'a bad man and a bad Jew', slapping Jessica around the face, thus corroborating her complaint 'our house is hell' and her need to leave. Peculiarly, this more condemnatory approach at least avoids what the late Arnold Wesker in 1999 attacked as the play's hypocritical plea for 'humanity', hypocritical because even though it sells itself as collective and universal it ends up justifying Shylock's punitive exclusion. In Wesker's own version of the play *The Merchant* (1976), Shylock and Antonio are friends, who genuinely make the arrangement as a 'merry bond'. Shylock is only forced to go through with it to prevent the Jewish community losing face and presence in Venice. While Wesker's play is stridently revisionist, even the most 'faithful' production cannot help but guide interpretations of key questions in one way or another. We do not know, for example, if Jessica is ultimately accepted or rejected by the Venetian as a converted Jew: in Neil Sissons's 1997 Compass Theatre production Carolyn Bazely's Jessica is robbed, then ejected from Belmont. What happens to Shylock is also up for debate. Sometimes he endures forced baptism.

Miller's, Nunn's and Bogdanov's 1970, 1999 and 2003 productions had Shylock sing the Jewish Mourner's Kaddish to express his loss and sadness. Michael Radford's 2004 film ends with Jeremy Irons's Antonio alone, Al Pacino's Shylock ostracised from his Jewish peers, and Zuleikha Robinson's Jessica guiltily, sadly, revolving her mother's stolen ring around her finger.

Critical reception

Kenneth Gross's book-length study of Shylock as 'Shakespeare's double' (2006) contains incisive, stimulatingly lyrical textual analysis and detailed performance history. Gross and others see in *The Merchant of Venice* analogies between inanimate commodities and animate objects of desire. Catherine Belsey (1992) thinks the opposition between fairy-tale Belmont and commercial Venice is largely illusory, just as the leaden casket conceals its real value. The leaden casket's role in Bassanio acquiring Portia, like Shylock's worryingly effortless exchange of money with real flesh, interrogates the symbolism of the money form itself. Lars Engle (1993) likewise argues the play introduces to the public realm newly intense patterns of credit, debit, payment and profit. Marc Shell (1993) relates it to the economics of 'human production'. Richard Halpern (1991) argues that legal protections for merchants, like those Portia digs out for the grateful Antonio, enable the process Karl Marx calls 'primitive accumulation', that is to say, the original accumulation of wealth which lets merchants make investments, kick-starting capitalism as a widespread way of doing things.

The Merchant of Venice has since been identified as a key play for 'new economic criticism' (see Grav 2012). Jill Phillips Ingram (2006) relates the play to an emerging ethic of 'self-interest', more fully realised in the seventeenth century. Robert Darcy (see Woodbridge 2003) compares financial hoarding with Portia's and Jessica's fathers' near-incestuous possessive hold on their daughters. Natasha Korda (2009) sees Portia as a creditor in a variety of currencies (trust, rings, favours) in relation to the surprisingly common historical figure of the female moneylender. Ellen M. Caldwell (2014) similarly argues that Portia is the real mercantile centre of the play, but relates her more to Renaissance iconographies of the goddess Fortuna.

Donovan Sherman (2013) and David Schalkwyk (2011) argue, however, that some theological categories stubbornly escape attempts to make everything the exchangeable equivalent of everything else. Sherman focuses on the soul, Schalkwyk on 'the quality of mercy', seeing Portia's punishment of Shylock as a 'mercifixion' (2011: 152). Julia Lupton (2005) and Amy Greenstadt (2013) read the foreskin circumcised in Jewish birth ritual, like Antonio's pound of flesh, as a residue which challengingly eludes Christian modes of conceptualising the world. François-Xavier Gleyzon (2013) also analyses the play's material symbolism, reading the pound of flesh as a parody of Eucharistic ritual. Howard Jacobson is currently producing a documentary film on the play for the BBC, entitled *Shylock's Ghost*.

Discussion questions

✳ Is there a single likeable character in *The Merchant of Venice*?

✳ How does *The Merchant of Venice* stretch the conventions of comedy?

✳ 'The multicultural Venetian republic, steeped in a venality that permeates all of its social institutions, produces subjects who are, in different ways, alienated from themselves' (ed. Drakakis 2010: 48). In what ways does this self-alienation manifest itself?

Bibliography and further reading

Editions

Shakespeare, W. (1993), *The Merchant of Venice*, ed. J. Halio, Oxford: Oxford University Press.
Shakespeare, W. (2010), *The Merchant of Venice*, ed. J. Drakakis, London: Arden Shakespeare.

Critical response

Belsey, C. (1992), 'Love in Venice', *Shakespeare Survey*, 44, 41–55.
Caldwell, E. (2014), 'Opportunistic Portia as Fortuna in Shakespeare's *Merchant of Venice*', *Studies in English Literature 1500–1900*, 54:2, 349–73.
Engle, L. (1993), *Shakespearean Pragmatism: Market of His Time*, Chicago/London: University of Chicago Press.
Gleyzon, F.-X. (2013), 'Opening the Sacred Body or the Profaned Host in *The Merchant of Venice*', *English Studies*, 94:7, 821–44.
Grav, P. (2012), 'Taking Stock of Shakespeare and the New Economic Criticism', *Shakespeare*, 8:1, 111–36.
Greenstadt, A. (2013), 'The Kindest Cut: Circumcision and Queer Kinship in *The Merchant of Venice*', *English Literary History*, 80:4, 945–80.
Gross, K. (2006), *Shylock is Shakespeare*, Chicago: University of Chicago Press.
Halpern, R. (1991), *The Poetics of Primitive Accumulation: English Renaissance Culture and the Genealogy of Capital*, Ithaca, NY: Cornell University Press.
Ingram, J. (2006), *Idioms of Self-interest: Credit, Identity and Property in English Renaissance Literature*, New York: Routledge.
Korda, N. (2009), 'Dame Usury: Gender, Credit, and (Ac)counting in the Sonnets and *The Merchant of Venice*', *Shakespeare Quarterly*, 60:2, 129–53.
Lupton, J. (2005), *Citizen Saints: Shakespeare and Political Theology*, Chicago/London: University of Chicago Press.
Middleton, I. (2015), 'A Jew's Daughter and a Christian's Wife: Performing Multiplicity in *The Merchant of Venice*', *Shakespeare Bulletin*, 33:2, 293–317.
Schalkwyk, D. (2011), 'The Impossible Gift of Love in *The Merchant of Venice* and the Sonnets', *Shakespeare*, 7:2, 142–55.

Shapiro, J. (1996), *Shakespeare and the Jews*, New York: Columbia University Press.

Shell, M. (1993), *Money, Language and Thought: Literary and Philosophical Economies from the Medieval to the Modern Era*, Baltimore/London: John Hopkins University Press.

Sherman, D. (2013), 'Governing the Wolf: Soul and Space in *The Merchant of Venice*', *Journal of Medieval and Early Modern Studies*, 43:1, 99–120.

Wesker, A. (1999), 'Theatre: Shame on You Shakespeare', 20 July, *Independent*, <http://www.independent.co.uk/arts-entertainment/theatre-shame-on-you-shakespeare-1107733.html> (accessed 9 August 2016).

Woodbridge, L. (ed.) (2003), *Money and the Age of Shakespeare: Essays in New Economic Criticism*, New York/Basingstoke: Palgrave Macmillan.

9 Twelfth Night, or What You Will

c. 1600, first performance c. 1602

Act, scene and line references are to the 2008 Arden Third Series edition, edited by Keir Elam.

Plot summary

Viola and Sebastian, as identical a pair of brother–sister twins as there could possibly be, are separated in a shipwreck. Viola is washed up on the shores of Illyria and does not know if her brother has survived (I, ii, 3–4). Without shelter, she decides to disguise herself as a man, calling herself 'Cesario', and serve the Duke of Illyria, Orsino (I, ii, 52). Orsino is in love with Olivia, a Lady still in mourning for her father and brother who 'died some twelvemonth since' (I, ii, 34). Olivia lives with her snooty, grumpy steward Malvolio, her maid Maria, her clown Feste, her fun-loving uncle Sir Toby Belch, and his friend Sir Andrew Aguecheek. Andrew Aguecheek wants like Duke Orsino to marry Olivia. Viola falls instantly in love with Duke Orsino ('myself would be his wife', I, iv, 42). But the unwitting Orsino asks 'Cesario' to 'unfold the passion of my love' to Olivia on his behalf (I, iv, 24). 'Cesario' does so, so eloquently that Olivia falls in love with 'him' instead: 'this youth's perfections [...] creep in at mine eyes' (I, v, 289–90). Olivia gives 'Cesario' a ring as a love token. As Viola complains, this is all 'too hard a knot for me t'untie' (II, ii, 41). Several plot strands, which later interweave, are introduced at this point. On the one hand, Sebastian, who happily survived the shipwreck, befriends the wanted criminal Antonio (II, i), who lends Sebastian some money (III, iii, 38). On the other, tensions are developing in Olivia's household. Malvolio interrupts Sir Toby, Andrew Aguecheek and Maria's late-night merry-making (II, iii, 81). In revenge the three concoct a plan to disgrace him (II, v, 9–168). They forge a letter in Olivia's hand, implying that she is in love with him, and asking that if he returns her love he should smile continuously at her and wear yellow stockings: 'a colour [Olivia] detests' (II, v, 190). Malvolio follows these instructions to the letter, sniffing an opportunity for social advancement. He is humiliated before a horrified Olivia, who cries 'this is very midsummer madness' (III, iv, 53). Sir Toby seizes the opportunity to have Malvolio clapped up 'in a dark room and bound' (III, iv, 131). While Malvolio is thus constrained, Feste and Maria torment him further (IV, ii). Meanwhile, Andrew Aguecheek is jealously angry (III, ii, 1–6) after seeing the lovestruck Olivia asking 'Cesario' for his 'hand, sir' (III, i, 91). Sir Toby thinks Andrew Aguecheek could regain Olivia's favour by fighting 'him' in a duel: 'challenge [...] the count's youth to fight' (III, ii, 32–3). This duel leads to much confusion and comic business. Sir Toby and his man Fabian terrify the duellists by convincing first 'Cesario' that Andrew Aguecheek is 'quick, skillful and deadly' (III, iv, 220), and then Andrew Aguecheek that 'Cesario' is 'a very devil' (III, iv, 167). As the duellists draw their swords on each other, quivering with fear, Antonio leaps in, mistaking 'Cesario' for Sebastian and fearing for his friend's life (III, iv, 304). As Antonio is a wanted criminal, his interruption soon draws attention. Orsino's officers quickly come to arrest him. Antonio asks Viola for the money he had lent her identical twin brother: 'my necessity / Makes me to ask you for my purse' (III, iv, 331–2). Viola of course has no idea what Antonio is talking about. Antonio spits 'Thou hast, Sebastian, done good feature shame' (III, iv, 357). The officers lead Antonio away. Viola now knows her brother is alive. Feste, likewise confusing the identical twins, guides Sebastian back towards Olivia's house (IV, i). There, an angry Andrew Aguecheek strikes him (IV, i, 24). Sebastian retaliates vigorously and Sir Toby can only just hold him back. Sir Toby and Sebastian draw on each other, ready to fight, but Olivia, alerted by Feste, rushes in to interrupt, calling Sir Toby an 'ungracious wretch' (IV, i, 43). Almost instantly a lovestruck Sebastian and Olivia decide to marry (IV, iii, 32). When Orsino and Viola encounter Olivia, therefore, Olivia is confused by Viola's behaviour, crying 'husband, stay' (V, i, 140). This revelation shocks both Orsino and Viola. Orsino is angry with the 'dissembling cub' for marrying his beloved (V, i, 160), and Olivia feels 'detested' and 'beguiled' (V, i, 135). Then Andrew Aguecheek rebukes 'Cesario' for wounding him and Sir Toby ('you broke my head for nothing', V, i, 180). These mysteries are, however, all cleared up as Sebastian enters and Viola and Sebastian come face to face with each other for the first time in the play. The siblings reveal to the others the story of the shipwreck. Realising 'Cesario' is a girl, Orsino vows to make Viola his mistress (V, i, 378) and Olivia orders the release of Malvolio, about whom she had quite forgotten (V, i, 276). Malvolio hisses 'I'll be revenged on the whole pack of you' (V, i, 369). It is left open as to whether Orsino's request to have him called back succeeds. Sir Toby marries Maria (V, i, 355), and the play ends with Feste's song 'And the rain it raineth every day'.

Characters

Viola/'Cesario' (I, ii; I, iv; I, v; II, ii; II, iv; III, i; III, iv; V, i)

Lost and shipwrecked on her first appearance, Viola soon and resourcefully has the idea to serve the Duke Orsino (I, ii, 50–2). Stephen Orgel suggests the alias 'Cesario' refers to Viola's disguise as a eunuch, via the Latin *caesus*, cut. The character's androgyny is clearly emphasised. Orsino observes, almost at first glance, 'Diana's lip / Is not more smooth and rubious. Thy small pipe/Is as the maiden's organ [...] all is semblative a woman's part' (I, iv, 31–4). As if self-consciously overcompensating for this effeminacy, 'Cesario' soon asserts 'his' courtly credentials. Feste takes coin, but 'he' by contrast is 'no fee'd post' (I, v, 274). 'Cesario' even rebukes Olivia, who might otherwise be Viola's social superior: 'you are too proud' (I, v, 239). This 'scorn' and 'contempt and anger of his lip' charms Olivia (III, i, 143–4), as does 'his' fashion-ably ornate, imagistic and allusive language, which she compares to 'music from the spheres' (III, i, 108). Here is one of the most famous examples:

> If I did love you in my master's flame
> [...] I would [...]
> Make me a willow cabin at your gate
> And call upon my soul within the house;
> Write loyal cantons of contemned love
> And sing them loud even in the dead of night;
> Hallow your name to the reverberate hills
> And make the babbling gossip of the air
> Cry out 'Olivia!'
> (I, v, 256–66)

This speech plays on the old poetic idea that the nymph Echo, who pined away with love for the cruel Narcissus, accompanies similarly unrequited lovers' lonely laments in solitary woods and caves. The carefully constructed conceit contrasts with Viola's own voice, which is often more direct and straightforward, even monosyllabic. When receiving Olivia's ring, for example, she ponders: 'What means this lady? [...] she loves me sure [...] I am the man' (II, ii, 17, 22, 25). But even though the style differs, 'Cesario's' allusion to the lovelorn Echo shows how Viola's own often melancholy wit may sometimes peep through the effeminate, eloquent voice that she creates. She confides to Feste 'I am almost sick' for a beard, as if being a man would free her from her frustrated love for Orsino (III, i, 45). And, when describing this love *to* Orsino, she hides behind the story of a fictional sister (II, iv, 107) who 'never told her love' and 'pined in thought' (II, iv, 110, 112). This melancholy tone predominates in the first half of the play, while Viola thinks her brother is still dead. Her palpable joy at his possible survival announces the later resolutions and climax ('O prove true,/That I, dear brother, be now ta'en for you', III, iv, 373).

Olivia (I, v; III, i; III, iv; IV, i; IV, iii; V, i)

Olivia's entrance is artfully delayed until after most of the other major characters have heard or talked about her. She and Malvolio, who enter together, are the last of the major characters to be seen onstage. Her mourning for her father and brother recalls Viola's own suspected bereavement. Yet, from the first she is seen as intelligently appreciative of Feste's wit, defending him against Malvolio's jaundiced cynicism and 'ill will' (I, v, 86–93). In her first dialogue with 'Cesario' (I, v, 211) she is initially wary ('Your will?', 'Whence came you?', I, v, 164, 172). But she soon grants 'Cesario's' request 'let me see your face' (I, v, 222). Her decision to take off her mourning veil, presumably refused to previous suitors like Orsino, symbolises a return to living, sexuality, and more specifically her attraction to the young messenger (I, v, 227). Olivia's soliloquy soon after 'Cesario's' departure repeats parts of their conversation, as if prolonging it in fantasy (I, v, 281–3). And she seems careful to protect this fantasy from the threat of rejection. Her eventual, blurted declaration of love for 'Cesario' ('I love thee so', III, i, 149) only comes after a more tentative, yet still seductively suggestive conversation. As if to gauge 'his' affection for her, Olivia tentatively asks 'Cesario' 'What might you think?' about the ring she gave him (III, i, 115). On 'Cesario's' curt response 'I pity you', she first seems to accept disappointment ('methinks 'tis time to smile again./O world, how apt the poor are to be proud!', III, iv, 124–5). But then her desire resurfaces with redoubled force: she cries, almost involuntarily, 'stay'! (III, i, 115). Most modern editors give this important word a whole verse line to itself. Olivia thus seems to shift, movingly, between desire, disappointment and decorum (III, i, 109–62). This increases the emotional stakes of the later confusions between her husband and his sister, and the sense of release at their resolution.

Feste (I, v; II, iii; II, iv; III, i; IV, i; IV, ii; V, i)

Feste's name plays clearly on 'festive', tying in with the traditions of Twelfth Night as a time for celebration and mischief. 'Festus' was the name of the Lord of Misrule elected for 6 January. He was apparently played by Robert Armin, a countertenor who could 'sing both high and low' (II, iii, 40): like Lear's Fool, another of Armin's roles, Feste sings the song 'And the rain it raineth every day' (V, i, 382–401). Feste is one of the play's most complex and contradictory roles. He can verge from heartfelt friendliness to genuine cruelty. In his first appearances he flirts with Maria: 'thou wert as witty a piece of flesh as any in Illyria' (I, v, 26), and then uses his wit to console Olivia: if her brother is in heaven, she, not he, is the fool for mourning him (I, v, 64–8). This 'consolation' however, takes the form of a provocative verbal game, resembling the question-and-answer structure of catechism. This is characteristic of how Feste challengingly parodies authoritative discourses, basing his arguments on invented philosophers like 'Quinapalus', as if scorning the silliness of basing your ideas on others' (I, v, 33).

Feste's clowning, as often in Shakespeare, is therefore frequently drily critical ('many a good hanging prevents a bad marriage', I, v, 18–19). He is a marginal figure, moving rootlessly between households and unafraid to criticise powerful figures like Orsino: 'thy mind is a very opal. I would have men of such constancy put to sea' (II, iv, 72–7). More cruelly, perhaps, Feste taunts the imprisoned Malvolio in the guise of 'Sir Topas'. Malvolio's dark cell has 'bay windows transparent as barricadoes, and the clerestories toward the south-north are as lustrous as ebony' (IV, ii, 36–8). This is arguably just straightforward irony: 'barricadoes' are obviously not 'transparent', 'ebony' not 'lustrous'. But, more sinisterly, Feste is trying almost to brainwash Malvolio into misreading the outside world, consistent with his suspicion that language can determine reality ('what is "that" but "that", and "is" but "is"?', IV, ii, 15–16), or that reality itself is somewhat unstable, as in his bewildered response to Sebastian: 'your name is not Master Cesario, nor this is not my nose neither. Nothing that is so is so' (IV, i, 7–8). Feste's sustains this torment by mocking Malvolio for being 'no better in your wits than a fool' (IV, ii, 89–90) and reading his letter to Olivia and the others in a mad voice ('I do but read madness', V, i, 287). As Feste scornfully reveals to Malvolio that he was Sir Topas all along, he pointedly spits Malvolio's insult (I, v, 80) back at him. These are Feste's last spoken lines: 'do you remember [...] "barren rascal" [...?] And thus the whirligig of time brings in his revenges' (V, i, 368–70). This note of bitter loneliness lingers into Feste's epilogue-like song, with its refrains of 'raineth every day' and men 'shut[ting] their gate' on him (V, i, 385, 388).

Malvolio (I, v; II, ii; II, iii; II, v; III, iv; IV, ii; V, i)

This comedy, while often zany, thus touches on some dark moments, especially in the treatment of Malvolio. Is it fully deserved? It is clear Malvolio is not a sympathetic character. Even his name, 'mal-voglio' (*malavoglio*), means 'ill will'. Olivia tells him he is 'sick of self-love' (I, v, 86) and Maria thinks 'he is a kind of Puritan' (II, iii, 136). Puritans scorned other people's pleasure (such as going to the theatre) in the name of Christian virtue. And Malvolio certainly interrupts the others' late-night revels: 'Have you no wit, manners nor honesty but to gabble like tinkers at this time of night?' (II, iii, 85–6). But Malvolio's puritanism is perhaps less the problem than his snooty contemptuousness for others. As well as dismissing Feste as a 'barren rascal' (I, v, 79) he throws, rather than gives, Olivia's ring to 'Cesario' ('there it lies', II, ii, 15). His (eavesdropped) soliloquy, in markedly non-aristocratic prose, further illustrates his pretentious 'self-love': he fantasises that Sir Toby 'curtsies there to me' (II, v, 58–9) and calls Andrew Aguecheek 'a foolish knight' (II, v, 76). Then, thinking he has wooed Olivia and thus 'cast [his] humble slough' (III, iv, 66), he scorns the rest of the household: 'I am not of your element' (III, iv, 120). Malvolio's humiliation deploys the class-based behavioural conventions he tries to manipulate and exploit. He is too embarrassingly old (and low-born) to carry off the courtly behaviour practised by Orsino and 'Cesario'. His oily invitation 'To bed? Ay, sweetheart, and I'll come to thee' (III, iv, 29) seems even grotesquely to parody it. The play refuses, however, to justify Malvolio's humiliation fully. Perhaps the class-based system that does the humiliating is worse than the pretentious social climber being humiliated. It is up to directors and actors to decide if the 'most notoriously abused' steward (V, i, 372) is reconciled with the others, or left forever to his embittered solitude.

Sir Toby Belch (I, iii; I, v; II, iii; II, v; III, i; III, ii; III, iv; IV, i; IV, ii; V, i)

Sir Toby seems, at least at first, one of the play's major sources of comedy and jollity. He criticises Olivia's mourning of their kinsman ('I am sure care's an enemy to life', I, iii, 2), shifts the tone to feasting, drinking and merriment after Feste's 'mellifluous' song ('shall we make the welkin dance indeed?', II, iii, 56), and rebuts the sleepy Malvolio's complaints that the revellers are making too much noise: 'dost thou think, because thou art virtuous, there shall be no more cakes and ale?' (II, iii, 112–13). The use of the familiar 'thou' form when addressing Malvolio, as if to a social inferior, is deliberate: Sir Toby scoffs 'Art any more than a steward?' (II, iii, 112). An element of cruelty thus sometimes underlies the jolliness. He orchestrates the duel, for example, so as to maximise terror in both combatants, rewriting one letter because the old one 'will breed no terror in the youth' (III, iv, 184). His own swordfight, with the younger, stronger Sebastian, misguidedly and comically tries to regain a long-lost youthful bravado (IV, i, 42). This violent frustration perhaps comes through in his final insult to his unwitting cash cow Andrew Aguecheek: 'An ass-head and a coxcomb and [...] a thin-faced knave, a gull' (V, i, 201–2). These are the last words we hear either Sir Toby or Andrew Aguecheek say. They exit straight after, so do not take part in the closing reconciliations, but we hear that Sir Toby and Maria have married offstage (V, i, 358).

Sir Andrew Aguecheek (I, iii; II, iii; II, v; III, i; III, ii; III, iv; IV, i; V, i)

The 'thin-faced knave's' hair 'hangs like flax on a distaff' (I, iii, 98), yellow like Malvolio's stockings ('a colour [Olivia] abhors', II, v, 193) and cowards. Andrew Aguecheek is of course comically, absurdly anxious during the duel. Even before he appears, Maria calls him a 'very fool' (I, iii, 22). But Sir Toby is interested in his 'three thousand ducats a year' (I, iii, 20). Andrew Aguecheek himself says he is a 'great eater of beef' and, like physicians of the time, thinks this 'does great harm to my wit' (I, iii, 83–4). While he says he cares 'not for good life' (II, iii, 37) – his name plays on 'ague' or fever – he shallowly delights in expensive 'masques and revels sometimes together' (I, iii, 109–10). He therefore sends Sir Toby money more or less on demand (e.g. II, iv, 170). Sir Toby boasts to Fabian that he has received from Andrew Aguecheek 'some two thousand [ducats]' (III, ii, 51–2). Despite Andrew Aguecheek's gullible stupidity, he utters one of the play's most touching lines. When Sir Toby boasts that Maria loves him Andrew Aguecheek replies 'I was adored once, too' (II, iii, 169). The name of this great lost love remains a mystery.

Maria (I, iii; I, v; II, iii; II, v; III, iv; IV, ii; V, i)

Maria is Olivia's trusted maid. She enjoys witty dialogues with Feste (I, v, 1–29), but dislikes the 'fool' and 'prodigal' Andrew Aguecheek (I, iii, 22), whose 'dry hand' she mocks as a sign of a lack of virility (I, iii, 65–77). She invents the plan to 'gull' Malvolio (II, iii, 131–4). Maria mysteriously exits while Malvolio reads the forged letter, but gleefully witnesses his absurd behaviour in yellow stockings. 'In recompense' for this jest, Sir Toby marries her (V, i, 358), as Feste predicts (I, v, 25–6).

Orsino (I, i; I, iv; II, iv; V, i)

Utterer of the play's famous opening lines ('If music be the food of love, play on ...'), Orsino introduces and in part personifies the play's exploration of love and creativity. It may be argued that Orsino is not really in love with Olivia: he thinks after all that women 'lack retention' (II, iv, 96), a medical term relating humoral balance with emotional constancy. Orsino seems more in love with love itself, with Olivia as he imagines her in his own love-powered mind. Orsino's love for Olivia is certainly introspective, perhaps even narcissistic. Olivia's rejections are dismissed as 'uncivil' (V, i, 108), then met with excessive if soon forgotten fury: 'Why should I not [...] kill the thing I love' (V, i, 113–15). Yet it is also true that Orsino's love for Olivia has to be imperfect in some way to make his subsequent love for Viola credible. From the very first act a confusedly homosocial attraction is implied between Orsino and Viola/'Cesario', as when he praises, for example, his/her lip as 'rubious' (I, iv, 32). When the priest tells him 'Cesario' has married Olivia (V, i, 152–9), then, it is unclear which has hurt Orsino the most. But the twins' reconciliation seems magically to reconcile Orsino with both. Viola becomes Orsino's 'mistress' (V, i, 320), Olivia his 'sweet sister' (V, i, 377).

Sebastian (II, i; III, iii; IV, i; IV, iii; V, i) and Antonio (II, i; III, iii; III, iv; V, i)

Sebastian's first entry is mainly expository, recapping the news of the shipwreck (II, i, 14–21). His love for Olivia, completed in a matter of lines, leads on to and helps explain his soliloquy comparing love to madness and confusion (IV, iii, 1–21).

Antonio is sometimes played as in love with his new friend Sebastian, mirroring Orsino's admiration of his similarly androgynous page. Even though Orsino hunts Antonio as a fugitive, he 'adore[s]' Sebastian so much that 'danger shall seem sport' (II, i, 44), admitting 'By day *and night* did we keep company' (V, i, 92, my emphasis). Antonio also plays a key narrative function by bringing Viola and Sebastian into in-creasingly close contact with each other. He breaks up Sir Toby's orchestrated duel between 'Cesario' and Andrew Aguecheek, and is deeply hurt when Viola does not give him the purse he lent Sebastian ('how vile an idol proves this god!', III, iv, 362). Orsino calls him 'Notable pirate', 'salt-water thief' and an enemy (V, i, 65). But as Antonio remains onstage with the others at the end, by which time his dear friend is effectively the Duke's brother-in-law, he is presumably pardoned in the spirit of comedic reconciliation.

Fabian (II, v; III, ii; III, iv; V, i)

Fabian joins the play quite without warning midway through. Nobody mentions him before he enters. But he plays a surprisingly large role in the later acts. Fabian is in many ways similar to Feste: he is talkative with some witty lines: 'If this [Malvolio's madness] were played up on a stage now, I could condemn it as an improbable fiction' (III, iv, 123–4). But Feste's and Fabian's roles cannot be doubled because they share a scene (V, i, 276–372). Fabian helps with some of the livelier stage business, as when he plays 'go-between' for the duellists, frightening Viola (III, iv, 255–60), and convincing Andrew Aguecheek that courageous violence will redeem 'my lady's opinion' (III, ii, 25). But Fabian in many ways seems more peaceable than Feste, reading Malvolio's letter begging for help (V, i, 297–305), and graciously confessing the forged letter in an attempt to smooth the situation over (V, i, 349–62).

Play structure

Twelfth Night is often seen as a domestic comedy. We do not see much of Olivia or Orsino: the story focuses predominantly on servants, stewards and messengers. The space circumscribed by *Twelfth Night* is also relatively small: events tend to take place either in or around Olivia's house. And these events occur in more or less real time. True, *Twelfth Night* like *Othello* works according to a 'double time scheme': Antonio says he met Sebastian 'three months before' (V, i, 90), but this is often passed over in the speed of performance. It is not so much a serious plot detail as a way of emphasising the twins' resemblance: Antonio still cannot tell the difference between them after all this time. Twin-like dualities structure the play. It seems divided into two distinct halves by the long and eventful fourth scene of Act III, which suddenly and unexpectedly introduces Fabian, contains more intensely farcical stage business like the duel, and Malvolio's humiliating behaviour with Olivia, and sees Sebastian and Antonio becoming increasingly involved. The play's structure thus accentuates its interest in symmetrical and asymmetrical pairings. Act I sees Viola encountering Orsino's and Olivia's households; Act II sees Sebastian encountering Antonio. The bulky Sir Toby contrasts comically with the thin-faced Andrew Aguecheek. Olivia's desire for 'Cesario' mirrors Antonio's love for Sebastian. And Feste's confusion of Viola and Sebastian (IV, i) anticipates the more comically violent one, just afterwards, when Andrew Aguecheek, encouraged by 'Cesario's' inability to fight, strikes Sebastian instead. Other episodes of confusion run on in sequence, as if to compare them. Feste/'Sir Topas' warps Malvolio's sense of reality in his cell, just before Sebastian delivers a bewildered speech about his sudden infatuation with Olivia (IV, iii). The shared entry of Feste and Fabian, two hitherto separated clownish roles (V, i, 1), anticipates the reconciliation of Viola with Sebastian that takes place later in the same scene (V, i, 221). Extending the idea of confused dualities, whole plot strands interweave. The scenes that introduce and continue Malvolio's humiliatingly mistaken declaration of love to Olivia (II, v; III, iv) surround that recounting Olivia's similarly misguided declaration to 'Cesario' (III, i). Antonio, and then Olivia, mistake 'Cesario' for Sebastian (IV, i, 330; V, i, 135). Conversely, when Viola and Sebastian see each other for the first time since the shipwreck their dialogue is evenly balanced, uninterrupted, as if this moment of peace and reconciliation throws the surrounding chaos into sharper relief (V, i, 222–59). The ending leaves actors and directors with real decisions to make. We do not quite know how Antonio responds to his beloved friend's marriage to Olivia, for example, nor how Malvolio responds to the others' appeal to return. This very open-endedness may contribute to the overall sense of melancholy relayed by Feste's song.

Language

Feste tells 'Cesario': 'I am not [Olivia's] fool, but her corrupter of words' (III, i, 34–5). Language in *Twelfth Night* also accentuates its themes of confusion, doubleness and division. Antonio's rhyming couplets (mind/unkind, evil/devil) signal his intense hurt when he thinks himself betrayed by Sebastian (III, iv, 364–7). Frequent rhetorical figures include *hendiadys*, the use of two words to refer to one thing, and *ploce*, where words are repeated in different contexts with different meanings, as when Feste uses 'dry' to mean 'dull' then 'thirsty' (I, v, 40–1). Olivia's confused love for Viola reflects their names' near-anagrams of each other. The play explores language as an agent for love, seduction and changes in social classes via marriage. The key example here is Malvolio's belief that Olivia has written him a love letter. He delightedly (mis)recognises Maria's forgery as Olivia's handwriting, identifying 'her very c's, her u's and her t's, and thus makes she her great P's' (II, v, 85–6), and thus believes the beloved addressee of the letter, 'M.A.I.O.', is a coded reference to him: 'to crush it a little it would bow to me, for every one of these letters is in my name' (II, v, 137). Psychoanalytically minded critics, noting that the letters Malvolio points out spell out 'cut', observe here an allusion to castration, like Viola's disguise as 'Cesario'. Malvolio is soon to be deprived of his power, 'crushed' more perhaps than 'a little'. These letters also nearly spell out 'cunt', while 'great Ps' refer to the genitals via a pun on urination. Malvolio thus projects erotic desire onto and via, his 'crushing' of words. But this sexual desire is also bound up with social ambition, which is similarly linguistically determined and circumscribed. Malvolio's desire for Olivia is at least partially motivated by revenge: especially on the likes of Sir Toby who has contemptuously addressed him with the informal 'thou'. But in order to do this he has to master fashionable techniques of courtly, amorous communication, which can take non-verbal as well as verbal forms. He fails with both. His cross-garters are 'a fashion [Olivia] detests' (II, v, 194), words he uses like 'element' (III, iv, 120) have fallen out of fashion. Feste observes: 'you [...] are out of my welkin. I might say "element", but the word is overworn' (III, i, 55–7).

Social success thus depends on following, even predicting, such shifts in dress and language. This seems easier for characters like Viola who are blessed with 'soft and tender breeding' (V, i, 317). Andrew Aguecheek addresses 'Cesario' in French, a clumsy tactic to intimidate or embarrass 'him' which he immediately drops as Viola effortlessly and perfectly responds in the language (III, i, 69–70). 'Cesario' also innovates on the old myth, redescribing Echo as 'the babbling gossip of the air' (I, v, 265), displaying well-trained wit as well as well-born learnedness. This attracts the similarly well-born Olivia, who also likes 'echoing' literary conventions. She, for example, parodies the convention of the 'blazon', the reductive but conventional poetic description of a female body as a list of physical attributes: 'item, two lips, indifferent red; item, two grey eyes, with lids to them; item, one neck, one chin and so forth' (I, v, 239–40). Language thus operates seriously, linking themes of sexuality, culture and power, as well as playfully, as in Sir Toby's pun on 'cinquepace' (a kind of dance) and 'sink-apace' (cesspool or sewer) (I, iii,

125), or the revellers' song 'Hold thy peace' which ironically makes a dreadful racket (II, iii, 69).

Themes

Joy and melancholy

The revellers' song is one of seven in *Twelfth Night*, which relay a blend of joy and melancholy. Sir Toby briefly sings 'Three merry men are we' (II, iii, 75) but the rootless Feste's songs often contain more morbid images: 'in sad cypress let me be laid [...] I am slain by a cruel fair maid' (II, iv, 52–4). The shift in sentiment and tone follows on from Orsino's famous opening speech about 'music' being 'the food of love', which may be seen as the play's thematic overture. Orsino compares love to music because both are slippery and effervescent, impossible to sustain fully and wholly in time: pitch has to rise and fall in time for music to be music at all. Orsino stops his players precisely because music thus changes: ''Tis not so sweet as it was before' (I, i, 8–9). His second comparison continues this idea: like love, like music, the sea also changes constantly: 'naught enters there [...] But falls into abatement and low price/Even in a minute' (I, i, 11–13).

Self-love

This stress on love as a dynamic force perhaps explains why Orsino's apparent love for Olivia so quickly and frequently mutates into a form of self-love. His metaphor of Olivia as a 'hart' plays on his own 'heart' (I, i, 16): 'when mine eyes did see Olivia first [...] That instant was I turned into a hart/And my desires, like fell and cruel hounds,/E'er since pursue me' (I, i, 18, 20–2). The comparison with the mythical Actaeon, set upon by his own hounds by a goddess he unwittingly glimpsed bathing, is internalised. Olivia's face, seemingly a mere stimulus, seems nowhere near as important as Orsino's self-examination of his own 'desires'. Perhaps, then, Orsino links love with the sea because they share a watery, self-reflective surface. Malvolio, 'sick of self-love' (I, v, 86), similarly envelopes Olivia in his narcissistic fantasy of social grandeur. Maria spies on him 'practising behaviour to his own shadow' (II, v, 15), a Shakespearean word for mirror image ('Narcissus so himself himself forsook/And died to kiss his *shadow* in the brook', ed. Burrow 2002: ll. 161–2, emphasis added). For Orsino and Malvolio, then, the precise difference between love and self-love is as difficult to establish as that between the twins whom Orsino calls a bewildering 'apple cleft in two' (V, i, 219) and 'one face, one voice, one habit and two persons' (V, i, 213). Viola and Sebastian resemble for Orsino a 'perspective': a painting which only makes sense when viewed from an angle (compare *Richard II*, II, ii, 18–20). Perhaps, then, Orsino's love for Viola likewise reframes and redirects his self-love, turning it outwards, to another.

Texts and contexts

There is only one early text of *Twelfth Night*: it is contained in the 1623 Folio. Attributed to Compositor 'B', the text is relatively clean, offering few quibbles or cruces for the modernising editor. The play's main cultural context, as signalled by its title and alternative *What You Will*, is the liberal celebration that conventionally marks Twelfth Night, the last day of Christmas. 'Twelfth Night merriments' were common and often involved comic theatrical elements, such as the mad 'Feast of Fools', echoing Feste, Andrew Aguecheek and Sir Toby's late-night rowdiness, and the 'Lord of misrule', who inverts social hierarchies. Sir Toby's praises of 'cakes and ale' remind us such disruption was often communicated via metaphors of the pleasured, deregulated body (II, iii, 113). The play's main literary context is Barnaby Riche's tale of twins *Of Apollonius and Silla* (1581). But this is much softer and less violent in Shakespeare's version. Perhaps there is an autobiographical element. Shakespeare had twins, Hamnet and Judith. Hamnet's death aged eleven would chime with Viola's fears of losing Sebastian and the melancholy strands of unrequited love that run through the play.

The play in performance

Twelfth Night is a popular play. Keir Elam's intrepid survey in the Arden Third Series edition, to which this account is indebted, traces over seventy important productions since 1920. Elam's distinction between 'Twelfth Night' and 'Illyria' productions is useful. 'Twelfth Night' productions tend to have a cosy, English, even Christmassy, feel: such productions are invariably good business for theatres over the holiday season. Examples include the young Orson Welles's 1932 production, where with each scene change a huge backstage picture book turned a page and showed a new backdrop, Kenneth Branagh's 1987 RSC/Renaissance Theatre Company production (televised by Paul Kafno), and the 1996 film (Trevor Nunn), which suggested a war between Messaline and Illyria, resolved ultimately by Viola's and Orsino's love. 'Illyria' productions tend rather to use warm colours and exotic costumes, taking their lead from allusions to foreign lands like Sir Toby's allusion to the 'Sophy': the Shah of Persia (III, iv, 272). Ariane Mnouchkine's 1982 Avignon production was influenced by Asian theatre and Indian costumes, reflecting the slightly different nuance of the title translated into French, *La nuit des rois*. Tim Supple's 2003 Channel 4 TV film offered a politicised reading of motifs of exile and disorientation, seeing Viola and Sebastian as asylum-seekers driven out by a military coup; while Stephen Beresford's 2004 Albery production drew on Indian imagery and costume to suggest affiliations with Indian caste system and soothsayers. 'Illyria' productions may allude to *commedia dell'arte* to reflect related social and sexual transgressions. Evidence that same-sex marriage was sanctioned in countries like Albania (*adelphopoiia*) also offers a framework for the play's suggestive treatments of androgyny. Whatever its overall conceptual feel, productions of *Twelfth Night* have to address specific logistical or characterological problems. *Twelfth Night* is largely a domestic drama: a lot of it takes place indoors or close to Olivia's household. It makes lots of references to doors and the entrances and exits can be intricate, especially during the scenes of high farce like the duel. Characterological questions often centre on Malvolio and Feste. Actors and directors have to ask whether Malvolio's imprisonment has by the end turned him irreversibly mad. Bill Alexander's 1987 production contained one of the 'maddest' Malvolios, played by Antony Sher, striking a surprisingly frightening note. Likewise, decisions have to be made about Malvolio's tormentor Feste. In Peter Hall's RSC production (1958–60) Feste's 'Sir Topas' roleplay was a fundamentally good-intentioned attempt to cure Malvolio of his sick self-love, weeping when it failed. Feste was slightly more ambiguous in John Barton's 1969 production, also for the RSC. The set deployed optical illusions to confuse the audience's perception of depth, encouraging the audience to see things from Feste's skewed perspective. In recent productions the focus has shifted from Malvolio to Viola. Themes of androgyny and sexual ambivalence have correspondingly come to the fore. Adrian Noble's 1997 RSC production set homosexual attraction – Orsino and his court emerged onstage half-naked after showering – in wider and more important themes of metamorphosis. Costumes came from a variety of periods and the sets were spectacular. Viola was hooked up to a drip after the accident, a huge fridge full of alcohol was brought onstage for the party scene, and the humiliated Malvolio was sent, literally, to a doghouse. Lindsay Posner's 2001 RSC production likewise juxtaposed suggestions of homosexuality, showing Sebastian and Antonio getting dressed by an unmade bed as if they have just made love, and using comically flamboyant costumes. It continued a long tradition where the sleepy Malvolio wears hairnets or curlers, hinting at an inner life at odds with his fussy, strait-laced exterior, by dressing him in a fabulous red dressing gown. Tim Carroll's 400th-anniversary production at the Middle Temple (2002) used an all-male cast to replicate Elizabethan conditions, leading to much libidinally intricate stage business. Olivia's androgynous beauty as s/he casts off her mourning veil infatuates Viola/'Cesario' almost as much as Viola/'Cesario' infatuates him/her.

Critical reception

D. J. Palmer (1979) offers a good survey of the Ovidian influence on the play. More recently, Nick Hutchison and Donald Jellerson (2014) have focused on Feste to argue for the importance of dramatic 'character', a concept long scorned in literary criticism after generations of post-structuralist scepticism. Suzanne Penuel (2010) offers a rich psychoanalytical reading, focusing on 'the ambivalently longed for figure of the early modern father' and mourning after the Reformation. A recent pair of essays by David Schalkwyk on the play looks first at the female friendship (2010), and then at love (2011), as a Renaissance physiological phenomenon or 'passion' and a way of rethinking contemporary concepts of the 'emotion'. The 2011 collection *Twelfth Night: New Critical Essays* edited by James Schiffer offers a full critical history and valuably varied and still relatively up-to-date set of readings which focus on, for example, the play's structure, themes of gender, historical context, intersections with festivity and ritual, and non-English-language productions.

Discussion questions

* 'Twelfth Night is a hypocritical comedy, cloaking cruelty in joy.' Is this criticism fair?

* 'The different elements in the play are hard to balance properly' (John Gielgud, directing the play in 1955, in Gielgud et al. [1979] (1997): 118). Do you agree? If so, can we say the play makes a virtue of its imbalances?

Bibliography and further reading

Edition

Shakespeare, W. (2002), 'Venus and Adonis', in The Complete Sonnets and Poems, ed. C. Burrow, Oxford: Oxford University Press, pp. 6–39.
Shakespeare, W. (2008), Twelfth Night, or What You Will, ed. K. Elam, London: Arden Shakespeare.

Critical response

Gielgud, J. with J. Miller and J. Powell [1979] (1997), John Gielgud: An Actor and His Time, New York/London: Applause Books.
Hutchison, N. and Jellerson, D. (2014), '"I do care for something": Twelfth Night's Feste and the Performance of Character', Shakespeare Bulletin, 32:2, 185–206.
Palmer, D. J. (1979), 'Twelfth Night and the Myth of Echo and Narcissus', Shakespeare Survey, 32, 73–8.
Penuel, S. (2010), 'Missing Fathers: Twelfth Night and the Reformation of Mourning', Studies in Philology, 107:1, 74–96.
Schalkwyk, D. (2010), 'The Discourses of Friendship and the Structural Imagination of Theater: Montaigne, Twelfth Night, De Gournay', Renaissance Drama, 38:1, 141–71.
Schalkwyk, D. (2011), 'Is Love an Emotion? Shakespeare's Twelfth Night and Antony and Cleopatra', Symplokē, 18:1–2, 99–130.
Schiffer, J. (ed.) [2011] (2013), Twelfth Night: New Critical Essays, New York: Garland Publishing.

10   *Measure for Measure*

Composition c. 1603, first performance c. 1604

Act, scene and line references are to the 2006 New Cambridge edition, edited by Brian Gibbons.

Plot summary

Duke Vincentio of Vienna leaves his post ('to Poland', I, iii, 15), offering no real explanation for this decision. He leaves the prudish Angelo in his stead, alongside his trusted advisor, Escalus. This is a subterfuge. Unknown to everyone except a few confidants, the Duke will actually remain in Vienna, disguised as a friar ('Friar Lodowick', V, i, 125), to observe his people and their governors. In Mistress Overdone's brothel Pompey announces the brothels and game-houses 'must be plucked down' on Angelo's decree (I, ii, 80). And one Claudio's head is 'to be chopped off' for 'getting Madam Julietta with child' outside wedlock (I, ii, 56, 60). Claudio is betrothed to Julieta by 'true contract', but they await the 'denunciation of outward order' because her 'friends' or kinsmen have yet to release her dowry (I, ii, 126, 129–32). An alarmed Lucio, gambler and brothel-goer, warns Claudio's sister, Isabella, a nun, that her brother's 'life / Falls into forfeit' (I, iv, 66). Isabella visits Angelo and at Lucio's urging asks for her brother to be spared (II, ii, 85). Eventually Angelo agrees, but only if Isabella has sex with him: 'redeem thy brother / By yielding up thy body to my will' (II, iv, 164–5). A furious Isabella refuses, even as her imprisoned brother begs her to accept ('Sweet sister, let me live', III, i, 133). The disguised Duke comforts Isabella. Once, he says, Angelo had promised to marry a lady called Mariana, but he then left her when 'her brother Frederick was wrecked at sea', leaving her without a dowry (III, i, 207–8). Mariana lives alone in a 'moated grange' (III, i, 247–8). 'Friar Lodowick' advises Isabella to perform a 'bed trick', that is, to swap places with Mariana under cover of darkness, so that Angelo might *think* he has had sex with Isabella and so have her brother spared. This plan is carried out successfully (offstage) but Angelo still goes ahead with the death sentence. Claudio is to 'be executed by four of the clock' (IV, ii, 106) before his fellow prisoner Barnardine. Angelo adds, 'For my better satisfaction let me have Claudio's head sent me by five' (IV, ii, 108). At this point occurs 'an accident that heaven provides' (IV, iii, 68). Ragozine, a 'notorious pirate' who looks like Claudio dies that very same morning 'of a cruel fever' (IV, iii, 61–2). Angelo is sent Ragozine's head instead. The Duke deliberately keeps Isabella unaware of this stroke of fortune, however, 'to make her heavenly comforts of despair/When it is least expected' (IV, ii, 101–2). Isabella thus of course thinks her brother dead and curses Angelo (IV, iii, 113–14). The Duke then writes to Angelo and Escalus, announcing his return to Vienna and to power (IV, v). As he reappears, Isabella sues for justice against Angelo (V, i, 25), and Mariana corroborates Isabella's terrible story (V, i, 251). The Duke pretends not to believe them, leaves (V, i, 255), then returns once more disguised as Friar Lodowick to hear the continued dispute (V, i, 275–347). Lucio, arrested for his ribald comments, pulls away in desperation the Friar's hood and reveals the Duke (V, i, 348). The Duke soon passes sentence on Angelo for his crime. On the Duke's orders, Angelo marries Mariana 'instantly' (V, i, 570). Angelo is then sentenced to death (V, i, 393–409). But Mariana begs the Duke for mercy, pleading with Isabella to 'lend a knee' (V, i, 435). Even though Isabella still thinks Angelo responsible for her brother's death, she joins Mariana. Angelo is eventually, grudgingly, spared ('your evil quits you well', V, i, 489). Lucio (who throughout the play has been unwittingly slandering the Duke to his face) is forced to marry the prostitute he constantly mistreats and with whom he fathered a child (V, i, 505). The Duke invites Isabella to marry him as the play ends (V, i, 528).

Characters

Angelo (I, i; II, i; II, ii; II, iv; IV, iv; V, i)

Absent for all of Act III and the best part of Act IV, Angelo is nonetheless a key character. The title refers largely to his harsh treatments of Claudio, Isabella and Mariana and corresponding punishment by the Duke. Angelo's very name suggests a fallen angel, and his rise and fall is the play's central plotline. Angelo is an irredeemable hypocrite in the Greek word's original sense, 'actor' (Angelo of course pretends to be someone he is not), and, more currently, as someone who acts badly according to precepts he sets for others. Apparently 'a man of stricture and firm abstinence' (I, iii, 13), Angelo's desire for Isabella contrasts radically with his zero-tolerance policy to prostitution and non-marital sex ('fornication'). He justifies this policy to his doubtful secondary Escalus in terms of example-making. The law must actively punish, as originally intended, and not serve as the mere 'scarecrow' it has become under the Duke (II, i, 1). As Claudio clapped in irons gloomily notes, a governor 'newly in the seat' must come down hard to show 'he can command' (I, ii, 141–6). Lucio calls Angelo's blood 'very snow-broth', and tells the disguised Duke he thinks Angelo 'was begot between two stock-fishes' (dried cod, cold and bloodless), and 'his urine is congealed ice' (III, ii, 96–7). It seems that Angelo strives to link his sexless polity with his own sexual attitude. He is setting up a cult of personality in Vienna. He is the law.

This politically motivated projection of chastity is of course exposed as false by Angelo's courtship of Mariana, and attempted sexual blackmail of Isabella. But it may be argued that Angelo is less condemnable than (or at least differently condemnable from) other Shakespearean Machiavellians like Richard III or Iago. Angelo feels and laments the clash of natural erotic impulse with the sexless persona necessitated by public office. Power wrenches 'awe from fools' through '*false* seeming' (II, iv, 14–15, emphasis added): political duty clashes with personal desire ('I have had such faults', II, i, 27–30). Angelo's soliloquies describe this internal conflict between sex and its politicised repression with an intensity perhaps unique in Shakespeare. In one of the play's dramatic high points, his first soliloquy (II, ii, 166–91), Angelo complains that his hunger for Isabella, presumably radically different from that for Mariana, is not a simple matter of 'forbidden fruit'. His sexual desire is precisely the desire *not* to desire: guilt itself becomes erotically exciting. Angelo's jumpy speech patterns seem here to reflect the resulting confusion ('what's this? What's this?', 'Dost thou desire her foully for those things / That make her good?' (II, ii, 178–9). This feverishness only intensifies when he makes his 'indecent proposal' to Isabella (II, iv, 31–171). This is the dramatic and structural centre of the play. Isabella fails, or refuses, to understand his euphemistic conditionals: 'might there not be a charity in sin / To save this brother's life?' (II, iv, 63–4). He needs to make his meaning plain. He explodes in frustration:

> I have begun,
> And now I give my sensual race the rein.
> Fit thy consent to my sharp appetite,
> Lay by all nicety and prolixious blushes
> That banish what they sue for, redeem thy brother
> By yielding up thy body to my will,
> Or else he must not only die the death
> But thy unkindness shall his death draw out
> To lingering sufferance.
> (II, iv, 160–8)

Angelo's cruelty here is clear. Isabella's threat to denounce him to the authorities, Angelo's mere subordinates, has been chillingly waved away ('who will believe thee?', II, iv, 155). Now he threatens to 'draw out' her brother's execution as painfully as possible. But there is regret, too. Even here, Angelo admits his appetite is 'sharp' and that Isabella is forced to give up her 'nicety'. The near-uncontrolled fluidity of this long sentence expresses palpable torment. Angelo's regretful fourth soliloquy (IV, iv, 18–32) links once more guilt with rhetorical intensity:

> This deed unshapes me quite, makes me unpregnant
> And dull to all proceedings. A deflowered maid,
> And by an eminent body that enforced
> The law against it?
> (IV, iv, 18–20)

The implication that Angelo intimately links guilt with (sexual) release continues when his misdeeds are discovered and he begs (unsuccessfully) to be executed: 'let my trial be mine own confession: / Immediate sentence then, and sequent death / Is all the grace I beg' (V, i, 365–7). He remains silent after he is forgiven. Rather than

just an unambiguous villain, Angelo may more helpfully and interestingly be seen as
an exploration of guilt's eroticised adventures. Where does sex go, psychologically,
when it is consciously and actively repressed?

Isabella (I, iv; II, ii; II, iv; III, i; IV, ii; IV, iii; IV, vi; V, i)

For practically the whole play, the 'votarist' Isabella – 'one given up by vow to a
service or worship' (*OED*) – is uncompromisingly and determinedly chaste. Isabella
personifies what Angelo wants to be. In her first appearance she is told that once
her vows are complete she will be unable to 'speak with men / But in the presence of
the prioress' (I, iv, 10–13). But Isabella begs only 'more strict restraint' (I, iv, 4). She
approves Angelo's response to prostitution and fornication as 'just but severe' (II, ii,
42), and persists for Claudio's life only at Lucio's insistence (I, iv, 74–6; II, ii, 44–8).
In the distraught soliloquy following Angelo's 'indecent proposal' she resolves her
brother should die: 'Isabel live chaste, and brother die: / More than our brother is
our chastity' (II, iv, 185–6). This resolution only persists when Claudio begs her desperately to accept Angelo's blackmail. '[d]ishonest wretch', she snaps: 'die, perish'
(III, i, 137, 144).

The interviews leading up to Angelo's sexual bribery not only reveal Isabella's
early noted eloquence ('well she can persuade', notes Claudio, I, ii, 167) but also
three strongly held values. First, Isabella deems ideal justice (a word she later
screams four times before the Duke, V, i, 25) to be impersonal. All are equal before
the law (a rule Angelo, of course, notoriously abuses). Second, this is because earthly
law is subservient to Christian teachings of 'pity' and 'mercy', words that Isabella
repeats throughout (e.g. II, ii, 51, 64, 80) and which recall the biblical verse that
gives the play its title: 'with what judgement ye judge [on earth], ye shall be judged
[by God]' (Matt. 7: 2). Third, earthly governance, always and ultimately exercised by
men, must always recall this mortal subservience and imperfection. Isabella deems
naïve and dangerous Angelo's insistence 'the law, not I, condemn your brother' (II, ii,
82). The writing and enforcement of any law (or 'authority' as she calls it) is due to
'man, proud man' who 'plays such fantastic tricks before high heaven / As make the
angels weep' (II, ii, 121–7).

Isabella's discourse on the contrast between ideal law and human weakness
strangely mirrors Angelo's lament about governors' 'false seeming'. And her discourse about men's failure to emulate divine perfection similarly, and seductively,
reflects back to him his deep beliefs or suspicions. Her famously suggestive insistence on her chastity shares, even intensifies, the idea that so frightens him: guilty
rejections of sex may themselves contain hidden sexual energy:

> Were I under the terms of death,
> Th'impression of keen whips I'd wear as rubies,
> And strip myself to death, as to a bed
> That, longing, have been sick for, ere I'd yield
> My body up to shame.
> (II, iv, 100–4)

The ambivalence Angelo and Isabella weirdly share towards sexualised purity and sex itself – note the 'whips, rubies, strip, bed, longing' – culminates with the Duke's marriage proposal to Isabella at the end. Given Isabella's insistence throughout on chastity, it is perhaps surprising that the Duke proposes to her. Marriage would entail the nun giving up her orders and taking up a sexual life. The fact the Duke makes this proposal twice, and Isabella still says nothing, suggests her indecision lasts right up to, and perhaps beyond, the play's open ending.

Duke Vincentio (I, i; I, iii; II, iii; III, i; III, ii; IV, i; IV, ii; IV, iii; IV, v; V, i)

The proposal by the 'duke of dark corners' (IV, iii, 148) to Isabella is one problematic gesture amongst many. As he confesses to Friar Thomas, he has been too lax, will now leave Angelo to redress the balance, and will spy on him as a 'true friar' to test his validity (I, iii, 35–55). This is arguably the plan of a weak ruler, not a just one. His desire to spy means he does not intervene when Claudio is arrested or Angelo orders his execution. Did he even orchestrate Claudio's arrest in the first place? We are also not told how long he knew of Angelo's sad history with Mariana. In an often-cut passage (it is absent, say, from the 1979 BBC film), Mariana recognises the disguised Duke as a 'man of comfort' who sees her 'often' (IV, i, 8–9). The Duke may therefore have learned of Angelo's cruelty even before he decides to leave Vienna. Does this influence his whole plan? Is the whole play just an elaborate ruse to test Angelo, perhaps in revenge? Is, therefore, his spectacular unveiling at the end nothing more than an elaborate PR exercise, intended to re-establish his shaky authority? Simon McBurney's 2004 production implies he plots the whole set of events just to get Isabella into bed.

The Duke not only raises uncertainties, he is uncertain himself, especially about political rule. His opening speeches to Escalus (I, i, 3–21) and Angelo (I, i, 26–47) are tongue-twistingly awkward and a headache for editors. He confesses he has 'let slip' his rule of state (I, iii, 19–32) and complains of the burdens of 'place and greatness' (IV, i, 56). His letters to Escalus and Angelo are 'uneven and distracted' (IV, iv, 2). Such uncertainty arguably leads to ethically dubious decisions: perhaps the Duke is not just weak, but even worse a villain than Angelo. He seems, for example, eager to do away with Barnardine (IV, iv, 56). He also uses his disguise to hear Angelo's and Mariana's private confessions, only then to make them public (III, i, 164; V, i, 519). His admittedly beautiful consolatory speech to Claudio ('Be absolute for death …', III, i, 5–41) is uttered with the full knowledge he could pardon and free the desperate prisoner whenever he liked. Yet more problematically, he tests Isabella. He tells her Claudio's 'Head is off, and sent to Angelo' (III, i, 108) despite knowing the contrary, and prolongs Isabella's pain by persisting in this pretence well into Act V. He even pretends to side with Angelo. The Duke thus develops the play's searching examination of divine and earthly forms of authority. James I, like the monarchs before him, was crowned by the will of God, the Lord's anointed and representative. Here we have onstage a ruler who perhaps abuses this divine right by testing people and making them suffer. This surely complicates the Duke's bid to orchestrate a situation where Angelo is pardoned by those he hurts the most and engineer thereby a kind of 'pure forgiveness' which resembles more Christ's sacrifice than an ethics of 'measure for measure'. The Duke's marriage proposals to Isabella thus retrospectively throw his previous deeds into question. He seems effectively to have been testing whether Isabella is good enough for him to have sex with, completely ignoring her wish for chastity, under a somewhat hypocritical guise of moral improvement, to which he feels entitled through rank alone.

The problems the Duke raises, in terms of believability and ethical judgement, lead to the question of just what kind of play *Measure for Measure* is. It is not, at least not always, a verisimilar or plausible depiction of how people might actually behave, or how things might actually happen. The death of Ragozine, which releases the Duke from the dilemma of killing Barnardine, is, for example, much too convenient (IV, iii, 68). Perhaps we are dealing more therefore with a hypothetical exploration of how justice and morality might work in certain conditions, a kind of embodied 'essay', which operates less according to principles of believability than dramatic tension, suspense, excitement and the asking, not answering, of thorny questions.

Lucio (I, ii; I, iv; II, ii; III, ii; IV, iii; V, i)

Lucio is a vocal mouthpiece for such questions, especially of sexual morality. For him, Isabella – 'enskied and sainted' (I, iv, 34) – is the awe-inspiring opposite of the world he inhabits and embodies. Brothel-goer, gamer, homewrecker (IV, iii, 161), Lucio is wittily dismissive of soldiers (I, ii, 16), venereal 'diseases' (I, ii, 36) and even his own death sentence (V, i, 514–15). But alongside this self-interested cynicism Lucio shows a passion for tolerance in his sustained concern and affection for Claudio, his asides commending Isabella's suit to Angelo (II, ii, 92), and his later outburst to the disguised Duke:

> Would the Duke that is absent have done this? Ere he would have hanged a man for the getting of a thousand bastards, he would have paid for the nursing of a thousand. He had some feeling of the sport, he knew the service, and that instructed him to mercy. (III, ii, 101–5)

The humour here depends on the mixed messages. Lucio effectively calls the Duke a lecher, which insults him on his terms but not on Lucio's. Lucio defends sexual desire as universal, pleasurable ('the service', 'the sport') and natural (the 'downright way of creation', III, ii, 92). Debunker of puritanical moral pretension, Lucio is the most important articulator of an earthy, flexible, pragmatic morality voiced also by Pompey, Mistress Overdone and Barnardine, which the play never quite silences.

Claudio (I, ii; III, i; V, i)

The imprisoned, condemned Claudio is ruefully astute about irresistible sexual compulsion (I, ii, 107–12) and a new magistrate's need to establish authority (I, ii, 137–52). His powerful, often-anthologised speech ('Ay, but to die and to go not where …', III, i, 118–32) reminds readers/playgoers, especially secular, modern ones, of the terrifying stakes of the afterlife. Such fears help explain Claudio's quick shift from defiant pride when his sister refuses Angelo ('Thou shalt not do't', III, i, 102) to him desperately begging her 'let me live' (III, i, 133). But they also explain Isabella's ferocious response: 'I'll pray a thousand prayers for thy death, / No word to save thee' (III, i, 146). It is perhaps telling that he and Isabella say nothing to each other after he is unmasked near the very end of the play (V, i, 482).

Mariana (IV, i; V, i)

Mariana is in her way as puzzling as the Duke. Her first mention (III, i, 200) comes as a complete surprise. She is totally absent even when Angelo in soliloquy (and thus with nothing to hide) talks expressly about his previous loves: 'Ever till now / When men were fond, I smiled, and wondered how' (II, ii, 190–1). The Duke's backstory of Angelo and Mariana, full of shipwrecks, lost treasures and jilted brides, is perhaps improbable (III, i, 204–18). But Mariana helps Shakespeare deepen the story's exploration of forgiveness, especially when she calls for Angelo's pardon as powerfully as Isabella does for Claudio's, craving 'no other, nor no better man' (V, i , 419) and begging Isabella to 'lend a knee' (V, i, 435). There is no equivalent figure in *Measure for Measure*'s source texts.

Escalus (I, i; II, i; III, ii; IV, iv; V, i)

Escalus is the voice of political reason: the 'moderate' who perhaps matches best the play's overall outlook. Experienced in political 'art and practice' (I, i, 12), Escalus applies a severe law correctly to Pompey and Mistress Overdone (II, i, 210–15; III, ii, 164–76). And his worried criticisms of Angelo ('so severe that he hath forced me to tell him he is indeed Justice', III, ii, 215–17) turn out to be sound. His final speech justly expresses disappointment at his disgraced colleague's 'lack of tempered judgement' (V, i, 463–6).

Provost (II, ii; II, iii; III, i; IV, ii; IV, iii; V, i)

The Provost enables crucial plot events like the 'head trick' (IV, ii, 145). Like Escalus he voices a gentle, temperate objection to Angelo's dogmatically (and duplicitously) sexless radicalism, which he is nonetheless too low-born to action. He reassures Claudio, for example, that he is not arresting him 'in evil disposition' (I, ii, 100).

Mistress Overdone (I, ii; III, ii)

The madam and former prostitute Mistress Overdone is over-done, a bawdy phrase mixing sex and fatigue (compare 'shagged out'). Overdone only appears in two scenes but as the first woman to appear onstage forms a counterpoint with Isabella. Overdone personifies the underworld. She owns a brothel, and is put in prison (III, ii, 176). As such she illustrates the hidden, crime-ridden sexuality trembling beneath the surface in Angelo's Vienna.

Pompey (I, ii; II, i; III, ii; IV, ii; IV, iii) and Froth (II, i)

Pompey is a 'tapster' (barman) and 'bawd' (pimp). Like Lucio he protests sexual repression is unnatural ('does your worship mean to geld and splay all the youth of the city?', II, i, 198). And, standing trial with his fellow fool Froth, his clownish impudence veers from active defiance to bored dismissiveness:

> Escalus: Is [prostitution] a lawful trade?
> Pompey: If the law would allow it, sir
> (II, i, 193–4)

A shrewd witness of the social repercussions of Angelo's new rule, the newly imprisoned Pompey wryly notes in soliloquy: 'I am as well acquainted here as I was in [...] Mistress Overdone's own house, for here be many of her old customers' (IV, iv, 3). Angelo's repressive measures do not eliminate vice, they merely transfer it from one place to another.

Elbow (II, i; III, ii)

The constable Elbow, like Dogberry in *Much Ado About Nothing*, idiotically muddles his words: 'benefactors' for 'malefactors' (II, i, 47), 'detest' for 'attest' (II, i, 63). He is also prone to jaundiced bigotry, fearing sexual licence may cause miscegenation ('we shall have all the world [...] brown and white bastard', III, ii, 2–3). Elbow thus silently encourages sympathy with the Lucios, Pompeys and Overdones he strives to victimise.

Abhorson and Barnardine (IV, iii)

In his only appearance (IV, iii, 17–56) the prison executioner Abhorson forms a kind of comedy double act with Pompey. Their mission to execute the fearsome prisoner Barnardine (so that his head might be swapped for Claudio's) allows for morbidly comic business. Barnardine flatly refuses to be executed ('I have been drinking all night, I am not fitted for't', IV, iii, 36–7), and Pompey retorts: 'he that drinks all night, and is hanged betimes in the morning, may sleep the sounder all the next day' (IV, iii, 38–9). Harold Bloom controversially calls 'Sublime Barnardine' the play's 'greatest glory' for sheer heroic stubbornness: 'a minimal hope for the human against the state, by being unwilling to die for any man's persuasion' (Bloom 1999: 380, referencing IV, iii, 51).

Juliet (I, ii; II, iii; V, i)

Juliet has very few lines, speaking only to repent her 'evil' (II, iii, 20–42) but her onstage presence is powerful. In Act I, scene ii, separated from Claudio, her heavily pregnant, vulnerably isolated body silently condemns Angelo's absoluteness (in Michael Boyd's RSC 1998–9 production she carried the shaming placard 'Fornicator' around her neck). At Juliet's last entrance she is often holding her baby (V, i, 470), one of the variables through which directors make the play's ambiguous ending more or less joyous.

Ragozine (IV, iii)

Ragozine, like Yorick, is only ever seen onstage as a bodiless head (IV, iii, 92). This 'over-determined, over-convenient sign' enables for Jacques Lezra otherwise impossible events – especially Barnardine's survival – thus contributing to the play's allegorical treatment of subversion (Lezra 1989: 265). For Richard Wilson, Ragozine's head swap for Claudio's is the ultimate expression of the play's theme of (political) headlessness and recurrent motif of substitution, replacement and deputy (Wilson 2015). *Measure for Measure* is full of such strenuously, rigorously organised patterns.

Play structure

Like all Shakespeare plays, *Measure for Measure* is carefully and intricately structured. The first two scenes quickly, economically and urgently clarify details of plot exposition, such as the Duke's departure, Angelo's replacement, the closing down of the brothels, and Claudio's execution. They also map out the two clearly defined spheres within and between which Isabella, Lucio and the Duke will move: the court, marked by Angelo's anxious, rigid maintenance, and the sexily violent underworld. *Measure for Measure* is a play of two spaces and two halves. In the first, the exchanges between Angelo and Isabella predominate. We never hear of, let alone meet, Mariana. In the second, Angelo and Isabella never meet: the play's driving forces are the 'bed trick' and the 'head trick'. The boy's song to Mariana – the only one in the play – thus serves as a kind of fulcrum. This overarching dualistic structure is the large-scale equivalent of the story's various reciprocated exchanges: Angelo's punishment for Angelo's crime; Claudio's life for Isabella's chastity; Isabella's marriage for the Duke's help, measure for measure. The play's biblical title ripples through the play, replicated in even its smallest-scale dualisms and parallelisms. Lucio and Claudio both get unmarried women pregnant. Angelo and Pompey commit crimes which mirror Claudio's. Angelo (and Mariana) and Claudio (and Juliet) transgress pre-contracted marriages, Escalus imprisons Pompey, and Angelo condemns Claudio: an irony all the more acute as Pompey is asked to cut off Claudio's head. The play's frequent use of reversal accentuates this interest in symmetry. Angelo and the Duke 'reverse' power and humility. Lucio's pride over 'Lodowick' is 'reversed' when he sweeps back the cassock to reveal the Duke.

Language

The play's interest in reversal marks also the punning use of language. In puns verbal meaning sways in one direction and back again. For example, in a passage famously analysed by William Empson in *The Structure of Complex Words* (1951), Angelo's word 'sense' links persuasiveness with sexual arousal: 'She speaks, and 'tis such sense / That my sense breeds with it' (II, ii, 146–7). Such shifting meanings enact in miniature the strange force of Angelo and Isabella's interviews: their rapid inter-changes (e.g. II, ii, 35–40) and hypothetical empathising with each other's position (II, iv, 90–5) arguably emulate sexual intimacy linguistically.

The language of *Measure for Measure* is similarly dense and varied throughout. Theological terminology like Isabella's 'concupiscible' (V, i, 98), alluding to sinful, hell-burning lust, and biblical cadence like the Duke's 'thou knowst not what thou speakst' (V, i, 105), echoing Christ's 'they know not what they do' (Luke 23: 34), intimate larger-scale tensions between divine and earthly authority. 'Authority' is uttered eleven times, and always prominently. Likewise, 'justice' plays on the dif-ference between its abstract, even holy, ideal (V, i, 25) with the mortal 'justice' or magistrate who imperfectly enforces it (III, ii, 216). 'Law' is personified so often as to become a kind of character itself. Effective laws are often described in living terms: the Duke calls them 'biting' and a 'lion' (I, iii, 20, 23). A dangerous paradox is thus established between these (already aggressive) hotly living laws and their (seemingly) cold guardian. The words that cluster around Angelo include 'ice' (III, ii, 98), 'seeming' (II, iv, 151), 'glassy' (II, ii, 124) but also 'blood' ('blood, thou art blood', II, iv, 15). The different meanings packed in this short word 'blood' hint at the mur-derously sexual pressure in Angelo's mind. Also prominent is the word 'pregnant', juxtaposing Juliet's pregnancy and by extension the fecund naturalness of sexual desire with competence and truth: Escalus is 'pregnant' in 'the terms of common justice' (I, i, 11), and Angelo stresses his arguments are 'very pregnant' (II, i, 23). A subtle suggestion is established. The 'pregnant', competent thing for Angelo to do is to spare Claudio and his pregnant wife.

Different linguistic forms – prose and verse – demarcate powerful and powerless halves of society, as is common in Shakespeare. In character as 'Friar Lodowick' the Duke speaks prose but often in his private asides speaks verse. One example here is a speech, attributed to Thomas Middleton, in rhymed tetrameter, which lends an aphoristic, even proverbial, tone, as if there is a kind of folkloric timelessness to his wisdom. Language individuates the characters within, as well as between, their re-spective spheres. Lucio breaks his characteristic use of prose to speak in respectful verse to Isabella. Elbow's malapropisms by contrast reveal sycophantic, pretentious aspirations. There is a wide gap between what he says and what he means, and thus between what he is and what he wants to be. And Pompey's continuous stream of innuendo, for example 'groping for trouts in a peculiar river' (I, ii, 75), expresses his urge to see sex everywhere, an urge that laws and threatened punishments only briefly and weakly hold in check.

As well as individual words and expressions, however, certain syntactical structures are also used with especial force, as here, the speech which gives the play its title:

The very mercy of the law cries out
Most audible, even from his proper tongue:

An Angelo for Claudio, death for death;
Haste still pays haste, and leisure answers leisure;
Like doth quit like, and measure still for measure
(V, i, 400–4)

This passage is very symmetrical: its last three lines each contain two balanced and doubled clauses, and it concludes with a resounding rhyming couplet. In this it performs as well as describes the pure reciprocity of Talion justice ('eye for eye, tooth for tooth', Deuteronomy 19: 21), over which Isabella and Mariana's supplication for Angelo's life wins a kind of triumph. The play's exhaustive concern with reciprocity and justice marks even the verse's tiniest rhythmical pulses.

Themes

Sex, suffering and the afterlife

Measure for Measure continuously juxtaposes sex with power and suffering, as exemplified by Claudio and Juliet, Angelo and Isabella, and the Duke and Isabella. Recent productions have staged orgies and used fetishist costumes. But the play's treatment of sexuality is not reducible to mere sadomasochistic kinkiness. In the paper 'A Child Is Being Beaten' (1919) another Viennese, Sigmund Freud, theorised masochism as violence chiefly to an internalised other, such as a persecuting father, whose image lay dormant in the masochist's unconscious memory. The sadist, therefore, paradoxically seeks to help his or her masochistic 'victim' exorcise childhood demons with orgasmic release. Pleasure and pain are easily exchangeable, even synonymous, and in the sheer intensity of the practice the boundaries between its practitioners become comparably fluid. This play anticipates the Freudian intuition that sadomasochistic pleasure in sexual suffering intermingles actual, imagined and remembered persons, but does so with the theological force afforded by Shakespeare's historical moment. Isabella represents everything Angelo wants to be. His public policy strives towards the complete sexlessness that she practises and signifies. But his wish to be her is irresistibly sexual. The sex act, that fierce intermingling of bodies, is readily understandable in this context. Isabella's sexlessness is, dreadfully paradoxically, only available to Angelo via sex. Yet more confusingly, Angelo's desire to fuse with Isabella also takes the form, via his 'indecent proposal', of projecting aggressively his own conflicted sexuality onto her. This raises a question: given the close connection throughout between sex and suffering, of passion with submission, is Angelo offering Isabella a perverse kind of love gift? After all, Angelo is giving Isabella, via the loss of her brother, a chance to prove her chastity as few other women have or could, and thus perhaps a better chance of tasting the undying bliss of heaven.

As Claudio makes especially clear, the afterlife, continuously pleasing an all-seeing, ever-seeing God, is a predominant concern. Isabella's apparently innocent designation of 'true prayers' as 'bribes' (II, ii, 150–1) implies that divinely witnessed deeds in this world may be cashed in for bliss in the next. Testing love and virtue before an authoritative witness is, of course, a recurrent motif. 'Friar Lodowick' excuses Angelo's foul deeds as 'making assay of [Isabella's] virtue' (III, ii, 161). And the Duke of course does precisely the same thing. Angelo's and the Duke's respective 'indecent proposals' – Angelo's sexual blackmail, the Duke's marriage proposal – both align masochistic power with surveillance. Arguably, Angelo tests Isabella, albeit hard and self-interestedly, in the eyes of an all-seeing God, while the Duke tests her before his own disguised eyes. The play thus observes an intimacy between power, especially the power to judge, and earthly and divine surveillance. God sees all. But does it mean his divinely anointed representative (the watching James I) should do likewise? And how does this relate to our own positions as viewers or readers of the play?

Authority and surveillance

The play thus treats 'authority' and surveillance as inseparable: appearance is often reality and vice versa. This challenges Lucio's comforting proverb *cucullus non facit monachum* ('the cowl doesn't make the monk') (V, i, 259). Vienna is a duplicitous city where juries are 'guiltier than him they try' (II, i, 21) and where Angelo's desperate need to reinforce the law displays a self-conscious awareness of public communications. 'Thieves for their robbery have authority/When judges steal themselves' (II, ii, 180). The skilful manipulation of appearance permits the continuance of power according to which people like Claudio, Lucio, Overdone, Pompey, Barnardine and Ragozine live or die. Lucio sharply observes that Angelo makes an 'example' of Claudio (I, iv, 68) and Claudio's arrest seems less immediately disheartening than its humiliating visibility: 'Fellow, why dost thou thus *show* me to the world?' (II, ii, 98, my emphasis). The relationship between power and seeing is pervasive, seeping through the lowliest on death row to the highest in the dukedom. The Duke does not like 'to *stage* me to their [the people's] eyes' (I, i, 68) and complains later 'millions of false eyes' are 'stuck' upon him (IV, i, 56–7). It is only after reversing the relationship of who sees whom, disguising himself as a 'looker-on' (V, i, 313), that he may reassert his authority. Conversely, Angelo's chilling speech 'Who will believe thee, Isabel?' (II, iv, 155–71), asserts his power through an identity created in and by the eyes of others: his 'unsoiled name' and 'place in the state' (II, iv, 156–8). But perhaps the play's most powerful statement about the relationship between authority and voyeurism is the very way the play is built. Shakespeare's improbable additions to the sources, accelerating the timeframe and adding plots of shipwreck may be seen less as artistic 'failings' than as a sly comment on how people will believe anything if it is exciting and spectacular enough.

Texts and contexts

Texts

Modern editions of *Measure for Measure* take as their source text that found in the 1623 First Folio. It is the fourth play in the Comedies section. No earlier versions were to our knowledge circulated in Shakespeare's lifetime. The Folio text is largely clear and of a good condition. There are, however, some cruces. The Duke's opening speech requires emendation to be legible and Mistress Overdone seems to forget Claudio's crime ('well, what has he done?', I, ii, 72) even just after she has explained it to Lucio. A strange word, 'prenzie' (III, i, 93, 102), is often rendered and performed as 'precise'. Recent scholarship has ascribed some of the play, such as the Duke's rhymed soliloquy (III, ii, 222–44), to Thomas Middleton (see Middleton 2010: 1542–86). For readings and variants consult the Cambridge University Press (ed. Gibbons 2006: 193–211) and Oxford University Press (ed. Bawcutt: 2008: 231–7) editions of the play.

Sources: Cinthio, Whetstone and Matthew: 7: 2

Two related texts are often quoted as sources for *Measure for Measure*. The first is in the compendium of stories *Gli Hecatommithi* (*One Hundred Tales*) by Giovanni Battista Giraldi Cinthio (1504–73), later turned by Cinthio into a play. In this story Epitia, Juriste, Vico and the Emperor Maximilian correspond to Isabella, Angelo, Claudio and the Duke respectively. Cinthio's story differs from Shakespeare's play in some important respects: Epitia actually submits to Juriste's lustful request; and Juriste's order to execute Vico anyway is carried out. Nonetheless, as in Shakespeare, the wronged sister ultimately (and problematically) wins mercy for her tormenter.

The second source text is George Whetstone's play *Promos and Cassandra*, which was published in 1578 and alluded to in *Love's Labour's Lost* (1594). The equivalent figures for Isabella, Angelo and Claudio are Promos, Cassandra and Andrugio. Shakespeare shares with Whetstone's play a 'head trick', where the brother's head is substituted for another prisoner's, a hangman scene and frequent use of soliloquy. The audience, moreover, knows well before Isabella/Cassandra that her brother is alive. Critics have detected an influence on Shakespeare in Whetstone's distinctive and interrelating plots, which take the action to various parts of the city, including the prisons. Moreover, like Shakespeare's Vienna, Whetstone's city 'Julio' strongly resembles the London of the time.

But *Measure for Measure* adds much to Cinthio's and Whetstone's source material. Absent from both Cinthio and Whetstone is the story of Mariana and the 'bed trick' motif, and the 'disguised ruler' motif (in both sources the rulers only reappear at the very end). Shakespeare's verse also accentuates greatly the psychological and inward entanglements of his characters. In Whetstone the characters' soliloquies seem merely to illustrate an established opinion or position whereas Angelo's soliloquies especially witness a psychology evolving in real time. And, as mentioned above and as Shakespeare's church-going audience would have realised, the title refers directly to passages from the Gospels: 'For with what judgement ye judge, ye shall be judged: and with what measure ye mete, it shall be measured to you again' (Matt. 7: 2). Shakespeare's title shifts the focus away from the plight of individual persons and towards universal moral questions.

King James, *Basilikon Doron* and the Royal Entry

Measure for Measure was performed in Whitehall on 26 December 1604, before the recently crowned James I. Composed and performed at the same time as the King's Royal Entry to London, its themes of a ruler's absence and presence would have been topical. Some critics (e.g. ed. Gibbons 2006: 21–2) have observed thematic parallels with James I's book *Basilikon Doron*, which stresses temperance as a key quality of a good ruler, and, in Lucio's critiques of the Duke, allusions to King James's fondness for young men (see Bergeron 1999).

Puritanism

Measure for Measure sees political power intertwining with religious devotion and sexual desire. The right relationship between these three forces was keenly contested in the sixteenth and seventeenth centuries. From the 1560s the word 'Puritan' emerged to denote 'extreme' Protestants, urging extreme punishment, even death, for sexual practices like prostitution, adultery and incest. Angelo's description as 'precise' (I, iv, 50), of which Folio's 'prenzie' (III, i, 93, 95) is arguably a corruption, recalls contemporary nicknames for Puritans as 'precisemen' and 'precisians'. The play may be seen as a sophisticated comment on the psychology of Puritanism: it depicts the complicated forms of desire which remain, or mutate, when sexual instinct is ostensibly repressed.

Epicureanism

As well as sex, pleasure and its repression, *Measure for Measure* also deals urgently with questions of the afterlife. The Duke, comforting Claudio in his famous speech 'Be absolute for death …' (III, i, 5–41), seems to echo certain tenets of an atheistic, Epicurean outlook, perhaps surprisingly for a Friar. Epicurus (341–270 BC) held that pleasure was the central good. Such pleasure was defined as the absence of pain and anxiety, as caused ultimately by the fear of death and what comes after. But, Epicurus reasoned, if we mortals can have no knowledge of the experience of death, or what it is to be dead, then we cannot know that it is any worse than life. The Duke's resigned Epicureanism is one of the 'shades' in the play's subtle spectrum of thinking about the afterlife.

The play in performance

Measure for Measure was rarely staged unaltered from its earliest performances to the twentieth century. Peter Brook (RSC 1950), introduced a long (two-minute) pause before Isabella decides to help Marianna plead for Angelo. John Barton (RSC 1970) introduced an 'open' ending, where Isabella does not accept the Duke's marriage proposal but is left 'wondering, puzzling about what to do' (Hampton-Reeves 2007: 110–19). Since then there have been over ten productions by the RSC alone. This frank treatment of sex and power has become increasingly topical. In some productions Angelo has groped Isabella, forced her to touch him or attempted rape (Hampton-Reeves 2007: 109). Underage prostitutes (Steven Pimlott, RSC 1994), porn videos, masturbation and fellatio (Simon McBurney, Complicité 2004), and sadomasochism (Roxana Silbert, RSC 2011) have also featured prominently. Onscreen versions include Desmond Davis's traditionalist 1979 BBC/Time-Life film, dismissed as 'overly conservative' (Hampton-Reeves 2007: 130) and 'insipid' (Angela Stock in ed. Gibbons 2006: 83); and David Thacker's 1996 BBC Television film, which resituated the story in a darkly dystopian world of depression, alcoholism and CCTV cameras: motifs taken up in McBurney's 2004 production. Bob Komar's 2006 film, like many recent stage productions (three in 2004 in London alone), viewed the story through a lens of torture and religious conviction. He put the story in an army barracks and strengthened the play's thematic parallels with a political landscape haunted by 9/11 and Guantánamo Bay prison.

Critical reception

John Dryden called *Measure for Measure* 'meanly written' (1672); Samuel Johnson deemed some aspects 'trite and vulgar' (1773[?]); Samuel Taylor Coleridge called it 'hateful' (1827); and for William Winter it was 'unfit for the modern theatre' (1913) (quoted in Geckle 2001: 1, 4, 80, 336). Important defences were, however, published in the early to mid-twentieth century. In *The Wheel of Fire* (1930), George Wilson Knight argued for the play's moral worth according to the New Testament precepts of grace and mercy implied by its title. F. R. Leavis agreed 'there is no play in the whole canon remoter from "morbid pessimism" than *Measure for Measure*' (Leavis 1964: 164). Knight and Leavis premise their defences on artistic harmony or ethical integrity, as Terence Hawkes points out in 'Take me to your Leda' (1988). But mid- to late twentieth-century interest tends rather to focus on the play's exploration of social fragmentation and, via Michel Foucault's *Discipline and Punish*, how surveillance (disguised Dukes) and spectacle (public punishment) work together to reinforce power. Key essays on such topics include those by Jonathan Dollimore (1994), Kiernan Ryan (2001) and Richard Wilson (1996). Foucauldian readings have since been attacked as 'anachronistic': Foucault's observations pertain to later historical periods than Shakespeare's. Julia Lupton (1996) and Richard Wilson (2015) thus offer more theological readings of the play's politics. Ewan Fernie (2012) embarks on a self-invested, even autobiographical, form of literary criticism in his close reading of art, beauty and Angelo.

Discussion questions

* Who, if anybody, does the play ultimately side with?

* Is the Duke a better ruler than Angelo? Or are they both bad for different reasons?

* You are Isabella. The Duke holds out his hand for marriage. What would *you* do?

Bibliography and further reading

Editions

Shakespeare, W. (2006), *Measure for Measure*, ed. B. Gibbons, with additional material by A. Stock, Cambridge: Cambridge University Press.
Shakespeare, W. (2008), *Measure for Measure*, ed. N. W. Bawcutt, Oxford: Oxford University Press.

Critical response

Bergeron, D. (1999), *King James and Letters of Homoerotic Desire*, Iowa City: University of Iowa Press.
Bloom, H. (1999), *Shakespeare and the Invention of the Human*, New York: Riverhead.
Dollimore, J. (1994), 'Transgression and Surveillance in *Measure for Measure*', in J. Dollimore and A. Sinfield (eds), *Political Shakespeare: New Essays in Cultural Materialism*, Manchester: Manchester University Press, pp. 72–87.
Empson, W. (1951), *The Structure of Complex Words*, London: Chatto and Windus.
Fernie, E. (2012), '"To sin in loving virtue": Desire and Possession in *Measure for Measure*', in W. McKenzie and T. Papadopoulou (eds), *Shakespeare and I*, London/ New York: Continuum.
Foucault, M. (1977), *Discipline and Punish: The Birth of the Prison*, trans. Alan Sheridan, Harmondsworth: Penguin.
Freud, S. (1997), '"A Child Is Being Beaten" (1919)', in E. S. Person (ed.), *On Freud's 'A Child Is Being Beaten'*, London: Karnac Books, pp. 1–30.
Geckle, G. L. (ed.) (2001), Measure for Measure: *The Critical Heritage*, London/New York: Continuum.
Hampton-Reeves, S. (2007), Measure for Measure: *A Guide to the Text and Its Theatrical Life*, Basingstoke: Macmillan.
Hawkes, T. (1988), 'Take Me to Your Leda', *Shakespeare Survey*, 40, 21–32.
Knight, G. W. [1930] (1964), *The Wheel of Fire: Interpretation of Shakespeare's Tragedy*, New York/Cleveland: Meridian Books/World Publishing.

Leavis, F. R. (1964), *The Common Pursuit*, New York: New York University Press.

Lezra, J. (1989), 'Pirating Reading: The Appearance of History in *Measure for Measure*', *English Literary History*, 56:2, 255–92.

Lupton, J. (1996), 'Saints on Trial: The Genre of *Measure for Measure*', in *The After-Lives of the Saints: Hagiography, Typology, and Renaissance Literature*, Stanford: Stanford University Press, pp. 110–40.

Middleton, T. (2010), *The Collected Works*, ed. G. Taylor, J. Lavagnino, M. P. Jackson, J. Jowett, V. Wayne and A. Weiss, Oxford: Oxford University Press.

Ryan, K. (2001), '*Measure for Measure*: Marxism before Marx', in Jean E. Howard and Scott Cutler Shershow (eds), *Marxist Shakespeares*, London/New York: Routledge, pp. 227–44.

Wilson, R. (1996), 'Prince of Darkness: Foucault's Shakespeare', in Nigel Wood (ed.), *Measure for Measure*, Buckingham: Open University Press, pp. 133–75.

Wilson, R. (2015), 'As Mice by Lions: Political Theology and *Measure for Measure*', *Shakespeare*, 11:2, 157–77.

Part III. Histories

11 'The Henriad' (*Richard II, Henry IV Part 1* and *Part 2, Henry V*)

1595–9

Act, scene and line references are to the Oxford Shakespeare editions: *Richard II*, edited by Anthony B. Dawson and Paul Yachnin (2011); *Henry IV Part One*, edited by David Bevington (1987); *Henry IV Part Two*, edited by René Weis (1997); and *Henry V*, edited by Gary Taylor (1982).

Plot summary

These four plays cover together events that take place from 1398–1422. Near the beginning of *Richard II*, King Richard banishes Henry of Bolingbroke, Earl of Hereford ('Bolingbroke') for ten years for feuding with fellow aristocrat Thomas Mowbray and disturbing the public peace (*RII*, I, iii, 139–40). Mowbray and Bolingbroke accuse each other of murdering Gloucester, also known as Thomas of Woodstock, an affair in which the King himself seems suspiciously, mysteriously involved (*RII*, I, ii, 37–9; II, i, 131). Richard soon proves an ineffective as well as suspicious king. He levies unpopular taxes (*RII*, II, i, 246–8) and takes for himself the possessions of the dead John of Gaunt, Bolingbroke's father and Duke of Lancaster (*RII*, II, i, 161–2). Bolingbroke was due to inherit his father's possessions, so Richard's seizing them invalidates the selfsame hereditary principles on which his own reign is founded. Bolingbroke claims that, now his father is dead, he no longer has the legal identity under which he was banished, and is thus entitled to return ('As I was banished, I was banished Hereford / But as I come, I come for Lancaster' (*RII*, II, iii, 112–13). Bolingbroke executes Richard's chief allies Bushy and Green for 'deceiving' the King, using them as scapegoats for Richard's unpopular policies (*RII*, III, i). This isolates Richard to the point where even Richard's most loyal ally York reluctantly turns to Bolingbroke (*RII*, III, ii, 200). At Flint Castle Bolingbroke gives Richard an ultimatum: repeal my banishment and return to me the lands I am entitled to, and I shall leave you alone; if not, I shall reluctantly attack you (*RII*, III, iii, 30–46). The King realises that if a mere subject can command him in this way then he is no longer really King. Richard relents, broken and powerless (*RII*, III, iii, 131–206). The crown passes from King Richard – ancestor to the Yorkist line – to the Lancastrian Bolingbroke. Bolingbroke is crowned King Henry IV of England (*RII*, IV, i, 113). This is the single most important event of the two tetralogies. The second tetralogy will see descendants from the York and Lancaster houses, symbolised respectively by white and red roses, bitterly and violently dispute the legitimacy of this action, causing the famous Wars of the Roses. Richard II, by now a political inconvenience, is assassinated (*RII*, V, vi, 112). King Henry IV claims ignorance of this act, 'though I did wish him dead', and vows to 'make a voyage to the Holy Land / To wash this blood off from my guilty hand' (*RII*, V, vi, 49–50).

As *Henry IV Part 1* starts, the fledgling reign of the new King is already in trouble. He has just finished fighting the Welsh leader Owen Glendower. Harry Percy ('Hotspur'), son of Northumberland who had helped Henry to the crown in *Richard II*, disputes Henry's refusal to pay Glendower a ransom for his prisoner, and Hotspur's brother-in-law, Lord Mortimer Earl of March. Henry thinks Mortimer a traitor. Hotspur thinks Mortimer's acts were just an inevitable result of 'the chance of war' (*1HIV*, I, iii, 94). The angered Hotspur mounts a rebellion against Bolingbroke, whom he calls a 'vile politician' (*1HIV*, I, iii, 240). He is joined by Mortimer, Glendower, and various friends and allies of those the King had killed or deposed on his way to power (*1HIV*, I, iii, 257–300; II, iii, 1–32). Meanwhile, King Henry summons his son Hal (later to become Henry V) to upbraid him for wasting his time in the pubs of Eastcheap, East London, with dissolute friends like Sir John Falstaff. He reminds his son that his kingship was taken, not inherited. A more disciplined fighter or politician could in turn strip the crown from him. It is therefore up to Hal to behave impeccably and retain public goodwill (*1HIV*, III, ii, 1–91). Hotspur's rebellious forces mobilise against the King towards Shrewsbury. Hotspur learns his father is sick and his forces cannot join them (*1HIV*, IV, i, 16). He fights on anyway. During the Battle of Shrewsbury Hal saves his father's life ('Thou has redeemed thy lost opinion', *1HIV*, V, iv, 47). Hal then kills his friend Hotspur (*1HIV*, V, iv, 85). Hotspur's rebellion has failed. At the end of *Henry IV Part 1*, much like at the beginning, the relieved King finds 'a time for frighted peace to pant' (*1HIV*, I, i, 2).

Henry IV Part 2 sees Hotspur's loving, devastated wife Kate rebuking her father-in-law, who seeks revenge on the King for Hotspur's death, for deserting her husband at the crucial moment ('him did you leave', *2HIV*, II, iii, 33). The play covers the last nine years and eight months of Henry's reign. The Archbishop of York and Earl of Northumberland mount a rebellion (*2HIV*, I, ii, 199). The plotters know the King's forces are scattered 'in three heads', fighting France and the Welsh as well as them: their 'five and twenty thousand men of choice' could therefore potentially win (*2HIV*, I, iii, 71, 11). The Archbishop vows vengeance for Richard II's death (*2HIV*, I, iii, 85–108). Meanwhile the King is worried again about Hal's involvement with Falstaff and the tavern-goers. But he is reassured that 'The Prince but studies his companions / Like a strange tongue, wherein, to gain the language' (*2HIV*, IV, iii, 68–9). The King grows ill (*2HIV*, IV, iii, 110–11). Hal, by his father's bedside, thinks him dead ('This sleep is sound indeed'). He therefore puts on the crown and, full of 'heavy sorrows of the blood', takes it away with him (*2HIV*, IV, iii, 166, 169, 173). But the King awakes and chides his son for wishing him dead ('I weary thee', *2HIV*, IV, iii, 223). Hal protests his 'duteous spirit' and begs 'pardon' just as his father's condition worsens (*2HIV*, IV, iii, 277, 268, 370). The rebellion is defeated as Hal's younger brother Prince John tricks and captures the Archbishop and his co-conspirators (*2HIV*, IV, i, 335–6). The play concludes with Henry IV's reported death (*2HIV*, V, ii, 5). Hal is crowned King Henry V (*2HIV*, V, ii, 42). A joyful Falstaff approaches the new King, confident their long-standing friendship will win him 'dignities' and 'offices' (*2HIV*, V, iii, 121–2). But Henry V dismisses him: 'I know thee not, old man' (*2HIV*, V, v, 46). The 'wanton and effeminate boy' (*RII*, V, iii, 10) has 'throw[n] off' his 'loose behaviour', just as he promised (*1HIV*, I, ii, 196).

As *Henry V* begins, the newly crowned young King asks his counsellors if his family lineage entitles him to reclaim French territories 'with right and conscience' (*HV*, I, ii, 96). The advisors, who secretly and worriedly want to protect their own lands and monies, say yes (*HV*, I, i, 9–24, I, ii, 97). The question is settled when the French King sends King Henry a taunting gift of tennis balls, a provocative allusion to war (*HV*, I, ii, 258). The English army sets sail for France, but not before the King executes three traitors at the harbour town of Southampton: further proof of his developing firmness of statecraft (*HV*, II, ii, 76–141). Falstaff dies (*HV*, II, iii, 5). The English army takes possession of the walled town of Harfleur (*HV*, III, iii, 128–30), crosses the River Somme (*HV*, III, v, 1) and meets the French army at Agincourt [1415]. The French army is much bigger ('five to one. Besides, they are all fresh', *HV*, IV, iii, 4) but the English win (*HV*, IV, vii, 81). The disgusted French kill the unarmed English boys who carry arms and supplies to the soldiers (*HV*, IV, vii, 1–4). The King is furious (*HV*, IV, vii, 50–1) but to prevent future enmity marries Princess Catherine of France (*HV*, V, ii, 333–57). The Chorus soon undercuts this happy ending. The Epilogue, in sonnet form, tells us Henry's son King Henry VI and his governors 'lost France and made his England bleed' (*HV*, Epilogue, 12).

Characters

Henry Bolingbroke, later Henry of Lancaster, later King Henry IV
(*RII, 1HIV, 2HIV*)

The man crowned Henry IV just after halfway through *Richard II* is included first in this list of characters simply because he is in terms of stage time the longest-reigning king in the tetralogy. His role over its first three plays traces a fairly symmetrical arc, rising from disgrace to royal power then falling to weakness, illness and death. Richard II banishes him and his enemy Mowbray for 'sky-aspiring and ambitious thoughts' (*RII*, I, iii, 130) but Bolingbroke claims that his return to England four scenes later when his father dies is legal: 'Attorneys are denied me / And therefore personally I lay my claim / To my inheritance of free descent' (*RII*, II, iii, 134–5). It is unsure if Bolingbroke wants to become King all along. He certainly denies it in the text, offering 'allegiance and true faith of heart' to Richard if he returns his lands (*RII*, III, iii, 36). Some actors, however, have interpreted this as mere show. Bolingbroke is certainly capable of decisive political action, leaving Richard isolated by disposing of his key allies Bushy and Green (*RII*, III, iii). On the other hand, the dubious way Bolingbroke becomes King haunts him through the next two plays. He exiles Sir Pierce Exton for murdering Richard (*RII*, V, vi, 43–4), even though Exton claims he himself had ordered someone to 'rid me of this living fear' (*RII*, V, iv, 2). The audience never actually sees Henry IV utter these words. His precise responsibility for Richard's death is thus shrouded in mystery, as is Richard's for Gloucester's at the beginning of the play. Note, however, the new King's closing allusion to his 'guilty hand' (*RII*, V, vi, 50).

Such anxieties mark Henry IV's frequent warnings to his son and heir Hal, for example: 'even as I was then is Percy [Hotspur] now [...] He hath more worthy interest to the state/Than thou the shadow of succession' (*1HIV*, III, ii, 96–9). A path from anger to fragile reconciliation structures both parts of *Henry IV*, but there are slight differences in this overall narrative shape. Henry IV dominates the beginning of *Part 1* but is much less present in *Part 2*, not entering until Act III, scene i. This helps emphasise the King's sickness and lethargy and the Prince's struggle with his growing independence and power. Henry's dying advice to Hal to 'busy giddy minds/With foreign quarrels' (*2HIV*, III, i, 343–4) casts a somewhat Machiavellian light over Henry V's conquest of Agincourt. Arguably the exploit is based not on honour but on making people forget that Hal inherited his crown from a usurper.

Hal, later Henry V (*1HIV, 2HIV, HV*)

Hal's father describes him before he appears onstage. King Henry criticises Hal's tavern-going 'riot and dishonour', wishing Hotspur was his son, that a 'night-tripping fairy' had swapped them at birth (*1HIV*, I, i, 84, 86). Hal's first appearance, however, modifies this initial impression somewhat: he mocks the just-woken Falstaff for the very indolence his father sees in him: 'What a devil hast thou to do with the time of the day?' (*1HIV*, I, ii, 5–6). His famous first soliloquy acknowledges but contradicts his father's report, predicting his 'reformation' to the sterner leadership illustrated later in rejecting Falstaff and fighting the French (*1HIV*, I, ii, 183–205). Similar hints come through even in the most raucous moments of Hal and Falstaff's drunken roleplay. Hal promises he will indeed 'banish plump Jack' (*1HIV*, II, iv, 463). Hal also makes sure the victims of Falstaff's attempted thefts suffer no loss (*1HIV*, II, iv, 527–8). Yet Hal's relationship with his father remains uneasy. His brave showing in the battle of Shrewsbury in *Part 1*, redeeming his 'lost opinion' by saving his father and killing Hotspur, seems exhausted by the time he enters, quite late, in *Part 2*. He is 'exceeding weary' (*2HIV*, II, ii, 1). His father is sick, his duties becoming real. No one believes he is sad to inherit the crown: his friend Poins even calls him a 'princely hypocrite' (*2HIV*, II, ii, 51). But Hal's soliloquies as he first puts on the crown ('polished perturbation, golden care'), and before he goes into battle against the French, show real anxiety at the 'hard condition' of royal responsibility (*2HIV*, IV, iii, 152–78; *HV*, IV, i, 218–72). These military and psychological struggles are, perhaps, figured by Hal's defeat of Hotspur in *Part 1* and rejection of Falstaff in *Part 2*.

By moments Henry V shares his father's clear-minded, even cold-hearted, political pragmatism. As Bolingbroke quickly dispatched Bushy and Green, so Henry V unhesitatingly executes the three traitors at Southampton: 'Touching our person seek we no revenge, / But we our kingdom's safety must so tender' (*HV*, II, ii, 171–2). Likewise he shows no favouritism to his old friend Bardolph, hanged for looting: 'We would have all such offenders so cut off' (*HV*, III, vi, 108). *Henry V* may be seen as a guide to the different military, psychological, rhetorical and relational competencies of a successful Renaissance king. He of course delivers famous speeches to his soldiers ('Once more into the breach, dear friends', *HV*, III, i, 1–34; 'This day is called the Feast of Crispian', *HV*, IV, iii, 18–67). But in disguise he also tries to justify, and often fierily, his fight as 'just' and 'honourable' to the impoverished but astute, concerned soldier Williams (*HV*, IV, i, 84–217). And in a completely different rhetorical key, including humble, broken French, he woos his betrothed Catherine, the French Princess (*HV*, V, ii, 98–271).

Sir John Falstaff (*1HIV, 2HIV*, death reported *HV*)

Falstaff was first called 'Oldcastle' but Sir John Oldcastle's descendants the Brookes protested after the plays' first performances in 1594. The Epilogue of *Part 2* apologetically clarifies 'Oldcastle died martyr, and this is not the man' (*2HIV*, Epilogue, 30–1). Traces survive of the old name, however, as when Hal calls him 'my old lad of the castle' (*1HIV*, I, ii, 40–1). The Brookes' concern is partially explained by Falstaff's increasing fame. Falstaff was so popular in Shakespeare's day he had his own spin-off *The Merry Wives of Windsor* (text first published in 1602). Perhaps Falstaff was – and is – so popular because audiences wishfully identify with his unapologetically, uncompromisingly selfish quest for pleasure, visible onstage via his huge size: he is a 'hill of flesh', and 'stuffed cloak-bag of guts' (*1HIV*, II, iv, 236, 435). Merrily claiming 'A good wit will make use of anything' (*2HIV*, I, ii, 241–2), Falstaff is forever in debt (*2HIV*, II, i, 116–17), chomps 'capons' (chickens) and glugs 'sack' (sherry) (*1HIV*, II, iv, 516–20), and generally lies, disguises and performs his way through life, dismissing honour as a 'mere scutcheon', or tombstone inscription (*1HIV*, V, ii, 139). He commits a robbery at Gad's Hill (*1HIV*, II, ii, 86), mockingly roleplays the King and then Hal (*1HIV*, 2, iv, 362–462), and, at the Battle of Shrewsbury, fakes his own death before claiming undeserved credit for Hotspur's (*1HIV*, V, iv, 109–60). Falstaff seems to inhabit a self-willed, optimistic play world all his own which, at the beginning of *Henry IV* at least, is tempered only rarely by reality.

Falstaff's is by far the largest role in *Part 2* and his jests do not take long to start. 'I am not just witty in myself but the cause that wit is in other men' (*2HIV*, I, ii, 9–10). He fakes deafness and insults the Lord Chief Justice ('it is the disease of not listening', *2HIV*, I, ii, 118–19). We then learn Falstaff has exploited Mistress Quickly's love for him by asking her for money, assuring her he will pay her back and marry her (*2HIV*, II, i, 89–91). She has him arrested for his debt but Falstaff audaciously only asks for more ('Let it be ten pound if thou canst', *2HIV*, II, i, 144). But from this point Falstaff seems progressively to mirror the tetralogy's increasingly serious tone. His 'gout' or 'pox' which plays 'the rogue' with his 'great toe' (I, ii, 238–9) foreshadows his fatal sickness. His callous streak, already implicit in the Gad's Hill robbery and calling his soldiers mere 'food for powder' who'll 'fill a pit as well as better' (*1HIV*, IV, ii, 62–4), grows more evident. He drunkenly fights Pistol (*2HIV*, II, iv, 200). He recruits as soldiers unfit, scared men and then accepts their bribes to excuse them from military service (*2HIV*, III, ii, 94–180, 211–43). And his reminiscences with Justice Shallow about their youthful escapades on the 'chimes at midnight' strike a melancholy note: 'that's fifty-five year ago' (*2HIV*, III, ii, 203–11). When King Henry V rejects him, his customary bravado ('I will be the man yet that shall make you great') rings hollow. Shallow replies 'I cannot perceive how' (*2HIV*, V, v, 78–80). Falstaff's final line is unfinished, interrupted by a dismissive Lord Chief Justice (*2HIV*, V, v, 91). It is left to Hostess Quickly, who thinks 'the king has killed his heart', to recount his last words (*HV*, II, i, 84; II, iii, 9–28).

Richard II (*RII*)

Richard II's deposition ignites the whole story of the two tetralogies. He is often caricatured as a weak king, due to negative portrayals by the chronicles Shakespeare took as his sources. But Shakespeare's play *Richard II* allows for a more charitable reading, illustrating the contradictions underlying the very structures and principles of medieval and Renaissance hereditary rule. Richard is confident he has been chosen by God himself to be King, as belief at the time dictated, and that this divinity extends to a kind of enchanted relationship between a sovereign and the land he rules: 'This earth shall have a feeling and these stones / Prove armed soldiers ere her native king / Shall falter under foul rebellion's arms' (*RII*, III, ii, 24–7). Richard therefore thinks God himself would step in to save him ('God save the King!'); the fact he does not ('Will no man say "amen"?', *RII*, IV, i, 173) radically weakens fundamental preconceptions about the King's relationship with his people.

Richard thus comes bitterly to mock the idea and symbolism of the 'King's Two Bodies', whereby the King's physical body is a mere representation of the symbolic body of the kingdom. In a scene absent from earlier editions of the play, where the continuation of Elizabeth I's reign was a dangerously sensitive issue, the deposed Richard smashes a mirror, killing off symbolically his regal 'reflection', but also implicitly rejecting the 'political theology' that he had such a supernatural power in the first place (*RII*, IV, i, 288). The idea of the 'King's Two Bodies' is shattered forever. Richard, bewildered and imprisoned, turns the idea inside out. Once his body symbolised a whole kingdom; now he sees a whole kingdom in his own body: 'these same thoughts people this little world [...] Thus play I in one person many people / And none contented' (*RII*, V, v, 9, 31–2). Not only is an individual king deposed, then, the whole system that supports the King's role is thrown into jeopardy. No king for the next eight plays will ever truly be secure.

Hotspur (1HIV)

As his nickname suggests, 'Hotspur' (Harry Percy) is hot-headed and impulsive. He constantly interrupts Worcester as he tries to explain their plot (1HIV, I, iii, 233), and mocks and annoys his potential ally Glendower (1HIV, III, i). He is, however, affectingly tender with his wife Kate (1HIV, II, iii) and delivers a dignified speech, dying, at the end of his fight with Hal (1HIV, V, iv, 76–85). Kate's beautiful lament, for his life and the fact he was betrayed in battle by his father, is sadly often cut in production (2HIV, II, iii, 9–45).

Northumberland (RII, 1HIV, 2HIV)

Hotspur's father Northumberland plays a dominant, 'Kingmaker' role in Richard II. He is indispensable to Bolingbroke's taking of the crown: supplying soldiers, helping Bolingbroke's passage back to England, and intimidating Richard and his allies (RII, II, i, 277–98; II, iii, 2–18; IV, i, 151–227). But Northumberland soon thinks the King ungrateful and plots against him (1HIV, I, iii, 125–300). Sick, he fatally leaves his son to face the King's forces alone (1HIV, IV, i, 16). In Part 2 he discusses mounting another rebellion, this time with Richard's old ally the Archbishop of York, but again he fails to see the project through, listening to his wife's and daughter's protests and fleeing to Scotland (2HIV, II, iii, 67).

Mortimer (1HIV)

Mortimer is the rival claimant to the throne supported by Hotspur and Northumberland after Richard II. Crucially, he is descended from a son of the Black Prince that is older than the son from whom Bolingbroke's line is descended. This makes his family line's claim to the throne stronger than that of Henry IV and the Lancastrians born after him. These issues dominate Shakespeare's other historical tetralogy.

Princess Catherine (HV)

Princess Catherine of France is married to the king at the end of Henry V. Her brief, French-language interludes with her lady-in-waiting, where she misconstrues normal English words as rude French ones, comically counter-balance the occasional graphic violence of the war scenes (HV, III, iv). She responds lovingly to Henry's suit after his victory, leading to a peace between England and France (HV, V, ii, 99–271).

Language

Richard II is the only play in the tetralogy written entirely in verse. A quarter of the lines form part of some kind of rhyme scheme. The language's conscious formality reflects the play's main themes and issues. The extensive use of feminine endings, where lines end relatively gently on an unstressed syllable, imply the fragility of any king's grip over the English crown. The carefully organised imagery illustrates the highly symbolic nature of the regal system that Richard's deposition nearly destroys. Images and movements of ascent and descent are especially prominent. Richard mocks Bolingbroke's anger with unwitting prescience – 'how high a pitch his resolution soars' (*RII*, I, i, 109) – before bemoaning his own fall: 'down, down I come' (*RII*, III, iii, 177). Images of melting and liquidity are also frequent. Richard compares himself to a melting 'king of snow' (*RII*, IV, i, 260), likening his fall and Bolingbroke's rise to 'two buckets filling one another' (*RII*, IV, i, 185).

Richard's fall also seems to affect language itself as a system of meaning and communication. Mowbray complains he will be unable to speak in his 'native English' while banished (*RII*, I, iii, 160). This nostalgic link of language with homeland is fragmented as Richard loses the crown. The Duchess of York rebukes Henry IV for 'set[ting] the word itself against the word' (*RII*, V, iii, 121). Words no longer correspond with their meanings, much as the deposed king no longer corresponds symbolically with his kingdom. The ominous idea of systemic breakdown is also relayed via metaphors of sight. The deposed Richard's tears cloud his vision (*RII*, IV, i, 244) and Bushy likens 'grief' to 'perspective' paintings that must be 'eyed awry' to 'distinguish form' (*RII*, II, ii, 21).

Richard II's exclusive use of verse mirrors Richard's ultimately destructive courtly haughtiness and introspection. The next three plays mingle verse and prose, reflecting the tension between Hal's duty to his father's court and his desire to explore the kingdom he will inherit. The Eastcheap characters' prose is richly, if often confusingly, inventive. It contains, for example, mangled proverbs or Bible verses (Falstaff twists St Paul's word 'vocation' to justify his fondness for thieving), comic verbal distortions (Mistress Quickly's 'pulsidge' for 'pulse'), elaborate insults (Doll Tearsheet calls Pistol a 'basket-hilt stale juggler') and pretentiously overblown poetic diction (such as Pistol's 'Nay, rather damn them with King Cerberus,/And let the welkin roar', *1HIV*, I, ii, 99–100; see also *2HIV*, II, iv, 23, 127, 166–7). Hal himself moves smoothly from verse to prose, either to join in with Eastcheap's near-the-knuckle banter – Falstaff is, for example, a 'trunk of humours', 'bolting-hutch of beastliness' and 'swollen parcel of dropsies' (*1HIV*, II, iv, 433–5) – or to converse with his French betrothed Catherine in a simpler English that she might understand.

Themes

Stagecraft and statecraft

The theme of theatricality itself is absolutely central to Shakespeare's plays. For Jaques in *As You Like It*, of course, 'All the world's a stage/And all the men and women merely players' (II, vii, 138–9). The *Henry IV* tetralogy explores stagecraft's relationship with statecraft. The very idea of the 'King's Two Bodies' is theatrical, simply because one thing represents another. Material 'reality' is only half the story.

The King's flesh is only a bodily metaphor: his real identity is his kingdom's power and strength and the divine hierarchy that set him on the throne on the first place. King is to subject as God is to King. This theological backdrop helps explain why York 'weep[s]' about Richard's fate and his allegiance with Bolingbroke (*RII*, V, ii, 2), why Henry IV and his son atone so often for Richard's death (*RII*, V, vi, 49–50; *HV*, IV, i, 277–93) and why arguments about 'conscience' surface in the second half of *Henry V* (*HV*, IV, i, 171–2). If 'all the world's a stage', then God is our critical audience.

Accompanying this theological outlook, however, is a more worldly strand of Renaissance political theory, exemplified most famously by Machiavelli's *The Prince*. Moralists stressed that worldly glory or fame was transitory and unimportant, but Machiavelli disagreed, arguing it was the chief motivating factor for human action. Bolingbroke's popularity with the subjects, carefully cultivated by theatrical events like processions, is key to his rise to the throne. As York recounts, the people 'darted their desiring eyes/Upon his visage [face]' (*RII*, V, ii, 15–16), while Richard is like a mere bit-player: 'him that enters next [...] his prattle [...] tedious' (*RII*, V, ii, 25–6).

The successful King must therefore be a competent actor, playing his role convincingly to God and to his people. Hal seems to intuit this in his frequent use of disguise. He tricks Falstaff during the Gad's Hill robbery (*1HIV*, II, ii, 97) and infiltrates his drunken conversations with Tearsheet and Quickly (*2HIV*, II, iv, 232). He also ably, comically, plays his own father to entertain the Eastcheap drinkers (*1HIV*, II, iv, 418–63). But there is an underlying sense that this consummate actor only pretends to jest with his subjects so as better to rule them. The future King's 'I know you all' is arguably directed to the audience itself, living under the state's silent, beady eye. As King he undertakes such surveillance at night in France, assuming aliases 'Harry *le roi*' (*HV*, IV, i, 50) or nameless soldier '[u]nder Sir Thomas Erpingham' (*HV*, IV, i, 92) to gauge the morale of his troops. Thus disguised he grows angry with commoner Michael Williams for doubting his cause (*HV*, IV, i, 181–218), but after his victory rewards him with gold for his honesty (*HV*, IV, viii, 56–7). It is unsure however, if the King's threat of a later 'challenge' is meant wholly in jest (*HV*, IV, viii, 59). And Williams's apparent refusal to take money from Henry's Welsh captain Fluellen, who had wanted him hanged for treason, undercuts the idea that this situation has been fully and happily resolved (*HV*, IV, viii, 66, 43–4). Sometimes the exercise of spectacular power is arguably cruel, as when Henry V's old friend Bardolph is hanged as an example to others (*HV*, III, vi, 108), or when the English kill their French prisoners (*HV*, IV, vi, 38). The plays thus scrutinise, rather than fully advocate or reject, Machiavellian precepts like 'it is much safer to be feared than to be loved, when one of the two must be lacking' (Machiavelli 2005: 58).

International relations and a 'useable past'

As the French war so clearly shows, the tetralogy deals head-on with the kinds of international and ideological conflicts characteristic of early modern *Realpolitik*. The Welsh King Glendower is appalled when the Englishman Hotspur orders the use of explosives to divert the course of the river Trent and give him a larger continuous stretch of land. 'I'll not have it altered' (*1HIV*, III, i, 112). The natural world for Glendower is its own law. The river 'must' wind its own way, simply because 'it doth' (*1HIV*, III, i, 103). *Henry V* deals with English–Irish conflict past and present. In a brief but memorable appearance Henry's aggressive captain Macmorris, Shakespeare's only Irish character, assumes that as an Irishman he will be called a 'villain and a bastard and a knave and a rascal' (*HV*, III, v, 63–4). The Chorus says Henry's homecoming is welcomed with 'much more cause' than that of the Earl of Essex, Robert Devereux, who in 1599 sought (and failed) to suppress Irish rebellion (*HV*, V, Chorus, 29–34): 'the only explicit, extra-dramatic, incontestable reference to a contemporary event anywhere in the canon' (ed. Taylor 1982: 7). Such references were rare because it was often dangerous, if not illegal, for playwrights and theatres to depict contemporary events or persons directly. In the introduction to his 2003 Oxford edition of *Henry VI Part 2* Roger Warren even suggests 'it is more accurate to speak of "political plays" than "history plays"' (ed. Warren 2003: 36). Historical kings and queens thus helped Shakespeare explore current affairs: his theatre offered a space for collective thought for an often illiterate populace, where no countrywide school system was in place.

The idea that the past may usefully instruct action on present problems or conflicts, or, more generally, that history is a kind of allegory of the present, is implicit throughout the tetralogy. In 1601 Elizabeth I apparently told the Kentish antiquarian William Lambarde 'I am Richard II, know ye not that?' (but this has recently been contested; see Scott-Warren 2013). Like Richard, Elizabeth had no heir and the resulting power vacuum led to threats of deposition, most notably from the Earl of Essex. Strands of discussion emerging from the Protestant Reformation were, moreover, challenging the monarch's automatically religiously sanctioned legitimacy. Some religious extremists mooted the possibility, if not necessity, of regicide in certain circumstances. On the other hand, the *Homily Against Disobedience* politicised religion by forbidding rebellion against the (Christ-like) monarch. Successive audiences have found powerful reflections of their own political situations in these plays. For example, Northumberland's lines 'The king is not himself but basely led / By flatterers' (*RII*, II, i, 241–2) in John Rich's 1738 Covent Garden production met with wild applause by those who disliked King George II's entourage.

Royal families

The plays' exploration of kingship, heredity and succession also has a more acutely personal, familial element, especially in their treatments of father–son relations. Richard II's self-absorbed isolation is compounded by the fact we do not see his parents, a difference accentuated by the play's foregrounding of paternal relationships between Aumerle and York, and Bolingbroke and John of Gaunt. It is often noted that the structure of the Henry IV plays, especially *Part 1*, artfully poises Hal between two radically opposed father figures: Henry IV and Falstaff. The way the scene moves so regularly between the court and Eastcheap perhaps suggests a kind of oscillatory indecision in Hal's mind. If so, his 'I know you all' speech is in fact a nervous attempt to convince himself he will become the king his father and country expect.

Texts and contexts

Texts

Richard II was first printed in 1597 but the deposition scene does not appear in print until 1608, nearly fifteen years after the play's first performances and, perhaps more than coincidentally, the first version printed after Elizabeth I's death. *Henry IV Part 1* first appeared in 1598 in Quarto, with relatively few variants in the Folio text. *Part 2* causes more problems for the modern editor. The 1600 Quarto has two different versions, one with a scene containing King Henry's speech 'How many thousand of my poorest subjects / Are at this hour asleep', one without. And these Quartos themselves both differ from the Folio text. There are fourteen 'Quarto-only' passages, and eight 'Folio-only passages' that often discuss the ramifications of Richard's deposition and assassination. Like the deposition scene of *Richard II*, these scenes may have stayed out of print for political reasons. *Henry V* was first printed in Quarto in 1600, but all editions after 1623 have been based on the Folio. The French nobles' angrily ashamed response to defeat differs in the two versions (IV, v), as does Henry's ambivalent attitude to honest dissenter Michael Williams (IV, viii). Editors must also decide whether to agree to Lewis Theobald's famous emendation of Falstaff's death as described by Mistress Quickly, from 'A table [likeness] of green fields' to 'A [He] babbled of green fields' (II, iii, 16).

Sources: Shakespeare and Holinshed

Shakespeare drew much of his material from Raphael Holinshed's *Chronicles of England, Scotland and Ireland,* published in 1577 and 1587, and drawing on seventy years of work by precedent Tudor historians. Holinshed unambiguously assigns the conflicts portrayed in Shakespeare's two tetralogies to one root cause: Bolingbroke '*wrong* usurped the crowne [and] *cruellie* procured [Richard's] death' (quoted in ed. Weis 1997: 18, my emphasis). By moments Shakespeare follows Holinshed closely, as in Archbishop of Canterbury's long (and quite frankly dull) speech on Salic law (*HV*, I, ii, 33–95). Often, however, he shapes the historical material to help narrative flow and stress thematic parallels. In *Richard II* Shakespeare accelerates Richard's decision to banish Bolingbroke and Mowbray while reducing the murdered Gloucester's reputation as a troublemaker, making Richard seem more capricious and unstable. Bolingbroke returns sooner from exile, accentuating his ominous threat. Richard's transfer to Pomfret and his wife's departure for France, two separate historical events, are assimilated for dramatic effect (*RII*, V, i). Gaunt and York function almost like a Greek chorus, commenting despairingly on events (*RII*, II, i; V, v). The symbolic scenes with portraits (II, ii), mirrors (IV, i), and two gardeners once Bolingbroke chops away 'Bushy' and 'Green' (III, iv), are apparently Shakespearean inventions.

Shakespeare also stresses in *Henry IV Part 1* the relationship between Hal and Hotspur. He makes them roughly the same age even though the historical Hotspur was twenty-three years older, and calls Hotspur's wife 'Kate', like Henry V's Queen Catherine, even though her actual name was Elizabeth. The Hal–Hotspur rivalry gives the play structural focus and balance. The story sways rhythmically between Hal and Hotspur scenes and culminates in a duel that never historically took place. Hal was only sixteen at the Battle of Shrewsbury. At the beginning of *Part 2* 'Rumour' and Morton's speech to Northumberland recap the story left hanging at the end of *Part 1*. This dramatic impetus continues when battles fought in 1405 and 1408 are conflated to a single scene set in 1413 (*2HIV*, IV, i). *Henry V* shows the king in a more positive light by minimising historical factors that worked in his favour, like the French King's madness and French forces' infighting, while quietly suppressing the strategic blunder that left Henry stranded at Agincourt in the first place.

The plays in performance

Consecutive performance

Some theatre companies have staged the whole tetralogy. The English Shakespeare Company, for example, even staged the whole 'octology' (2–4 September 1988), an achievement matched by the RSC for the 'Glorious Moment' (13–16 March 2008, see Dailey 2010). *Richard II* and *Henry V* are, however, most often staged alone. The *Henry IV* plays can be played separately (*Part 1* much more frequently than *Part 2*) or together, sometimes abridged as a single show. Falstaff-centred productions have brought in material from *The Merry Wives of Windsor*.

Richard II

Richard II productions have been varied, even subversive, in their interpretations. In 1951 Michael Redgrave played Richard as homosexual while homosexuality was still illegal. Joan Littlewood's 1964 production and Michael Bogdanov's 1986–9 English Shakespeare Company production saw the play in broadly Marxian terms: Richard was an unwitting victim of the irrevocable power of money that he himself had unleashed. John Barton's 1973 production alternated leads, Ian Richardson and Richard Pasco swapping the roles of Richard and Bolingbrooke each performance, stressing the two characters' reciprocity. Richard's handing over the crown ('On this side my hand, and on that side thine', IV, i, 183) emerged from the play's themes of mirroring and symmetrical structures. Death crowned them both at the end. Ariane Mnouchkine's experimental 1981 five-hour version (Théâtre du Soleil) made extensive use of doubling to portray 'bodies traversed by a single voice' (see ed.

Dawson and Yachnin 2011: 96). Fiona Shaw played the lead in 1995 (televised 1997) as an overgrown child, sucking her thumb when telling 'sad stories of the deaths of kings' (III, ii, 156), and throwing tantrums when things did not go her way. Recent high-profile Richard IIs, hinting at a resurgence after relative neglect, include Ralph Fiennes (Almeida 2000), Mark Rylance (Globe 2003), Kevin Spacey (Old Vic 2005), Eddie Redmayne (Donmar Warehouse 2011), John Heffernan (Tobacco Factory 2011), an absolutely excellent David Tennant (RSC 2012), and Ben Whishaw in the accessible and very worthwhile 2012 televised BBC tetralogy *The Hollow Crown*.

The *Henry IV* plays

Anthony Quayle's 1951 RSC star turn as Falstaff was taken up again for the 1979 BBC films. Orson Welles's 1965 film *Chimes at Midnight*, with Welles as Falstaff, is a distinctive contribution to the plays' performance history, famous for its impressive battle scenes and distinctive, high-contrast black and white cinematic style. In Dominic Dromgoole's 2010 Globe production Jamie Parker's Hal and Roger Allam's Falstaff came in for special praise. In Greg Doran's 2014 RSC production, with Antony Sher as Falstaff, Alex Hassell as Hal and Jasper Britton as Henry IV, the figure of dead King Richard looked down, perhaps accusingly, from above. *The Hollow Crown* versions of the plays cast Jeremy Irons as Henry IV, Simon Russell Beale as Falstaff, who shades the role with cruel melancholy, Tom Hiddleston as an accomplished Hal, and Paul Ritter as a lively but aggressive Pistol, one of the plays' earliest favourite characters, but whose appeal can be hard to communicate to modern audiences.

Henry V

One of the twentieth century's most famous versions of *Henry V* is Laurence Olivier's 1944 film, which cut 1,700 lines to maximise the play's patriotism and raise morale in the Second World War. As if to rival Olivier's Technicolor chivalry, Kenneth Branagh's 1989 film is dark, muddy and bloody. In the Globe 2012 production, with Jamie Parker as Henry V, the King is so moved by news of Bardolph's hanging he becomes less autocratic, and a better leader. The all-male company Propeller's 2011 modern-costume production encouraged analogies with contemporary and trench warfare. Tom Hiddleston's Henry V in the *Hollow Crown* series delicately balances seriousness with vulnerability.

Critical reception

Richard II

Collections edited by Harold Bloom (1988), Charles Forker (1998) and Kirby Farrell (1999) together offer a good selection of earlier criticism. Richard Halpern

(2009) revisits *Richard II*'s treatment of the 'King's Two Bodies' to critique Ernst Kantorowicz's classic 1957 study of the same name. Richard's 'Two Bodies' tragically intertwine: he is like all mortal men too subject to 'creaturely passions' to inhabit his symbolic role appropriately, a fluidity is figured by new, precarious forms of money. Jeffrey Doty (2010) historicises *Richard II*'s attention to statecraft and stagecraft in terms of a new 'public sphere'. In the 1590s the theatre becomes increasingly a space for 'non-elite' political thought and discussion: theatre and politics inform each other. Christopher Pye (1988) and Richard Ashby (2015) examine this idea via attention to the play's motifs of visuality and a 'politics of the gaze'. For Donovan Sherman, Richard 'mobilizes theater's ineffectiveness as powerful because it is paradoxically self-defeating' (2014: 26). Jason Scott-Warren (2013) challenges the view that Elizabeth I compared herself to Richard II. See also the recent collection of essays edited by Jeremy Lopez (2012).

The *Henry IV* plays

Stephen Greenblatt's 'Invisible Bullets' (1985; see Greenblatt 1994), a classic of new historicist criticism, draws analogies between Hal's management of his inherited kingdom and sixteenth-century techniques used to keep the colonised peoples of the New World in check. Greenblatt echoes Kafka in concluding that glimmers of radical change are always deferred: 'There is subversion, there is no end of subversion, only not for us' (1994: 45). Simon Palfrey (2005) suggests Hal's 'I know *you* all' is also addressed directly to the audience, a metatheatrical anticipation of how he intertwines surveillance and power (Palfrey 2005: 236, emphasis mine). Harold Bloom (1999), consciously distancing himself from avowedly political criticism, prefers to celebrate Falstaff as perhaps Shakespeare's greatest creation: 'the true and perfect image of life itself' (Bloom 1999: 283). Lucy Munro (2013) argues that Pistol, another massively popular figure in Shakespeare's day, reflects Shakespeare's broader approach to historical narrative in his lively intermingling of archaic and invented words. Meghan C. Andrews's historical reading suggests Hal dramatises 'Elizabethan society's longing for a fully masculine heir to the throne' (2014: 382), while Jacqueline Vanhoutte (2013) sees similar resonances between the ageing Falstaff and the waning of Elizabethan power.

Henry V

Andrew Hiscock's critical survey of 'Shakespeare and the Theatre of War' (2011) usefully summarises recent lines of argument. Graham Holderness argues that *Henry V*'s transfer of action to France offers critical distance, which lets the English commonwealth safely evaluate itself (quoted in Hiscock 2011: 225). For David J. Baker, *Henry V* is 'a patriotic work, written in time of colonial war to justify the expansionism and xenophobia of a nation consolidating an empire' (quoted in Hiscock 2011: 223). And for David Scott Kastan, national coherency in Elizabethan England is 'fashioned [...] largely by reference to the alterity and inferiority of the Irish' (quoted in Hiscock 2011: 226). In Ewan Fernie's 'Action! *Henry V*', the play emerges as 'an exemplum of human action: available in the struggle against fascism and in the invasion of Afghanistan and Iraq' (Fernie 2007: 118). And Etienne Poulard (2013) reads *Henry V* as forerunner of a consumerist 'interpassivity' exemplified by reality TV or internet pornography: the audience does not 'enjoy' the entertainment, it watches someone *else*, the Chorus, doing so.

Discussion questions

❋ Harold Bloom says Falstaff is 'the authentic teacher of wisdom' (1999: 283). What kind of 'wisdom' could a liar and thief possibly teach us?

❋ How has *Henry V* influenced modern ideals of authority and leadership?

❋ Is Shakespeare a patriot?

Bibliography and further reading

Editions
Shakespeare, W. (1982), *Henry V*, ed. G. Taylor, Oxford: Oxford University Press.
Shakespeare, W. (1987), *Henry IV Part One*, ed. D. Bevington, Oxford: Oxford University Press.
Shakespeare, W. (1997), *Henry IV Part Two*, ed. R. Weis, Oxford: Oxford University Press.
Shakespeare, W. (2003), *Henry VI Part Two*, ed. R. Warren, Oxford: Oxford University Press.
Shakespeare, W. (2011), *Richard II*, ed. A. B. Dawson and P. Yachnin, Oxford: Oxford University Press.

Critical response
Andrews, M. (2014), 'Gender, Genre, and Elizabeth's Princely Surrogates', *Studies in English Literature 1500–1900*, 54:2, 375–99.
Ashby, R. (2015), '"Pierced to the soul": The Politics of the Gaze in *Richard II*', *Shakespeare*, 11:2, 201–13.
Bloom, H. (ed.) (1988), *William Shakespeare's 'Richard II': Modern Critical Interpretations*, New York: Chelsea House Publishers.
Bloom, H. (1999), *Shakespeare and the Invention of the Human*, New York: Riverhead Books.
Dailey, A. (2010), 'The RSC's "Glorious Moment" and the Making of Shakespearian History', *Shakespeare Survey*, 63, 184–97.
Doty, J. (2010), 'Shakespeare's *Richard II*, "Popularity" and the Early Modern Public Sphere', *Shakespeare Quarterly*, 61:2, 183–205.

Farrell, K. (ed.) (1999), *Critical Essays on Shakespeare's* Richard II, New York: G. K. Hall.

Fernie, E. (2007), 'Action! *Henry V*', in H. Grady and T. Hawkes (eds), *Presentist Shakespeares*, London/New York: Routledge, pp. 96–120.

Forker, C. (ed.) (1998), *Richard II: Shakespeare: The Critical Tradition*, London New York: The Athlone Press.

Greenblatt, S. (1994), 'Invisible Bullets: Renaissance Authority and Its Subversion, *Henry IV* and *Henry V*', in J. Dollimore and A. Sinfield (eds), *Political Shakespeare: Essays in Cultural Materialism*, 2nd edn, Manchester: Manchester University Press, pp. 18–47.

Halpern, R. (2009), 'The King's Two Buckets: Kantorowicz, *Richard II*, and Fiscal Trauerspiel', *Representations*, 106, 67–76.

Hiscock, A. (2011), '"More warlike than politique": Shakespeare and the Theatre of War – a Critical Survey', *Shakespeare*, 7:2, 221–47.

Kantorowicz, E. (1957), *The King's Two Bodies: A Study in Medieval Political Theology*, Princeton: Princeton University Press.

Lopez, J. (ed.) (2012), *Richard II: New Critical Essays*, London: Routledge.

Machiavelli, N. (2005), *The Prince*, trans. and ed. P. Bondanella, Oxford: Oxford University Press.

Munro, L. (2013), 'Speaking History: Linguistic Memory and the Usable Past in the Early Modern History Play', *Huntingdon Library Quarterly*, 76:4, 519–40.

Palfrey, S. (2005), *Doing Shakespeare*, London: Thomson/Arden Shakespeare.

Poulard, E. (2013), '"After the takeover": Shakespeare, Lacan, Žižek and the Interpassive Subject', *English Studies*, 94:3, 291–312.

Pye, C. (1988), 'The Betrayal of the Gaze: Theatricality and Power in Shakespeare's *Richard II*', *English Literary History*, 55:3, 575–98.

Scott-Warren, J. (2013), 'Was Elizabeth I Richard II? The Authenticity of Lambarde's "Conversation"', *Review of English Studies*, 64:264, 208–30.

Sherman, D. (2014), '"What more remains?": Messianic Performance in *Richard II*', *Shakespeare Quarterly*, 65:1, 22–48.

Vanhoutte, J. (2013), '"Age in love": Falstaff among the Minions of the Moon', *English Literary Renaissance*, 43:1, 86–127.

12 The *Henry VI* trilogy and *Richard III*

c. 1591–7

Act, scene and line references are to the Oxford Shakespeare editions: *Henry VI Part One*, edited by Michael Taylor (2003); *Henry VI Part Two*, edited by Roger Warren (2003); *Henry VI Part Three*, edited by Randall Martin (2001); and *Richard III*, edited by John Jowett (2000).

Plot summary

The historical period portrayed by the *Henry VI* tetralogy lasts from 1422 (Henry V's death) to 1485 (Richard III's death). *Henry VI Part 1* starts with Henry V's funeral. The new king is a minor. Henry VI was crowned at 'nine months old' (*3HVI*, I, i, 113). The French exploit this by crowning their own Prince, Charles, to rule over the French territories Henry V had conquered. Two incident-packed stories intertwine in *Henry VI Part 1*: one in France, one in England. In France, the English captain John Talbot struggles to regain control of the lost English territory, even as the French are emboldened by the seemingly magical presence of the young country maid Joan of Arc. The English lose Orleans, the Earl of Salisbury killed by cannon shot (*1HVI*, I, v–vii). Talbot eludes an attempted trap by the Duchess of Auvergne (*1HVI*, II, ii–iii); the Duke of Bedford is killed but the English regain Rouen (*1HVI*, III, ii); and the Duke of Burgundy, a Frenchman, turncoats back from the English to the French (*1HVI*, III, iii). In England, the child king's Protector the Duke of Gloucester, also known as Duke Humphrey, competes for power with the unscrupulous Bishop of Winchester. Their soldiers clash in the City of London (*1HVI*, I, iii). Against this already fraught backdrop a further source of conflict emerges. Richard Plantagenet, dubbed Duke of York (*1HVI*, III, i, 173), is grandson to the *third* son of Edward III, whereas King Henry VI is grandson only to Edward III's *fourth* son. York thinks that by rights he should be King. The fact that Henry's grandfather took the crown, rather than inherited it (as Shakespeare recounts in *Richard II*), only makes York's claim all the stronger. In a law-court garden, York invites those who support his claim to the throne to pluck a white rose. The Earl of Warwick accepts. The Duke of Somerset and Earl of Suffolk refuse, taking red roses instead. The 'French' and 'English' strands of the play are brought together as young King Henry VI comes to Paris to be crowned (*1HVI*, IV, i). Burgundy's treachery is discovered, and Somerset and York – still furious with each other after the rose-garden episode – are called upon to replace the soldiers that are missing as a result. But as Talbot marches on Bordeaux, and finds himself outmanoeuvred and surrounded by the French, Somerset refuses to send along reinforcements to York. This is an attempt to embarrass York, his enemy (*1HVI*, IV, iv, 9). The loss of Bordeaux and the slaughter of brave John Talbot and his son are thus directly down to Somerset and York's quarrel. At Paris, however, the English defeat Joan of Arc and York condemns Joan of Arc to be burnt. A truce is struck (*1HVI*, V, v). Gloucester seeks to make peace with France by marrying the young King Henry to the daughter of the Earl of Armagnac, but the Earl of Suffolk intervenes, convincing him to marry Margaret, Princess of Naples. Suffolk is in love with Margaret and hopes to use her as political leverage to influence the King (*1HVI*, V, vi, 107–8). To Gloucester's disbelief and dismay, Suffolk's eloquence prevails. King Henry VI marries Queen Margaret as *Henry VI Part 2* begins, 'without having any dowry' (*2HVI*, I, i, 61).

The second part of the tetralogy is made up of five other key incidents. First, Gloucester is disgraced, and ultimately murdered, when it is discovered that his haughty, ambitious wife Eleanor has committed witchcraft (*2HVI*, II, iv). Second, Gloucester's enemy, the Bishop of Winchester, grows mad and dies soon after Gloucester's death, babbling near-confessions to Gloucester's murder on his deathbed (*2HVI*, III, iii). Third, Suffolk, the Queen's adulterous lover, is banished for his part in Gloucester's death (*2HVI*, III, ii, 299). On the way to France he is captured and decapitated by pirates who are sympathetic to Gloucester, and who resent Suffolk's part in the loss of Anjou and Maine to the French (*2HVI*, IV, i). Fourth, the Duke of York, striving as always to advance his claim to the throne, tries secretly to destabilise King Henry's reputation by funding and encouraging the commoner Jack Cade to rebel against the King, pretending he (like York) is descended from an elder son of Edward III (*2HVI*, IV, ii–viii). Cade is unseated by his own followers and, as fugitive, discovered and killed by minor noble Alexander Iden (*2HVI*, IV, ix–x). The fifth and final incident is the first battle between white-rose York and the red-rose Lancastrian King: the first War of the Roses, which takes place at St Albans, Hertfordshire (*2HVI*, V, i–iii). York's son, the hunchback Richard (later Richard III), kills his father's long-standing enemy Somerset (*2HVI*, V, ii, 65). York kills the King's ally Clifford (*2HVI*, V, ii, 28). The King flees to the London Parliament; York's forces give chase.

Henry VI Part 3 begins with the two sets of leaders confronting each other in Parliament. York reminds Henry his own grandfather was a rebel, not a hereditary king. The embarrassed, threatened Henry offers a deal: the crown will pass to York and his sons on Henry's death (*3HVI*, I, i, 172–5). Henry's allies, wife Margaret and disinherited son ('Ned') are appalled at this apparent cowardice and defeatism: Margaret 'divorces' her husband (*3HVI*, I, i, 247–51) and sets off to fight. Meanwhile, York's sons Edward, Richard and Clarence urge their father to strike while the iron is hot and take the crown immediately (*3HVI*, I, ii, 11–35). Margaret's Lancastrian forces win the battle that ensues, in York. They kill York's youngest son Rutland (*3HVI*, I, iii, 47), then York himself (*3HVI*, I, iv), humiliatingly setting his head above his own town gates. Warwick reports sadly to his Yorkist allies that another battle, the second to take place at St Albans, has similarly gone against them (*3HVI*, II, i, 135–7). The furious young Yorkists fight back, and this time prevail: the prominent Lancastrian young Clifford's head replaces the Duke of York's over the town gates (*3HVI*, II, vi, 84). York's eldest son Edward is effectively now the King of England. To consolidate their strong position, Warwick suggests Edward should marry Lady Bona. Marrying thus into the French royal family would assure their continued support (*3HVI*, II, vi, 89). With France onside, the threat of the Lancastrians, already weakened, would disappear forever. But Edward marries instead the English widow Lady Elizabeth Grey (*3HVI*, III, ii, 105–6) This strategic folly infuriates Edward's brother Clarence, who later defects to the Lancastrians (*3HVI*, IV, i, 123). Richard stays with Edward but confides to the audience in soliloquy that he will happily kill his brothers and their sons to become King (*3HVI*, III, ii, 124–95). The news of Edward's marriage to Lady Grey reaches France just as Warwick finishes praising Lady Bona on Edward's behalf, just as Lady Bona's father accepts Edward's offer of marriage, and just as Queen Margaret bemoans 'Henry's hope is done' (*3HVI*, III, iii, 57). But the message changes everything. The French King takes Edward's snub as an insult, as does the humiliated Warwick, who switches allegiance instantly to Henry's grateful Queen. On his return to England Warwick surprises Edward and takes him captive (*3HVI*, IV, iii, 27–57). But Edward escapes with Richard's help (*3HVI*, IV, v), and is crowned Edward IV (*3HVI*, IV, vii, 75). News of Edward's escape makes the Lancastrians fearful for their children and heirs. One such, Richmond (the future Henry VII, first of the Tudor line), is evacuated to Brittany (*3HVI*, IV, vi, 97). Warwick and the Lancastrians fight the Yorkists at Coventry. The Yorkist Clarence returns to his family side (*3HVI*, V, i, 81–102). Richard captures the former King Henry and takes him to the Tower of London (*3HVI*, IV, viii, 52–64). Another battle takes place at Barnet, just north of London, as the Lancastrians go south to recapture Henry. These battles are somewhat mingled by the play's action-packed ending. But Barnet is especially costly for Margaret, Henry and the Lancastrians. Warwick is killed (*3HVI*, V, ii, 49). At the final battle, at Tewkesbury, the Yorkists score a decisive victory over the weakened Lancastrians. Margaret's son 'Ned' is killed (*3HVI*, V, v, 38–67). Richard kills the imprisoned Henry at the Tower (*3HVI*, V, vi, 57).

As *Henry VI Part 3* ends, then, it seems King Edward IV enjoys a 'glorious summer' (*RIII*, I, i, 2). The Lancastrian threat is quashed, and Queen Elizabeth has just given birth to a prince. But the famous opening soliloquy of *Richard III* makes clear that this stability is not to last. Richard wants the crown for himself. He quickly frames his brother Clarence for treason (*RIII*, I, i, 56–9). This is relatively easy because Clarence had already once proved himself disloyal by briefly siding with the Lancastrians. Clarence is murdered in the Tower (*RIII*, I, iv, 245). Richard claims Edward IV's revocation of the death warrant simply arrived too late (*RIII*, II, i, 86–90). An appalled Edward IV, who has grown sick since the triumph at Tewkesbury, dies in the very next scene. Despite Queen Elizabeth's and her brothers' complaints, this makes Richard the Lord Protector over Edward's two sons. Richard quickly takes advantage of this strong position. He arrests Elizabeth's brothers on suspicion of Clarence's death and has them executed at Pomfret Castle (*RIII*, III, iii). He then executes the Earl of Hastings, a dissenting voice, for siding with a reputed witch Mistress Shore and causing his disabilities (*RIII*, III, iv, 81). He conveys the young princes, rival claimants to his throne, to the Tower (*RIII*, III, i, 149). Meanwhile, with the help and enthusiastic public praises of his ally Buckingham, to whom he has promised land and rewards should he become King, Richard secures the approval of the City of London and is crowned Richard III (*RIII*, IV, ii). Once crowned, Richard III's first thought is to prolong his reign. He arranges the murder of his wife Lady Anne (*RIII*, IV, ii, 51), whom he has 'wooed' and 'won' through a mixture of emotional blackmail and implicit threats (*RIII*, I, ii). This is to clear his way to marry his niece Elizabeth, daughter to Edward IV, and whose sons with another husband would have stronger claims to the throne than his. He also asks Buckingham to kill off the young boys in the Tower (*RIII*, IV, ii). When Buckingham balks at the idea, Richard refuses him the land he had been promised and dismisses him (*RIII*, IV, ii, 41–2). Richard finds someone else do the deed for the right price: James Tyrrell (*RIII*, IV, iii, 1–22). The betrayed Buckingham hastily assembles an army to unseat Richard, but it is no match for the royal forces and Buckingham is executed for treason (*RIII*, V, i). As Edward IV's widow, Richard's mother and ex-Queen Margaret lament together, Richard has killed practically everyone (*RIII*, IV, iv, 40–73). The only real rival to his crown is Richmond, whom we remember was evacuated to Brittany as a child in *Henry VI Part 3*. The double agent Stanley, despite Richard's threats to his young son (*RIII*, IV, iv, 412–13), gives Richmond secret intelligence. Edward's widow Elizabeth has given her consent for him to marry her daughter, Princess Elizabeth (*RIII*, IV, v): if Richmond defeats Richard and marries Princess Elizabeth, then the crown will unambiguously be his. At Bosworth Field, Richard's troops are defeated, leaving the solitary Richard to scream – famously – 'A horse, a horse! My kingdom for a horse!' (*RIII*, V, vi, 13). The victory of the Earl of Richmond, Henry Tudor, ends the dispute between Yorkists and Lancastrians, or the Wars of the Roses, and ushers in the Tudor dynasty, of which Shakespeare's own Queen, Elizabeth I, is the latest (and, as it turns out, last) royal representative (*RIII*, V, vii).

Characters (Lancastrians)

Princess Margaret (*1HVI, 2HVI, 3HVI, RIII*)

Princess Margaret is mentioned first in this list of characters because she is the only one present in all four plays. Her role, encompassing political craftiness, military grandeur, bitter ferocity and pride even in disgrace, has been called a 'King Lear for women' (Adrian Noble, quoted in ed. Martin 2001: 82). But her silent entry, near the end of *Henry VI Part 1*, offers little indication of just how important she is going to be. Here, she charms the Earl of Suffolk, William de la Pole, even as Suffolk has been sent to arrange the marriage between her and the King. Actors playing Margaret consider this a key scene. If she comes across here as entirely innocent, her later violence is partially excusable, a mere product of the culture she has been plunged into; any seeming strategising on her part, however, suggests that she is a more active, and therefore responsible, contributor to this culture. Does Margaret always have a 'tiger's heart wrapped in a woman's hide' (*3HVI*, I, iv, 137) , or does she acquire one? If the latter, she certainly acquires one quite quickly. She rapidly, seductively, gains control in her relationship with Suffolk (*2HVI*, I, iii, 43–101), using his help and instruction to unsettle Gloucester's Protectorship over the King, making the whole political system unsteady. Margaret's political ambition, partially realised through Suffolk, is entangled with her love for him. Power and lust are represented via Suffolk as two faces of the same desire. A devastated Margaret cradles Suffolk's severed head in her arms (*2HVI*, IV, iv, 1–24), and directors have seen this as a psychological turning point: the strategist transforms into one of Shakespeare's most militaristic heroines. Margaret is a formidable military leader and shrewd tactician, rabidly committed to the pride of her house, furious when Henry decides to make the Duke of York his heir instead of their own son 'Ned' (*3HVI*, I, i, 216–26). She therefore savours a vengeful pleasure in killing her captured enemy, humiliating York by setting a paper crown on his head (*3HVI*, I, iv, 95) and wiping his face with a napkin dipped in his dead son's blood (*3HVI*, I, iv, 79–80). Her fierce distress at her own son's death is one of the tetralogy's dramatic high points (*3HVI*, V, v, 51–67). Margaret has come to rival, if not supersede, Richard Gloucester (i.e. the later Richard III) as the main role in *3HVI*. Even after the Yorkist victory, she still plays a powerful role, cursing the York court (*RIII*, I, iv, 194–302) and bitterly comforting the women whose children and husbands Richard slaughters (e.g. *RIII*, IV, iv, 77–109). The historical Margaret died in 1482, three years before Richard, but we do not see her die on Shakespeare's stage. She therefore sometimes reappears as a silent, haunting presence in the play's (and tetralogy's) final scenes.

Henry VI (*1HVI, 2HVI, 3HVI*)

James I dismissed Henry VI as a 'sillie weake King' (Moretti 2008: 275), and contemporaries thought 'he lost his wits and memory for a time' (see ed. Warren 2003: 34). Henry VI is certainly too mild and piously Christian to bear or control the vengeful bloodshed around him. Yielding the inheritance of his crown to York leads to a dangerously uncertain power vacuum, where the only way of establishing power is brute force. He is ultimately easy prey for Richard Gloucester (*3HVI*, V, vi, 60). His soliloquies about royal responsibility and military destructiveness illustrate a touching but unworldly idealism (*3HVI*, II, v, 1–54, 73–8, 94–124). These speeches are delivered in near-solitude, adrift from the fighting, in a pastoral location. This is the Edenic space which is now lost, torn apart.

Characters (Yorkists)

Richard Duke of York (1HVI, 2HVI, 3HVI)

Richard Duke of York is behind the claim leading to the Wars of the Roses: this overarching strand of the tetralogy is carefully introduced in *Henry VI Part 1*. York's argument with Somerset in the rose garden, 'too loud' for the 'Temple hall', soon escalates to outright animosity: 'this quarrel will drink blood' (*1HVI*, II, iv, 2, 134). Their sulking with each other leaves Talbot and his son without reinforcements and doomed to die at the hands of the French. York is, however, capable of improvising and turning political situations to his advantage. For example, in *Henry VI Part 2* the other nobles, distracted by their common need to weaken the Lord Protector Duke Humphrey of Gloucester, give him soldiers to put down an Irish rebellion, but York plots to use them to 'stir up in England some black storm' and reinforce his claim to the crown (*2HVI*, III, i, 348). When York is trapped at the start of *Henry VI Part 3* by the Lancastrian forces, his death scene, with its motifs of mocking bowing and false crowns, seems clearly to echo Christ's crucifixion. His death, however, only intensifies his sons' aggressive attempts to avenge him by continuing the claim he initiates.

Richard Duke of Gloucester, later Richard III (2HVI, 3HVI, RIII)

York's son, Richard Duke of Gloucester, later Richard III, is of course much more significant than his older brothers, especially in dramatic terms. He dominates the tetralogy's final play that bears his name in a way that no one character does in any of the others. He enters in Act V, scene i of *Henry VI Part 2*, a kind of 'cliffhanger' to signal the importance of the next generation of Yorkists who will take the struggle into the next play. Clifford attacks Richard almost as soon as he sees him ('foul indigested lump,/As crooked in thy manners as thy shape!', *2HVI*, V, i, 157–8), revealing just how aggressively Richard's hunchback is perceived. But Richard's rise is irresistible over much of the next two plays. He kills York's long-standing enemy Somerset (*2HVI*, V, ii, 65), secretly and astutely mocks his brother Edward's love for Elizabeth Grey (e.g. *2HVI*, III, ii, 21–3) and, crucially, kills off once and for all the imprisoned Henry VI (*2HVI*, V, vi, 57). Richard's soliloquy, at the precise midpoint of *Henry VI Part 3* and the longest in all Shakespeare's plays, affirms his willingness to sacrifice principles for power, to kill all who stand in his way: 'I can smile and murder whiles I smile [...] Can I do all this and cannot get a crown? (*3HVI*, III, ii, 182, 194). Directors often transfer this speech into productions of *Richard III*, the play where Richard's plans so spectacularly and murderously come to fruition. Like Iago, Richard has often been compared to the medieval Vice. He is frequently downstage, close enough to the audience to confide with them, almost boastfully, about the terrible deeds he is about to perform. It is perhaps more than coincidence, then, that Richard III is the only play to start with its main protagonist soliloquising directly to the audience. If in *Henry VI Part 2* he vowed to send even 'the murderous Machiavel to school' (*2HVI*, III, iii, 193), then soon in *Richard III* he orchestrates his elder brother Clarence's execution, which brings his sick eldest brother Edward yet closer to death. But as well as duplicitous scheming, Richard's Machiavellianism takes the form of what Machiavelli himself termed *virtù*. *Virtù* should not be translated as merely Christian 'virtue'. In many ways it is precisely the opposite, relating glory to a kind of self-reliant, self-willed manliness (*virtù* shares a root with the Latin word for *vir*, man). Machiavelli (in)famously claims that:

> Fortune is a woman, and if you want to keep her under it is necessary to beat her and force her down. It is clear that she more often allows herself to be won over by impetuous men than by those who proceed coldly. (Machiavelli 2005: 87)

Richard's 'impetuous' *virtù* is powerfully illustrated in the astonishing scene where he convinces Lady Anne, furious, grieving for the relatives Richard himself has killed and spitting in his face, to marry him (*RIII*, I, ii, 208–10). The odds of Richard's success are overwhelming: 'all the world to nothing' (*RIII*, I, ii, 223). Even Richard is surprised at overcoming Anne's anger and resistance. But his abilities to demonstrate *virtù* and overcome principles of loyalty and mourning, such as Lady Anne's, are perhaps related to his isolation from any such ethical, social, familial or religious codes. He is 'not shaped for sportive tricks' (*RIII*, I, i, 14) and condemned 'to hate the idle pleasures of these days' (*RIII*, I, i, 31). Key to his rejection of society, then, is the way society makes him define *himself* as a rejection. Sigmund Freud saw Richard as an archetype of a wounded narcissist, suffering from a lack of maternal love. Richard indeed spits 'Love foreswore me in my mother's womb' (*3HVI*, III, ii, 153). And in this surprisingly feminine play, with three queens and a queen mother, powerfully choric all-women scenes curse Richard for his bloodthirstiness (e.g. *RIII*, IV, iv). From this psychoanalytical perspective, Richard internalises deep societal and maternal rejection, violently dragging his victims, even child princes, into the deathly emptiness that lies in place of a healthily narcissistic sense of self. The crown of England would therefore be merely a fragile symbolic replacement for Richard's gulf-like void of self-esteem. Recently, however, other, more theological paradigms have illuminated Richard's behaviour. Ken Jackson (2005), for example, noting that Richard swears frequently by St Paul and by no other saint, argues that Richard resembles Paul in the way he radically, riskily and wholeheartedly commits to a cause. This is despite the fact that, unlike Paul, Richard is resolutely without grace or divine help, as the ghosts that later torment him warn. Richard therefore becomes a kind of anti-Paul, Paul's demonic counterpart. Interpreting Richard's psychological contradictions in theological terms may have had an extra nuance for Shakespeare's early Tudor audiences: Richard unwittingly starts the Tudor dynasty by killing all potential rivals to the throne, however young they may be. The path is therefore clear for his own conqueror, Richmond, to become the first Tudor king, Henry VII. Perhaps, then, Richard is God's plaything, the agent of Tudor providence.

Edward Duke of York, later Edward IV *(2HVI, 3HVI, RIII)*

Richard Duke of York's eldest son, Edward IV, turns to Warwick after his father's death as a political mentor, even surrogate father. As mentioned above, his key error is marrying the relatively poor landowner Lady Elizabeth Grey instead of Lady Bona of the French dynasty, whose power and soldiers would secure his family's rule against the Lancastrian threat (*3HVI*, III, ii). Warwick, sent by Edward to plead for Bona's hand on his behalf, is appalled by the 'dishonour' and 'shame' this change of heart has caused him in front of the French King, especially as Warwick's father died for the Yorkist cause: 'I here renounce him and return to Henry' (*3HVI*, III, iii, 181–98). Edward's mistake also increases the existing rivalry between him and his brothers. It makes Clarence change sides, albeit temporarily ('I mind to leave you', *3HVI*, IV, i, 65), encourages Richard ('I stay not for the love of Edward but the crown', *3HVI*, IV, i, 125), and leads ultimately to exhaustion and fatal sickness (*RIII*, II, ii, 39).

George Duke of Clarence (*2HVI, 3HVI, RIII*)

Audience viewpoints of Clarence may alter depending on whether they see him throughout the tetralogy or in *Richard III* alone. As seen above, in *Henry VI Part 3* Clarence betrays his brothers, changing sides and changing back again ('I will not ruinate my father's house', V, i, 83). In *Richard III*, though, Clarence is Richard's first victim, largely anonymous apart from a terrifying speech about his nightmare foreboding death ('methought what pain it was to drown [...] jewels [...] lay in dead men's skulls [...] in scorn of eyes', *RIII*, I, iv, 9–60). Clarence is therefore often seen more sympathetically in the delimited context of *Richard III*. As Richard warns the executioners, 'Clarence is well spoken, and [...] May move your hearts to pity' (*RIII*, I, iii, 348–9).

Characters (others)

The Earl of Richmond, later Henry VII (*3HVI, RIII*)

Richmond, crowned Henry VII, is not as prominent in *Richard III* as Hastings, Buckingham or Lady Anne, but unlike them is included here because by founding the Tudor line he brings the tetralogy, and indeed the whole eight-play cycle, to a close. As a child he makes a brief appearance in *Henry VI Part 3*, where King Henry prophesises 'This pretty lad will prove our country's bliss' (*3HVI*, IV, vi, 70). Richmond concludes *Richard III* by promising to 'unite the white rose and the red' (*RIII*, V, vii, 19), part of Shakespeare's praise of the Tudor line. Shakespeare's much later, co-written play, dealing with Henry VII's son and heir (*Henry VIII, or All is True*), continues the story up to the birth of Elizabeth I.

The Earl of Warwick (*1HVI, 2HVI, 3HVI*)

Warwick, 'the Kingmaker', is a powerful and influential soldier. Honour is paramount for him, hence his sudden defection from the Yorkist party when Edward IV humiliates him in front of the French King. His death, however, seems almost humiliatingly undignified and messy: 'my glory smeared in dust and blood [...] this cold congealed blood [...] glues my lips and will not let me speak' (*3HVI*, V, ii, 23, 37–8). The chivalric codes Warwick personifies seem irrevocably swept away by the Lancastrian deposition and the Wars of the Roses.

Humphrey Duke of Gloucester (*1HVI, 2HVI*)

John Barton, co-director of perhaps the plays' most influential twentieth-century production, named Humphrey Duke of Gloucester the principal character of *Henry VI Part 2*. Lord Protector of the boy King, he struggles with the courtiers' 'spiteful false objections' (*2HVI*, I, iii, 156): they each seek to weaken Humphrey and exploit the King's youth to their own ends. He eventually falls when his wife Eleanor, who dreams 'Henry and Dame Margaret kneeled to me' (*2HVI*, I, ii, 39) is arrested on charges of witchcraft (*2HVI*, I, iv, 40). Even as Humphrey protests 'I banish her my bed and company' (*2HVI*, II, ii, 192), Henry decides to end Humphrey's Protectorship (*2HVI*, II, iii, 24). Margaret, in love with Gloucester's enemy Suffolk, and the Bishop of Winchester take advantage of Gloucester's newly weakened position to arrest him on nameless 'mightier crimes [...] whereof you cannot easily purge yourself' (*2HVI*, III, i, 134–5). The King complains but does not act. Gloucester is quickly assassinated before he can stand trial (*2HVI*, III, ii, 1).

Bishop of Winchester, later Cardinal Beaufort (*1HVI, 2HVI*)

Winchester is Gloucester's main, unscrupulous rival. He seeks at all costs to win the Protectorship and become thereby the effective ruler of the kingdom. He even leads troops against Gloucester outside the gates of London until the Mayor interrupts (*1HVI*, III, i, 1–142). Made Cardinal near the end of *Henry VI Part 1* (V, i, 27), he plots Gloucester's downfall with Margaret and Suffolk (*2HVI*, III, i, 223–330) but dies himself, sick and anguished, soon after Gloucester's murder. For a suspicious Warwick, 'So bad a death argues a monstrous life' (*2HVI*, III, iii, 30).

Jack Cade (*2HVI*)

The Cade rebellion does not take up much stage time relative to the rest of the play, but it is memorable for its sheer energy and spectacle. At one point two decapitated heads on poles are made to 'kiss' each other (*2HVI*, IV, vii, 124). The onstage Jack Cade is much more brutal than that reported by York. Cade undermines confidence in Henry's royal birthright on York's behalf by setting up a rival claim. Cade 'proclaims himself Lord Mortimer, / Descended from the Duke of Clarence' house' (*2HVI*, IV, iv, 26–7), appealing thereby to monarchist and hereditary traditions. His short-lived revolution generates a heady mix of comedy, revolutionary sentiment and the anti-intellectual fury of mob rule: 'The first thing we do, let's kill all the lawyers' (*2HVI*, IV, ii, 71). Those who set up printing presses and grammar schools have 'traitorously corrupted the youth of the realm' (*2HVI*, IV, vii, 30). As with the riot that follows the emperor's assassination in *Julius Caesar* (III, iii), it is the innocent, not the real repressors, who get killed.

William de la Pole, Earl of Suffolk *(1HVI, 2HVI)*

Suffolk is a failed, or unlucky, political schemer. In love with Princess Margaret, he praises to King Henry her 'peerless feature [...] valiant courage and undaunted spirit' (*1HVI*, V, vi, 68–70), because he hopes Henry will marry her. That way, he thinks, 'I will rule both her, the King, and realm' (*1HVI*, V, vi, 107–8). This ambition and self-interest resurfaces when he evicts common people from his land. His tenants petition him for 'enclosing the commons of Melford' or seizing previously 'common' land by sheer force (*2HVI*, I, iii, 23). *Henry VI Part 2* thus begins and ends with scenes of acute class struggle. Marxist critics have paid detailed attention to this scene because it exemplifies the idea of 'Primitive Accumulation' set out in chapter 16 of *Capital* (Marx 1992). Landowners were starting to use their land increasingly as sources of private income, which they could then reinvest as capital, sparking the ever-accelerating process of capitalism we recognise today. Banished on suspicion of Gloucester's murder (*2HVI*, III, ii, 300), and decapitated while sailing away by the pirate Walter Whitmore – Suffolk gasps 'A cunning man [...] told me that by "water" I should die' (*2HVI*, IV, i, 36) – the economic processes that Suffolk helps inaugurate arguably live on.

John Talbot *(1HVI)*

John Talbot is one of the key characters of *Henry VI Part 1*: a great military hero tragically struck down when Somerset and York refuse to cooperate and send through reinforcements (*1HVI*, IV, iii, 9–16). The Countess of Auvergne tries to trap him, as an enemy Englishman, but he is forward-thinking enough to set up reinforcements to protect him (*1HVI*, II, iii). Like Warwick, he personifies a fragile, vulnerable, chivalric ideal.

Joan of Arc *(1HVI)*

Joan is nicknamed the 'pucelle', French for virgin, but echoing also 'puzzell', Elizabethan English slang for whore. She is an almost magically powerful feminine presence, physically besting the Dauphin and Talbot (*1HVI*, I, ii, 102–4; I, vi, 8–10). Princess Margaret's first entrance occurs just as York's guards carry off the defeated Joan (*1HVI*, V, iii, 43; V, iv, 1). Joan's fierce, feminised combativeness thus seems to transfer to Margaret, who will carry it through the rest of the tetralogy.

Language

Gary Taylor estimates that only about 20 per cent of *Henry VI Part 1* is definitely by Shakespeare (ed. Taylor 2003: 10). Its often regular pentameter and end-stopped verse lines certainly contrast with the fluid, intricate density of later work like, say, Macbeth's soliloquies. Such regular verse patterns mark even the play's more linguistically ambitious set pieces, such as the stichomythic (one-line) argument between Talbot, who wants his son to flee to safety, and his son, who wants to fight and die with his father (see IV, v, 34–42). Robert Greene's famous criticism that Shakespeare was 'well able to bombast out a blanke verse as the best of you' follows an echo from *3 Henry VI*: Shakespeare's heart is 'wrapped in a player's hide' as Margaret's is 'in a tiger's hide'. Such 'bombastic' blank verse is perhaps uninteresting to read, but in performance it gains a speed and cumulative force. The thudding syllables often match the grimly determined sounds of the fighting, as with Richard Gloucester's appeal to Warwick:

> Ah Warwick, why hast thou withdrawn thyself?
> Thy brother's blood the thirsty earth hath drunk,
> Broached with the steely point of Clifford's lance,
> And in the very pangs of death he cried,
> Like to a dismal clangor heard from far,
> 'Warwick revenge, brother revenge my death!'
> (*3VI*, II, iii, 14–19)

Henry VI Part 2 contains probably the tetralogy's most noteworthy uses of prose. The armourer Horner's dispute, then fight, with his apprentice Peter Thump (I, iii, 176–220; II, iii, 59–94) offers a glimpse into the daily lives of the ordinary people caught up in the aristocrats' quarrels. Many of Cade's and his rebels' speeches are also set in prose. Cade's followers desert him, however, when Clifford promises them money in verse (IV, viii, 34–52), leaving a disillusioned Cade to ask: 'was ever feather so lightly blown to and fro as this multitude? (IV, viii, 55–6). Such passages may be read as prototypes for the *Henry IV* plays' elaborate, polyvocal blends of verse and prose.

Themes

A 'useable past'

As with the *Henry IV* plays, Shakespeare is arguably using historical material to interrogate concerns topical for him and his early audiences. The plays warn of the violent public consequences of courtiers' private quarrels, especially when in *Henry VI Part 3* a nameless son, pressed into military service, unwittingly kills his father (II, v, 61). Forced conscription was a hot topic in the vexed geopolitical situation of the 1590s. Political issues in Shakespeare's era, and in the period these plays depict, are inseparable from theological ones. But in this world, where everyone hates everyone else, the plays brood on the sheer difficulty of reconciling Christian values with the hard realities of state. The saintly but ineffectual Henry VI is mirrored by the astute Bishop of Winchester, whose dubious morals do not prevent him from becoming

Cardinal. The plays arguably critique the Catholic England of the fifteenth century from a late-sixteenth-century revisionist English Protestant perspective.

Texts and contexts

Texts

Were these plays originally conceived individually, or as part of an overarching, continuous project? There seems to be a clear narrative link from the end of *Henry VI Part 3* to the start of *Richard III*, but for other connections the evidence is hazy. Michael Taylor's discussion in his introduction to the Oxford University Press edition is useful. Taylor suggests *Henry VI Part 1* was actually written *after* the others, capitalising on the commercial success of the others as a kind of prequel, while attempting to set the bloody tales of the later plays in international context (see ed. Taylor 2003: 10–15). *The First Part of Henry the Sixth* was not published until the 1623 Folio, some thirty-one years after first performances. But the original composition has been dated to 1591–2. Revisions were perhaps made in 1598–9, suggesting a revival coinciding with 1599, and performances of *Henry V*. The play called in the Folio *The Second Part of Henry the Sixth, with the Death of the Good Duke Humphrey* was originally printed in 1594 as a Quarto text ('Q') called *The First Part of the Contention Betwixt the Two Famous Houses of York and Lancaster*. The Folio play *The Third Part of Henry the Sixth, with the Death of the Duke of York* was originally printed in 1595 in Octavo ('O') as *The True Tragedy of Richard Duke of York and the Death of Good King Henry the Sixth*. Note how the Folio titles, probably not Shakespeare's, help shape the plays into an overarching framework. *Part 2* is difficult for modern editors because the versions differ significantly: King Henry's regrets that he cannot help Humphrey, for example, are much diminished in Q, making him seem colder. Roger Warren offers a full account of the textual variations in his Oxford edition of the play (see especially ed. Warren 2003: 75–100). *Part 3* also differs from version to version: O is about one-third shorter than F, and takes out several minor roles. The 1623 F version of *Richard III* contains thirteen passages that are absent from the 1597 Q text (*The Tragedy of King Richard the Third*), including a lengthy speech by Richard, augmenting his request for Princess Elizabeth's hand in marriage, and the Queen's touching prayer to the stones of the Tower of London to 'use my babies well'.

Shakespeare's revisionism: sources and their shaping

Even though the tetralogy's constituent plays undergo variations from version to version, differences survive between Shakespeare's plays and his historical sources such as Edward Hall's *The Union of the Two Noble and Illustre Families of Lancaster and York* (1548, 1550), Raphael Holinshed's *Chronicles of England, Scotland and Ireland* (1577, 1587) and Thomas More's *History of Richard III*, printed in the Holinshed.

Shakespeare's scene where the nobles pick roses in a garden to represent their allegiance (*1HVI*, II, iv) is unhistorical, but it helps Shakespeare as a playwright establish relationships quickly, economically and dramatically. Priorities of theatrical storytelling also help explain why historical battles are telescoped into one longer war scene, as in Act II of *Henry VI Part 3*. Shakespeare's characterisation is also often unhistorical. Henry VI's ill-fated Protector Humphrey Duke of Gloucester did not in fact get on especially well with the young king (a fact perhaps better reflected by the shorter 1595 'Q' text of *Henry VI Part 2*), but Shakespeare stresses Humphrey's kindness and good sense to follow the common opinion of his time. By contrast, Shakespeare's sources praise Edward IV's reign but the plays show him as sexually rapacious, weak-minded and a bad decision-maker. Shakespeare tones down Buckingham's revolt against Richard III, as if to ascribe Richard's aggressiveness more to personal malice than political expediency, and conversely depicts Richard's eventual enemy Stanley in a more favourable light. This may be because Stanley was an ancestor of Lord Strange, of Lord Strange's Men, the theatre group in which Shakespeare may have been involved prior to the formation of the Lord Chamberlain's Men in 1594.

The plays in performance

The *Henry VI* trilogy

Roger Warren notes that 'almost all the productions of *Henry VI* since the 1590s have occurred within the last fifty years' (ed. Warren 2003: 7). The benchmark production is John Barton and Peter Hall's 1963 *The Wars of the Roses* (RSC, Stratford-upon-Avon). Barton rewrote some 1,450 lines to fit the whole trilogy into a single one-day performance. The production drew analogies between the plays' political violence and its own vexed post-war/cold-war situation. David Warner's Henry stressed the paradox that well-meaning Christian passivity led ultimately to destruction and bloodshed. Terry Hands sought to tell the trilogy's story as simply as possible in his minimally cut and minimalist RSC 1977 production. One-day performances lasted nine hours, divided into morning, afternoon and evening sessions. Alan Howard's Henry used balletic movement to relay his growth from boy to man, and was conscientious rather than incompetent, hampered by bouts of madness. Michael Bogdanov's and Michael Pennington's modern-costume *The Wars of the Roses* (English Shakespeare Company 1987–1990) implied parallels between Princess Margaret and the then Prime Minister Margaret Thatcher, while Pennington's Cade was a nihilistic punk rocker, and decapitated heads were kicked around like footballs.

The Plantagenets, directed by Adrian Noble (RSC 1988–9) made powerful use of special effects (Joan was burnt onstage) and accentuated Humphrey's paternal relationship with Henry. Michael Boyd's two-part production (RSC 2000), which on eight occasions staged the whole story in a ten-hour performance, was deliberately gory. Some reviewers complained of being showered with blood and body parts.

Talbot's son John returned as a decomposed zombie to play the son who unwittingly kills his own father, stressing the continuity of war. When characters died, they rose again and solemnly followed a sinister red figure offstage, as if to the afterlife, and sometimes silently returned, as if they haunted the present still. The battles were given movement and energy via the use of trapdoors, trapezes and ropes, and the triumphalism of Edward's victory speech at the end contrasted eerily with the onstage blood staining the hem of his robe. When the production was revived in 2006, a black actor once more played Henry (David Oyelowo in 2000, Chuk Iwuji in 2006), suggesting a racial dimension to Henry's estrangement from his violent courtiers.

Edward Hall's *Rose Rage* (Propeller, Watermill Theatre, Newbury 2001/2) largely cut *Part 1*. Its set, designed by Michael Pavelka, copied an abattoir from Smithfield market, London, emphasising the plays' political butchery. During the 2012 'Globe to Globe' season the trilogy was staged by companies from Serbia, Macedonia and Albania, regions for whom themes of civil war are only too acute: in *Part 1* the set pointedly resembled the United Nations Security Council. The plays' topicality is also stressed by their most recent high-profile production, directed by Trevor Nunn for the Rose Theatre, Kingston (2015). The *Henry VI* tetralogy directed by Jane Howell for the BBC (1983) is readily available on DVD. It is clear, pacey and engagingly stylised. In 2016 the BBC returned to the Henry VI/Richard III tetralogy in the second instalment of *The Hollow Crown*, but the decision to reduce these four plays to three films (unlike the much fuller treatment of 'The Henriad') led to some disappointing omissions. The Cade rebellion was mystifyingly entirely cut, Princess Margaret's role much reduced, and Suffolk's and Somerset's roles conflated. While beautifully shot, then, these films lacked to my mind the energy and force of the Howell productions.

Richard III

Productions of *Richard III* come under a separate heading because this play has enjoyed a long performance history independent from the preceding plays. Notable early Richard IIIs include Richard Burbage (the role's first player), David Garrick in the eighteenth century and Charles Kean in the early nineteenth. From the twentieth century, Laurence Olivier's performance filmed in 1955 is still influential, as is Antony Sher's scuttling, spidery, crutch-ridden Richard (RSC 1984), Ian McKellen's uniformed proto-fascist (stage 1990, film 1995), Kevin Spacey's violent self-hater (Old Vic 2011), and Mark Rylance's and Richard Clothier's suave, seductive sociopaths for the 2012 Globe all-male production and gory 2011 Propeller production respectively.

Critical reception

A good starting point is *Shakespeare's History Plays*, edited by Robert Watt (2002), which contains a clear introduction and good selection of influential essays. Elizabeth

Harper (2016) offers a thorough survey of infanticide in the plays, in relation to time as the great devourer of its own children. Alan Finlayson and Elizabeth Fraser (2011) discuss the Cade rebellion's self-conscious theatricality. Catherine Sanok (2010) argues the plays were influenced by a saintly or popular cult around 'Good King Henry [VI]'. Eric Heinze (2009) reads the tetralogy as a sustained exploration of the (im)possibility of reconciling effective and just systems of rule. Feminist critics have focused stimulatingly on Shakespeare's attention to Joan of Arc. Leah Marcus (1988) argues the 'puzzell' Joan and then Queen Margaret resonate powerfully with Elizabethan iconographies of the strong queen. H. Austin Whitver (2015) responds that the French can only praise and commemorate Joan in an imagined future, when she will already be dead, because her feminine strength threatens their patriarchal present. Jennifer A. Rich (2002) historicises the treatment of Joan via early modern anxieties about feminine 'counterfeit' dissimulation, and the increasing economic role of credit and debt. Influential recent readings of *Richard III* include Philip Schwyzer's analysis of the symbolic histories of Richard's favourite objects (2012), Mark Robson on the ghost as image for the effervescence and unpredictability of historical time (2005) and Katherine Schaap Williams on Richard as offering new performative possibilities for bodies unthinkingly dismissed as 'disabled' (2009).

Discussion questions

* Do the histories depict 'The world we have lost'? If so, how?

* Is history for Shakespeare cyclical, or a steady upward or downward path, or radically unpredictable?

Bibliography and further reading

Editions

Shakespeare, W. (2000), *Richard III*, ed. J. Jowett, Oxford: Oxford University Press.

Shakespeare, W. (2001), *Henry VI Part Three*, ed. R. Martin, Oxford: Oxford University Press.

Shakespeare, W. (2003), *Henry VI Part One*, ed. M. Taylor, Oxford: Oxford University Press.

Shakespeare, W. (2003), *Henry VI Part Two*, ed. R. Warren, Oxford: Oxford University Press.

Critical response

Finlayson, A. and E. Fraser (2011), 'Fictions of Sovereignty: Shakespeare, Theatre and the Representation of Rule', *Parliamentary Affairs*, 64:2, 233–47.

Harper, E. (2016), '"And men ne'er spend their fury on a child" – Killing Children in Shakespeare's Early Histories', *Shakespeare*, 12, 1–17.

Heinze, E. (2009), 'Power Politics and the Rule of Law: Shakespeare's First Historical Tetralogy and Law's "Foundations"', *Oxford Journal of Legal Studies*, 29:1, 139–68.

Jackson, K. (2005), '"All the World to Nothing": Badiou, Žižek and Pauline Subjectivity in *Richard III*', *Shakespeare*, 1:1–2, 29–52.

Machiavelli, N. (2005), *The Prince*, trans. and ed. P. Bondanella, Oxford: Oxford University Press.

Marcus, L. (1988), *Puzzling Shakespeare: Local Reading and Its Discontents*, Berkeley: University of California Press.

Marx, K. (1992), *Capital: A Critique of Political Economy Vol. 1*, trans. B. Fowkes, London: Penguin.

Moretti, T. (2008), 'Misthinking the King: The Theatrics of Christian Rule in *Henry VI, Part 3*', *Renascence*, 60:4, 275–94.

Rich, J. A. (2002), 'Gender and the Market in *Henry VI, I*', in Yvonne Bruce (ed.), *Images of Matter: Essays on British Literature of the Middle Ages and Renaissance*, Proceedings of the Eighth Citadel Conference on Literature, Charleston, South Carolina, 2002, Newark: University of Delaware Press, pp. 206–7.

Robson, M. (2005), 'Shakespeare's Words of the Future: Promising *Richard III*', *Textual Practice*, 19:1, 13–30.

Sanok, C. (2010), 'Good King Henry and the Genealogy of Shakespeare's First History Plays', *Journal of Medieval and Early Modern Studies*, 40:1, 37–63.

Schaap Williams, K. (2009), 'Enabling Richard: The Rhetoric of Disability in *Richard III*', *Disability Studies Quarterly*, 29:4, <http://dsq-sds.org/article/view/997/1181> (last accessed 29 June 2016).

Schwyzer, P. (2012), 'Trophies, Traces, Relics, and Props: The Untimely Objects of Richard III', *Shakespeare Quarterly*, 63:3, 297–327.

Watt, R. (ed.) (2002), *Shakespeare's History Plays*, Harlow: Longman.

Whitver, H. A. (2015), 'Erecting a Pyramid in France: Tomb Symbolism in *1 Henry VI*', *Journal for Early Modern Cultural Studies*, 15:3, 82–101.

Part IV. Late plays

13 *The Winter's Tale*

Composition c. 1610, first recorded performance **1611**

Act, scene and line references are to the 2010 Arden Third Series edition, edited by John Pitcher.

Plot summary

Leontes, King of Sicilia, fears his as-yet-unborn second child – sibling to his son Mamillius – is not in fact his (II, i, 62). He suspects his wife Hermione of adultery with his childhood friend Polixenes, King of Bohemia (I, ii, 109–19, 184–206). Leontes' confidant Camillo warns Polixenes of these suspicions (I, ii, 412–13). Camillo and Polixenes flee Sicilia (I, ii, 460–1), and Hermione is imprisoned (II, i, 125). Hermione gives birth to a girl shortly before her trial (II, iii, 63). Leontes asks his man Antigonus first to kill the baby but then, softening at Antigonus's protests, to desert the baby in some far-off place to die (II, iii, 171–7). At the end of the trial an oracle acquits Hermione of wrongdoing (III, ii, 130–3), just as news arrives of Mamillius's death, which makes Hermione swoon in despair (III, ii, 141–6). Leontes suddenly concedes he had been in the wrong all along (III, ii, 150–69). But the sooth-sayer Paulina, Antigonus's wife, announces Hermione's offstage death (III, ii, 197–8). Meanwhile Antigonus has sailed to Bohemia, where he lays the baby down with a box and some letters (III, iii, 45). A Bohemian Shepherd discovers the child as a bear devours poor Antigonus (III, iii, 69). Sixteen years pass (IV, i, 5–6). The story resumes in Bohemia during a sheep-shearing festival (IV, iv, 68). The baby has grown into a maid 'of most rare note' (IV, ii, 42), 'Perdita', whom the Shepherd pretends is his daughter. During the festival the disguised Polixenes, accompanied by Camillo, spies on his son Florizel, whom he suspects of wasting his time with Perdita, a mere country girl below his station (IV, iii, 45–6). When he catches Florizel with Perdita he casts off his disguise, rebuking them and the Shepherd (IV, iv, 422–46). The lovers despair, but Camillo suggests they could 'make for Sicilia' (IV, iv, 548), where they can be free and happy in their love, especially as Leontes still feels indebted to Polixenes and his family for the wrongs he had done sixteen years earlier. Florizel swaps clothes with the crook and ballad-seller Autolycus so he might pass through to Sicilia unobstructed (IV, iv, 638–9). Autolycus uses Florizel's courtly attire to pass himself off as a rich courtier (IV, iv, 717–18). Thus disguised, Autolycus frightens the

Bohemian Shepherd and his son with stories of Polixenes' likely wrath once Florizel's flight is discovered (IV, iv, 776–804). The terrified shepherds flee to Leontes' Sicilia so that Perdita's true rank may be revealed and that they may be absolved from blame (IV, iv, 823–5). Autolycus follows, sniffing an opportunity for 'advancement': the shepherds might receive courtly gold that he may then trick them out of (IV, iv, 835–47). The scene passes back to Sicilia (V, i). Leontes still bitterly regrets his folly of sixteen years ago (V, i, 1–19). As Florizel and Perdita arrive (V, i, 122), Polixenes sends a message to Leontes, asking him to arrest his fugitive son (V, i, 180–1). Florizel suspects Camillo of betraying him (V, i, 192). Leontes agrees to try and broker a reconciliation between Florizel and his father (V, ii, 230–1). The scene then moves outside, where some excited gentlemen recount the rediscovery of Perdita (V, ii). The Bohemian Shepherd has presented as proof a 'fardel' (bundle) with Hermione's 'mantle' (cloak) and 'jewel' (V, ii, 31–2), and 'letters', 'handkerchief' and 'rings' (V, ii, 65–6), which Paulina recognises as belonging to Antigonus. Perdita's royal blood means also that she is free to marry Florizel, unimpeded by Polixenes. The Shepherd and his son, now made gentlemen, turn the tables on Autolycus, mocking him for his now-inferior social status (V, ii, 149–50). A statue is unveiled that day to commemorate Hermione's life. The viewers, awestruck by its likeness, are stunned to see it come to life on Paulina's command (V, iii, 99). The surviving members of Hermione's family are thus reconciled. As the play closes, Hermione asks Perdita how she has spent the last sixteen years (V, iii, 123–5), and Leontes asks Camillo to marry Paulina (V, iii, 143–4).

Characters

Hermione (I, ii; II, i; III, ii; V, iii)

Hermione frames this experimentally long story, as both the target of Leontes' mad jealousy and, much later as the awakening statue, the sign of their reconciliation. Her husband's jealousy is awakened merely by Hermione trying to persuade Polixenes to stay a week longer: Leontes complains 'at my request he would not' (I, ii, 88). This gesture, which Leontes finds so provocative, seems all the more innocuous as elsewhere, and throughout, Hermione seems only to live for her husband's love and praise, eagerly and excitedly asking him 'Have I twice said well? When was it before?' (I, ii, 90–108). Hermione's three speeches at her trial (III, ii, 21–53, 58–76, 89–114) are powerful in their contrasting tone, striking a dramatic balance of bewildered innocence and fierily wounded indignation, centring on the accusatory 'My life stands in the level of your dreams' (III, ii, 79–80). Her next appearance, as a prophesising, ghostly apparition in Antigonus's dream (III, iii, 26–33), raises questions about whether Hermione is simply hidden away by Paulina, or whether there is a more mysteriously spiritual story going on, where Hermione actually dies and she is truly resurrected. Her final appearance gives few clues: she merely says 'Knowing by Paulina that the oracle / Gave hope thou [Perdita] wast in being, have preserved / Myself to see the issue' (V, iii, 127–8). And the quality of this 'preserva-tion' is somewhat mysterious. It is certainly more than the mere preservation of the body: Hermione as a shrieking dream vision presents herself to Antigonus, cursing 'For this ungentle business / Put on thee by my lord, thou ne'er shalt see / Thy wife Paulina more' (III, iii, 33–5). This spiritual Hermione's vindictiveness seems a little out of keeping with her tragically victimised earthly counterpart, whose dismissal of Antigonus as collateral damage, to be sacrificed to the inexorable unfolding of the fairy-tale plot, seems concerning.

Leontes (I, ii; II, i; II, iii; III, ii; V, i; V, iii)

The first two syllables of Leontes' name echo the national symbol of Bohemia, a lion, hinting at the reunification of the royal families by the end of the play. But in the first scenes his violent behaviour does little to suggest such a happy ending. The warning signs are introduced early with Leontes' strange comparison, unheard or ignored by Hermione, between Hermione's entreating Polixenes to stay with them and their own marriage (I, ii, 104). The famous 'Too hot, too hot' speech (I, ii, 108–18) represents a new Shakespearean exploration of compulsive male jealousy. Othello needs Iago to convince him of his wife's infidelity; Leontes' suspicions are much more powerfully self-sourced. The tenderness he intermittently shares with his son Mamillius (I, ii, 121–46), and sudden request that Camillo kill Polixenes, adds to the sense of emotional instability and lack of control. His figurative language is wild, eccentric, even illogical, explaining and justifying his jealousy via an analogy of purely psychosomatic ill effects, such as vomiting at the mere sight of a harmless spider in a drink (II, i, 37–53). He seems desperate for his courtiers to support his accusations against Hermione ('Have I done well?', II, i, 55–125). Leontes oscillates between rage and distress throughout the first two acts. His speeches are often jerky and self-interrupting (I, ii, 178–206) and he confesses he is continually restless, 'a feather for each wind that blows' (II, iii, 152). He softens his insistence that the 'bastard' 'issue of Polixenes' be committed 'to the fire' (II, iii, 94) when he asks Antigonus merely to desert it (II, iii, 180–1). His refusal to believe even the oracle's acquittal of Hermione is likewise suddenly transformed when news reaches him of Mamillius's and Hermione's deaths (III, ii, 150–69), a speech which is noticeably clearer, syntactically and lexically, than his earlier ones. His regret endures until next we see him, two acts and sixteen years later.

Perdita (II, iii (actress not onstage); IV, iv; V, i; V, iii)

At Perdita's birth (her name means 'the lost one'), Paulina stresses the baby's likeness to Leontes, in a failed bid to convince him the child is his (II, iii, 96–106). Perdita is then, of course, deserted by Antigonus in a storm that destroys the ship bearing her: a loss that accentuates by contrast the rejuvenating effects of her first entry as a sixteen-year-old 'queen' of the sheep-shearing festival (IV, iv, 5). Despite the obvious connotations of fertility and sexuality this role affords her, Perdita remains wary of Florizel's advances. This wariness is not only sexual, it is political. Her first speech is full of addresses like 'my gracious lord' and 'your high self' (IV, iv, 5, 7). As she is a low-born shepherd girl (or so she thinks), she is worried that Florizel's father will see through Florizel's disguise as 'Doricles' (IV, iv, 146) and punish their courtship. Perdita is often witty and articulate, especially in her exchange with the disguised Polixenes and Camillo about grafted flowers, 'art' and 'nature' (IV, iv, 79–112). Upset by Polixenes' discovery and anger over her love ('I told you what would come of this', IV, iv, 452), she speaks only rarely as Camillo and Florizel hatch their plan to leave for Sicilia. She is similarly quiet in the final act, speaking only to express her fear for her shepherd 'father' (V, i, 201–3) and, in the final scene, to ask to kiss her mother's hand (V, iii, 42–6). Her silent onstage reactions may, however, signal much about changing perceptions of family and class identity, and the relationship between royalty and the rural.

Polixenes (I, ii; IV, ii; IV, iv; V, iii)

Childhood friends innocent as 'twinned lambs' (I, ii, 67) – perhaps a pre-echo of the sheep-shearing festival – Polixenes is quickly aware of Leontes' sudden change of attitude. 'Methinks / My favour here begins to warp' (I, ii, 361–2). As Camillo warns Polixenes that Leontes thinks he has had sex with Hermione and wants to kill him, Polixenes is appalled, stunned ('how should this grow?', I, ii, 427) and afraid ('Fear o'ershades me', I, ii, 453). After this perhaps cowardly flight from Sicilia, Polixenes' next contribution, save for a brief expository recap with Camillo (IV, ii) and conversation with Perdita (IV, iv, 79–112), occurs just as the disguised Florizel and Perdita are about to marry. Polixenes, likewise disguised, concedes Perdita seems 'greater than herself, / Too noble for this place' (IV, iv, 158–9), and observes the festivities she rules over as 'queen' for much of this long scene silently, apparently contentedly (IV, iv, 162–347). But he still disapproves of his son marrying her. He gleans information about his son's disguise from the unwitting Shepherd (IV, iv, 168–82) and waits until Florizel takes Perdita's hand in marriage before asking 'Have you a father?' (IV, iv, 396). It is not until Florizel insists on keeping his marriage secret from his father that Polixenes throws off his disguise, threatening Florizel with 'divorce' (IV, iv, 422), the Shepherd with 'hanging' (IV, iv, 427), and Perdita with having her 'beauty scratched with briars' (IV, iv, 430) and a 'cruel' 'death' (IV, iv, 445), accusing her of 'excellent witchcraft' (IV, iv, 428) and 'enchantment' (IV, iv, 439). The fury suggests a violently possessive streak 'twinning' that of his childhood friend and fellow-king Leontes. This, however, is soon forgotten with the revelation about Perdita's royal birth: Polixenes gladly reconciles with Leontes in the final scenes.

Camillo (I, i; I, ii; IV, ii; IV, iv; V, iii)

Camillo is present from the very first scene. As a messenger and go-between he helps establish the plot and relationship between the two kingdoms. Protesting Hermione's and Polixenes' innocence, Leontes spits: 'Camillo was his help in this, his pander [assistant, pimp]' (II, i, 46). Camillo's reasonable voice emphasises by contrast Leontes' irrationality. Camillo also serves useful expository functions. In Act IV, scene ii he reminds the audience that sixteen years have passed, and in Act IV, scene iv comes up with the idea to take Perdita to Sicilia (IV, iv, 513–18), even though he does not yet know that Perdita is the King's lost daughter, and risks Polixenes being angered by Leontes' sheltering his disobedient child. Camillo's desire to see his homeland again influences this risky decision ('I desire to lay my bones there', IV, ii, 6). Camillo is less visible in the final act, although he offers consolation to Leontes, still at this point mourning Hermione (V, iii, 49–53), and briefly, astonished, praises the statue's animation. It is up to actors and directors to decide how he responds to the joyous Leontes' closing request 'Come, Camillo,/And take [Paulina] by the hand' (V, iii, 143–4): the text offers no indication.

Florizel (IV, iv; V, i; V, iii)

Polixenes' son Florizel is eloquent and resourceful. He compares himself, when describing his love for Perdita and his disguise, to Jove and other dissembling gods, contributing to the play's artfully constructed mythological backdrop (IV, iv, 24–35). His repeated praises of Perdita, addressed to or in full earshot of his disguised father, accentuate his love (IV, iv, 135–46, 361–9, 375–83). Florizel apparently respects Polixenes; he never once insults or condemns him even though, as far as he is concerned, he is not present. He even admires his 'health' and 'strength' (IV, iv, 408); and only says to his prying, disguised father that 'for some other reasons, my grave sir,/Which 'tis not fit you know, I not acquaint/My father of this business' (IV, iv, 416–18). Polixenes remains resolute – 'nothing altered' – even after his father's furious exit (IV, iv, 469), but Camillo notes his anguish ('This is desperate, sir', IV, iv, 490). Florizel is desperate 'not to see [Polixenes] any more' (IV, iv, 499–500) and 'put to sea/With her who here I cannot hold on shore' (IV, iv, 503–4), giving Camillo the idea to 'make for Sicilia' (IV, iv, 548). He follows unhesitatingly Camillo's instructions to 'change garments' with Autolycus (IV, iv, 638–9). Arriving in Sicilia, he remains, once more, defiant despite Polixenes' warrant for his arrest: 'power no jot/Hath [Fortune] to change our loves' (V, i, 216–17). Florizel is present, but silent, in the final scene. His behaviour towards his love, his father and his new parents-in-law is a matter for conjecture and directorial vision.

Paulina (II, ii; II, iii; III, ii; V, i; V, iii)

Even though Leontes calls Paulina a 'mankind [manly] witch' (II, iii, 66), her magical powers are not revealed immediately. Not mentioned in the first act, and only briefly just before her first appearance (when Antigonus mentions a 'wife', II, i, 135), there is little indication of how important she will turn out to be. In her first entry, however, her impact is powerful and immediate: she is aggressive to the Gaoler who prevents her from gaining direct access to Hermione (IV, iv, 9–11) and resolves to rebuke the King herself ('The office/Becomes a woman best; I'll take't upon me', II, ii, 30–1). She is fiery in Hermione's defence, cursing Leontes strongly enough for nameless Lords to accuse her of impropriety (II, ii, 25; III, ii, 213–15). Even at the beginning of the final act, sixteen years on, she is stern with Leontes, reminding him he 'killed' his wife (V, i, 15). But her proposed marriage to Camillo contributes strongly to the overall sense of reconciliation, even perhaps of loss overcome.

Antigonus (II, i; II, iii; III, iii)

Antigonus's first line comes immediately as Hermione is led away, signalling the strong bond between him and his queen that will last until his death. Despite this loyalty, his language is often tinged with misogyny. He vows to 'geld' (make barren) his 'three daughters', whom we never see, if Leontes' suspicions prove true (II, i, 140–9). Even if this is a way of stressing Antigonus's sheer disbelief, the violence of the image perhaps gives cause for concern. His relationship with his wife Paulina is interestingly ambivalent. He publicly rebukes her ('That's enough', II, iii, 29; 'I told her [...] she should not visit you', II, iii, 43–5), but often finds himself agreeing with her despite himself: 'When she will take the rein I let her run, / But she'll not stumble' (II, iii, 50–1). He is perhaps resignedly aware husbands cannot control their wives, mocking Leontes' threat to hang him if he cannot get Paulina to be quiet ('Hang all the husbands / That cannot do that feat, you'll leave yourself / Hardly one subject', II, iii, 109). Perhaps a sense of strain with Paulina, as well as his urge 'to save the innocent' (II, iii, 165), makes up his mind to flee Sicilia with the baby. Such marital tension would help explain Paulina's marriage to Camillo, which otherwise might appear too glib and sudden (especially in terms of elapsed onstage time, rather than the sixteen years depicted). It should be recalled, though, that the very last words Paulina utters in the play mourn her husband ('my mate, that's never to be found again', V, iii, 134). These underlying issues complicate the way the final scene is played.

Autolycus (IV, iii; IV, iv; V, ii)

The clownish ballad-seller and thief Autolycus, the first character to speak in the play's second half proper, comically counterpoints the first half's tragic events. His first song talks of the spring and budding sexuality ('set my pugging tooth an edge', IV, iii, 7), and he gulls the Shepherd's son (IV, iii, 74–5), and most of the feasters, out of 'their festival purses' (IV, iii, 619). Even honesty is for Autolycus a useful stratagem or policy. After swapping clothes with Florizel, and eavesdropping the Clown and Shepherd talking about Perdita's discovery, he concedes 'Though I am not naturally honest, I am so sometimes by chance' (IV, iv, 715–16). His witty, duel-like exchanges with these 'rustics' (IV, iv, 718) are often concerned with social pretension. Whether we believe or not Autolycus's claims that he was once Florizel's courtier ('now out of service', IV, iv, 14), his parodies of 'court-odour' and 'court-contempt' are acute (IV, iv, 734–42). Perhaps his begging the newly ennobled 'rustics' 'to pardon [...]

all the faults I have committed' (V, ii, 146–7) and his promise to 'amend [...] to all my power' (V, ii, 151, 166) – his last words in the play – are similarly ironic. A truly contrite Autolycus would certainly be surprising.

Shepherd (III, iii; IV, iv; V, ii) and Clown (III, iii; IV, iii; IV, iv; V, ii)

The Shepherd and his son, despite the son's foolishness, are both sympathetic characters. The Shepherd, after all, kindly takes in Perdita, saving her life, and makes often shrewd, if grumpy, observations: 'I would there were no age between ten and three-and-twenty, or that youth would sleep out the rest; for there is nothing in the between but getting wenches with child, wronging the ancientry [their elders], stealing, fighting ...' (III, iii, 58–63). Perhaps this is a frustrated description of his own son. His later observation about Autolycus in Florizel's clothing is also bitingly acute: 'His garments are rich, but he wears them not handsomely' (IV, iv, 753–4). The Shepherd sees Perdita as continuer of traditions upheld by his late wife as 'mistress o'th'feast' (IV, iv, 68), and urges her to carry out these duties with enthusiasm (IV, iv, 64–8). He happily 'give[s his] daughter' to 'Doricles' (Florizel's fake name), but is broken-hearted by Polixenes' threats, lamenting to Florizel: 'You have undone a man of fourscore-three [eighty-three years old], that thought to fill his grave in quiet' (IV, iv, 458–60). The Clown his son is repeatedly referred to as 'boy' in Act III, scene iii. He could therefore be played by a child in the first 'half' of the play, a young adult in the second, when Autolycus gulls him effortlessly out of his pocket money. It is the Clown, however, in his gullible susceptibility to Autolycus's stories, who suggests that 'We must to the king and show our strange sights' (IV, iv, 824), crucially developing the plot. Their exchanges with Autolycus, which draw frequently on duelling terminology like 'give [...] the lie' (V, ii, 131), that is, the slander that duellists would challenge, are a kind of 'duel' of social pretension: Autolycus pretends to be a gentleman to dupe the two 'rustics'; the 'rustics' once ennobled respond. The Clown loses no opportunity to gloat, albeit with unwitting ironic stupidity ('I am [...] now a gentleman born [...] and have been so [...] these four hours', V, ii, 131–4), while his father, older and wiser, counsels 'we must be gentle now we are gentlemen' (V, ii, 149–50).

Mamillius (I, ii; II, i)

Mamillius, whose name perhaps evokes mother–child relations in its echo of 'mammary', is a happy, fun-loving, story-loving child, which makes his death all the sadder. In expository terms, he helps illustrate the increasing strain and distance between Leontes and Hermione ('I am glad you did not nurse him', II, i, 56–7). But, perhaps more importantly, his loss makes the play's 'happy' ending dramatically complex. To what degree can the newly reunited Hermione, Leontes and Perdita, and we the audience, forget him? Often directors will allude to Mamillius in some way to shade emotionally the play's closing tableau, recollecting his line 'A sad tale's best for winter' (II, i, 25–6). Is Mamillius, like Antigonus, mere 'collateral damage'?

Play structure

'A winter's tale' was another term for 'an old wife's tale'. Shakespeare's use of the definite article – **The** Winter's Tale – implies this play operates at the very limit of belief and disbelief. It is certainly one of the most, if not the most, structurally experimental plays Shakespeare ever wrote, with his most famous stage direction ('*Exit, pursued by a bear*', stage direction after III, ii, 57). The play's timeframe is deliberately long, depicting events over a period of sixteen years, and Time itself is personified with a speaking role (IV, i). Time's speech is a kind of central pivot or fulcrum that links the two temporally distant halves of the play. The symmetry of the overall structure is stressed when Time turns an hour-glass at more or less the central line of this central speech (IV, i, 16). This rotation hints at a kind of carnivalesque reversal from stiff, paranoid Sicilia to unbridled, festive, rural Bohemia, a reversal suggested as the Shepherd says to the Clown his son 'thou met'st with things dying, I with things newborn' (III, iii, 110–11). The audience is encouraged to feel time slightly differently once the glass is turned: the action of the first half is brisk, unpredictable, intense, while the sheep-shearing festival scene (IV, iv) is the second longest in all Shakespeare's plays (just behind the last of *Love's Labour's Lost*). There is perhaps a subtle wordplay on Time's 'glass' as a mirror, as well as an hourglass, a word use more common in Shakespeare's time: subtle motifs in the first half reflect those in the second. The raging Leontes' description of Hermione as a promiscuous country girl or 'flax-wench' (I, ii, 275) contrasts with the later portrayal of fun-loving but prudent country girls Mopsa and Dorcas (IV, iv, 235–319). Dorcas protests 'Bless me from marrying a usurer' (IV, vi, 268) and they sing together a 'merry' ballad to a rascal who has betrayed them both (played, aptly enough, by Autolycus, IV, iv, 298–313). Autolycus's complaint when fooling the Clown that 'his shoulder-blade is out' (IV, iii, 72–3) echoes the bear '[tearing] out' Antigonus's 'shoulder-bone' (III, iii, 93) (see ed. Pitcher 2010: 62–4). The play invites comparisons and contrasts within scenes, as well as between scenes and acts, as when Hermione's play with Mamillius (II, i, 21–32) echoes Leontes' (II, i, 118–27). This emphasis on family togetherness only makes Leontes' desire for sole possession of 'the boy' all the more sadly destructive (II, i, 56–7).

Language

The use of language in *The Winter's Tale* emphasises its sense of formal experimentation. Leontes' soliloquies describing his jealousy are full of strange imagery, as if he is in the grip of a madness that is stronger than him. Like Othello, his language is shot through with insanity. One of his mad speeches contains 'The most obscure lines in Shakespeare' (ed. Pitcher 2010: 40):

> Sweet villain,
> Most dearest, my collop! Can thy dam? May't be
> Affection? – Thy intention stabs the centre,

Thou dost make possible things not so held,
Communicat'st with dreams – how can this be?
With what's unreal though coactive art,
And fellow'st nothing. Then 'tis very credent
Thou mayst co-join with something, and thou dost,
And that beyond commission, and I find it,
And that to the infection of my brains
And hard'ning of my brows
(I, ii, 136–46)

The precise meaning of this passage has long foxed critics and editors, who have often repunctuated the passage extensively; and the problem is not helped by the fact that the original text seems somewhat garbled or misprinted. But the play's recent Arden editor John Pitcher explains it via the specific Renaissance sense of 'affection' as brain fever (*affectio*). 'The senses (sight, touch) communicated impressions to the mind in the normal way but memory and judgement failed to interpret them correctly' (ed. Pitcher 2010: 41). Reading 'fellow'st nothing' as the speech's 'key phrase', 'affection produces [...] unreal imaginings [...] from out of itself'; Pitcher adds: 'the delusions might attach themselves to real things, and reveal Hermione and Polixenes attached as lovers' (ed. Pitcher 2010: 41). If the very obscurity of the language suggests something of Leontes' mental state, there is also a suggestion that Shakespeare is experimenting with verse rhythm and phonetic sound. Leontes' speech is jerky and abrupt, accentuated by conspicuous alliteration. Compare the repeated 'b' sounds in Leontes' later, similarly agitated, barely logical speech: 'It is a *b*awdy planet [...] No *b*arricado for a *b*elly [...] It will let in and out the enemy / With *b*ag and *b*aggage' (I, ii, 200–5, emphasis added).

The Bohemian rural world is differentiated from Leontes' Sicilian court by its own, no less distinctive, linguistic characteristics, slang and rhythms. Despite some rare uses of verse, as when the Shepherd ceremonially opens the sheep-shearing festival (I, iv, 55–69), this world mainly communicates in prose. Many comic allusions refer obscurely to a culture now lost to us, such as 'Mistress Tale-Porter' (IV, iv, 269–70), which puns bawdily on 'story' and 'penis', but in performance the Clown's malapropisms (comic misuses of a word) still raise a laugh: 'advocate's the court word for pheasant' (IV, iv, 745–6). The rural community takes great joy in buying, sharing and singing ballads, as the ballad-seller (and pickpocket) Autolycus delightedly observes (IV, iv, 609–15). Ballads offer a way of collectively articulating ideas, and they often have some ethical or cultural resonance. One topically satirises usurers, for example (IV, iv, 262–5), and the gentleman Rogero later remarks that Perdita's rediscovery has caused 'such a deal of wonder [...] that the ballad makers cannot be able to express it' (V, ii, 23–5). *The Winter's Tale* also explores the sociological connotations of language in its use of register: Autolycus overemphasises courtly language to an almost parodic degree as he delightedly finds himself wearing aristocratic clothing: 'How blest are we that are not simple men! Yet Nature might have made me as these [the Shepherd and Clown] are. Therefore I will not disdain' (IV, iv, 749–51).

As well as such rich variations in language, distinct prosodical features can also be identified throughout the play. Rhythmically, the language is much less rigidly regular than, say, the rounded, martial blank verse of the *Henry VI* tetralogy, written much earlier in Shakespeare's career. This is achieved through regular use of feminine endings, where the line ends on an unstressed syllable; of enjambed, or run-on lines, where the sentences 'run on' over the end of a line of verse; and of hypermetrics, where lines potentially contain more than ten syllables, and as such need to be elided, or run together, to make them fit the metre. Perhaps we could say, then, that words flow through the verse line much like Hermione's statue melts into movement and life. The spirit of experimentation therefore pervades the language as well as the structure of the play. Pitcher interestingly sees the story as a fantasia on the metamorphic, semantic possibilities of the 'presiding word' 'bear' (ed. Pitcher 2010: 133): endure, carry, support, give birth, as well as the animal who devours Antigonus.

Themes

Time and consolation

Most of the characters in this tragicomedy have crosses to bear. Leontes and Hermione have to endure Leontes' madly jealous possessiveness; Perdita and Florizel have to endure Polyxenes'. Hermione is of course resurrected but Mamillius and Antigonus are 'gone for ever' (III, iii, 57, Antigonus's last words). The play seems preoccupied with the proverbial idea that time heals all wounds, perhaps even that time has a plan that we do not see. After all, the 'oracle' implies that time and the events unfolding within it are fixed in advance (III, ii, 130–3) and, as seen above, Hermione's perhaps cruel dream vision warns Antigonus he 'ne'er shalt see' Paulina again (III, iii, 34–5). The suggestion that time consoles as it passes is more central to *The Winter's Tale* than perhaps any other play by Shakespeare. It certainly foregrounds tensions between represented time (sixteen years) and the real time of actual theatrical performance (three or so hours). In his introduction to *Shakespeare's Sonnets* John Kerrigan writes:

> Each day of the medieval year – summer and winter alike – was divided into twelve hours. So the hours were long in summer and short in winter [...] As clocks and watches became cheap and compact, however, during the sixteenth century, the new music of time – cold, mechanical, inexorable – encroached on the lives of ordinary men and women. (ed. Kerrigan 1986: 34–5)

The Winter's Tale could be seen as a nostalgic response to this historical development. While time was often vilified as the universal destroyer of all things (*tempus edax rerum* in Ovid's proverbial Latin tag), the play personifies it rather as a guide through the play's bittersweet events. To personify an abstract idea like time is to imply it has a human agency and frailty and to embody it unavoidably as gendered: the actor must depict 'Time' as somehow 'male' or 'female', and this cannot help but suggest time itself is gentle, aggressive, fertile or barren. And actors and directors have responded imaginatively to this stimulating challenge.

Seasonal renewal

The play's nostalgic, consolatory approach to time is also expressed via its depiction of the seasons. Polixenes at the beginning of the play compares himself and Leontes to spring-like 'twinned lambs' (I, ii, 67) – as if anticipating their ultimate reunion – but the first half is quite clearly wintry in its cold-hearted themes; recall Mamillius's 'a sad tale's best for winter' (II, i, 25). The second half by contrast starts with Autolycus's song about spring and burgeoning sexuality (IV, iii, 1–12) and continues with the richly colourful, floral symbolism of the sheep-shearing festival. Florizel stresses the floral etymology of his name by mentioning Flora in his very first speech (IV, iv, 2); and Perdita likewise links flowers to myths with creation and cyclical natural rhythms as she hands 'rosemary and rue', which last through the winter, to 'reverend sirs' Camillo and Polixenes (IV, iv, 73–9), 'lavender, mints, savory, marjoram', which are flowers 'of middle summer [...] To men of middle age' (IV, iv, 104–8), and laments she has no 'flowers o'th'spring' for her younger love (IV, iv, 113–14), nor to commemorate Mopsa's and Dorcas's 'maidenheads' (IV, iv, 115–16). She therefore prays to Proserpina, who in myth was imprisoned by Pluto god of the underworld for the autumn and winter and only released in the spring, for 'Daffodils', 'violets', 'primroses', 'oxlips', 'crown imperial', 'lilies', and 'flower-de-luce' (IV, iv, 118–27). The offers of flowers seem to symbolise a larger belief that the seasons are directly keyed into broader patterns: life and death, loss and reconciliation like Perdita's rediscovery, and fertility like Perdita's love, marriage and (implied) children with Florizel. Florizel sees Perdita's beauty in these cyclical, harmonious terms: 'When you do dance, I wish you / A wave o'th'sea, that you might ever do / Nothing but that, move still, still so, / And own no other function' (IV, iv, 140–3). This praise is set in the context of Perdita's status as 'queen' of a feast celebrating the return of natural fecundity ('all your acts are queens', IV, iv, 146). Perdita's costume as 'queen' gives her not only a new role but also a new identity ('this robe of mine / Does change my disposition', IV, iv, 133–4) – hinting, in a rural mode, at the truly royal identity she is to discover.

Costume, court and country

Yet even though the sheep-shearing festival replicates a courtly hierarchy, with Perdita as 'queen', the rural and royal worlds are markedly separate. The Bohemian Shepherd's prose is perhaps surprising after the Sicilian court's elaborate verse, as is his grim description of his and his son's rude lives, full of unwanted pregnancy, crime and fighting (III, iii, 58–62). This helps explain Polixenes' horror at his son's request to marry Perdita, and why some form of disguise is essential to cross from royal to rural realms and back again. Florizel plays Doricles, of course, Polixenes and Camillo are also disguised, and Autolycus disguises himself four times: as a destitute beggar

(IV, iv, 62), a pedlar (IV, iv, 220), a pseudo-courtier (IV, iv, 651), and a gentleman when discussing the statue and the reunion (V, ii). This preoccupation with costume and disguise, which includes the Shepherd's and Clown's new clothes, comments subtly on 'sumptuary laws', then in force, which ascribed materials or garments to members of different social rank. But it also contributes to the play's wider concern with the relationship between 'art' and 'nature'. The Shepherd, for example, suspects Autolycus despite his courtly garments ('he wears them not handsomely', IV, iv, 753–4), as if there is an underlying nature that art cannot hide.

Art and nature

The play's most explicit exchange on art and nature occurs, however, in Perdita's and Polixenes' discussion on 'gillyvors' (gillyflowers) or 'nature's bastards', which are created via horticultural grafting (IV, iv, 86–98). Polixenes thinks such grafting is not unnatural because the raw material is natural, as ultimately is everything: 'Nature is made better by no mean / But Nature makes that mean [...] the art itself is nature' (IV, iv, 95–7). This does little, however, to reassure Perdita's concerns that such 'art' may make nature itself 'unnatural', or that, by analogy, Florizel may only want to desire her enough to have a child by her because she is wearing make-up ('painted', IV, iv, 101). Just as Polixenes' figurative language echoes his fear that his son might wed Perdita 'we marry / A gentler scion to the wildest stock / And make conceive a bark of *baser* kind / By bud of nobler race' (IV, iv, 92–5, my emphasis), so Perdita's concern about 'Nature's bastards' resonates unwittingly with Leontes' repeated claims that she herself was such a 'bastard' (II, iii, 153–9). As with *King Lear*, then, 'nature' denotes not only organic matter, nor only the inherent quality of a thing, but also a 'correct' relationship between family members. This is relevant to the play's ending. When Hermione's 'statue' comes back to life, 'art' becomes 'nature' because the marble statue turns out to be organically 'warm' ('O she's warm', V, iii, 109) but also because her family unit has become 'natural' again. Perhaps Polixenes' line 'The art itself is nature' has a metatheatrical element: in the statue scene the audience must make a 'leap of faith' to take this highly stylised theatrical 'art' as 'naturally' real. The play extends the very horizon of the believable.

Texts and contexts

Texts

There is only one early version of *The Winter's Tale*: the 1623 Folio text (F). Ralph Crane transcribed a manuscript for printing. His input is recognisable from his distinctive scene headings and repunctuation. Overall, the text compositors 'produced a clean text from Crane's transcript' (ed. Pitcher 2010: 365) and 'In the three seventeenth century Folios derived from F, the text of *The Winter's Tale* changes very little' (ed. Pitcher 2010: 366).

Sources

The most immediate source for *The Winter's Tale* is Robert Greene's *Pandosto, or the Triumph of Time*, a very successful 1588 prose narrative. Greene's characters Pandosto, Bellaria, Fawnia, Garinter and Egnistus correspond, respectively, to Shakespeare's Leontes, Hermione, Perdita, Mamillius and Polixenes. In Greene's version, however, Pandosto unwittingly tries to seduce his daughter and kills himself when he finds out her real identity. The much happier, more redemptive statue scene thus seems to be a Shakespearean addition. Just when it was added, however, remains a matter for critical debate. It is not mentioned in Simon Forman's 1611 eyewitness account of the play: perhaps it was added later.

Contexts and influences

Shakespeare's transformations of Robert Greene's source text illustrate other forms of cultural influence. Like so many other Shakespeare plays and poems, *The Winter's Tale* contains echoes of Ovid's *Metamorphoses* and the mythological universe from which Ovid's text itself originates. The name Autolycus, first known to us from Homer (*Odyssey* 19.447–9) is found in the *Metamorphoses* (1.303–17), as is the story of Proserpina (5.341–571). The clearest Ovidian reference, however, is to Pygmalion (*Metamorphoses* 10.244–95). Pygmalion's sculpture, like Hermione's, comes to life in a context of forgiveness and love. Pygmalion falls in love with his own statue of a woman, whom the pitying Venus brings to life as 'warm' Galatea.

'Tragie-comedie'

Reversing the narrative line of *Romeo and Juliet* by moving from tragedy to comedy, *The Winter's Tale* is a radically experimental blend of influences, characters and tones. It challenges Sir Philip Sidney's attack on the mixture of 'kings and clowns', and develops the 'tragie-comedie' as exemplified by *Il Pastor Fido* and defined by Beaumont and Fletcher: it actually stages persons dying. Slightly more tragic than a 'tragicomedy', then, it has been categorised by critics as a 'late play', or 'romance', which appeals to a slightly more metaphorical or allegorical mode of belief or reception. Pitcher even suggests that Shakespeare seeks to encourage in his audience something like a child's-eye view (ed. Pitcher 2010: 26).

The play in performance

Two of the most influential productions of *The Winter's Tale* are Peter Brook's 1951 Phoenix Theatre production, which ran for a massive 167 performances, and Trevor Nunn's stylised, expressionistic production for the RSC, inspired by Peter Brook's *The Empty Space*, running from 1969–71. The bright white robes of the nobles contrasted starkly against the black background, and Christopher Morley's set design involved a white box, as if to communicate Barrie Ingham's Leontes' jealous, hallucinating solipsism. By moments, the lights changed and the audience shared Leontes' paranoid visions of Hermione and Polixenes flirting. In the final scenes Leontes had a slight limp, as if he still bore the psychosomatic scars of his trauma sixteen years on. Richard Eyre's RSC production (Barbican 1982) gave Hermione a garland and floral robes, strengthening the links between Sicilia's courtly world and Bohemia's more rural one and anticipating her daughter's later role as the queen of the feast. Adrian Noble's RSC 1992 production made tremendously fun, clownish use of lots of balloons in the sheep-shearing scenes. Simon McBurney's Théâtre de Complicité's 1992 production made the most of the play's potential for doubling roles, like Leontes and Autolycus, or Antigonus and Autolycus, by sharing the twenty-two roles out among only nine actors, who each played two, three or even four characters, blurring the roles. Another notable production took place at the St Petersburg Maly Theatre (1997–9) in collaboration with Declan Donnellan and designer Nick Ormerod. The production alluded to the Russian winter and juxtaposed Leontes' near-tyrannical paranoia with the Soviet past. It was remarkable for casting 'Time' as a young woman, who only reveals herself from beneath old woman's robes when she speaks for the only time in Act IV, scene i, reconceiving Time, just before the sheep-shearing festival, as a universal renewer, not destroyer. At the end, however, with the cast frozen, Time leads Mamillius past them and away, as he stretches his hand desperately, uselessly, to his parents.

The bear is often the high point of the performance, a test of theatre companies' conceptual and technical ingenuity. Great bears have included that of the 1981 RSC production directed by Ronald Eyre, with Patrick Stewart as Leontes: in almost total darkness, a single flash of lightning illuminated a twenty-foot monster at the back of the stage, just before the house lights went up for the interval. In the 1991 English Shakespeare Company production, directed by Michael Bogdanov, the 'bear' was a glove manipulated by Michael Pennington, playing Leontes, as if his malice still exerted a quasi-supernatural grip over the others. David Farr's 2009 RSC production used a large puppet bear, starkly illuminated from below, made out of pages of paper. Another interesting recent production (2013), a 'promenade' where spectators walk through the set, was directed by Anirudh Nair and Neel Chaudhuri for The Tadpole Repertory and Wide Aisle Productions in New Delhi, India. Autolycus spoke in English, Hindustani and Urdu, imitating Dastangoi (sixteenth-century Indian storytellers), while the rivers, trees and white robes together recalled Hindu traditions of penitence.

Critical reception

John Dryden in 1672 dismissed The Winter's Tale for its lame plot and lack of 'vigour and maturity', and Alexander Pope doubted that Shakespeare had written the entire play at all (see Hunt [1995] 2010: 4–5). William Hazlitt, however, was one of its earliest important sympathetic readers: 'I do not know any body but [Shakespeare] who could produce [its] beauties' (quoted in Hunt [1995] 2010: 8). Important twentieth-century readings of the play include G. Wilson Knight's [1947] (2014) 'Great Creating Nature', which argued for the play's structural continuity: delicate, complex webs of imagery helped interconnect its providential narrative with a quasi-Wordsworthian pantheism: the idea that nature itself contained her own godliness. Northrop Frye in 1965 read the pastoral scenes as archetypally symbolic of Plato's ideal realm, or Eden, affirming that *The Winter's Tale* 'perhaps [...] expresses the cyclical imagery of comedy most clearly' (quoted in Hunt [1995] 2010: 34). Stanley Cavell's 'Recounting Gains, Showing Losses' (2003) argued that Leontes' jealousy is premised on sceptical philosophies of radical doubt: he cannot actually believe that his son Mamillius has come into existence, that something this close to him can actually not *be* him. *The Winter's Tale: Critical Essays* (Hunt [1995] 2010), contains a helpful summary of the play's critical reception and a good selection of important criticism written up until that date.

More recent work demonstrates new interest across the field of humanities in cognitive science as a way of establishing consistent 'character' or discussing emotion, issues discussed influentially by Sarah Beckwith in *Shakespeare and the Grammar of Forgiveness* (2011). Cognitive readings include those by James Lambert (2013), Hannah Chapelle Wojciehowski (2014) and Donald R. Wehrs (2011). Essays on forgiveness as a historically changing kind of power relationship include those by Lysbeth Em Benkert (2015), Michael Fischer (2012), Renuka Gusain (2013), Maurice Hunt (2011), Julia Lupton (2014), Paul Stegner (2014) and Beckwith herself (2015), who compares *The Winter's Tale* with Eric Rohmer's 1992 film *Conte d'hiver*, based on Shakespeare's play.

Discussion questions

* By the end, do we forgive Leontes for the death of Mamillius, and, less directly, Antigonus? If so, how does the play work to encourage such forgiveness? And would such forgiveness simply be a kind of disguised callousness?

* Written during a period of uncertainty and paranoia about witchcraft, how does the play present questions of magic?

* How does the play compare, or contrast, magic with other forms of enchantment?

Bibliography and further reading

Editions

Homer (1996), *The Odyssey*, trans. Robert Fagles, New York/London: Penguin.
Ovid (2002), *Ovid's Metamorphoses*, trans. Arthur Golding, ed. M. Forey, London/New York: Penguin.
Shakespeare, W. (1986), *The Sonnets and A Lover's Complaint*, ed. John Kerrigan, London: Penguin.
Shakespeare, W. (1996), *The Winter's Tale*, ed. S. Orgel, Oxford: Oxford University Press.
Shakespeare, W. (2010), *The Winter's Tale*, ed. J. Pitcher, London: Arden Shakespeare.

Critical response

Beckwith, S. (2011), *Shakespeare and the Grammar of Forgiveness*, Ithaca, NY: Cornell University Press.
Beckwith, S. (2015), 'Are There Any Women in Shakespeare's Plays? Fiction, Representation, and Reality in Feminist Criticism', *New Literary History*, 46:2, 241–60.
Benkert, L. M. (2015), 'Faith and Redemption in *The Winter's Tale*', *Religion and the Arts*, 19:1, 31–50.
Cavell S. (2003), 'Recounting Gains, Showing Losses', in *Disowning Knowledge in Seven Plays of Shakespeare*, updated edn, Cambridge: Cambridge University Press.
Fischer, M. (2012), 'Forgiveness and Literature', *Philosophy and Literature*, 36, 504–12.
Gusain, R. (2013), '"With what's unreal thou coactive art": The Problem and Possibilities of Beauty in *The Winter's Tale*', *Shakespeare*, 9:1, 52–75.
Hunt, M. (ed.) [1995] (2010), *The Winter's Tale: Critical Essays*, London/New York: Routledge.
Hunt, M. (2011), 'Syncretistic Religion in Shakespeare's Late Romances', *The Journal of the South Central Modern Language Association*, 28:2, 57–79.
Jones-Davies, M. (2010), 'Suspension of Disbelief in *The Winter's Tale*', *Études Anglaises*, 63:3, 259–73.
Knight, G. W. [1947] (2014), 'Great Creating Nature', in *The Crown of Life: Essays in Interpretation of Shakespeare's Final Plays*, London/New York: Routledge.
Lambert, J. (2013), 'The Pedagogy of Emotional Response: Feeling Shakespeare's *The Winter's Tale*', *This Rough Magic*, June, <http://www.thisroughmagic.org/lambert%20 article.html> (last accessed 29 June 2016).
Lupton, J. (2014), 'Judging Forgiveness: Hannah Arendt, W. H. Auden, and *The Winter's Tale*', *New Literary History*, 45:4, 641–63.
Stegner, P. (2014), 'Masculine and Feminine Penitence in *The Winter's Tale*', *Renascence*, 66:3, 189–202.
Tambling, J. (2015), '*The Winter's Tale*: Three Recognitions', *Essays in Criticism*, 65:1, 30–52.
Wehrs, D. (2011), 'Placing Human Constants within Literary History: Generic Revision and Affective Sociality in *The Winter's Tale* and *The Tempest*', *Poetics Today*, 32:3, 521–91.
Wojciehowski, H. (2014), 'Statues that Move: Vitality Effects in *The Winter's Tale*', *Literature and Theology*, 28:3, 299–315.

14 *The Tempest*

Composition c. 1610–11, first recorded performance 1611

Act, scene and line references are to the 1999 Arden Third Series edition, edited by Virginia Mason Vaughan and Alden T. Vaughan.

Prospero, formerly Duke of Milan and now presiding over a nameless island, magically causes the skies to roar tempestuously with the aid of his servant, the airy sprite Ariel (I, i; I, ii). This is to make run aground on his island a ship containing his brother Antonio, who had betrayed him and stolen his dukedom, Alonso King of Naples, Alonso's brother Sebastian, and Alonso's son Ferdinand (I, ii, 66–151). As the confused, shipwrecked nobles and their attendants try to navigate through the island, Prospero asks Ariel to make himself invisible and follow them (I, ii, 302–5). Ariel protects the sleeping Alonso and Gonzalo from Antonio and Sebastian who plot to kill them (II, i, 298–9), and later torments them with visions (III, iii, 53–82). The lords who had wronged Prospero are thus avenged. But Ariel's work is also a way of repaying Prospero. Prospero had freed Ariel from the witch Sycorax's 'cloven pine' (I, ii, 277) in exchange for Ariel's service. But the conditions of this service cause tensions between Prospero and Ariel, who now requests 'liberty' (I, ii, 245). Sycorax's son Caliban is Prospero's other grudging servant. Caliban had once tried to rape Prospero's daughter Miranda (I, ii, 348–9), and is now punished by having to carry out hard physical tasks like getting wood in for the fire (I, ii, 312–13). Ariel draws Ferdinand into Miranda's view and she falls in love with him on first sight. (I, ii, 418–19). Prospero seems to disapprove of the match but is secretly delighted (I, ii, 494–5; IV, i, 1–11). Ferdinand and Miranda's love develops and culminates in a masque-like marriage ceremony presided over by three Goddesses, Ceres, Iris and Juno (IV, i, 60–142). Meanwhile Caliban meets two shipwrecked clowns, Stephano and Trinculo, and after having drunk some of Stephano's alcohol, begs to serve Stephano as once he had served Prospero (II, ii, 15–182). The three of them attempt to wrest power from Prospero by stealing his magical books and gowns (III, ii, 86–103). But Ariel foils their plot (IV, i, 181–3), luring them to a 'filthy' pool and leaving them stinking of 'horse-piss' (IV, i, 199). The play ends with the young lovers married, Prospero forgiving his 'unnatural' brother, who says nothing in response (V, i, 78–9), and the ship bearing everyone except Ariel and Caliban back home. Prospero's Epilogue – delivered directly to the audience – begs them to 'set him free', and propel him back home through the power of their applause (Epilogue, 19–20).

Characters

Prospero (I, ii; III, i; III, iii; IV, i; V, i; Epilogue)

Prospero is the 'prime mover' of *The Tempest*. He exerts more power over his fellow characters than perhaps anyone else in Shakespeare. His authoritative tone is established from his first entrance, consoling his daughter, who is worried about the shipwreck she has just witnessed, and rebuking her at the same time. He causes the storm but does no real harm to the mariners (I, ii, 217). Prospero strikes this uneasy balance of sternness, kindness and authority throughout the play. With Ariel he veers from fearsome threats to loving praise. Near the beginning Prospero reminds Ariel that he had liberated Ariel from Sycorax and threatens him, 'moody' for his freedom, of being locked once more into the 'cloven pine' (I, ii, 295). He only sets Ariel free near the very end of the play (V, i, 252). Prospero controls Caliban yet more forcefully, threatening him throughout with spells and 'pinches' (I, ii, 329–30). Ferdinand and Miranda are fearful on witnessing his anger at Caliban's rebellious plot (IV, i, 143–5). Prospero orchestrates with similarly strict authority his daughter and son-in-law's courtship and marriage. Via Ariel he brings Ferdinand into contact with Miranda but then pretends to be angry with Ferdinand, and even as he approves the wedding warns sternly and harshly against sex before marriage, or 'fire in the blood': 'be more abstemious' (IV, i, 53). Such examples illustrate that Prospero's power is based as much on emotional control as it is on magic spells: he deliberately leads Alonso to believe Miranda and Ferdinand are dead, for example, before he draws back the barrier to reveal them playing chess (V, i, 171). By avenging his brother, assuring his daughter's marriage and seeing off Caliban's rebellion, Prospero ultimately 'prospers'. But in the Epilogue he asks the audience to decide if he should enjoy his home again or stay stranded on his island. The audience becomes a kind of Prospero to Prospero.

Ariel (I, ii; II, i; III, ii; III, iii; IV, i; V, i)

Ariel's name echoes 'Uriel', glossed as 'lyon of God' in marginal notes to Isiah 29. Ariel is likewise a magical agent doing a godlike master's bidding, and a mysterious being. As a shape-changing 'spirit', it is not clear whether Ariel is a man or a woman, or even whether such distinctions are important. Very few clues, such as gender-specific pronouns, offer any answer to this question. Ariel's first speech to 'his' 'master' is very respectful, but cracks later appear as he insistently requests his 'liberty' (I, ii, 240–56). It is up to the actor to decide whether Ariel's submission to Prospero's threats and promises ('do my spiriting gently', I, ii, 297) is genuinely meant or hissed through gritted teeth. It is true, however, that Ariel carries out Prospero's requests effectively, even taking intelligent initiative, like awakening Gonzalo just as Antonio and Sebastian are about to kill Alonso, or mimicking Stephano's and Trinculo's voices so as to start fights between them (III, ii, 40–53). Ariel is at the centre of the play's most spectacular and terrifying moment, pretending to be a 'harpy' to torment the 'three men of sin' (Sebastian, Antonio and Alonso) who persecuted Prospero in Milan (III, iii, 53–83), and quashes Caliban's rebellion. Ariel even seems desperate for Prospero's approval, or reassurance that s/he will ultimately be freed ('do you love me, master?', IV, i, 48). Sometimes actors play Ariel as reacting scornfully, violently when freedom is finally granted, as if it is too little, too late.

Caliban (I, ii; II, ii; III, ii; IV, i; V, i)

As has often been noted, 'Caliban' is an at least coincidental near-homophone with 'cannibal'. In the Folio *Dramatis Personae* he is described as a 'savage and deformed slave'. In the play proper, negative epithets and describers cluster around him. Stephano and Trinculo repeatedly call him, for example, 'monster' and 'mooncalf', a term for a still-born or deformed farm animal (III, ii, 16–35). Caliban is marked out and marginalised from the other characters by his noticeably different use of language. His diction is different from that of the other characters, and some of his words, like 'pignuts' and 'scamels' (II, ii, 164–9), are unique to him, not only in *The Tempest* but in all Shakespeare. The Arden editors speculate that a 'scamel', a word hitherto unknown and unused, may be a kind of shellfish, but the very mystery as to its meaning is a powerful reminder of who we are dealing with. Caliban's strange language corresponds to his dissident behaviour. The son of Sycorax, the witch who once ruled Prospero's island (I, ii, 284), Caliban remains unapologetic for his attempted rape of Miranda ('I'd have peopled the world else with Calibans', I, ii, 352) and only grudgingly concedes that Prospero is more powerful than he (I, ii, 373–4), grumbling in soliloquy about the hard, menial work Prospero forces him to do (II, ii, 1–13). It is therefore all the more surprising, then, that as Caliban seeks to overthrow Prospero he installs Stephano in Prospero's place. It is as if Caliban has internalised so strongly and naturally his condition as slave that he can only understand freedom itself in terms of a new master ('Ca-caliban / Has a new master, get a new man', II, ii, 179–80).

Miranda (I, ii; II, i; III, i; IV, i; V, i)

Miranda's name derives etymologically from the Latin verb *mirare*, wonder, a key theme of another late play, *The Winter's Tale*. Ferdinand plays on this nuance as he praises her: 'ad-mired Miranda!' (III, i, 37). Miranda's associations with an admirably wondrous mirror (*miror* is the first person conjugation of the verb, 'I wonder') comes through when Prospero reveals the stage tableau of Miranda and Ferdinand playing chess, facing each other as if they are each other's lovingly admired reflections (V, i, 172–7). In her first appearance Miranda contributes to Prospero's backstory, dimly remembering her past life ('Had I not/Four or five women once, that tended me?', I, ii, 46–7), but she is more than a mere plot device. She is visibly gentle, caring and perceptive, suffering 'with those [she] saw suffer' (I, ii, 5–6), and anticipating from the very beginning that the storm-tossed ship contains a 'noble creature' (I, ii, 7). Her devotion to Ferdinand is clear from her loving speech (III, i, 47–92) and as she protects him against a seemingly defensive Prospero (I, ii, 460–75). An aggressive speech directed at Caliban is given to Miranda in the Folio text (I, ii, 353–63), but since the eighteenth century it has been ascribed to Prospero on grounds of decorum and characterological consistency. Editors' and directors' decisions here greatly influence our understanding of Miranda.

Ferdinand (I, ii; III, i; IV, i; V, i)

The first time we see Ferdinand he is drifting, lost on the island. He is confident, even by moments somewhat cocky, as Prospero observes, wondering what Ferdinand's father would say if he heard Ferdinand boasting he is 'the best' of those who speak his language (I, ii, 431–2). Sebastian also helps illustrate the sheer extent of Prospero's magical and paternal power. He is 'charmed from moving' (I, ii, 467) and by Act III, scene i, has taken over Caliban's functions, such as getting wood for the fire. He cheerfully admits, however, 'The mistress which I serve ... makes my labours pleasures' (III, i, 7). And the revelation of him and Miranda playing chess to the bewildered but delighted Alonso is one of the play's dramatic highlights.

Gonzalo (I, i; II, i; III, iii; V, i)

Wise, gentle, perhaps at times a little doddery, the old Gonzalo is the most straightforwardly sympathetic of the shipwrecked mariners. In the first scene he is merely critical of the lower-born Boatswain (pronounced 'bosun'), while Sebastian and Antonio are snootily dismissive, even violent ('you whoreson, insolent noise-maker!', I, i, 42–3). In Prospero's long recitation of the backstory it emerges that Gonzalo had helped Prospero: it is due to him that Prospero still has his books (I, ii, 161–8). Prospero confesses as much as he 'freezes' the usurpers and addresses each one: he acknowledges Gonzalo is an 'honourable man' and 'loyal sir' (V, i, 62). Gonzalo's speech on 'the Commonwealth' (II, i, 148–65), the ideal political system that the island allows him to envisage, is taken via the French essayist Michel de Montaigne's 'Des cannibales', itself adapted from the Latin poet Ovid's description of the perfect, now-lost Golden Age.

Alonso (I, i; II, i; III, iii; V, i)

Despite his role in Prospero's overthrow (I, ii, 121–7), Alonso, like Gonzalo, is one of the more sympathetic of the shipwrecked party. Like Prospero, Alonso is a target of a plot by Antonio, which Ariel halts just in time (II, i, 258–306). He is despondent about his missing son ('No, no, he's gone', II, i, 123) and devastated by Ariel's 'three men of sin' speech (III, iii, 95–101). He feels punished for his role in Prospero's fall, begging forgiveness not only from him (V, i, 111–19), but also later from his own son and Prospero's new son-in-law Ferdinand ('O how oddly will it sound that I/Must ask my child forgiveness', V, i, 197–8).

Sebastian (I, i; II, i; III, iii; V, i)

Sebastian's unpleasantness is established from the very first scene, when he attacks the Boatswain who is trying to save them all as a 'bawling, blasphemous, incharitable dog' (I, i, 39–40). After being washed ashore, Sebastian tells Alonso with breezy callousness 'We have lost your son, I fear, for ever [...] The fault's your own' (II, i, 133, 136). He is rebuked by Gonzalo: 'you rub the sore/When you should bring the plaster' (II, i, 139–40). Sebastian is, moreover, only too willing to follow Antonio's advice to kill Alonso and take his crown, much as Antonio had done with Prospero (II, i, 292–3). He and Antonio remain mostly *silent* in the final scene, even as Prospero's immobilising spells wear off at the end of the play (V, i, 104–319). This is a key question in performance. Are they ashamed, grudgingly repentant or surly and defiant? Simon Russell Beale recently argued the latter, thinking the bookish Prospero would have made an ineffectual ruler (BBC Radio 4 interview, 28 December 2015).

Antonio (I, i; II, i; III, iii; V, i)

Antonio is perhaps the least sympathetic of the shipwrecked mariners. Antonio wants the Boatswain hanged for disagreeing with his higher-born betters, even though they do not know the sea as well: 'Hang, cur! Hang, you whoreson' (I, i, 40). His aggressive power hunger also comes through with his plot to do away with Alonso as he sleeps, a replication of his earlier usurpation of Prospero. These earlier misdeeds unavoidably affect Antonio's silent response to Prospero's perhaps pompous final speeches of forgiveness, either explaining his anger or accentuating his regret.

Trinculo (II, ii; III, ii; IV, i; V, i)

Trinculo's name plays on 'trink', the clinking of glasses, and French or Italian words for 'arse': *cul* or *culo*. This clownish drunkenness is evident in all the japing with Caliban, especially when they both unwittingly form a 'strange fish' as their legs protrude from beneath a ship (II, ii, 27). Trinculo is, however, lucid enough to see through Caliban's delusion of his beauty and greatness. 'Servant monster? The folly of this island! They say there's but five upon this isle; we are three of them. If th'other two be brained like us, the state totters' (III, ii, 4–7).

Stephano (II, ii; III, ii; IV, i; V, i)

Stephano forms a comic counterpoint with Trinculo: he is only all too flattered by Caliban's praise and belief that he will become the new leader of the island. Critical debate is lively as to whether the play's depiction of Caliban's and the clowns' foiled rebellion, and their joyous seizure of the lavish gowns, is ultimately subversive or reactionary and authoritarian.

Play structure

The excellent introduction to the Arden Third Series edition of *The Tempest* analyses carefully the play's intricate structural symmetries (see ed. Vaughan and Vaughan 1999: 14–17). The play contains nine scenes in total. The central scene is, appropriately, Ferdinand and Miranda's betrothal (III, i). The play begins and ends with the ship's destruction and reconstruction. Scenes two (I, ii) and eight (IV, i) stage Prospero, Miranda and Ferdinand. In scene two Ferdinand 'loses' a father and in scene eight he 'gains' a father-in-law. Scenes three (II, i) and seven (III, iii) both represent Antonio and Sebastian's attempts to usurp Alonso's throne; in both they are thwarted by Ariel. Scenes four (II, ii) and six (III, ii) present Caliban, Stephano and Trinculo's failed 'revolution'. This markedly concentric structure corresponds to the play's adherence to Aristotelian unities of time, place and action. Unlike sprawling plays like *Hamlet* or *Anthony and Cleopatra*, *The Tempest* depicts events lasting no longer than twenty-four hours, taking place in a single location and centring on a single event. The action of *The Tempest* takes place approximately between 2p.m. and 6p.m., as temporal markers like 'What is the time o'th'day?' (2p.m.) (I, ii, 240) and 'Some three hours since' (V, i, 136) make clear. Such a structure necessitates a skilful balance between action and narration. After the dramatic first scene, which stops with a cliffhanger, a ship on the brink of breaking up and sinking, the second scene is more narrative in focus, and perhaps a little dull, as Prospero recounts to Miranda his studious rule at Milan and usurpation by Antonio and Alonso. The middle act is divided up, advancing three separate but simultaneous plot strands: Ferdinand and Miranda's love story, Caliban and the clowns, and the shipwrecked mariners, confronted with Ariel's visions of banquets and dances, while the fourth act is given over wholly to the wedding ceremony, which in some performances can take up to half an hour.

Language

(This discussion is indebted to the introduction of the 1999 Arden Third Series edition, edited by Virginia Mason Vaughan and Alden T. Vaughan.)

Language is often raised as an explicit issue or theme in Shakespeare's plays and *The Tempest* is no exception. The use of language is, for example, key to tensions between Prospero and Caliban: it is a sign of the one's power over the other. Caliban spits to his master: 'Thou hast taught me language and my profit on't/Is I know how to curse. The red plague rid you/For learning me your language' (I, ii, 364–7). Caliban's language is distinctive, containing many new or unique words, and sometimes it is rich with verbal melody. Consider, for example, how the overlapping 'f', 'n', 's', 't', 'um', 'p' and 'z' sounds, italicised below, seem to imitate the harmless and beguiling noises that Caliban rapturously describes:

> Be not afeard. The isle is full of noises,
> Sounds and sweet airs that give delight and hurt not.
> Sometimes a thousand twangling instruments
> Will hum about mine ears; and sometimes voices,
> That if I then had waked after long sleep,
> Will make me sleep again; and then in dreaming,
> The clouds, methought, would open and show riches
> Ready to drop upon me, that when I waked
> I cried to dream again.
> (III, ii, 135–43)

The wedding speeches similarly create specific atmospheres via poetic techniques like rhyme or other phonetic patterns, such as Ceres' bouncily bountiful four-beat lines blessing the wedded lovers ('Vines with clustering bunches growing,/Plants with goodly burden bowing', IV, i, 112–13). The use of lexis (word choice) and alliterative plosives ('burden bowing') corroborates the atmosphere of fertility and sensuality. Ferdinand and Miranda run on and interrupt each other's verse lines, as if linguistically to perform their togetherness (III, i, 15–67). Enjambed, or run-on, lines (where sentences or clauses 'run on' over lines of verse) are similarly used frequently and to varied effect, as when Prospero struggles through his rage and confusion to explain his story to Miranda (I, ii, 66–132). Senses of love, magic and strangeness are furthered by new, rare compound words like 'spell-stopped' (V, i, 61), or 'cloud-capped' (IV, i, 152). Some of The Tempest's rhetorical patterns and discernible characteristics echo those of The Winter's Tale, pointing to a recognisably late Shakespearean style. Lines are compressed via contractions and apostrophes, for example 'hearts i'th'state' (I, ii, 84); words are missed out for the audience to fill in, for example 'urchins shall [go] forth' (I, ii, 337–8). Likewise, keywords can often be delayed, encouraging momentary anticipation, even confusion, in the mind of the listener (I, ii, 263–6 delays the key verb 'banished'). These techniques are juxtaposed to great effect in one of the play's rhetorical high points, when Prospero, having now achieved his aims, decides to give up magic:

> Ye elves of hills, brooks, standing lakes and groves,
> And ye that on the sands with printless foot
> Do chase the ebbing Neptune, and do fly him
> When he comes back; you demi-puppets that
> By moonshine do the green sour ringlets make,
> Whereof the ewe not bites; and you whose pastime
> Is to make midnight-mushrooms, that rejoice
> To hear the solemn curfew, by whose aid –
> Weak masters though ye be – I have bedimmed
> The noontide sun, called forth the mutinous winds,
> And twixt the green sea and the azured vault
> Set roaring war; to the dread-rattling thunder

> Have I given fire and rifted Jove's stout oak
> With his own bolt: the strong-based promontory
> Have I made shake, and by the spurs plucked up
> The pine and cedar; graves at my command
> Have waked their sleepers, ope'd and let'em forth
> By my so potent art. But this rough magic
> I here abjure...
> (V, i, 33–51)

Much of the first half of this speech describes Prospero's addressees: the 'elves', 'demi-puppets' and 'weak masters'. It is not until line 41 that we realise he wants to describe his magical powers to them. And even then, Prospero tends to delay the verb when boasting about each magical act: 'set roaring war' comes after ''twixt the green sea and the azured vault'; 'I made shake' comes after 'the strong-based promontory'. Compressed lines ('ope'd and let'em forth') are set alongside neo-logistic compounds ('dread-rattling') and melodic phonetic patterning – for example, repetitions of the cooing 'oo' sounds in 'brooks', 'foot', 'Neptune', 'moonshine', 'mushroom', 'noontide', 'mutinous' and 'azured' – give way in the fiercer second half to harsher consonants like prominent 'f' and 'k' sounds and more expansive, literally roaring assonances ('*roaring war*'). One might say the speech reaches a crescendo to make the vow of abjuration all the more sudden and irrevocable.

This attention to rhythm, incantation and linguistic melody extends into the play's frequent use of song. Songs include 'Come upon these yellow sands' (I, ii, 375–87), which guides the shipwrecked Ferdinand onto and through the island; 'Full fathom five' (I, ii, 397–405), which 'tells' Ferdinand about his missing father; and 'Where the bee sucks, there suck I' (V, i, 88–94). This last song stresses Ariel's magical power: he can shrink himself down to the size of an insect. Indeed, Ariel's singing blends music and magic together. If the songs' words seem to seep into their hypnotised onstage listeners as if in a dream, then perhaps this is the implied ideal effect on the audience, too. Like Prospero's direct address to the audience in his Epilogue, the play's 'Dispersed music' and Caliban's 'sounds and sweet airs' (III, ii, 136) blur the boundaries of the stage space, bringing the audience closer into its world. As the rapt Ferdinand dreamily asks: 'where should this music be' (I, ii, 388)?

Themes

Power and rank

From its very first scene *The Tempest* problematises questions of power and rank. The captain mocks the nobles who obstruct the sailors, assuming their aristocratic status makes them the more competent seafarers: 'what care these roarers [waves] for the name of king?' (I, i, 16–17). Prospero tells us in the next scene these same characters, similarly pridefully, stole his dukedom. Antonio turns Prospero's court against him, using Alonso's help to 'extirpate me and mine / Out of the dukedom and confer fair Milan,/With all the honours, on my brother' (I, ii, **79–87**). Gonzalo's speech on 'the Commonwealth' (II, i, **148–65**) sees the island as an idyllically equal space where no such ambitious rivalry exists, but such hopes are of course belied by the tensions between Prospero and his increasingly rebellious slave Caliban. Prospero grudgingly admits 'We cannot miss him; he doth make our fire,/Fetch in our wood ...' (I, ii, **312–14**). Caliban's enslavement is a punishment following his attempted rape of Miranda. But it also flies in the face of the hereditary principles that underpinned in Shakespeare's time the transmission of land and titles, such as Prospero's dukedom of Milan. In other words, Prospero usurps Caliban like Antonio usurped Prospero. Caliban repeatedly bemoans this state of affairs (I, ii, **332–44**; III, ii, **40–53**). But his later rebellion is undermined by its apparent absurdity. Trinculo protests 'A most ridiculous monster – to make a wonder of a poor drunkard!' (II, ii, **162**), and not only are they led to a puddle of 'horse-piss' (IV, i, **199**), they are then chased offstage after stealing Prospero's costumes, which they mistakenly thought would give them his magical powers. Caliban at the end is forced to grovel 'how fine my master is' (V, i, **263**) and spit 'What a thrice-double ass/Was I to take this drunkard for a god,/And worship this dull fool' (V, i, **296–8**). Perhaps Caliban learns a truer sense of freedom just as the play ends.

Knowledge, power and forgiveness

Prospero's prospering over Caliban raises the issue of how his power relates to his magical knowledge. In many ways *The Tempest* puts in a more magical setting the Machiavellian themes of the Histories and Tragedies, which at their darkest moments further the idea that knowledge is power, that might makes right. Prospero's distracted dedication to books and 'the bettering of [his] mind' (I, ii, **89–90**) only seems to count as knowledge when, on the island, he uses it to gain power over Ariel, Caliban and his shipwrecked betrayers. This strange foreign land sees a kind of challenge to the strict association of knowledge with power when in the final third of the play Prospero willingly abandons his magic, frees Ariel and forgives his usurpers, promising his affections will 'become tender' and stating 'the rarer action is/In virtue than in vengeance' (V, i, **27–8**). But traces of the old, authoritarian Prospero remain. He is contemptuous of Caliban and the conspirators ('these three have robbed me', V, i, **272**) and even in the act of pardoning retains a note of high-handed, pious pomposity: 'I do forgive thee, unnatural though thou art' (V, i, **78–9**). In the end, it is we the audience who are begged to absolve Prospero, setting him 'free' through the 'indulgence' of applause (Epilogue, **19–20**). This direct address to the audience can be seen as the final, explicit manifestation of the play's latently metatheatrical strand, most prominent when Prospero famously compares the spirits to actors, and the festivities of the wedding to this 'great globe' (IV, i, **153**). As the audience witnesses the play 'dissolve', die away and 'leave not a rack behind', they are left, as if in a 'dream', with Prospero's urgent need to be forgiven (IV, i, **154**).

Texts and contexts

There is only one early version of *The Tempest*: that printed as the first play of the 1623 Folio. Early readers would have thought this was one of Shakespeare's first works, not one of his last. The text is relatively clean but there are two problematic cruces. As mentioned above, the first is the speech about Caliban, 'Abhorred slave' (I, ii, 353–63), which the Folio text ascribes to Miranda. Stylistic analysis reveals this speech is more appropriate to Prospero, and the authoritative tone is certainly more like Prospero than Miranda. Nonetheless, Miranda's response is plausible, given that she is a young, vulnerable woman enveloped by a powerfully masculine world, and victim of attempted rape. The second crux concerns Act IV, scene i, lines 122–4. Editors are unsure whether it should read 'Wife' or 'wise': it was easy to confuse the long 's' with 'f'. Nicholas Rowe introduced the second reading in 1709. This crux is important because Ferdinand's attitude to his wife influences the sense of male–female equality in the play. Is he praising her, or the 'wise' Prospero? If the latter, does Ferdinand neglect his wife in the name of masculine solidarity with his new father-in-law? And, if so, is Miranda's marriage just a continuation of the masculine entrapment she has already suffered on the island? Taken together, then, editors' readings of these two lines can affect our understanding of Miranda quite strongly.

There is no one identifiable source for *The Tempest* and the story is most often deemed to be of Shakespeare's invention, like *A Midsummer Night's Dream*, *The Merry Wives of Windsor* or *Titus Andronicus*. There are, however, strong echoes of other texts. We have already seen that Gonzalo's idea that 'the Commonwealth', an ideal community without greed, rivalry or strain, echoes Montaigne's description of the Brazilians in 'Des cannibales', which itself echoes the description of the Golden Age in Ovid's *Metamorphoses*. The Ovidian influence is evident also in Prospero's speech quoted above, 'Ye elves of hills, of brooks, of woods alone' (*Metamorphoses* 7.265–8), which echoes Medea's invocation to Hecate in Golding's English translation. The use in the wedding scene of mythological figures like Iris (the Rainbow), daughter of Thaumante and allegory of admiration, and Ceres, goddess of natural fertility and mother of Proserpina, draws on Ovid as did Renaissance mythographers like Vincenzo Cartari. The portrayal of the island is also influenced by reports like William Strachey's 1609 'True Reportory of the Wracke, and Redemption of Sir Thomas Gates', while the uses of special effects, high spectacle and elaborately patterned verse are all influenced by the fashion in James I's court for the masque (see ed. Orgel 1987). The resonance with the Jacobean court extends to the play's narrative: like James I with Prince Henry and Elizabeth's marriage to the Elector Palatine, Antonio loses a son and marries off his daughter. Peter Hall's 1974 National Theatre played on such historical resonances as it quoted masque imagery and lighting, making Prospero look like the Elizabethan magician John Dee, and Juno like Elizabeth I. Hall, however, interwove such historical detail with more modern gestures like putting Ariel on a trapeze above, and making up Caliban with half-and-half face painting, like a Jekyll and Hyde. In its historically eclectic approach

Hall's production helped illustrate some of the central issues that have stimulated practitioners throughout the play's performance history.

The play in performance

The Tempest contains what the Arden editors usefully call 'narrative gaps' (ed. Vaughan and Vaughan 1999: 75). These include the obscure backstories of Antonio's son and Prospero's wife ('a piece of virtue'), the fate of Claribel and Sycorax, and how Antonio, silent in the text, responds to Prospero's rebukes in the final scene. The play also stimulates interesting casting problems: men or women, boys or girls, can play Ariel. In a 1995 production in New York Aunjanue Ellis playing Ariel shared a sense of sexual chemistry with Patrick Stewart's Prospero. It is customary for older actors like Stewart to play Prospero but, as a Renaissance father of a sixteen-year-old, he could be as young as thirty-five. Prospero's protectiveness is strict or judicious depending on how sensually actors play the roles of Ferdinand and Miranda. A sensual Miranda can be provocative, even uncomfortable, given her history with Caliban. Via such issues performances of The Tempest often, consciously or not, betray wider cultural preconceptions about race relations. In the early half of the twentieth century The Tempest was a kind of theatrical experimentation space for (pseudo-)Darwinian ideas. Caliban was even portrayed as a kind of 'missing link', Frank Benson basing his gestures and movements on monkeys and baboons he had studied at a nearby zoo (see ed. Vaughan and Vaughan 1999: 93). The rewriting by Aimé Césaire, Une Tempête (1969), with Caliban as an African field hand and Ariel a mulatto house servant, sought to reappropriate Shakespeare and challenge the racist cultural weight with which he was being increasingly loaded, while Clifford Williams's RSC 1978 production cast David Suchet as Caliban: a 'sympathetic emblem of imperialistic exploitation [...] speaking the language with the too-perfect precision of an alien' (Times, 3 May 1978; see ed. Vaughan and Vaughan 1999: 114). Adrian Noble's RSC 1998 production saw Caliban and Ariel in (literally) black and white terms, colour-coded by body paint.

Since the mid-twentieth century influential productions have been characterised by experimentations with theatrical form and radical progressive political statements. Peter Brook's 1968 production at the London Roundhouse replaced practically all the Shakespearean text with mime and sought to expose the play's latent violence, showing Caliban appearing to rape Prospero who then in turn represses the attack. American Shakespeare Theatre's 1981 production took a no less loosely allegorical approach, interpreting the play in terms of Freud's 'second topography' with Prospero as ego, Caliban as id and Ariel as superego, compressing libidinal rage into art.

Jonathan Miller's 1970 Mermaid Theatre production highlighted Prospero's potential colonialist cruelty and Derek Jarman's 1979 film displayed strong punk imagery and gay sensibilities, with Caliban played by blind, gay actor Jack Birkett ('The Incredible Orlando'), as if to equate with racial difference other forms of otherness and marginality. Ron Daniels's 1982 RSC production, like Jarman's, absorbed iconography drawn from the counter-culture of the time, with Mark Rylance with a punk haircut and Bob Peck as a half-naked cross between Tarzan and a Rastafarian.

The minimalist, balletic Italian production *La Tempesta*, directed by Giorgio Strehler in 1983, has been held up as one of the most inventive theatrical reim-aginings of Shakespeare's script. A topsail crashed down upon the mariners in the opening storm, the clowns were based on Harlequin and *commedia dell'arte*, and a freed Ariel, mad with joy at liberty, danced blissfully across the stage. On some nights of Sam Mendes' RSC 1993 production, Simon Russell Beale's Ariel spat at Alec McCowen's Prospero the moment he was free enough to do so. Mendes directed *The Tempest* again in 2010, basing the set design on paintings like Edouard Manet's *Le déjeuner sur l'herbe* to evoke a pastoral idyll. Peter Greenaway's wonderful 1991 film *Prospero's Books* similarly draws on art history. The set is filled with Renais-sance and Baroque imagery like flying cherubs with angel wings and comically large ruffs and hats as worn by the shipwrecked nobles. John Gielgud voices all the roles, speaking as he writes the play out. Greenaway offers a postmodern variation on the common, dearly held (but false) idea that Prospero is a thinly veiled autobiography of Shakespeare himself, saying goodbye to his audience with his last play.

The Tempest has remained just as popular with audiences in the twenty-first century, with a variety of high-profile productions. Jonathan Kent's 2000 Almeida production was noted for its powerful use of water and special effects which made Aiden Gillen's Ariel seem like he could teleport around the stage. Rupert Goold's 2006 RSC production focused on the theme of madness: Prospero and Miranda's years of isolation and confinement had made them erratic, a sense relayed also by the harsh modernism and cold colours of the post-industrial set, and by Julian Bleach's Ariel's shocking emergence from a whale(!). The late Pete Postlethwaite was praised for his thoughtful, authoritative 2007 Prospero at the Royal Exchange, Manchester. Postcolonialist themes were reawakened by productions by a small company, Tara Arts, in 2007–8 and by a 2009 performance at the Stratford-upon-Avon Courtyard, which used puppets to evoke the natural landscape and played on African mythology and costume, in opposition to white-suited imperialists like Alonso. Prospero (played by Antony Sher) directed his plea at the end for forgive-ness to Caliban (played by John Kani), who was able to retake, proudly, his island as his own. In David Farr's 2012 RSC production Jonathan Slinger's Prospero was visibly moved by Ariel's unthinking charity, as if Ariel was part of his own moral journey to absolution. More recently, Roger Allam's movingly protective, paternal Prospero in Jeremy Herrin's 2013 Globe production saw the play as being about the difficulty of letting go. And Julie Taymor's 2010 film version reverses profoundly the island's power balance by casting Helen Mirren as 'Prospera': an interestingly gendered variation on the racial, politicised radical experimentation the play has stimulated over its recent performance history. Virginia Mason Vaughan's 2011 book in the *Shakespeare in Performance* series is a useful supplementary resource for students interested pursuing further research on such matters.

Critical reception

The Tempest has inspired literary art as well as criticism. Feminist revisions include H[ilda] D[oolittle]'s *By Avon River* (1949), which sees Claribel (Alonso's unseen, soon-to-be married daughter) as allegory of the contemporary female artist. Marina Warner's *Indigo* (1992) gives Sycorax a voice and personal perspective. Other famous rewritings include Robert Browning's *Caliban upon Setebos* (2015) and W. H. Auden's *The Sea and the Mirror* (2003). Oscar Wilde cryptically alludes to Caliban in the Preface to *The Picture of Dorian Gray*:

> The nineteenth century dislike of realism is the rage of Caliban seeing his own face in a glass.
>   The nineteenth century dislike of romanticism is the rage of Caliban not seeing his own face in a glass. (Wilde 2000: 3)

This suggests *The Tempest* shapes powerfully Wilde's thinking about creativity, representation and self-construction: readers see themselves in Caliban, and the rage that results can lead to internal and external violence. These themes have been taken up in critical literature about Caliban, especially postcolonialist criticism, which since the mid-twentieth century has been lively and prolific: Duke Pesta's 2014 article is a useful follow-up, and Moslem Zolfagharkhani and Zahra Heshmatifar (2012) trace how *The Tempest* was itself used in colonialist curricula. Perhaps, however, the starting point here is Octave Mannoni's 1950 study *La psychologie de la colonisation*, which was retitled in English translation *Prospero and Caliban* (1956) in reference to discussions of Prospero's paranoid 'inferiority complex' and Caliban's 'dependency complex', where freedom is never quite fully thinkable. Mannoni's thought has influenced more recent theoretically focused criticism of the play. One important example here is Jonathan Goldberg's 'Under the Covers with Caliban' (1997), which examines the play's potentially liberating treatments of gender, sexuality and reproduction by analysing its often subversive restaging of childbirth, like Ariel's delivery from the cloven pine, or Caliban's from Sycorax. Another is Paul Brown's '"This thing of darkness I acknowledge mine": *The Tempest* and the Discourse of Colonialism' (1994), which relates the Prospero–Caliban relationship to early seventeenth-century prejudices, preconceptions and stereotypes about the 'foreign' other.

More recently, Christopher Pye's 'Storm at Sea: *The Tempest*, Cultural Materialism and the Early Modern Political Aesthetic' (2013) examines Caliban as a meeting point for political and aesthetic discussion, as the 'revulsion' he stimulates falls into both categories. Ingo Berensmeyer (2014) proposes that *The Tempest*, and Shakespeare in general, is a 'media ecology': a kind of collage of meaning from the play's (or plays') earliest source texts to the eclectic citations from 'high' and 'low' art which may mark the most recent performances. Julia Lupton (2013) examines the play's 'soundscape'. As a more conventional example of 'eco-criticism', Shannon Kelly (2014) examines early modern uses of coral as a symbol for self-regenerating political authority, using as an example Ariel's song about the Neapolitan King Alonso ('Of his bones are coral made', I, ii, 398). Gillian Woods (2014) revisits the

Catholic nuance of Prospero's plea for 'indulgence' in the context of sectarian controversy, while Jacqueline Cowan (2016) examines Prospero as a kind of empirical, quasi-scientific experimenter, an early proponent of an intellectual tradition associated more readily with Francis Bacon.

Discussion questions

* What are the thematic and linguistic characteristics of Shakespeare's 'Late Plays' (or 'Romances' or 'Tragicomedies')? Are they so readily 'detachable' from the rest of his work?

* Does *The Tempest*, as a meditation on the psychological, even magical, effects of omniscience, power and control, have a special relevance in our era of search engines and instant information?

* '*The Tempest* is a romance containing built-in criticism of romance; not a rejection of it, but an appreciation of both its glories and limitations' (Wells 1966: 76). What forms might this 'in-built criticism' take? What are the 'glories' of romance and how does the *Tempest* uphold them?

* 'Prospero's masque serves *The Tempest* [...] as an allegorical core that symbolises ideas which pervade the play' (ed. Vaughan and Vaughan 1999: 70). What are these ideas?

Bibliography and further reading

Editions

Ovid (2002), *Ovid's Metamorphoses*, trans. Arthur Golding, ed. M. Forey, London/New York: Penguin.
Shakespeare, W. (1987), *The Tempest*, ed. S. Orgel, Oxford: Oxford University Press.
Shakespeare, W. (1999), *The Tempest*, ed. V. M. Vaughan and A. T. Vaughan, London: Arden Shakespeare.

Critical response

Auden, W. H. (2003), *The Sea and the Mirror: A Commentary on Shakespeare's* The Tempest, ed. A. Kirsch, Princeton/Oxford: Princeton University Press.
Berensmeyer, I. (2014), 'Shakespeare and Media Ecology: Beyond Historicism and Presentism', *Poetics Today*, 35:4, 515–38.

Brown, P. (1994), '"This thing of darkness I acknowledge mine": *The Tempest* and the Discourse of Colonialism', in J. Dollimore and A. Sinfield (eds), *Political Shakespeare: Essays in Cultural Materialism*, 2nd edn, Manchester: Manchester University Press, pp. 48–71.

Browning, R. (2015), 'Caliban upon Setebos', in R. Cronin and D. McMillan (eds), *Robert Browning*, 21st-Century Oxford Authors Series, Oxford: Oxford University Press, pp. 425–32.

Cartari, V. (2012), *Vincenzo Cartari's Images of the Gods of the Ancients: The First Italian Mythography*, trans. and annotated John Mulryan, Tempe, AZ: Arizona Center for Medieval and Renaissance Studies.

Cowan, J. (2016), 'The Imagination's Arts: Poetry and Natural Philosophy in Bacon and Shakespeare', *Studies in Philology*, 113:1, 132–62.

Goldberg, J. (1997), 'Under the Covers with Caliban', in D. C. Greetham (ed.), *The Margins of the Text*, Ann Arbor: University of Michigan Press, pp. 105–28.

H.D. (1949), *By Avon River*, New York: Macmillan.

Kelly, S. (2014), 'The King's Coral Body: A Natural History of Coral and the Post-tragic Ecology of *The Tempest*', *Journal for Early Modern Cultural Studies*, 14:1, 115–42.

Lupton, J. (2013), 'Shakespeare by Design: A Flight of Concepts', *English Studies*, 94:3, 259–77.

Mannoni, O. (1956), *Prospero and Caliban: The Psychology of Colonisation*, London: Methuen.

Pesta, D. (2014), 'Acknowledging Things of Darkness: Postcolonial Criticism of *The Tempest*', *Academic Questions*, 27:3, 273–85.

Pye, C. (2013), 'Storm at Sea: *The Tempest*, Cultural Materialism and the Early Modern Political Aesthetic', *English Studies*, 94:3, 331–45.

Vaughan, V. M. (2011), *The Tempest*, Manchester: Manchester University Press.

Warner, M. (1992), *Indigo, or, Mapping the Waters*, London: Chatto and Windus.

Wells, S. (1966), 'Shakespeare and Romance', in J. R. Brown and B. Harris (eds), *Later Shakespeare*, London: Edward Arnold, pp. 49–79.

Wilde, O. (2000), *The Picture of Dorian Gray*, ed. R. Mighall, London: Penguin.

Woods, G. (2014), 'Indulgent Representation: Theatricality and Sectarian Metaphor in *The Tempest*', *Literature Compass*, 11:11, 703–14.

Zolfagharkhani, M. and Z. Heshmatifar (2012), 'Pedagogical and Colonial Power Discourses in William Shakespeare's *The Tempest*', *Cross-Cultural Communication*, 8:2, 7–14.

Index